The Petals of a Kansas Sunflower

The Petals of a Kansas Sunflower

A Mennonite Diaspora

Melvin D. Epp

RESOURCE *Publications* • Eugene, Oregon

THE PETALS OF A KANSAS SUNFLOWER
A Mennonite Diaspora

Copyright © 2012 Melvin D. Epp. All rights reserved. Except for brief quotations in critical publications or reviews, no part of this book may be reproduced in any manner without prior written permission from the publisher. Write: Permissions, Wipf and Stock Publishers, 199 W. 8th Ave., Suite 3, Eugene, OR 97401.

Resource Publications
An Imprint of Wipf and Stock Publishers
199 W. 8th Ave., Suite 3
Eugene, OR 97401
www.wipfandstock.com

ISBN 13: 978-1-62032-064-8

Manufactured in the U.S.A.

Scripture quotations taken from The Holy Bible, New International Version®, NIV® Copyright © 1973, 1978, 1984, 2011 by Biblica, Inc.™ Used by permission. All rights reserved worldwide.

Scripture quotations taken from the New Revised Standard Version Bible, Copyright 1989, Division of Christian Education of the National Council of the Churches of Christ in the United States of America. Used by permission. All rights reserved.

Scripture quotations taken from the *The Message*. Copyright © by Eugene H. Peterson 1993, 1994, 1995, 1996, 2000, 2001, 2002. Used by permission of NavPress Publishing Group.

*For David S. and J. Terence
Beatrice, Charlie, and Riley*

and my Harder family:

An historical reference point

and

A heritage to embrace

Each of our lives is a fragile flower,
a bud blooming briefly in the ceaseless seasons of time.
We exist at the branch tip of a generational tree of ancestors,
who though long dead,
still live in the cores of our beings.
In many ways, we are what they have been
and experiencing their lives
enriches our own.

—MAX R. TERMAN in *HIRAM'S HONOR*

Contents

List of Figures / ix
Acknowledgments / xi
Preface / xiii

1. "Why Don't You Write Poetry?" / 1
2. This is My Land / 12
3. History as a Reference Point / 20
4. The Sparrows in the Fields / 75
5. But God! / 81
6. In the Days before Hallmark Cards / 91
7. For a Good Laugh / 100
8. Request for Poems / 106
9. Wedding Invitation / 111
10. *Polterabend* / 112
11. Celebration of Marriage / 117
12. Celebration of Sustained Bonding / 157
13. Celebration of the Golden Wedding Anniversary / 209
14. Celebration of Birthdays / 263
15. Remembering Special People on Their Birth Dates / 291
16. Honoring the Patriarch / 316
17. The Mission of Parochial Education / 319

Contents

    18   Encouraging Missionaries as They Say Goodbye / 334

    19   A Commercial Jingle, i.e., Song / 339

    20   The Celebration of Christmas / 342

    21   The Art of Saying Grace / 353

    22   Mother is Dying / 357

Appendix 1: History of My Mennonite Family / 377
Appendix 2: Passage to America / 392
Appendix 3: Tornado of June 8, 1941 / 401
Appendix 4: Eye on the World / 427
Chronological List of Marie's Poems / 430
Bibliography / 435
Subject/Name Index / 449

List of Figures

Figure 1—School picture of Marie Harder / 5
Figure 2—Physiographic map of Kansas / 15
Figure 3—Bernhard Harder / 21
Figure 4—Map of Vistula Delta in 1876 / 22
Figure 5—Native American Artifacts / 29
Figure 6—The family communion set / 36
Figure 7—Bernhard Harder farm in 1915 / 37
Figure 8—Emmaus Mennonite Church buildings / 38–39
Figure 9—Suitcase of Bernhard Harder Jr. / 44
Figure 10—Bernhard Harder Jr. with brother Gustav / 46
Figure 11—Souvenir vases / 62
Figure 12—Tien with daughter Margaretha / 64
Figure 13—Andres Powolski / 71
Figure 14—Susan Thiessen / 86
Figure 15—Susan's graduation picture from Grace University / 88
Figure 16—Susan at work at "Go Ye" Mission / 88
Figure 17—Marie's milking stool / 103
Figure 18—Marie's children / 109
Figure 19—Wedding invitation for John and Marie Epp / 119
Figure 20—Wedding portrait of John and Marie Epp / 122
Figure 21—Wedding portrait of Bernhard Harder Jr. and Helene Wiebe / 160
Figure 22—Gustav and Helene Harder's twenty-fifth wedding anniversary portrait / 169
Figure 23—John and Marie Epp's twenty-fifth wedding anniversary invitation / 184
Figure 24—Family portrait for the twenty-fifth wedding anniversary / 184

List of Figures

Figure 25—John and Marie Epp's fiftieth wedding anniversary invitation / 209

Figure 26—B. W. and Minna Harder's twenty-fifth wedding anniversary portrait / 226

Figure 27—Anna Regier / 255

Figure 28—John Epp Sr. / 256

Figure 29—Peter and Agnethe Epp / 258

Figure 30—Wedding portrait of John Harder Sr. and Marie Regier / 266

Figure 31—Sister Helen Ruth Epp / 276

Figure 32—Justine Bergmann Harder / 292

Figure 33—Floor plan of Bernhard Harder Sr. house of 1877 / 293–294

Figure 34—The farmyard / 295

Figure 35—Diagram of garden / 297

Figure 36—Fiftieth wedding portrait of Cornelius and Anna Regier / 305

Figure 37—Photos of the Brainerd School buildings / 320

Figure 38—Peppernut cutter / 345

Figure 39—*Springerle* cookie rolling pin / 347

Figure 40—Marie's pansy quilt / 361

Figure 41—Wedding cake for Alice and Herald Thiessen / 362

Figure 42—The Overland / 363

Figure 43—Marie on April 21, 1988 / 366

Figure 44— The Harder Cemetery gate on July 10, 1998 / 375

Figure 45—Marie's newly filled grave covered with cedar boughs / 376

Figure 46—Hand-operated can sealer / 379

Figure 47—Land Sales Flier / 391

Figure 48—*Lloyd Wartenhalle* in 1869 / 395

Figure 49—The Passenger List of the Mail Steamship Rhein / 397

Figure 50—The Manifest of passengers disembarking on July 1, 1876 / 399

Figure 51—Path of tornado on June 8, 1941 / 405

Figure 52—Devastation to John Epp Jr. farm / 410–411

Figure 53—Mennonite community sharing / 417

Figure 54—Marie's Brownie Box Camera / 428

Figure 55—Marie taking a picture of her family in 1928 / 429

Acknowledgments

I ACKNOWLEDGE WITH FONDNESS the legacy that Mother left for me to recall and admire. Her laughter and energy permeate this manuscript. And now, since I am no longer a child, I thank her posthumously for listening to me read German from *Der Fibel* as my father attempted to mold me into a better person. I was empowered to enjoy Mother's poetry in whichever language she used.

I wholeheartedly thank many others for making resource material available to me. Primarily, I commend Jean Thiessen, head librarian at the local Whitewater Memorial Library, for providing reprints, books, and microfilms from the world of libraries for my hermitage on the plains during the past twenty years. The Mennonite Library and Archives, Bethel College, North Newton, Kansas is a tremendous archival repository and made useful with the help of John Thiesen and James Lynch. The Frederic Remington Area Historical Society Library, housed in the local Frederic Remington High School library and maintained by Pam Haber, has been a trove of useful local history. Other local county and city historical libraries have been graciously accommodating: Harvey County Historical Society, Butler County Historical Society, Sedgwick Historical Society and Museum, and the Halstead Historical Society. With special appreciation, Ted Naylor, University of Nebraska Library, has also located some elusive factual information.

With particular fondness and gratitude, my sisters Martha and Phebe Ann shared recollections, photo albums, and encouragements uniquely sisterly. My cousins Susan and Lydia have shared memories of the Harder farm of the early 1920s and the experiences of surviving the life-altering tornado of 1941. Additionally, I thank the many other relatives and friends within the local community who confirmed dates, answered questions, and gave perspectives on local events and cultural mores.

A distinctive thanks to Gayle March for suggesting that I audit a seminar course, Memoir 399, at Wichita State University in which she

Acknowledgments

was enrolled. Professor Jeanine Hathaway and fellow students graciously cajoled a blooming botanist tending his linguistic shrubby thickets.

Mark Jantzen, professor of history, Bethel College, reviewed and commented on appendix 1; I appreciate his suggestions to bring the facts into historical accuracy. Merle Schlabaugh, professor of German, Bethel College, has methodically provided editorial expertise. I am indebted to both for sharing their academic prowess and I thank them.

The personnel of Wipf and Stock Publishers have been graciously helpful and I thank them for expediting the final phases of this endeavor.

My dear wife, Sylvia, has patiently endured the travail of this lengthy project. Her expertise of the German and English languages has been freely shared. I thank her wholeheartedly for her imprint on this manuscript.

Preface

I HAVE COLLECTED INTO one document the poems my mother wrote during her lifetime. The poems tell of her Harder family and the community within which they lived.

This is the story of West Prussian Mennonites from the Heubuden Church who left for America on June 15, 1876. They formed a church community in Kansas and joined the Western District Conference of the General Conference Mennonites as the Emmaus Mennonite Church. They purchased odd numbered sections of land from the Santa Fe Railroad. About one thousand Mennonite immigrants came to the United States from West Prussia during that time. The major settlements on the prairies were around Whitewater, Elbing, and Newton, Kansas; and Beatrice and Jansen, Nebraska.

These West Prussian Mennonites represented simply a very small enclave of all the Mennonites that came to the United States. Approximately 18,000 Mennonites immigrated to the midwestern prairies from southern Russia; many of these Russian Mennonites had their origins in West Prussia as well, but had been in Russia for 100 to 150 years, so their historical identities are in the Mennonite colonies in south Russia; however, familial relationships were cultivated and cherished. The political and religious tolerances in America were so deeply appreciated after the persecutions and political unrest experienced by these Anabaptists that the hardships of being pioneers seemed well worth the inconveniences.

Prior to 1683 there already were some Mennonites in New Amsterdam, later renamed New York City under British governance. In the time period of 1663–1664, a Plockhoy settlement near present-day Horekill, Delaware was settled by European Mennonites; however, this settlement did not survive. These peace-promoting Mennonites could have been from Switzerland, Germany, Moravia, and other places in Europe where believer's baptism and pacifism were not appreciated by the state church and governments.

Preface

On October 6, 1683, the ship *Concord* anchored at Philadelphia with the first Germantown settlers of forty to fifty Krefelders. Six miles northwest of Philadelphia this group established Germantown, the first ongoing Mennonite settlement in the new world. By the 1870s, the Mennonites of Pennsylvania, Ohio, Indiana, and Illinois relayed a positive experience in America to the twelve delegates sent from South Russia and West Prussia to check out North America. The immigration of my ancestors to Kansas resulted from the reports carried back to West Prussia of agricultural opportunities, and the religious and political freedoms observed in America.

1

"Why Don't You Write Poetry?"

She sat down in a chair in the back corner of the room. Her baby was fidgeting and in the quietness that a corner provides, she was coping and gently shushing, hoping her baby would soon fall asleep. It wasn't long and people were moving their chairs in close pinning her into the corner, and when these forty or more people started singing German Christmas carols, the sound was just overwhelming. The familiar and normally soothing refrains did not comfort her that evening: "*Stille Nacht, Heilige Nacht! Alles schläft, einsam wacht.* Silent Night! Holy Night! All is calm, all is bright." She clutched her baby claustrophobically and prayed, "Just get me out of here." She felt trapped and screamed into her own ear, "Why do I have to sit here in this corner all by myself with my baby? I cannot sing. What can I do? What can I do? Oh, what can I do?"

These were the questions that haunted my mother that night. Her frustration was sufficient that sitting there as a young woman, she looked squarely into the face of God and directed these questions at him as well. Mother felt that she sounded like a crow when she sang. She needed help to make her feel worthwhile and not relegated to an existence of solitude in a corner. She struggled for a feeling of productivity and accomplishment in her young married life and with all the singing around her she was getting no sense of reward.

As she implored the divine for an answer, her focus blocked out the sound of the singing around her. In the silence of concentration, her life, her abilities, and her interests flashed before her on the inside of her closed eyelids as she bowed her head as if looking at her sleeping child. With time, a quiet serenity permeated her whole being from her head to her toes. It then came to her, as if God responded, "Why don't you write poetry?"

"Why of course," she said to herself. "I love words. I love the rhyme and rhythms of words. I love the verbal dynamics of poetry. I easily memorize poetry and still remember many poems from my school days. Yes, I will focus on writing poems."

Mother embarked on her new focus of expression with enthusiasm and kept a journal that included a chronological sequence of poems. She also had a collection of loose scraps of paper on which she had penciled lines, as well as whole poems. The writing scraps included the backsides of business letters sent to my father or the inside of business envelopes cut open at the sides. Writing paper was scarce and thrift was paramount.

The first entries in her journal are short, personalized poems to accompany gifts presented by two brothers, Carl and Paul. How did these men know that Mother had found her poetic gift? It goes without saying that in 1929, my mother, as a Mennonite farm woman, would not have hung out a shingle. There is no record of the recipient of these gifts. The recipient could not have been their mother because she had already passed away in February 1923.

Für Carl J. Claassen zum Wassertopf

Wenn an Tagen schwül und heiß
Auf der Stern perlt er Schweiß
Ist gewißein kühler Trunk
Angenehm zu jeder Stund
Mög ein Trunk aus dieser Kanne
Dir und einem künftigen Manne
Wenn du daraus schenket ein
Stets eine rechte Labung sein

For Carl J. Claassen for the Water Pitcher

When the days are sultry and hot
Beads of sweat are on the forehead
It is known that one should
Take a cool drink every hour.
If you are willing to take a drink of our water

"Why Don't You Write Poetry?"

You and your lovely kin
When you use this gift
Will truly have a refreshing draught.

Für Paul U. Claassen zum Buttertermameter

Wenn du Käse und Butter machst
Dann musst du ja nicht vegessen
Daß du schon auf alles achtest
Und mit einem Ding tust messen.
Diesen Rat giebt die schon weiß
Was das Wirtschaften schon heiß
Ist es anfangs auch recht schwer
Gibt es leichter doch noch her
Ist dann alles gut geraten.
Lade uns dann einmal ein
Und wir werden dir dann sagen
Das dein Käse schmeckt sehr fein.

For Paul U. Claassen for the Butter Thermometer

When you make cheese and butter
You should not forget
That you need to be aware of everything
And with a thing like this you measure.
This suggestion gives a known product
When the process gets entailed enough
At the beginning it is difficult
But it gets easier quickly
Everything will then succeed
Invite us in sometime
And we will then tell you
That your cheese tastes wonderful.

To gain an appreciation of this divine directive, I am going to collect into one treatise and review the poems Mother wrote during her lifetime. The actual writing time spans the years from 1929 to 1991. The poems also reach back to 1876 when her family immigrated to America from West Prussia and continue forward through the twentieth century. Many of the poems express religious faith and so project forward throughout all eternity.

The Petals of a Kansas Sunflower

Mother was the last member of the first generation of Harders born in America. She was born in the farmhouse in which she lived her whole life until she walked out of the house at the age of eighty-nine to accompany my father's move to the local nursing home. As she left she said, "I have completed the list of my life's ambitions: I have been a good helpmate to my husband for sixty-five years; I have clothed, fed, and nurtured my eight children to adulthood; I was the surrogate mother to my nieces and nephews when my sisters passed away so young; I have rocked my seventeen grandchildren and baked cookies for them; I have decorated wedding cakes for my daughters and my nieces; I have designed eighteen pansy appliqué blocks and completed my lifelong aspiration of a pansy quilt; I have written down the story of my life so that my children and their children will not forget their heritage and who they are."

This move out of the old farmhouse was not an ordinary exodus. The emotional attachment was very strong. Mother was born in the southeast room on August 18, 1903. My father moved in with her and her mother several days after their wedding on April 21, 1927. Section 17, Milton Township, Butler County, Kansas was her world. Her grandfather purchased this land from the Atchison, Topeka & Santa Fe Railroad Company in 1876. Using a walking cane, Mother walked out of her home in December 1992, right after Christmas, dressed in her Sunday best.

I never sat in the parlor on a rocker to discuss with Mother her views of the creative process. I doubt if she ever once thought about the process or even asked herself if she felt a sense of creativity. She would have shrugged her shoulders and deferred those technicalities to scholars. She was too busy being helpful to contemplate her motives. Her poems were from her heart and intended for the communication of ideas. She wanted the listeners or readers to fully comprehend the concepts she was conveying. Rhymes, rhythms, word sequences, and imagination were her tools. She used all the skills acquired though the ninth grade in 1919–1920 at Bethel Academy in North Newton, Kansas, her final year of formal education, and a lifetime of learning as she read and studied with eight children as they went through elementary and secondary schools. Words fascinated her. The rhyme and rhythm of languages caught the attention of her ear.

"Why Don't You Write Poetry?"

Figure 1
A school picture of Marie Harder while attending Bethel Academy,
North Newton, Kansas for her 9th grade in 1919–1920.
Stovall Studio, Newton, Kansas. Source: Author's file.

I use the word "languages" plurally since the initial poems of the 1920s, 1930s, and into the 1940s were written in German. These were handwritten using the *Sütterlin* script, which I needed to transcribe into Roman script before I could translate her writings into English. Fortunately, Mother's handwriting was clear and beautiful, but the *Sütterlin* script was so laborious to read that I found translation difficult without the Roman-script transcription.

Until 1940, German was the language used in our home, our church, and in the immediate community. Commerce in the local towns was conducted mostly in English and an amalgam of English and German. Many local merchants and bankers were of non-Mennonite

German descent; additionally, the English merchants also learned a few German words and phrases to assist in the communication process with the Mennonite community to garner their business while the Mennonites were building their English vocabularies. Both Mother and Father learned English in elementary school since both went to the public school in Brainerd. Both were avid readers, so continuously became more fluent in English even though they communicated with each other in German when at home and in the nursing home at the end of their lives.

My oldest siblings also learned English during their early years in the Brainerd elementary school where most of the board members were members of our Mennonite church. Consequently, the language in our home during my preschool years was a mixture. Until entering the first grade, I too spoke a fusion of both, using English and German in the same sentence and was unable to specify which I was speaking if asked, much to the hilarity of my older siblings, and much to their embarrassment if a non-family member ever heard me.

Giving up German was difficult for my father. To encourage the learning of German, Father created a system of rewards, which seemed more like a regimen of punishment and cruelty since the emphasis was on the German and not the rewards. Reading German was a prerequisite for driving a car. When my father purchased a new Allis Chalmers tractor in 1946, my oldest brother was required to read out loud a prescribed number of pages of German before Father granted driving privileges. At Christmas in 1947 a shared gift of a full-sized bicycle for all the children was included in the festivities; reading German was again a qualifying prerequisite. Some of my siblings frantically read their assigned pages from the *Unterstufe* so they could at least tell their friends that they had ridden the bicycle before returning to school after the Christmas break. I was the youngest in the family and, along with being considered perpetually infantile, many of the early family rules did not apply to me as I grew up; however, I also had the audacity to lack any need to drive the tractor or ride the bicycle, so I was required to read a set number of pages from the primer, *Der Fibel*, just for character development.

In 1938 Mother wrote a humorous bilingual poem incorporating family names within the local German community using both English and German in the same poem. By switching back and forth, she could create the lines she needed.

"Why Don't You Write Poetry?"

Bilingual Poem

Two men were meeting on their way
   While gossiping I heard them say:
Who lives in the big house here?
   Oh yes, I know it's Mr. <u>Regier</u>.
And who lives in the one there farther?
   Well, don't you know that's Mr. <u>Harder</u>.
Is he planning a trip up the Rhine?
   No, that's Mr. <u>Thierstein</u>.
Is he the one that's fixing his fence?
   No, if I'm right it's Mr. <u>Entz</u>.
Was he insured for rain and hail?
   No, that was Mr. <u>Nightingale</u>.
Who is at the end of his wits?
   That must be Mr. <u>Busenitz</u>.
Did he preach in the church down yonder?
   Yes, he and Mr. <u>Neuenschwander</u>.
Wer braucht beim Melken gern viele Eimer?
   Kein anderer ist es als Mr. <u>Reimer</u>.
      Who prefers to use many pails while milking?
      It is none other than Mr. Reimer.
Ist er ein guter Menschenkenner?
   Nicht so gut wie Mr. <u>Penner</u>.
      Is he good at recognizing people?
      Not as good as Mr. Penner.
Wer reitet da denn auf dem Fuchs?
   Höchstwahrscheinlich Mr. <u>Brucks</u>.
      Who is mounted on that chestnut colored horse?
      With high probability, it's Mr. Brucks.
Wo wird denn das Öl bald fliessen?
   Bei keinen andern als Mr. <u>Thiessen</u>.
      Where will oil soon flow?
      For none other than Mr. Thiessen.
Wer kann nicht das singen lassen?
   Wie ich hörte ist es Mr. <u>Claassen</u>.
      Who will not permit singing?
      As I hear, it is Mr. Claassen.
Für wen sang er doch bloss von Liebe?
   Jedenfalls für Mr. <u>Wiebe</u>.
      For whom did he sing only of love?
      To commemorate Mr. Wiebe.

The Petals of a Kansas Sunflower

> *Mag der gern die Taube tot.*
> *Nein das ist der* Mr. <u>Voth</u>.
>> Did he prefer his squabs dead?
>> No, that is Mr. Voth.
> Who was hurt when the mule did kick?
>> People tell me it's Mr. <u>Dyck</u>.
> How long will this winter last?
>> No one knows says Mr. <u>Fast</u>.
> *Weiss er das den so genau?*
>> *Ja, er fragt* Mr. <u>Esau</u>.
>>> Does he know that for sure?
>>> Yes, he asked Mr. Esau.
> *Wer das nicht recht fassen kann?*
>> *Nein das ist wohl der* Mr. <u>Bergmann</u>.
>>> Who is it that cannot rightly comprehend this?
>>> No, that surely is Mr. Bergmann.
> Who can write and still have pep?
>> This time it was Mrs. <u>Epp</u>.

This poem was found handwritten on the inside of an opened envelope with "1938" stamped on the front. In the last two lines Mother acknowledges the boundless energy that allowed her to continuously write while fully engaged in farm life. In keeping with the prevailing attitudes and traditions of the 1930s, all names are prefaced with "Mr." and describe activities of men. Only in the last two lines does she digress to female activity and uses "Mrs." to formally refer to herself.

To retain the beautiful rhymes and meter that Mother created, I present all poems in their original language with translations of those in German emphasizing content rather than meter. The poems written in German are best read in German to extract their verbal beauty; their beautiful rhymes and meter are often (mostly) lost in translation.

Writing to be creative was not the issue here. Mother was creative and so she wrote. Writing workshops were not organized in prairie pastures convenient for her participation. Some of her poems expressed her sentiment or emotions. Often historical details were incorporated reflecting her keen memory of facts. She was an astute observer and was fascinated by birds and flowers. Kansas was beautiful and agriculture simply dynamic to her.

Each of us has a collection of secrets that we never share, and her interaction with God was one that Mother kept tucked hidden in her heart. She had not shared her conversation with God with anyone. One day, when she was in the nursing home nearing the end of her life, she was propped up in bed with pillows. Her checks were rosy again, now that she had had her right foot amputated to remove the infection after living in pain for many years with an ulcer resulting from the varicose veins in her legs. My sister living in Pennsylvania had just arrived for a visit. Mother was energized and anticipated an afternoon of old-fashioned visiting. It was during this visit that Mother confided in two of my sisters and told them of her talk with God. When I later asked for more detail, apparently my sisters were so stunned or so disbelieving that they did not ask any questions. Silently, they may well have simply said to themselves, "No one speaks to God that way. Neither does God talk back nor does he give such clear suggestions. Let's bring her back to reality."

I believe my mother was perfectly lucid as she was most of the time in her geriatric years. Presumably, it was after her late December 1928 interaction with the force of ultimate power that Mother discovered she had a talent for writing verse.

If I analyze what Mother told my sisters, perhaps her conversation was not as presumptuous as it might appear. Her first two poems presented above are dated October 1929. Checking the family files, I learn that these poems would have been written two years after my mother and father married and one year after my oldest sister was born. My second sister was born in October 1929. The divine directive to write poetry was indeed initiated after Mother already had one or more babies in her lap.

Where was the melodic corner in which my mother had her epiphany? My father's family celebrated Christmas at Grandfather Epp's house on December 26. This house was a mile east of where my parents lived. After supper the whole family gathered in the large dining room and the grandchildren recited one last time whatever pieces they had memorized for Christmas programs in school or church. The group then sang German Christmas carols around the 1908 Windsor reed pump organ that Grandfather Epp gave his daughters after Grandmother Epp passed away in 1907, having given birth to her ninth child and seventh daughter. My father's seven sisters prided themselves in being musically talented with great voices. The family sang in four-part harmony and with vibrato. Mother perceived herself as being vocally-challenged without the ability to carry a tune. However, she could play the piano with soul and gusto. When she played the "Black Hawk Waltz" or "Star of the East" for us children, she had rhythm and feeling in her music that the melodious harmony of the in-laws never expressed.

I surmise that Mother's talk with God may have been on December 26, 1928, the year before she wrote her first poems. Mother was the only daughter-in-law and was sufficiently intimidated that she never sang on December 26 or even in church. She would open the songbook and follow the words. When I asked her about not singing, Mother simply said, "If I do not sing, there is one less thing for my sisters-in-law to criticize." This did not diminish in the least her appreciation for good music, including both choral and instrumental. After she began writing poetry, Mother loved to surround herself with music.

I was really never aware that my mother did a lot of writing. She never shushed us children or locked herself in a room to write. It was just something she did while working at keeping the farmhouse and moving her farm family along. After marshalling her youngest children to bed and helping those in high school with their homework, she was free to spend several hours at the end of the day with a dictionary crafting words into poetic lines.

Focusing on poetry also distracted Mother from compulsively worrying about Father's safe return home. Father spent many weekday evenings away from home involved in his commitments to the local schools, the church, or the agriculture in our community. If Mother did not focus on words and rhymes as the evening got late, she would pace the floor from one end of the living room to the other checking at each window for car lights coming down the driveway or if the car with Father was entering the detached garage. Mother had lost her sisters to death while they were young, and the fear of losing her husband or any of her children was only marginally disguised. As the evening wore on, Mother, with heavy eyelids, would often reaffirm her attachment to Father and say to us children, "I will not go to bed until Father is home."

Along with God's suggestion of poetry, came the gift of writing prose and other verbal activity. Mother taught Sunday school for many years; for this preparation she would barricade herself in her bedroom for several hours on Saturday afternoons while her bread was rising in the kitchen. Mother did some other writing as well. She wrote a skit "Reasons for Immigration" that was presented at the seventy-fifth anniversary of Emmaus Mennonite Church on July 8, 1951. For the

"Why Don't You Write Poetry?"

ninetieth anniversary, Mother joined with Gladys Penner Ewy Regier to write a historical skit "The Decision." This was presented on July 3, 1966. When Mother was past her eighty-fifth birthday, she initiated a historical, autobiographical book, *Lest We Forget*. This book was printed locally in 1992 in a limited edition of fifty copies and distributed to family members.

I am so grateful that mother left a legacy of writings. Her epiphany as a new in-law created an enriched environment for her family. I have always sensed that mother enlarged our concepts of the world that surrounded us by drawing our attention to details of the natural world and by discussing ideas and beliefs within an historical perspective that she recalled so well. Her writings have contributed to the celebration of life's joys and sorrows within her community. She honored many people with personalized poems.

2

This Is My Land

Mother truly enjoyed Kansas and could not imagine living anywhere else. Her ability to observe the world around her and remember what she saw made her think of Kansas as fascinating. Since she lived her whole life in the same house, it is only natural that she began to claim that part of God's earth as her own. The world became defined by what was experienced in and around the house and the farm.

This too is where I began to observe the natural world around me. Much of what I saw in early life was at the end of Mother's pointing finger. With words she also helped me see and hear what she had learned from a lifelong fascination of elements within her world, Section 17, Milton Township. It is here that she lived her life on the farm. She expressed her interaction with her surroundings and recorded what she saw and felt by writing poems.

In Butler County on the Farm

Come with me to good old Kansas at an early morning dawn,
   Where the mocking bird will wake you with her sweet melodious song.
Faint, but clear hues of the morning now will spread the eastern sky,
   Where the sunbeams, though majestic, from our sight concealed still lie.
Soon the sun in all her splendor slowly rises to full sight,
   And the Kansas plains are flooded with her warm, comforting light.
Farmers now are busy choring, milking cows and feeding steers,
   Both in which we find them experts having practiced many years.

Visit me in good old Kansas in the spring time of the year,
   When the March winds still are blowing and the robins will appear,
When the lilac bush is blooming, tulips too in bright array,
   When the thunderclouds are rolling and the twisters have their way,
When the little pigs are squealing, and the baby chicks will peep,
   When in green the grass is clothed after months of winter sleep.

This Is My Land

Then we find the farmer busy and the plow will turn the sod.
   Precious seed he too will scatter, but the increase comes from God.

Work with me in good old Kansas on a bright, hot summer day,
   When the harvest fields are ripening midst the fields of fragrant hay.
Cultivators, too, are running up and down long rows of corn.
   Soon the combine will be humming from the early dawn of morn.
Lines of wheat trucks then are waiting at elevators to unload,
   Even the farmer's wife was drafted and speeds a truck load down the road,
Then we see the farmer grinning as the auger rolls the grain,
   This is where our good old Kansas as a wheat state got her fame.

Enjoy with me our state of Kansas when it's autumn on the plains,
   And the air is clean and lovely, washed by gentle autumn rains,
When the nights are cool and restful, and the days are warm and fair,
   Which the Indian summer gives us, while the cobwebs sail the air.
Children ride for miles on buses. (The school no longer is nearby.)
   Southward now wild geese are flying beneath the azure autumn sky.
Again the farmer runs his combine, milo filling every bin.
   This will help to fatten the cattle, which already he brought in.

Live with me in good old Kansas when the winter comes to stay,
   And "Jack-frost" will paint the windows in his own artistic way.
When the sunflower long has faded and the lark has flown south,
   Dark and drab the sky above us, gray and bare the trees about.
Snowplows now will clear the highways, for a blizzard came and went,
   And beneath a glittering whiteness every evergreen is bent.
With meat replenished in the larder and the farmer sells his steers,
   Which, throughout the state of Kansas, have been famous through the years.

Stand with me and see the beauty of the Kansas starlit sky;
   See the galaxy and planets in their aged course on high.
They have witnessed all the changes that were seen on Kansas plains,
   From the buffalos and Indians and the covered wagon trains,
To the "Rockets" on the railway and jets cruising overhead,
   With the autos on the highways that like network have been spread.
Then we see the farmer thankful (now retiring for the night)
   For the blessings that God gave him, and for freedom—still his right.
                                            —Mrs. John Epp Jr.

    In this poem, Mother would invite you to join her in the wide open spaces of south central Kansas, "Come with me to good old Kansas . . ." This is that part of your flight from Los Angeles to New York where, after crossing the Rocky Mountains and the Continental Divide, for an hour of looking down you see nothing but round circles of green and then unending, tiny squares of brown, green, and beige. Or if you are going across country by car, you might be on Interstate 70 in the middle of the state and you unconsciously set your cruise control over the speed limit because if you have seen it once, you think to yourself, why linger around to repeat the identical viewing experience for four hundred miles. I like this area best when I disembark from a plane or park the car and walk around.

In the details, Kansas expresses variation in geological impact with evidence of ice-age glaciations in the northeast 1.6 million years ago and the sea bottom of the ancient Western Interior Sea over most of the rest from at least 250 million years ago. The climate is continental. Temperatures can fluctuate widely within a day and the extremes include a record high of 121 degrees in Fredonia and Alton in 1936 to a record low of forty-below-zero in Lebanon in 1905. The average annual rainfall increases from seventeen to forty inches as one travels from west to southeast creating different ecological niches for plants, birds, and wildlife. The Kansas of Mother's world averages thirty to thirty-one inches of rain per year, but the timeliness of the rain greatly impacts agricultural productivity; praying for rain was a routine summer social and church activity for upland farming without irrigation. Two-thirds to three-fourths of the rain comes during the six months of April to September. This trend permits the success of summer crops such as corn, sorghum, soybeans, alfalfa, and hay.

The U.S. Geological Survey set a bench mark post in 1960 in the fencerow about one hundred feet south of the Harder Cemetery at the end of the farm driveway. The data plate on top of the 4" x 4" cement marker records that the elevation at the site is 1403 feet above sea level. I watched them create this marker and my father's employee embedded a penny (1944D) in a corner at the top of the post beside the round data plate.

Mother asks us to see Kansas from her perspective. Kansas is beautiful. She was equally enamored of agriculture. Through the seasons the agricultural emphases change with different crops being harvested and different animals taking the most attention. In the final segment she asks us to reflect on reasons for gratitude.

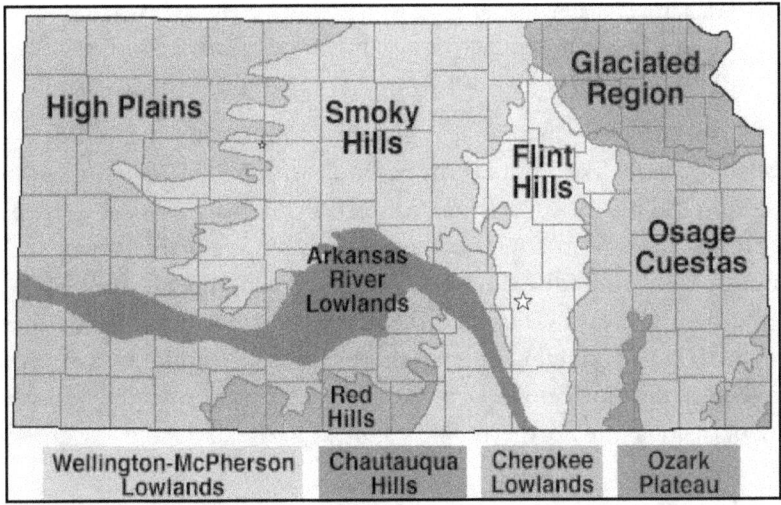

Figure 2
A physiographic map of Kansas. Butler County is the second county from the bottom within the Flint Hills area. Marie's world within Milton Township, Butler County is marked with a star. Source: Kansas Geological Survey, used with permission.

". . . And for freedom—still his right." Mother had listened to the immigrant generations. They were very conscious of the religious and political freedom that Kansas afforded her citizens. Freedom to practice their religious faith without political interference was the perpetual quest of the Mennonite diaspora and the reason they came to Kansas. Mother continued to consider Kansas divinely blessed and living in Kansas with its political and religious freedom a privilege. I am of the second generation born in America and know how quickly these freedoms are just assumed, rather than consciously cherished. The seductive tolerance of American democracy does not encourage, but rather diminishes, the intellectual analysis of one's personal beliefs and cultural heritage. After seventy-five years in America, the local church anniversary committee included in the foreword of their commemorative booklet:

> It has been said that the pioneers brought the sacrifices, that their children enjoyed them, and that their grandchildren are letting them slip by. God forbid that we and our children should regard lightly the faith, the convictions, and the courage of those who left established homes in search of new homes in a land in which they might enjoy freedom to worship according to the

dictates of their conscience... with the hope and prayer that our young people in coming years... may truly realize the cost and value of this precious heritage.

The skies still sparkle at night. In summertime the Milky Way stretches clearly like a broad white ribbon with frayed edges across the sky from the northeast to the southwest. In August, if we have the patience to look towards the northeast, we often see a shooting star. In autumn as the humidity drops with the lowered temperatures, the stars in the constellations clearly tell their stories. In the countryside there are few competing light sources, and prior to 1950, there wasn't even rural electrification on the farm, so it was very dark at night.[1] On very rare occasions, the northern lights danced in the darkened sky around the North Star.

The absence of the sounds of civilization is deafening on the farm. Even now in the twenty-first century, guests from the city are awed by the quietness when the wind isn't blowing. We can follow with closed eyes the progress of an eighteen-wheeler as it rolls down the state highway a half mile away. In summertime, it is possible to hear the community wake up in the morning as a neighboring farmer starts his tractor. The sounds of the trains whistling as they go through Whitewater or the ringing of church bells are heard on the farm several miles away.

At other times the prairie is anything but silent. When the wind velocity exceeds forty miles per hour an unsettling, eerie sound reverberates from trees and physical structures. The tree limbs groan and the leaves vibrate on a high note in unison. That is when I get a knot in my stomach. Or when the wind imitates the sound of a freight train that leaves its tracks and approaches from the southwest moving northeast, we know that a funnel cloud has formed and indiscriminate destruction is imminent. My parents heard these sounds the night of June 8,

---

1. My father established an account with the Butler Rural Electric Cooperative (REC) on March 7, 1939. The war effort of World War II made supplies, notably copper wire, unavailable for expansion of rural electrification. The house was wired for electricity after the end of the war and the account was activated January 1, 1950. The electric line for the farm came along the township road from the south under the auspices of REC. Electricity came into Whitewater in 1912 and this utility was taken over later by Kansas Gas & Electric Company (KGE). The town of Whitewater is one and a half miles west of the farm. The town of Brainerd is on the road one mile east of the farm and obtained electrical services in 1929. The farms one mile east or one mile west on the north-south roads were also on power grids with KGE lines.

1941, and in a few seemingly endless seconds, their farm became a disheveled mound of splintered aspirations and dreams. This event was the reference point of all activity in my childhood. I was the only p. t., i.e., post-tornado baby, born one year later and, upon reflection, prided myself in being a symbol of life returning to normalcy. Other relatives and friends also lived on the route of this runaway train and descriptive fragments evolve in several poems, but otherwise Mother wrote very little about this event. Perhaps she was just too overwhelmed and too involved with cleanup and simply trying to cope. More details of the June 8, 1941 tornado are included in chapter 5 and in appendix 3.

Other sounds play out the rhythms of nature on an annual cycle. At a point in early spring the frogs will begin croaking in the lagoons. The day before, all is quiet and the next day the world is filled with their song. The exact date varies from year to year and involves accumulated heat units. But on the day when the frogs begin to sing, the daffodils will be blooming, the Eastern Red Cedar will be in the final phases of shedding pollen, the maple and elm trees will begin to flower, and the daylilies will have new shoots erupting from the earth. This sequence of annual events is known in botanical science as "phenology."

Cicadas serenade during late July, August, and into September. The highpitched sounds of their vibrating wings can be deafening. Conversation under trees at dusk at times is almost impossible.

When the coyotes bark or howl at night, I think of laughing children who are giddy. But in the quiet darkness of early nighttime, the coyote's sounds were frightening to me as a child. As an adult, I still find that this sound jars even when the coyotes are over a quarter mile away.

It was not for lack of exposure to alternative places, but for Mother home and *gemütlichkeit* (comfort) were without doubt Section 17, Milton Township, Butler County, Kansas. During her lifetime she and my father traveled to California, as well as to New York City. They spent six months in Germany in the early 1960s helping with church relief work. On another occasion, they circumnavigated our planet visiting their children and Mother's niece and nephew with stops in Africa, Hong Kong, Japan, and Hawaii.

Mother wrote a second poem about Kansas, which reflects the pastoral aspects of living on the prairies. The expression of gratitude for what living in Kansas has encompassed permeates the entire poem. The first generation of immigrants sought a better place for their children. And this they achieved.

The Petals of a Kansas Sunflower

Kansas

In the midst of swaying wheat fields
   Where the sky is fair and blue,
Where the meadowlark is singing
   And the sunflower nods at you.
Where the blizzards sweep the prairie
   And the coyotes howl at night,
Where the sun in all her splendor
   Sets in colors radiant bright,
There we see our homesteads dotted
   Over Kansas fertile soil.
God has richly blessed our efforts
   As we labor, as we toil.
He has given us the sunshine,
   In due time the wind and rain,
He has given us the increase
   Of the precious golden grain.
We don't know the pangs of hunger,
   God gives us our daily bread.
We are not in need of raiment,
   We are clothed and we are fed.
Lovely are our homes—and spacious,
   Even though they'll fade away.
Rich and manifold these blessings
   We enjoy from day to day.
God blessed us through our fathers
   Whom he led with mighty hand.
As from overseas he brought them
   To this free and blessed land.
They looked not for earthly treasures,
   'Twas a sacrifice they brought
For the welfare of their children,
   Religious freedom here they sought.
Shall we take all this for granted,
   All these blessings from God's hand?
Knowing we are just sojourners
   To a great and better land.
Humbly then with love forever
   We shall bring our grateful praise,
And exalt our heavenly Father
   Until the end of our days.

—Marie Epp

I think that Mother wrote these two poems in the 1950s to early 1960s. In the first poem she mentions that "Children ride for miles on buses. (The school no longer is near by.)" The local schools were consolidated in stages with the comprehensive reorganization in 1963, which resulted in increased busing. The poems are written in English. Early in her writing career and in public forums she used Father's name, Mrs. John Epp Jr., and later in life she often simply initialed her poems M. H. E. for Marie Harder Epp.

During the same time period, *The Independent* (Whitewater, Kansas) newspaper on June 15, 1950 referred to Mother as the "poet laureate of the community." They published the poem she wrote for B. W. Harder's golden wedding anniversary included in chapter 13. Mother was honored that the poem was printed in the local paper, but "being published" held no meritorious value for her writing career. Her poem, "In Butler County on the Farm" was printed on a Tuesday in the column "Kernels and Cobs" of the Kansas City *Daily Drover Telegram*. She later changed the title of the poem to "In Kansas on the Farm" and distributed copies to her extended family. She never discussed or pursued getting other poems published. Less than ten poems were included in her autobiographical book and her only comment about poetry writing was "Over the years I have written many poems for wedding anniversaries, and this one is my latest. I wrote it for James and Lisa Epp's wedding August 1991." This poem is presented in chapter 11 and is the last poem she penned.

3

History as a Reference Point

When my great-grandfather Bernhard Harder arrived in Kansas, he was looking for high ground. Flooding had been a perpetual problem during the spring thaws in West Prussia as the ice floes clogged the Nogat and Vistula Rivers. The productive farm Great-grandfather Harder sold in Gurken in the Vistula Delta of West Prussia, just before their June 15, 1876 departure, lay between these two rivers. These lowlands were the drained areas that fellow Mennonites from Holland had reclaimed from swamplands by means of windmills, canals, and dikes beginning in 1530.

The spring thaws would begin farther south in Austria, sending flood waters with ice chunks flowing down rivers to the Baltic Sea. In colder, northern Germany spring arrived later, and the chunks of floating ice would often refreeze causing huge ice jams. These blocked the river channels and flooding would result. The floods of 1839, 1845, and 1855 were particularly devastating and inundated the fields; they also destroyed Great-grandfather's manicured garden. After each flood he reclaimed the fields and replanted his garden. He managed his farm and garden for forty-four years. It is little wonder that this beautiful property in West Prussia became very dear to his heart. After the 1855 flood the levees were raised and dynamite became available for breaking ice jams.

Whenever there were floods in West Prussia, some of the fields were covered with worthless sand. The Rev. Cornelius H. Regier, my paternal great-grandfather, whom we will meet again in chapter 15, and who also was Great-grandfather Harder's nephew, recounted that he once supervised a gang of forty men who, after laboriously digging a ditch four to six feet deep across a field, would then roll a strip of surface sand into the ditch, and cover the sand with good soil by digging the next ditch, thus reclaiming the area for agricultural production. Great-grandfather Harder's goal in America was to emphasize production and not reclamation.

Figure 3
Bernhard Harder (1811–1900) photographed in Wichita, Kansas in the studio of Nereus Baldwin, 118 East Douglas Avenue (second floor). Mr. Baldwin is a renowned photographer of early Wichita, beginning his work in 1873. The date of this photo is presumably ca. 1885 but before 1886 when the studio became N. Baldwin & Son. By 1885 train transportation from Brainerd to Wichita became available. Baldwin Photos, Wichita, KS. Source: Author's file.

The Petals of a Kansas Sunflower

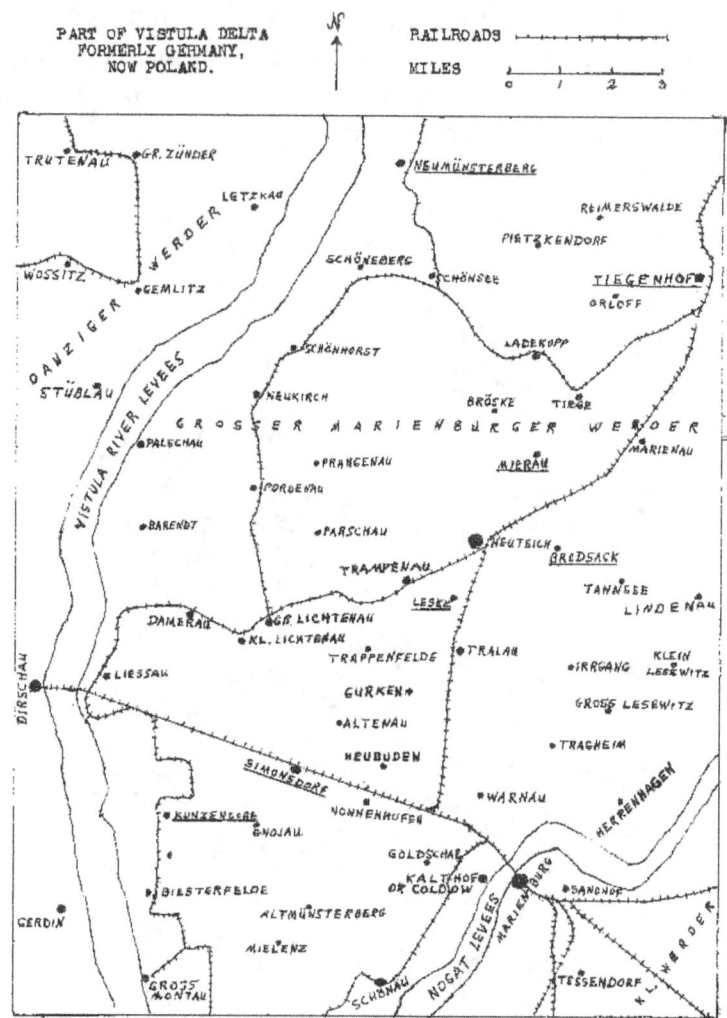

Figure 4
Map of the Vistula Delta in 1876.
Source: Claassen, Ernest. *Abraham Claassen, Vistula to Plum Grove*. **Whitewater, KS: privately printed, 1975. Used with permission.**

It was late July 1876 and with a group of other new immigrants, Great-grandfather was creating the future he desired for his three sons: Johannes (a.k.a. John Sr.) aged twenty-two, Gustav aged twenty, and Bernhard aged eleven. His sons were approaching the Prussian military draft age and this relocation was timely. They had just arrived by train in Kansas from New York City after eleven days on the Atlantic Ocean.

History as a Reference Point

It had not been easy leaving West Prussia after spending forty-four years developing a beautiful, prosperous farm and garden. The Prussian government passed a national conscription law in 1868, which abolished all previously arranged exemptions. Every able-bodied man between the ages of twenty and forty-five could be drafted for military service after 1870. This ended the privileges obtained through special taxation that the Mennonites enjoyed in West Prussia for more than three hundred years. The freedom to follow their conscience with reference to military service was no longer allowed, so Great-grandfather finally comtemplated seriously the idea of leaving his *Heimat* (homeland).

In 1869, he took a long trip to southern Russia to search for a new homeland, as so many other West Prussian Mennonites had done before, beginning in 1780 and again in 1860. The trip itself was arduous, and it took five weeks to travel from West Prussia to southern Russia by horse and wagon. But the Russian government was beginning to exert political influence in southern Russia, working to make Russian the language of commerce and education within the German Mennonite villages, and to convert locally operated Mennonite schools into governmental institutions with Russian curricula. Long-standing promises were ending, including the perpetual (eternal) right for self-governance issued by Czarina Catherine the Great with the Manifesto of 1793 that had enticed so many West Prussian Mennonites and other Germans to Imperialist South Russia. By the summer of 1870 compulsory military service was introduced in Russia as well, also making it no longer desirable for military freedom and self-governance. Great-grandfather Harder decided that the only viable option was to immigrate to America.

He and his family were among the first group of West Prussians from the Heubuden church to sell their properties. He was sixty-four years old at the time and it was not easy to leave the farm he had nurtured. However, he committed himself and his family to accompany the Prussian Mennonite immigrants leaving for America from the Simonsdorf train station, the nearest station to the villages of Heubuden and Gurken on June 15, 1876. It was a very gloomy day as they made their way to the station through the heavy rain. The train took them by way of Berlin to Bremen, Germany, where the group embarked a ship for New York City and then a train to Kansas (see appendix 2 for more details). Now that he was in America, he needed to locate a site for a new farm for himself and farms for his three sons.

The Petals of a Kansas Sunflower

On August 18, 1876, Carl Bernhard Schmidt (a.k.a. C. B. Schmidt), the German-speaking general agent of the German Department of the Land Office in Topeka of the Atchison, Topeka & Santa Fe Railroad (a.k.a. Santa Fe), came to Halstead, Kansas to take the new immigrants to see land available in Butler County. Mr. Schmidt was very influential in bringing Mennonites and others of German heritage from West Prussia, Russia, and across Europe to Kansas. At this time about 15 percent of the land of Kansas had been given to the railroads by the federal government through the Land Grant Legislation of 1863, and the Santa Fe Railroad had 3,200,000 acres to sell in order to finance the completion of the expansion of railroads and telegraph lines across Kansas from the Missouri River to the Colorado state line. By 1876, the Santa Fe Railroad had eight hundred miles of completed tracks.

To advertise the available Santa Fe Railroad land, Mr. Schmidt had letters appearing in newspapers in Europe, including the *Frankfurter Zeitung* (Frankfurt newspaper), and had established landsales offices in northern Europe. In 1875 he also personally traveled, with sales fliers in hand (see figure 47, appendix 1), to West Prussia, across Europe, and also into southern Russia targeting Mennonites and others of German heritage to encourage immigration to the lands he represented in Kansas. He wanted people with a well-established work ethic to develop Kansas with businesses that would utilize the services of the railroad. Mr. Schmidt was an excellent salesman and facilitator, and eventually sold nearly three hundred thousand acres to German settlers coming from various parts of America as well as from Europe.

When the ship *SS Rhein* docked at Hoboken in New York on Saturday, July 1, 1876, Mr. Schmidt, together with a Mr. Andres from Kansas, was there to greet and assist the weary immigrants; both men were fluent in German and English. Also meeting the ship were two male relatives from Beatrice, Nebraska who had emigrated earlier from Russia. All these greeters helped facilitate the transfer of the extensive amounts of luggage, chests, and farm and household goods to trains that took some immigrants to Halstead, Kansas and others to Mt. Pleasant, Iowa.

Prior to departure, Mr. Schmidt and Mr. Andres also took some of the newly arrived West Prussian immigrants into New York City to exchange their *Reichsthaler* notes for American dollars. Here for the first time they saw tall buildings of eight stories. Available on the streets would have been copies of the *New York Times*. Had these immigrants been able to read English they would have learned that the day before, the Yale crewing team won the Yale-Harvard regatta with superior strokes—"However, everyone got home at last, the Blues very exultant and the Crimson very blue." From Utica, New York, the Hamilton College team took last place at the Saratoga Lake regatta, because the students prefered oration to rowing. It probably would not have concerned them any more that the Serbian Prince Milan was threatening to place torpedoes in the Danube if the Turkish gunboats quit Widdin—negotiations were ongoing. The temperature in New York City at noon on Friday, the day before, had been a warm eighty degrees.

Mr. Schmidt got the weary ocean travelers onto the right trains with tickets in hand. Six families were facilitated on the continuation of their westward journey to a new and unfamiliar location in the very heart of America called "Kansas." The heads of these families were Dietrich Claassen, Edward Claassen, Bernhard Harder, Johannes Harder, Heinrich Penner, and Gerhard Regier. In Halstead, the travel-weary immigrants were welcomed by relatives, the Abraham Entz and the Peter Wiebe families, who had emigrated two years earlier from southern Russia. The relatives opened their homes and the new pioneers remained with them or in neighboring houses until farms were found. The assistance, hospitality, and sharing over an extended period of time reflected the concept of community that was and continues to be an integral part of pioneering, as well as of Mennonite culture.

In Halstead, Kansas, newspapers in the German language were available. These could be procured whenever they went to town for supplies. *Zur Heimat* began publication in February 1875, and the *Nachrichten aus der Heidenwelt* started in January 1877. Both were merged into the Newton, Kansas newspaper *Christlicher Bundesbote* in January 1882 and continued publication until July 1947. Thus my relatives always had access to a Kansas newspaper in their language of fluency. Additionally, Newton had the *Newton Anzeiger* from June 1887 to April 1892 and *Der Herold* from November 1897 to December 1941.

The immigrant men spent July and August of 1876 looking for land after they recuperated from their long journey with a short rest. When their travel companions, who had gone to Mt. Pleasant, Iowa, came to Kansas to look at land, C. B. Schmidt was ready to show them the railroad land available for purchase. The group, equipped with spades and augers, drove out from Newton, Halstead, and Peabody on six spring wagons, stopping to examine the soil when they came to available land. They viewed land in several counties, going as far west as the Pawnee Rock area where the soil was good, but the buffalo grass was too short. Trips were also made to view land in the Beatrice, Nebraska area.

But now, on August 18, Mr. Schmidt would take some of these potential landowners by train from Halstead to Peabody, a distance of thirty miles. In Peabody, they transferred to two wagons with teams of horses and drove south. Evaluating land on this excursion were my great-grandfather Bernhard Harder and son Johannes Sr., Dietrich Claassen and son Ed Sr., Heinrich Penner, and the Rev. Peter Dyck, with his son-in-law Jacob W. Regier. Rev. Dyck and his family had initially gone to Iowa, but had come with his family to Halstead from Mt. Pleasant, just days before and were staying with my Harder great-grandparents.

There were few if any roads, just mostly grass, and maybe a path. The prairie grass was so tall at places that, even when standing in the wagons, it was hard to get a bird's-eye view. Fortunately, Mr. Schmidt knew the way and at least had a sense of direction. As they were going south, apparently the wagons went over some rough terrain and Great-grandfather Harder unexpectedly fell backward off the wagon, knocking the wind out of him. He could hardly breathe for awhile, but recovered enough so the caravan could go on. This accident did not deter him from his objective. He had endured and survived the ocean voyage and now this fall, so with shovel and auger in hand, Great-grandfather intended to test the soil profile for himself. He also took note of the height of the grasses and the height of the sunflowers growing on the disturbed soil of the surveyor's Xs plowed at the corner of each section where a surveyor's stone had been placed five inches below the surface. By the previous year, 1875, all public land in Kansas had been surveyed using the system originated by Thomas Jefferson while he was a United States congressman representing the state of Virginia. His Land Ordinance of 1785 stipulated baseline meridians from which to survey, divided the land into townships six miles square, and then subdivided each township into thirty-six one-mile square sections.

This was a successful sales trip, because with time all of these men purchased land from the Santa Fe Railroad within an area six to fifteen miles south of Peabody. They tried to locate an area where they could all purchase contiguous parcels of land to recreate a community village patterned after their previous European experiences and large enough to also accommodate their travel companions from Mt. Pleasant. But Mr. Schmidt had only odd numbered sections of railroad land for sale in this area per the Land Grant Legislation of 1863 that Abraham Lincoln signed into law. The odd numbered sections ten miles on either side of the railroad right-of-way were railroad lands; the even numbered sections were available for homesteading. Homesteading was governed by the Homestead Act of 1862, which limited each farmer to a quarter of a section only. In time, most of the West Prussian immigrants who initially traveled to Mt. Pleasant purchased land in the Beatrice, Nebraska area, while those that traveled directly to Kansas purchased land in Butler and Harvey counties, near the present-day towns of Whitewater, Elbing, and Newton.

The new pioneers did not see any bison or Indians on this land sales trip, nor did they ever see any wild bison. The last wild bison in Kansas was killed in 1879 at Point of Rocks north of Elkhart in the far southwest corner of Kansas. And contrary to their European perception, Indians also did not roam freely in Kansas any more. Between 1873 and 1875, there was continued methodical and massive slaughter of the buffalo for their meat and hides, resulting in the virtual extermination of bison from Kansas. By 1875 most of the Indians had relocated to Oklahoma, some encouraged by the ongoing slaughter and annihilation of the bison, the basis for their traditional bison-based livelihood, and other eventually forced by the government. After the Little Bighorn battle in 1876, the U.S. government forced most Northern Cheyennes from the Northern Plains to a reservation in Indian Territory, present-day Oklahoma. In September 1878 a group led by Chiefs Dull Knife and Little Wolf attempted to return to their homeland. Angry and embittered, they killed settlers and herders as they fled through Kansas. Forty settlers and herders were killed in Kansas, nineteen were in Decatur County. Decatur County is two hundred seventy-five miles northwest of Butler County, but surely the early settlers in Milton Township read about this tragedy in local newspapers. A monument dedicated to those settlers killed in the September 1878 raid was erected in the Oberlin cemetery in 1911. The Cheyenne raid through Kansas resulted in a new government treaty and the Northern Cheyenne were moved to a reservation in eastern Montana.

The Petals of a Kansas Sunflower

As will be mentioned in chapter 13, in late August 1876, Gerhard Regier and his sons did see two Indians on horses with bows and arrows on their backs riding through the area as the Regiers were surveying their landholdings for the first time. The first encounter created fear, caused by lack of familiarity. They learned quickly that the few Indians that would ride through were very friendly and only a few individuals visited their farms asking for food. Using the handsigns of rubbing their tummies or repeatedly moving their hands to their mouth, the Native Americans communicated their hunger. The new Mennonite pioneers freely shared their sustenance.

Another European perception was that in the American heartland, a criminal element abounded. Free-wheeling cowboys and gun-slinging outlaws were considered lawless criminals to be feared by the pioneers. The Chisholm Trail from San Antonio, Texas north to Abilene, Kansas was important immediately following the Civil War until the expansion of the railroads and the introduction of barbed wire. The trail brought herds of Texas longhorn cattle to the Abilene railhead serviced by the Kansas Pacific Railroad. In 1871, the Atchison, Topeka & Santa Fe Railroad reached Newton, Kansas shortening the Chisholm Trail by about one hundred miles or fifteen to twenty days of driving the cattle. Along with the cattle came the cowboys who turned Newton into a cowtown of incredible violence. The railhead services overwhelmed effective city planning and there appeared to be a complete lack of enforcement of law and order. A local story is that passengers arriving in Newton by train during this period would crouch below the level of the train windows in the event that an overly exuberant cowboy would shoot for sport at the windows of the train. By 1872, the Santa Fe reached Wichita, Kansas, which shortened the trail another twenty miles and converted Wichita into the main cattle trading center on the Santa Fe line. Numerous mobile businessmen and women who catered to the cattle trade and needs of the drovers left for the Delano district in west Wichita and other shipping points; with them they carried much of Newton's unsavory reputation. By 1876, Newton was a model prairie town that did not discourage or distract peace-minded Mennonite immigrants from purchasing railroad lands in the area.

History as a Reference Point

Figure 5
Native American artifacts collected from Section 17, Milton Township. The projectile point on the left is 6.75 cm from tip to base and was picked up on the southwest quarter of the section. The point on the right is 10.25 cm long collected on the southeast quarter. These isolated finds are points chipped from Kansas Wreford chert (flint) and depict Late Archaic Williams points (ca. 1000 BCE—500 CE). Since Section 17 is not traversed with a creek where points are normally found, these points may have been dropped and lost as the hunters traveled through the area or the points were carried in animal bodies (most likely bison) until they perished. Private collections. Source: Author's file.

Kansas was opened for agricultural settlement in 1854 through the enactment of the Kansas-Nebraska Act. Territorial Kansas, as it was known from 1854 to 1861, became a pawn in the bloody clashes involving pro-slave versus Free State interest groups. Kansas entered statehood on January 29, 1861, joining the Union as a free state under the Wyandotte Constitution. These confrontational events predated the arrival of my ancestors who came fifteen years after the statehood of Kansas. Slavery, the trade in humans as a chattel commodity, would not have been compatible with the concepts of the teachings of Jesus for these new pioneers. They did have many employees for all the manual work of that era, and some employees did spend their whole lives working on the same farm per the mores of the time. The term in German used to describe these employees translates into English as servants, not slaves, but they were wage-earners and were never owned or even indentured.

The wagon caravan returned to Peabody in the afternoon and the men took a train to Wichita for the night. On one occasion during their land-viewing travels the group lunched at a local hotel in the town of Sedgwick. When the waiter asked what they wanted for lunch, they bumbled in German and communicated, "Just bring us food." It was corn season and the waiter brought them large roasting ears of corn on plates. The immigrants had no clue what to do with the roasted ears of corn, because in Europe maize was only grown in flower beds as a novelty from America and not consumed, nor did corn have any practical value at the time in Europe. They looked around to see what the locals at other tables did with the corn. Taking the ears by the ends with their fingers and nibbling off the kernels after applying butter and salt was not a familiar or a comfortable experience. John Harder Sr. wrote, "We did not follow their example." I have no clue how they handled the corn or what else they had for lunch that day.

The men in my family were all agronomists and traditionally had been in agriculture; some trace their beginnings to the Friesland area in northern Holland. The name "Epp" has Dutch origins. Mennonites viewed land as a divine instrument. Historically, their need to own land was not fixed to any specific country since they tended to avoid involvement in governmental affairs, but they idealized an agrarian lifestyle. This way of life had helped isolate and protect the Mennonites from non-Mennonite cultural influences; to be avoided were ostentation, avarice, vanity, and violence. My mother, in true Mennonite character, once shared that she considered farming the only honest profession; many other professions, particularly those in business, compromised honesty to achieve success.

The name "Harder" appears indigenous to West Prussian Mennonites but originated in northern Germany. The Harders, an old farming dynasty, were among those invited by the Teutonic Knights to colonize the Vistula Delta after the native *Preussens* were conquered in 1283. The Harders joined the Mennonite community after the arrival of the

Dutch Mennonites. By 1667–77, the name "Harder" appeared in baptismal records of the Danzig Flemish congregation in the Vistula Delta. Within twenty-five years many Harders living in the Vistula Delta were Mennonites, because persons with the Harder surname were on the membership rolls of the major Mennonite congregations. I am beginning to think that Mother, who was a Harder, inherited her affinity for agriculture. It surely was in her blood.

My family was also Anabaptist. I heard the word, Anabaptist, used in conversation since childhood, but in my mind it seemed vague, like an abstraction. I never really considered the implications of its meaning within the historical context of my family, except that I recall local preachers rallying the congregation to adhere to the traditions. As an adult, my curiosity led me to examine the concept. A dictionary definition is "any member of a radical sixteenth-century sect of the Reformation originating in Switzerland, often persecuted because they opposed the taking of oaths, infant baptism, military service, and the holding of public office." In appendix 1, I have traced the history of my Mennonite Anabaptist ancestors from Holland through West Prussia to America to better understand the attitudinal and religious nuances within Mother's poetry.

There were many activities needed to create a farm and a community on this Kansas ocean of endless grass. Of primary importance was the construction of wells for a water source. There was a need for houses, farm buildings, and fences. Additionally, there was a need for schools, a church, and a cemetery.

From the writings of the Rev. Peter Dyck, apparently my great-grandfather had some anxiety about finding a water source on his farm and was relieved when finally the well digger, Mr. Harms, found a good source of water. "With the well they had many troubles before they got water. For both Harders [Bernhard Sr. and son John Sr., whose farm was one-quarter mile south and one-half mile east of his father's farm] it was seventy feet deep, consequently they had to at times hammer through stone, but now there is a lot of water. The complete well worked [i.e., lined] with quarry stone cost $1.10 per foot and to chisel with hammer through the stone $1.90 per foot." Deep wells were a new concept because the water table in West Prussia was very close to the surface.

These new pioneers did have access to postal service if they went to the Holden farmhouse on Section 20, Milton Township, approximately three-fourths of a mile south of where Great-grandfather located his new farm. With the passing of the Kansas-Nebraska Act of 1854, as Kansas was organized as a territory and opened for settlement, the United States Postal Service immediately proceeded to establish mail delivery in the territory. Delivery time was measured in months, because the postal service would handle letters addressed to an individual with the address "Somewhere in Kansas." The Holden post office originated in Milton Township on Section 18, relocated to Section 8 and then Section 20. It was in operation from 1870 to 1886 and serviced from Towanda, Kansas once or twice a week. Mail was carried by horseback, wagon, or on foot. Towanda was an early Indian trading post and had a post office beginning in 1865. In 1886 the Holden Post Office was moved one mile east to the new town of Brainerd and remained active until 1907. In 1888, I. H. Neiman was named postmaster in the new town of Whitewater. Daily rural mail delivery from Whitewater started about 1902.

Also on Section 20, the section south of Section 17 purchased by my great-grandfather, was an elementary school. Mrs. E. T. Eaton taught the first term of school in a small house built on the southwest quarter of Section 20 in what became District 95. The Holden School was built later in 1871 and was located on the north side of Section 20, just west of the half-mile hedge row. As Whitewater organized, District 95 was relocated to town and the first school building was built there in 1889. My grandfather, Bernhard Harder, was eleven years old in 1876 when the family immigrated, so immediately he had access to an elementary school within a mile of the farm. Oral history relates that Grandfather was the only boy enrolled in the school and was mercilessly teased by the girls. One day he connived to retaliate and set a bucket of water on top of the door. When the girls would come, he would tip the bucket. He released the bucket when someone came, but it was the teacher who got wet. Whoops.

The commitment to purchase Section 17, Milton Township was made by the end of August. The deed for the sale of Section 17, Milton Township was actually dated November 29, 1876 and filed for record June 1, 1877 in the Office of the Register of Deeds at the Butler County Court House in El Dorado. The deed also traces the ownership of the land from the United State of America to the State of Kansas to the Atchison, Topeka, & Santa Fe Railroad Company to Bernhard Harder:

History as a Reference Point

Section Seventeen (17)
Township Twenty-four (24) South, Range 3 East.

UNITED STATES OF AMERICA
to
STATE OF KANSAS

Land Grant by Act of Congress approved March 3, 1863, entitled an act for a Grant of Lands to the State of Kansas in alternate sections to aid in the Construction of certain Railroads and Telegraphs in said State of Kansas accepting said Grant. Approved February 9, 1864.

STATE OF KANSAS
to
ATCHISON, TOPEKA & SANTA FE RAILROAD COMPANY

Consideration—Act of Legislature. Dated May 19, 1873. Filed for record May 1, 1880 and recorded in Volume "V" of Deeds at page 215 of the records of Butler County, Kansas.

ATCHISON, TOPEKA AND SANTA FE RAILROAD COMPANY
F. H. Peabody, Vice President,
E. Meder, Secretary
George C. Lord, O. W. Peabody, F. H. Peabody, Joseph Nickerson, Trustees
to
BERNHARD HARDER

CONSIDERATION—$4198.40. Dated November 29, 1876. Filed for record June 1, 1877 and recorded in Volume "O" of Deeds at page 198 of the records of Butler County, Kansas.

DESCRIPTION—All of Section No. Seventeen (17) in Township No. Twenty four (24) South, of Range No. Three (3) East of the Sixth Principal Meridian containing Six Hundred and forty (640) acres more or less, according to the United States Survey.

DEED RECITES—Reserving however to the said Atchison, Topeka and Santa Fe Railroad Company all that portion of the land hereby conveyed (if there be any such) which lies within lines drawn parallel with the fifty feet on each side distant from the center line of its Railroad as now constructed or hereafter to be constructed and any greater width where necessary permanently to include all their cuts, embankments and other works necessary to secure and protect the main line of said Railroad.

WRITTEN IN THE BODY OF DEED—The Atchison, Topeka and Santa Fe Railroad Company, a corporation doing business under the laws of the State of Kansas and Thomas Nickerson, Oliver W. Peabody and George C. Lord, F. H. Peabody, Joseph Nickerson and A. I. Benyon.

The Petals of a Kansas Sunflower

Great-grandfather Harder and his sons set out from Halstead on a Monday morning in September, 1876. It took all day to travel the twenty-eight miles, because they stopped in Newton to purchase horses, harnesses, wagons, and mowers. When they finally arrived at their newly acquired property later in the day, all they could see was blue sky and prairie grass. They began cutting the grass and making haystacks. They slept at the haystacks and leaned boards against the haystacks if they needed a bit of shelter. They survived on bread, syrup, and coffee. To break the monotony of this spartan diet, they had coffee, syrup, and bread. Within a short time, they purchased a cow and added milk to their diet. There surely was enough grass to support a cow.

The first building they built was a *Speicher*, a granary. They brought a carpenter along from Halstead, but the lumber and building supplies were hauled by horse and wagon from Newton or Peabody, each being fifteen to twenty miles away. Every trip was a long day of work. The limestone foundation stones were hauled from the quarries near Florence, east of Peabody. The women came in the autumn of 1876 from Halstead and set up their household in this granary while the house was being built.

Great-grandfather Harder invited the other West Prussian immigrants in the community to join him and his family for Sunday worship in this newly built *Speicher*. He had been a chorister (*Vorsänger*) in the Heubuden Church in West Prussia for forty years beginning in 1836. The Heubuden Church did not have an organ or a piano, nor did they have many songbooks. The few books available only had the words of the songs, but not the musical notes. However, the title of the appropriate melody was also included with the words. So the chorister would recite a line or two of the song and then sing the lines with the congregation of over one thousand members joining in the singing. The whole song was lined out even if there were fourteen verses. Being a chorister was a worship leadership position of some distinction and honor, because he needed almost perfect pitch to keep the singing on track.

The first service in the granary was led by the Rev. Wilhelm Ewert who formerly had been the elder of a church in Obernessau, West Prussia and had traveled to America as a representative of the Prussian Mennonites on the exploration trip of twelve men in 1873. He had come a year earlier and settled in the Hillsboro area, founding the Brudertal congregation composed primarily of Russian Mennonites. In the granary the old people sat on the few available chairs and the rest seated themselves on planks placed across nail kegs. The community continued to meet in the granary on Sundays until the farmhouse was completed the next summer. The Rev. Peter Dyck who purchased land about seven miles north of my great-grandfather's land also helped with those early Sunday worship services. A visitor to the farm from Pennsylvania in July 1877 mentions that the group met on the farm for church service in the newly constructed spacious house.

After Great-grandfather had completed his house, he is remembered for having said, "*Eck well met Gurken nu doch nich meha tusche welle.* I would not want to trade back for what I had in Gurken." His farm in West Prussia was in the village of Gurken. A floor plan of the house and the layout of the garden that he created south of the house was designed to emulate the house and garden he left behind in West Prussia and are included in chapter 15.

Another consideration for Great-grandfather was a cemetery. Among the family group that came to America was his mother-in-law Justine Claassen Bergmann Penner who was seventy-nine years old. She had left two husbands buried in the Heubuden Church cemetery and was concerned about a *proper* burial on the plains of Kansas amid the endless expanse of tall grass. So Great-grandfather set a parcel of land aside at the end of the east farm driveway in perpetuity as a cemetery. Eight red cedar trees were planted along a central aisle with the parcel periphery outlined with a hedge of Osage orange trees. A metal gate was placed at the entrance. Fortunately, great-great-grandmother was able to enjoy her family and the Kansas experience for another eight years and is the first interment in the Harder cemetery. Buried on her right is her daughter Justine Bergmann Harder, my great-grandmother, and to her left is her son Jacob Bergmann. There was no organized church in 1876 when the family arrived in Kansas; the church was organized in 1878, and the first interment in the Emmaus Mennonite Church cemetery was by 1880, but the Harder family cemetery had been set up prior to that time and consequently utilized.

Figure 6
The family communion set of a pewter chalice and plate was used on the Kansas prairies until the newly organized church purchased their own sets after 1878. The inscription is H. F. D. B. 1797, the initials of Heinrich Fast and Dietrich Bergmann. These two men were brothers-in-law and Dietrich Bergmann was my great-great-grandfather and the first husband of my great-great-grandmother Justine Claassen Bergmann Penner who came to America in 1876 with her daughter Justine and son Jacob and their families. The date, 1797, may represent the year this set was procured or a significant year in the life of the family house church in West Prussia where this communion set was used during worship services. Private collection. Source: Author's file.

History as a Reference Point

Figure 7
Bernhard Harder farm in 1915. The house on the left is my great-grandfather's house built in 1876–1877. The second building from the left is the horse barn built in 1877 and the third is the *Speicher*, granary, that was built in 1876 into which the family moved in the autumn of 1876 and where Great-grandfather invited his neighbors for worship services on Sundays. The house on the right was my grandfather Bernhard Harder Jr.'s house built prior to his marriage in 1887. Source: Author's file.

In 1877, C. B. Schmidt toured the German Mennonite settlements that he helped to establish through the brokering of Santa Fe Railroad lands and published a booklet of his observations in 1878. He reported that it was noticeable the West Prussian Mennonites in Harvey and Butler County had the necessary capital to build nice and comfortable homes. He was told by Dietrich Claassen that the West Prussian settlement by that time in Butler County consisted of twenty-four families who had acquired railroad land. He observed that their Butler County land was just as productive as the fertile Vistula Delta in West Prussia. He concluded that these settlers had chosen a favorable location and their financial resources and hired help would contribute considerably to their prosperity.

The immigrant group continued to meet in Great-grandfather's house for Sunday services until the first church building was completed in the autumn of 1878. It was located about three miles northeast of the farm and in the center of the fragmented community.

In the spring of 1877, Leonhard Suderman and family moved to the community. He had been an elder in his community church in southern Russia, but his roots were in the Heubuden Church in West Prussia. He too had been one of the twelve delegates who in 1873 toured and evaluated the possibilities of settling in America for the Russian and West Prussian Mennonites. Elder Suderman helped organize the local church. He simultaneously served as elder for the West Prussian contingency in Newton until 1886. Occasionally, in the early years he would also travel to Beatrice, Nebraska to perform elder functions like baptisms during periods when that church lacked an elder. He served the local church until his death in 1900.

Figure 8a
The first building of the Emmaus Mennonite Church built in 1878 to seat two hundred people costing $1,000 and was used for thirty years. Pictured standing in front of building are Elder and Mrs. Leonard Sudermann with Mrs. G. H. Regier Sr., as a child.
Source: William Regier Slides, The Frederic Remington Area Historical Society Library.

The architectural design of the entry doors of these three churches is fascinating. The first and third models have one central entry door. The second church had a women's door on the left and a men's door on the right. The women sat to the left of the central aisle with the men on the right. The Heubuden Church in West Prussia had two doors also, but the women and children sat on the main level and the men sat in the balcony. At the Heubuden Church the men also had a small adjacent building for a cloak room; this was the era of horses and barns and the male garments perpetually had the reek of horse and barn.

History as a Reference Point

Figure 8b
The second Emmaus Mennonite Church building was erected in 1908 with seating for four hundred at a cost of $6,000. It was dedicated on December 20, 1908 and used for twenty years. Note the hitching posts connected with a chain on the left and the parked car on the right. Source: Author's file.

Figure 8c
The third Emmaus Mennonite Church building was dedicated in January, 1929. Construction costs were $27,000 for a seating capacity of eight hundred. The hitching posts are still in place. This structure was completely destroyed by fire on January 28, 2008. Subsequently, a new church was built two miles south at 9070 NW Meadowlark Road. Source: Author's file.

The Petals of a Kansas Sunflower

When the local church here in Kansas celebrated its seventy-fifth anniversary on July 8, 1951, Mother was asked to write a poem. She, as a child, had listened by the hour as the first generations of immigrants reminisced about their beloved Germany (West Prussia) and the new life in America. No other woman was asked to speak in 1951. The voices of the subservient Mennonite women were often lost or minimized by the traditional louder, authoritarian voices of their male leaders. However, the feminine voices helped to maintain contact with family and friends within a dispersed and isolated Mennonite society that developed in America.

The poem Mother wrote reflected the style of a lecture, i.e., somewhat sermon-like. If presented in church, it should sound like church. The poem was recited by my seventeen-year-old sister Phebe Ann. Mother accomplished a serious review of the history of the church, but she also put a face and a heart on the events, including the mention of personal sacrifices that immigration engendered. The male speakers expressed masculine stoicism and philosophical directives. As Mother notes, the first business meeting involved seventeen brethren (men), but no women, even though they were baptized members of the church.

Early church leadership and organization was restricted exclusively to males; this was a patriarchal tradition inculcated in Germanic Europe. Did the women members feel like second-class members? They never gave it a thought—it just was the way things were. In fact, the women used the day the males were dealing with church business as a day of festivity to visit female relatives and cousins unencumbered by male domination. A few widows and aged spinsters did occasionally attend business meetings as observers, but these were described as women with nothing to do. It wasn't until about 1946, right after the war, when one of the young men took a wife from a more progressive church that this young woman shamed all the traditionally entrenched women in their lethargy. The church records do not record a motion to allow female participation. The concept was just brought to the floor once and everyone just shrugged and said, "Why not?"

Many of the Mennonite farmers in West Prussia were managers of their farms since they had employees to do the actual work, but when they came to America, they needed to become laborers themselves because the economic reality of the wages paid in America did not warrant bringing their servants. "Oh, many of us don't realize what it meant for them, I fear, / to leave their parental inheritance and to become a pioneer." Friends, relatives, servants, and treasured possessions were left behind. "It meant the breaking of friendship bonds, even families had to sever; / They disposed of many a treasured thing and said 'goodbye' forever."

These Seventy-five Years
Mrs. John Epp Jr.

God leads his people wondrously, on life's journey here below;
   But it's in love and mercy as past history clearly shows.
"Get thee out of thy country, from thy kindred thou shalt part;"
   This was the command to Abraham, and since, to many a human heart.
To our forefathers also, from God, came this command:
   And he has led them safely, by his Almighty Hand.
They bade farewell to loved ones; their farms were left behind.
   They crossed the big wide ocean a haven here to find.
God's blessing rested on them; a new home soon they found,
   Where they could serve their Master and be tillers of the ground.
Where they could train their children as their conscience would dictate
   And their sons need not bear arms, as in the older land of late.
Oh yes, things here were different, but little did they mind;
   They all were sharing in the task. The servants stayed behind.

It was in 1876, just seventy-five years ago;
   When our forefathers to Kansas came, as many of you may know.
A deputation of twelve men came first, so we are told;
   To see the land and then return, as Israel's spies of old.
And one of these, we'll not neglect, to make mention of it here,
   Became the first Elder of Emmaus and served for many a year.
Russian and German Mennonites were sending these men forth
   To travel here extensively and then bring their report;
And as a result of this, immigration had its start.
   Some left their homeland joyfully, others with heavy heart.
There were many things for them to pack before the ocean voyage
   And yet they did it heartily and full of hope and courage.
Their thoughts went to an unknown land, where Indian tribes would roam,
   And useful would be everything in starting a new home.
Oh, many of us don't realize what it meant for them, I fear,
   To leave their parental inheritance and to become a pioneer.
It meant the breaking of friendship bonds, even families had to sever,
   They disposed of many a treasured thing and said "good-bye" forever.

The Petals of a Kansas Sunflower

On the 3rd of July in '76, so we find it to be right,
    The first few families of our group in St. Louis spent the night.
They were surprised as there they heard, in what a noisy way
    America observed the 100th anniversary of Independence Day.
They, however, didn't linger long. They found it to be best
    To proceed as soon as possible and travel further west.
From Halstead, later, so we read, they to Butler County came;
    By paying six dollars per acre soon had six sections to their claim.
These were not as we see it now, with good farms everywhere,
    With roads and trees and fences and highways here and there.
The warm breeze was swaying the prairie thick and high
    And overhead was stretching the azure summer sky.
The women stayed in Halstead, but the men were busy here
    Hauling lumber and then building, before the winter of the year;
But first they cut the prairie. At the hay stacks slept at night.
    With a menu of coffee, bread, and syrup, they got along all right.
Six families constituted the early settlement here
    And more and more were added to these from year to year.
The first church service, that we have record of, we see
    Was held in Great-grandfather Harder's newly erected granary.
The first business meeting consisted of 17 brethren in all;
    And the first church house was completed in '78, in fall.
Though small was the beginning, yet steadily it grew;
    To nearly 400 members, where then we had but few.
One member of that little group is still with us today,
    The others have gone to glory to their eternal stay.

Fifty years after the first, this, the third church was erected
    And the Elder serving now is the sixth we have elected.
Today as we are looking back over seventy-five long years—
    We see days of rejoicing and we see days of tears.
Many happy couples walked this aisle by Mendelssohn's strain.
    Silently the graves bear witness of untold tears and pain.
Although church life continued somewhat in the same routine,
    Yet here and there some changes today are plainly seen.
Now the weight of the ministry rests on the shoulders of one;
    Years ago we had three or four by whom this work was done.
Some things have become dear to us, that once were strange and new;
    Such as having Sunday School and instruments, to mention only a few.
The rows of buggies and horses that were seen here so long
    We saw them slowly vanish, until finally all were gone.

Once more I wish you'd bear with me as over seventy-five years we glance
    And notice how God graciously has led us to advance;

History as a Reference Point

Our members include doctors, missionaries, and deaconesses too,
   We have relief and Christian workers, of these more than a few.
Now as we come to celebrate, our hearts are full of praise.
   We marvel at God's greatness; we marvel at his ways.
Our hearts are filled with gratitude for what our fathers wrought
   In leaving the old homeland, as a new home here they sought.
God has wonderfully blessed us, no one would now deny,
   Both spiritually and materially with blessings from on high.
So let us then press forward as our forefathers have done,
   That for others we win a blessing as they for us have won.
And asking God to choose the place that each one is to fill
   Having only one desire, to be in the center of his will.

As I review the poems that Mother wrote, I begin to understand why there are repeating themes about community and religion. She often points backwards and reminds those listening to the recitation of her poems that we are the product of our heritage. The people who passed away before us have all contributed to the life and philosophy that Mother held so dear. She also points forwards at times saying, "So let us then press forward as our forefathers have done; that for others we win a blessing as they for us have won." Young people need to know about their grandparents so they too can appreciate and perpetuate the collective philosophical treasury.

My grandfather, Bernhard Harder Jr., as an eleven-year-old boy, was a member of this first group of our community emigrating from West Prussia. On their train ride across America, their itinerary had them get off the train and sleep in a St. Louis hotel on the Monday night of July 3, 1876. The next day was Independence Day and the centennial of the United States; everyone in St. Louis was celebrating. "They were surprised as there they heard, in what a noisy way / America observed the one hundredth anniversary of Independence Day." The street activities with firecrackers and dancing lasted all night. In the morning they sleepily boarded the train once again and traveled westward. Exactly one hundred years later, my wife Sylvia and I, together with our two sons, David and Terry, aged two years and nine months, sat on picnic blankets on the banks of the Mississippi River in St. Louis and participated with one million other Americans in celebrating the bicentennial of the independence of the United States. We viewed a three-hour air show in the afternoon and later an hour of fireworks from a barge in the middle of the Mississippi River after it got dark. During the late afternoon, as the sun went down in the west, the shadow of the arch symbolizing the "Gateway to the West" passed over us. I took Sylvia's hand as we looked deeply into each other's eyes and reflected on our place in history; we paused to remember Grandfather Bernhard Harder who had circumstantially been in St. Louis one hundred years earlier and became initiated to American festivities.

Figure 9
Eleven-year-old Bernhard Harder Jr. carried this suitcase with his books and toys from West Prussia to Kansas. Private collection. Source: Author's file.

It did not take Mother long to get the prairie wind into her poetic sails. In the second year of writing, she wrote an epic historical poem, "Reminiscences on the Past," about the employees who helped on the farm. Manual labor was used to accomplish most work, requiring constant manpower. Some of the descriptions made me think of viewing an old western movie. You can almost hear John Wayne's gravelly voice. But no, this was real and Mother experienced much of it.

I was introduced to the next poem in a telephone call from a neighbor and cousin who called one day and said that a German poem was found among the papers of her husband's late grandfather, B. W. Harder, which she had sent off for translation. From the translation, she concluded that only my mother could have written this poem. I

History as a Reference Point

reviewed the poem and the translation and agreed, but sensed that the translator was unfamiliar with my mother and the family's history. The translation omitted a few interesting portions, so I translated the poem, line by line. I was awakened to the many concepts, historical attitudes, and events that depicted life in America for these new immigrants. I developed a need to review Mother's treasury of poems to see through her eyes what she considered sufficiently important to share in oral format and to write down on paper.

Later I learned that this poem is also handwritten in Mother's journal and dated 1930. The construction of this poem is noteworthy with 490 lines of rhyming couplets. The copy that my neighbor found appears to be a hurried handwritten copy of the original. Why B. W. Harder had a copy remains unknown, but he was a gregarious leader in the close-knit community and Mother's former school teacher, so it is probable that Mother read this poem at a birthday or wedding anniversary celebration at her cousin's home and left her reading copy with him. B. W. was the oldest of the first generation of Harders born in America; my mother was the youngest. What is described in this poem would have occurred at the farm of B. W.'s grandfather.

Mother writes that a review of history gives a reference point in time. Since farming and housekeeping in the late 1800s and early 1900s were very labor intensive, what better way to recall the past than to review those who were employed. Some of the farm and domestic help who worked for Mother's grandparents in West Prussia came with them when they immigrated to America. In exchange for the payment of a ticket to America, they were asked to remain in their employment for a number of years. Mrs. Meyer was one of these employees.

Mrs. Meyer had left employment on the farm by 1880 per the U.S. Census Household Record and moved to Newton. Two small bud vases survive that Mother identified as souvenirs that Mrs. Meyer later brought to my great-grandmother when she came by train for a visit, one with the touristy words "Newton, Kan." on it.

The visit of Mrs. Meyer to the farm coming by train was made possible because in 1884 and 1885, eight years after establishing the farm, the Ellsworth, McPherson, Newton, and Southeastern Railroad Company (later owned by the Missouri Pacific Railroad) built an east-west track a half-mile south of the farm. If you flagged the train, it would stop where the road crosses the tracks when you wanted to get on or if you wanted to get off. Passengers rode in the last car of the train, the caboose. There were two trains per day; the morning train went east to El Dorado and the afternoon train went west through Newton to McPherson. After some time the freight and passenger business was separated and so four trains passed daily.

Figure 10
Bernhard Harder Jr. with his older brother Gustav shortly before they left West Prussia. Gottheil & Sohn, Danzig. Source: Author's file.

History as a Reference Point

Several new towns were established along the track wherever a train station was built: McLains, Annelly, Brainerd and Potwin. With the establishment of these towns, shopping locally was possible, rather than driving a day by wagon to get supplies from Newton, Peabody, or El Dorado. The railhead in Brainerd with its stockyard of holding pens built by the railroad also served the community in providing a local conduit for moving farm animals to market. Cattle could be herded to the railhead from the surrounding community. Hogs too could be walked from farms located within two miles of the railhead or hauled in wagons from more distant farms. Because the hogs were raised to such a large size, only four or five hogs could be hauled in a farm wagon. One load of hogs owned by John Harder Sr. tipped the scales at 405 pounds each at the Oklahoma City market; these hogs were referred to as "little elephants" and would each yield at slaughter as much as twenty-two gallons of lard. On July 5, 1885, the day the railroad siding was completed, four railroad stockcars of hogs and one of cattle were shipped out.

Two years later (1887) a Rock Island Railroad subsidiary, Chicago, Kansas, & Nebraska Railroad Company constructed a north-south track two miles west of the farm. The local towns of Elbing, Whitewater, and Furley built up along this track.

The coal-powered steam locomotives of the early trains were a perpetual fire hazard. Sparks on occasion escaped the smokestack and could ignite the dry grasses along the tracks. Also, lightning often caused prairie grass fires during dry periods. The Rev. Peter Dyck wrote in 1876 that they secured themselves from threats of wild prairie fires in the hay and straw in the fields by creating a boundary around their homestead by plowing two lines and burning off the grass and debris between. He also mentioned that prairie fires were frequent during dry periods and that one time he could observe twelve fires in the surrounding area from his house window.

After Mrs. Meyer, a subsequent household helper for my great-grandmother was Katharina Kliewer (1850–1939), normally referred to as "Tien," who was talkative and occasionally ill-tempered. She would get the little black cow to stand still by hitting her with a board and had a good ear for a hen's cackle announcing that an egg had been laid; it was not important if the cackling hen was from my great-grandmother's flock or my grandmother's hen house, Tien pounced on all eggs.

From "Reminiscences on the Past" I learned that early on oleanders were planted on the Harder cemetery at the end of the farm driveway and during the summer Tien had to carry water to irrigate these plants. Because they were not winter hardy, a male employee would carry these oleanders to the basement of the farm house for the winter (late September) and return them to the cemetery the next spring when danger of frost was past (early May).

Tien remained employed by my great-grandmother until Great-grandmother passed away at the age of eighty-two in 1916. Tien then moved into the Goessel Old Folks Home, which is about thirty-three miles from the farm. Here Mother gives some insight into early twentieth-century geriatric care. In Goessel, they tried to teach Tien good manners and when she wandered away, the staff would lock her in her room. A comment in the poem is that she became more contented after a visit to the farm and spending time with people who appreciated her. Tien passed away in 1939 and is interred in the local Emmaus Mennonite Church cemetery.

There was a little house one-half mile west of the farm that was constructed to accommodate a farm laborer and his family as part of the compensation package. After the death of my grandfather in 1904, it appears the house was converted into a rental property which included land to farm on their own behalf in addition to working on the farm for wages. Mother describes the people and the lives of those who made use of the house.

The last half of this poem is reserved for Andres Powolski (1849–1928). Andres at the age of nineteen began working for my great-grandfather in West Prussia ten years before the family moved to America in 1876. Andres's father had just passed away and he had no family ties left, so he came also and stayed in the employment of the family until he went to a nursing home. He passed away in 1928 and is buried in the Harder cemetery. Being a Catholic by birth, he would take the train several times each year to Newton to the Catholic church for services. When he came home he would say, with a feeling of relief, "Well, that's over for another year." He had a simple room in the horse barn built specifically for his lodging when the barn was built in 1877, but he ate his meals in the warmth of the kitchen of the farmhouse and also read the German newspaper there. He did not like to eat with the family, because he felt uncomfortable, feeling as if he was taking food away from the children. There are a few elements in Mother's discussion of Andres that I would highlight. One was his trip to town to sell Grandmother's eggs with an old horse and "a wagon with weak bones." Another was the introduction of the automobile into a horse-powered economy. Still further, the expression of loyalty to his host family and the display of emotions at the celebration of his year of jubilee; only mother could describe the feelings inherent among immigrants. And finally, after Andres moved to the nursing home he pined for the farm and finagled a stay over the weekend to avoid yet another bath.

Rückerinnerungen

Wenn es mir doch mögt' gelingen,
Hier auf dies' Papier zu bringen,
Und zuvor in einem Reim geschrieben
Was hier früher wurd getrieben.
Über längst vergangenen Tagen
Ließe sich so manches sagen;
Denn sie hatten dazu Mal
Hier noch Dienstzpersonal.
Da war wohl zuerst Frau Meyer
Dann Die Tien Die sucht' gern Eier.
Dann war Yotter, Schmidt und Martin.
Und der Andres dem das Warten
Wenn er gar auf Post zu früh
Manchmal machte recht viel Müh.

Frau Meyer, eine Deutsche war,
Daß sagt der Name uns schon klar
War mit den Großeltern bekannt
Von Deutschland her, doch nicht verwandt.
Als' nach Amerika sie kamen,
Die Meyersche sie mit sich nahmen.
Schafft hier noch bei ihnen ein paar Jahr
Und später in Newton wohnhaft war.
Das dies war noch vor meiner Zeit,
Weiß daher nicht recht bescheit.
Will jetzt lieber da beginnen
Wo ich mir noch kann besinnen.
Weiß noch, daß sie früher kam

The Petals of a Kansas Sunflower

Manchmal her zur Eisenbahn,
Um nach Großmutter zu sehe,
Wie es ihr wohl tat ergehe.
Großmutter bekam von ihr
Dann jedesmal ein "Souvenir."
Ein Schmandtöpfchen war's gewöhnlich
Ein Blumenväschen oder dem so ähnlich.
Uns Kinder mit "candy" sie bedacht
Den sie gewöhnlich mitgebracht.
Von Newton ist sie jetzt schon fort
Hörten von ihr seit dem kein Wort,
Denn nach Chicago schon seit langen
Ist mit ihren Kindern sie gegangen.

Tien, ein altes Frauenzimmer,
Wusst' was zu erzählen immer
Sie, die schon so manches Jahr
Hier im Dienst bei "Großchen" war,
Hatte so manches durch gemacht
Das sie gern zur Geltung bracht.
Im Garten hat Tien viel gehackt
Für das Kalb Heu eingepackt.
Großmutter hatte eine Kuh,
Die Tien gern molk in großer Ruh,
Doch zuweilen das nicht ging,
Die Kuh ein kleines schwarzes Ding,
Sich nicht immer gut betrug,
Worauf Tien mit dem Brett sie schlug.
Aufgewischt hat Tien ein Zimmer,
Aufgewaschen auch wohl immer.
In dem Garten half sie sehr
Wie auch schon gesagt vorher.
Manchmal wurd Tien aufgebracht,
Scheinbar grad so über Nacht,
Lang nacher bis der Groll verschwunden
Schalt in eins dann einer Stunden.
Sollt dann oft von hier auch fort.—
Sprach sie jedoch ein versöhnent Wort
Wurd sie wieder aufgenommen
D'rum ist's ein so weit gekommen.
Tienchen tat es wohl verdrießen,
Daß Oleander sie musst' gießen,
Denn die waren weit von hier,

History as a Reference Point

Auf dem Kirchhof standen vier.
Von Ziehbrunnen im Pferdestall
Holt sie das Wasser dazumal
Schleppte mit dem Wasser dann so weit
Während der trockene Sommerszeit.
Tienchen hatte es immer drock
Ging so, daß ihr wipt der Rock.
Doch es war auch so zuweilen,
Daß sie sich nicht brauchte eilen.
Wenn im Stall ein Hühnchen kackelt
Kam sie auch gleich angewackelt
Holte sich das frische Ei
Lachte sich nach eins dabei.
Kam einmal wer Fremdes her
Machte sie schnell ein Eimer leer
Mußte zum Stall nach Wasser gehe
Bekam dadurch dann was zu sehe.
Tienchen fuhr auch mit dem Zug
Manchmal nach Newton auf Besuch.
Beim allein nach Entzen gehe
Ist ihr einmals was geschehe.
Das nach Newton ging das nicht
Sie konnte allein verbiestern sich
Also mit Begleitung nur
Durfte sie wagen eine Tour.
Hatte sie es so weit gebracht.
Sie auch gern Einkäufe macht.
Kaufte sich dann Gummiband,
Zwirn und sonst allerhand.
Und im Sommer kam per Bahn
Oft Magaretha Sudermann
Her nach Tiench auf Besuch
Doch davon ist wohl genug.
Auch dieses ist schon lange her
Tienchen wirtschaft hier nicht mehr
Darf sich schon ein bischen schonen
Und Goessel Altenheim bewohnen
Da arbeiten darf Tein nicht mehr
Sie schonen sie da sehr
Hatten ihr mit nichts hantieren
Lehren ihr nur feine Manieren.
Das trotz alle feien Manieren
Will sie manchmal nicht passieren.
Sperren ihr dann in ihr Zimmer ein

The Petals of a Kansas Sunflower

Was ihr soll sehr heilsam sein.
Eine wohl noch bessere Kur
Ist, wenn man mit ihr nach Butler fuhr
Zwei Wochen besucht sie Freunde hier
Besser gefällt dann Goessel ihr.

Eine Zeitlang hatten wir
Auch Kaete Friessen in Quartier
Und es war ihr sehr viel wert
Da sie eine deutsche Schule lehrt.
Das sie hatte dazumal
Eine große Schülerzahl.

Der erste Renter der hier war—
War Cornelius Schmidt zwar viele Jahr.
Der erst Renter war also "Schmidt"
Er und die Familie natürlich mit
Wohnten in der kleinen Wohnung.
Doch früher hatte für Belohnung
Schmidt gern bewiesen seine Kraft
Da er als Arbeiter hier schafft.

Als Renter war er ziemlich gut
Hatt' wie es schien stets guten Mut,
Hat "Fenzen" gern zurecht gemacht
Und gern Heu hier eingebracht
Er hat gepflügt, geeggt, gesäht
Geerntet und gedroschen was gemäht,
Auch anderes tat er auch nebenbei
Verstand er sich mit der Zimmerei
Doch wenn er dacht es war genug
Dann gings nach Missouri auf Besuch
Die Feldarbeit wurd' unterbrochen
Und er verweilt da ein paar Wochen.
Kam er dann zurück von dort
Arbeitet er wie vorher so fort
Denn seit dem er aufgehört
Hatte die Arbeit sich sehr gemehrt.
Doch mit einmal gings nicht mehr
Nach Missouri wollte er
Ist dann auch dort hin gegangen
Und hat sein eigenes angefangen.
Als fort zog ein Familie "Schmidt"

History as a Reference Point

Verschwand so manches von unserem mit.
Doch, daß wollen wir übergehe
Und den nächsten Renter uns besehe.

Mit Schmidts wurd also eine Wohnung leer.
Sein musste hier aber wer
Der besorgen tat das Land
Und uns half sacht allerhand.
Yotter hieß der nächste Mann
Der als Renter hierher kam
Weiß von ihm nicht viel genau
Kannte kaum die Kinder und die Frau.
Wenn Yotter pflügte oder so etwas
Ihm zu beider Seiten ein Kind dann saß
Ein Muster als Beschwerung dienen
Und saßen da mit trüben Mienen.
Da als daß eine Jahr war um
Gab er doch garnicht darum
Wieder von hier fort zu ziehe
Wir mussten uns recht darum bemühe.
Er sagt wir hatten ihm fort gejagt,
Daß hatte er nicht von Harders gedacht.
Das, daß solche schlecht Menschen waren
Und ihm nicht hielten mehre Jahren.

Der nächst Renter der hier war
Arthur Schmidt auch auf ein Jahr
"Art," von Cornelius Schmidt ein Sohn
War ein windiger Patron
Schoten hat er gern gemacht
Sich hinten noch eins gelacht.
Doch, daß ist hier noch zusagen
Für Arthur kamen schwere Tagen
Seine Frau starb ihm das Jahr
Auch zwei Kinder ein Zwillingspaar.

Gustav Martens ein alter Mann
Eines Tages zu Fuß ankam
Und konnte hier so bittet fragen
Wir mögten ihm doch nicht versagen
Das Arbeiterhaus zu beziehe
Er würd uns weiter auch nicht mühe.
Es wurde ihm hier nicht versagt

The Petals of a Kansas Sunflower

Und schon am aller nächsten Tag
Ist mit Hack und Pack er angekommen
Und hat eine Wohnung eingenommen.
Am Abend allein er Schachspiel trieb
Oder wohl auch las und schrieb
Denn mit dem Dichten verstand er sich
Tausendmal besser noch als ich.
Er war sein eigener Koch und dann
Schafte er wo er Arbeit bekam.
Die letzte Zeit die er hier weilt
Wurd ihm von county zugeteilt.
Andre konnten davon sagen
Von Deutschland kannte er bessere Tage
Wer nicht vorwärts kommt muß stille stehe
Und, daß heißt dann wohl rückwärts gehe.
So ist er auch mit ihm gegangen
Mit alles was er angefangen.
Martens konnte Andres nicht ausstehe
Ließ es auch von andere sehe
Martens tat ihm wohl beneiden
Wollte ihm auch gern vertreiben.
Doch so weit ist's nicht gekommen
Er würd' ins Altenheim genommen
Weil ein Leiden er am Kopf bekam
Daß sich verschlimmert der arme Mann.
Und man ihm dazu bewog
Daß er ins Hillsboro Altenheim zog
Doch er besserte dort nicht
Schlimmer wurde sein Gesicht
Und ihm blieb wohl keine Wahl
Er kam ins Hillsboro Hospital
War da jedoch nur kurze Zeit
Dann war von seinen Leiden er befreit.

Andres Powolski ein alter Knecht
Auf seiner Art anhänglich und zwar mit recht.
Denn noch als ziemlich junger Mann
Schon von neunzehn Jahren an
Ist nach den Großeltern er gekommen
Und hat dort Stellung angenommon.
Als die Großeltern mit vielen Andern
Sich rüsten mussten zum auswandern,
Sechsundsiebzig war das Jahr

Und im Juni es wohl war
Ließ Andres es sich nicht verdrießen
Den Auswanderzug sich anzuschließen
Sein Vater starb noch kurz vorher
So hielt ihm nichts in Deutschland mehr.
In Amerika angekommen
Wurd' Landbesichtigung vorgenommen.
Kansas gefiel das beste ihnen
D'rum entschlossen sie sich dort hin zu ziehe
Andres hat so alles durch gemacht
Was das Ansiedeln mit sich bracht.
Doch dieses weiß ich nur von fragen
Oder wie man sagt, "Von hören sagen."
Will es daher über gehe
Und Andres beschreiben wie ich ihn gesehe:
Klein und schmal war seine Figur.
Doch recht friedliebens seine Natur
Blau waren seine Augen etwas blas das Gesicht
Früher trug er einen vollbart doch späterhin nicht
Mit den Füßen ging er sehr nach außen sehr dünn waren die Beine
Darum brauchte er in Deutschland beim Militär nicht zu sein.
Mit uns Kinder hat er viel gespielt
Uns gern auf dem Schoß aufhielt
Doch wer ihm gar zu sehr tat necken
Dem wollt' er im Sack einstecken.
Andres war ein treuer Knecht.
Dem war immer alles recht.
Doch zu sich selbst hat er gesprochen
In einem fort ununterbrochen.
"Übt der Andres Predigt ein?"
Fragt einmal ein Jungchen klein
Und es ist nicht zu verneinen,
Daß man konnte so was meinen
Wenn man ihm so reden hörte
Was in einem fort so währte.
Andres besorgte treu das Vieh
Hühner, Pferde, Schwein und Küh'
Füttern tat er niemals knapp
Nur zu früh er oft sie gab
Und war dabei dann noch gewöhnlich
Eine Zeitlang unversöhnlich
Wurde ihm gesagt: "Das Vieh
Gaben sie doch rein zu früh."

The Petals of a Kansas Sunflower

Schweinchen hatten wir nur zwei
Oder vielleicht waren es auch drei
Daß wir nicht viel Arbeit hatten
Doch alljährlich was zum braten.
Auch etwas Rindvieh hatten wir
Kühe glaub ich waren vier:
"Schöngesicht" und Blaue das sind zwei
"Beauty" und eine Jersey war dabei.
Hatten damals noch fünf Pferde
Die ich hier jetzt nennen werde
"Molly", "Lady", "Prince", und "Saul"
Und die "Nellie" schrecklich faul.
Aber so im lauf der Jahren
Als wir wollten schneidiger fahren
Kauft Mutter noch dem "Tom" dazu
Doch vorbei war's mit der Ruh;
Denn der hat sich sehr gescheut
Für die Autos schon von weit
Und, daß machte uns sehr bang
Hielten ihm daher nicht lang.
Schafften dann das Auto an
Das für nichts sich ängsten kann.
Andres freute sich recht dazu
Hatte dann doch auch mehr Ruh
Braucht nicht mehr aus und angespannt
"Kamodetfahre" er das nannt.
Für Andres war's ein ganzer Greul
Wenn zur Stadt er fuhr mit dem alten Saul
Das Pferd war lahm und Andres alt
Und manchmal war es auch noch kalt.
Der Wagen hatte schwache Knochen
Und ist eins mit ihm zusammen gebrochen
Als von Großmutters Eier er umgeben saß
Da gabs ein Unglück nicht auf spaß
Der Wagen zerbrach mit einem krach
Andres fiel vorn über die Eier ihm nach
Weiter wurde zum Glück nicht was
Als das Andres im Rührei saß.
Nur gut das er nicht von Eierschallen
Sonst war auch er auseinander gefallen.
Doch nur einmal ging das so
Andres war wohl auch nicht froh,
Besser gings ihm in der Tat

History as a Reference Point

Wenn zu Fuß er ging zu Stadt
Doch ohne uns zu sagen ging er nicht:
"Will abschrapen lassen mein Gesicht,"
So sprach er und fügte dem stets bei
"Wollt ihn, daß nur sagen, das sie wissen wo ich sei."
Doch war das Stadtgehen ihm wohl gut?
Etwas schief saß oft sein Hut
Wenn er zurück getorkelt kam
Oder 1 ¾ lange Schritte nahm.
In der Küche er sich neider läßt
Und aus der Kann eingießt den Koffeerest.
Kam jemand dann saß er steil
Und eine Tasse Kaffee verschlang in eil;
Doch, daß den Vanilla nur auffrischte
Den man im Städtchen ihm auftischte
Somit sich ein jeder Freute
Wenn zur Tür hinaus er schritt ins Weite.
Andres musste auch einmal
Obzwar es ihm war recht fatal
Nach ElDorado vor Gericht.
Doch sehr schlimm ergings ihm nicht.
Er dacht jetzt gehts ins "finstere Loch."
War am nächsten Tag zurück jedoch
Hatte da nur sagen brauchen
Wo er so etwas konnt kaufen
Wie er ja gewöhnlich tat
Wenn er niemal kam zur Stadt.
Doch obzuwar schon vor Gericht
Viel sagt er wie gewöhnlich nicht.
Doch dieses nur so neben bei
Im ganzen war er doch recht frei
Hat rein gemacht den Hühnerstall
In einer Woche bis zweimal
Uns war es natürlich sehr viel wert,
Daß er die Hühner so viel ehrt.
Brennung schleppte er auch hinein,
Dem davon musste voll auch stets sein.
Winter war für ihn schlechte Zeit.
Dann schaufelt er Schnee während es noch schneit,
Oder am warmen Ofen er saß
Und in der Zeitung über dem Kaiser las.
In der Ernte hat er auch geschafft,
Öfters über seine Kraft

The Petals of a Kansas Sunflower

Denn er wolte da am meisten
Mehr noch als die Jungen leisten.
Und so zwei drei mal im Jahr
Weil ein Katholik er war
Fuhr zur Kirche er nach Newton
Musste sich dann schon sehr sputen
Wusch in großer eile sich dann
Und ging zwei Stunden vor Zeit zur Bahn.
Andres ertappte einst einen "Schafer"
Der sich hier bei uns stahl Hafer
Doch das Ponk, daß sich mal schlägt
Sich wohl lieber noch verträgt.
Denn gleich sagt er davon kein Wort
Jedoch noch Jahren glipt's ihm fort.
Einmal so im lauf der Zeit
Kam hier her und zwar von weit
Aus Cleveland seines Bruderssohn
Angemeldet hatte er sich schon
Er wollte Andres dazu bewegen
Sein Wohnsitz nach Cleveland zu verlegen
Brachte manch Flaschchen von Osten mit
Gab davon Andres und auch dem Schmidt
Doch Andres blieb wo er war
Auch nach dem noch so an zwölf Jahr.
Als Andres 50 Jahr war hier
Sein Jubiläun feierten wir
Mit Abendbrot und Festrede auch
Wie es bei so etwas ist Brauch
Dem Andres hat es schier gerührt
Als Onkel in der Red'anführt
Wie damals in dem ersten Jahren
Als von Deutschland sie gekommen waren
Es ihnen dann ergangen war
Und Andres immer mit dabei.
Und als Onkel auch noch dann
Deutsche Volkslieder führte an
Die Andres mit melodischem klang
Gern bei seiner Arbeit sang
Da war's für Andres doch zu viel
Trän' auf Trän' in dem Bart ihm fiel.
Das Singen blieb bis später auch
Wenn er allein war so sein Brauch.
Ganz besonders leicht und flink

Ihm dann auch das Stucken ging.
Krank ist Andres oft gewesen
Doch darauf auch wieder genesen
Einmal fing er zu Kränkeln an
Doch so, daß der Doctor kam
Konnt mit garnichts mehr hantieren
Musste sich lassen operrieren.
In den letzten Jahren hatte er dazu
Jeden Winter ein paarmal "Flu"
Dann im Stall in seiner Kammer er lag
So ganz allein denn ganzen Tag
Doch scheinbar stets ihm Freude macht
Wenn zur Mahlzeit man den tray ihm bracht.
Als so Jahr auf Jahr verrann
Und Andres wurde ein alter Mann
Wurde auch schon zu der Zeit
Das "Bethel Altenheim" eingeweiht.
Andres freute sich dazu
Setzte sich dort bald zur Ruh
Kauft nach langen überlegen
Mit einem Teil von dem Vermögen
Sich auf Lebenszeit dort ein
Wollt also fort an "Newtoner" sein
Was vom Vermögen überblieb
Er durch "Regiers" der Mission verschrieb.
Besuchten wir ihm war die Freude groß
Doch dann ging das Fragen auch gleich los:
"Wat mokt de Herr?" "Wo jeit it de Fru?"
"Ei Sus'ke?" "Säten sie schon Weizen zu?"
So fragt er dann und nach seiner Art
Wünscht er gleich zu Anfang "Glückliche Heimfahrt."
Doch wie das so mit unter geht
Auf einmal Heimweh ihm anweht.
War ganz zimperlich und krank
Wohl so ein paar Wochen lang
Es ist ja immer so gewesen
Wer von Heimweh will genesen
Dem ist's eine sichere Kur
Wenn er zurück nach Hause fuhr.
An Andres wurde dies auch wahr
Wurd' ganz und gar geheilt sogar
Freitag holte Schwager Hans ihn her
So für zwei Tag' dachte er

The Petals of a Kansas Sunflower

Doch Andres hatte sich's anders gedacht
Als nur zu bleiben eine Nacht.
"Montag will ich erst zurück."
Sagt er mit einem bedeutsamen Blick—
Und als er Sonnabend hier bei uns saß
Sagte er so halb auf spaß,
"Nah nu jeit dat da schon los."
"Was denn? "Noch das Baden blos."
"De sind mie dar doch ganz zu reinlich."
Große sauberkeit war ihm peinlich
War das also der Grund allein
Warum er am Sonnabend hier wollt sein?
Montag vergnügt er Abschied nahm
Und bangte sich nicht mehr fort an.
War da fast zwei Jahre lang
Dann wurde er auf einmal krank
Und auch seine Zeit lief ab
Lungenentzündung bracht ihm ins Grab
Auf dem Kirchhof ruht er hier
Unweit von der Eingangstür.
Und an dem Grabe sein
Steht ein einfacher grauer Stein
Auf dem Grabstein steht mit recht
Ein Kurze Inschrift, "ein treuer Knecht."
Die Zeit die er hier im Dienst verwand
Hat fünf Generationen er gekannt.
Er diente Großvater, Vater, Kind
Und deren Kinder am'ran wachsen sind
So lang auf einer Stelle wie er
Bleibt heutzutage keiner mehr
Denn nah an 60 Jahren ist
Gewiß eine recht lange Frist.

Doch zum Abschluß soll jetzt kommen
Was ich mir hat' vorgenommen
Habe schwach mir aufgefrischt
Was längst Vergangenheit schon ist
Denn unaufhaltsam eilt die Zeit
Fort ist mancher der einst hier weilt
Mög' ein jeder nur so leben
Daß sein Andenken bleibt ein Segen.
1930

History as a Reference Point

Reminiscences on the Past

If only I might succeed
To bring here to this paper
And to write this in rhyme
What used to happen here.
About days long past
So much could be said;
It would give a reference point
Here to describe just now the employees.
The first was probably Mrs. Meyer.
Then the Tien, who liked to look for eggs.
Then there were Yotter, Schmidt and Martin,
And Andres who found waiting
When he got to the mailbox too early
Sometimes hard to take.

Mrs. Meyer was a German
The name says that clearly to us
She was acquainted with my grandparents
Though not related. From Germany to here,
As they came to America
They brought the young Meyer with them.
She worked for them a couple of years
And later was a resident of Newton.
That was still before my time
Consequently, I really do not know much about it.
I would now prefer to begin
Where I myself can recollect.
I do know, that she previously came
Here by train sometimes
In order to check on Grandmother
To inquire how she was doing.
Grandmother would get from her
A souvenir each time.
Usually it was a little creamer,
A flower vase or something like that.
She remembered us children with candy
Which she normally brought along.
She is now no longer in Newton.
Have not heard a word from her since then
It has been quite a while since she went to Chicago
She went with her children.

The Petals of a Kansas Sunflower

Figure 11a   Figure 11b

Figure 11a & b
Souvenir vases given by Mrs. Meyer to Great-grandmother Harder when she came by train from Newton to visit: a. this bud vase is porcelain decorated with the words, "Newton, Kan." It is four inches tall and made in Germany; b. the white porcelain bud vase is six inches tall and made in Austria. Private collections. Source: Author's file.

Tien, an elderly woman
Always knew something to tell.
For many years she was
Employed here by Grandmother
Had lived through a lot
And she wanted this to be known.
Tien hoed a lot in the garden.
She gathered hay for the calf.
Grandmother had a cow
That Tien liked to milk in a calm way
But sometimes it did not happen that way
The cow was a little black thing
She did not always behave properly
Consequently, Tien hit her with a board.
Tien would dust a room
She certainly always washed the dishes
She helped a lot in the garden
As I have already said above.
Sometimes Tien would get irritated
Apparently as if for nothing and overnight.

History as a Reference Point

It took a long time for the ill-will to disappear
She would scold for too many hours
Including often that she should leave here—
But if she would then say a conciliatory word
She would again be in good standing,
Since she had come so far.
Little Tien surely did it with some sulkiness
She had to water the oleanders
Because they were far from here
There were four on the cemetery.
From the pull well in the horse barn
She would get water for there
She would schlep the water the whole distance
During the dry summertime.
Little Tien was always in such a hurry
As she walked her skirt would swish.
But it was also a fact
That she did not need to be in such a hurry.
When a hen cackled in the barn
She would immediately go
And get the fresh egg
Laughing as she did so.
Once a stranger came here
She quickly emptied the water bucket
So that she would have to go to the barn for water
Consequently, she could then see what was going on.
Little Tien also took the train
Sometimes to go visiting in Newton.
She went alone to the Entz's
One time and it happened to her
That the train did not go to Newton.
If alone, she could get lost
Therefore only with someone accompanying her
Would she venture on a tour.
Once there, since it had taken her so far
She gladly also went shopping
She purchased elastic band,
Thread and other miscellaneous things.
And in the summer, came by train
Often with Margaretha Sudermann
She visited Tien here.

The Petals of a Kansas Sunflower

Figure 12
Katharina Kliewer (Tien) (1850–1939) and her daughter Margaretha Sudermann
(1877–1937), a frequent summer visitor. Source: Author's file.

But surely this is enough of that.
Also this is already long ago.
Little Tien does not work here anymore.
Now she can take it easy
And lives in the Goessel Old Folks Home.
There Tien does not need to work anymore
They take care of her there
She has nothing to do
Only teach her fine manners.

History as a Reference Point

But in spite of all fine manners
She sometimes would like to wander around.
Then they lock her in her room
Which is to be very wholesome for her.
A much better cure
Is when someone would go with her to Butler
For two weeks she visited friends here
She then liked it better in Goessel.

For a period we also had
Kaete Friesen as a boarder
And it was worth a lot to her
Since she taught a German school
At which time she had
A large pupil enrollment.

The first renter that was here—
Was Cornelius Schmidt and that was for many years.
The first renter was "Schmidt"
He and naturally his family with him
Lived in the little house
Which formerly had been included in the wages.
Schmidt liked to demonstrate his strength
As he worked here as a laborer.

As a renter he was pretty good
He appeared to have a good attitude.
He willingly repaired fences
And gladly brought in the hay.
He plowed, harrowed, sowed
Harvested and thrashed what was mowed
And other things he did as needed.
He was competent with carpentry
But when he thought it was enough
Then he would go to Missouri to visit.
The fieldwork would be interrupted
And he stayed there a couple of weeks.
When he came back from there
He worked like he had before
Since from the time he stopped
The workload had piled up.
But suddenly it did not work any more
He wanted to go to Missouri
So he went there
And began his own business.

The Petals of a Kansas Sunflower

When the Schmidt family moved
Some of our things disappeared with them
However, we will over look that
And review the next renter.

With the Schmidts gone, the house became empty
But it was necessary
Someone was needed to take care of the land
And to help generally.
Yotter was the name of the next man
Who came here as renter.
Did not know much about him for sure
Barely know the children and the wife.
When Yotter plowed or did something like that
A child sat on either side of him
A model of grievant servitude
And sat there with grim countenances.
As the first year came to an end
He had no hesitations
About moving away from here.
We were really troubled by this
He said that we had chased him away
He had not thought this of the Harders
That they were such bad people
And would not keep him for many years.

The next renter that was here
Arthur Schmidt also stayed for one year.
"Art" a son of Cornelius Schmidt
Was a talkative fellow
He enjoyed playing tricks
And laughed again afterwards.
However, it needs to be said here
For Arthur sorrowful days came
His wife died during that year
Also two children, a pair of twins.

Gustav Martens was an old man
He came on foot one day
And asked in such a pleading way
Would we not refuse to give him permission
To move into the worker's house
He would not trouble us further.
Permission was not denied him

History as a Reference Point

And already the next day
He arrived with his belongings
And set up household.
In the evenings he played chess alone
Or liked to also read and write
But with writing poetry, he understood how
A thousand times better than I.
He was his own cook and then
Worked where he could find work.
Toward the end of the time that he spent here
His support was augmented by the county.
Some concluded from all this that
He had known better days in Germany.
Whoever does not move forward stands still
And, really that means going backward.
That is the way it went with him.
In everything he did
Martens could not stand Andres.
It was obvious to others also
Martens truly envied him
Would have gladly driven him away
That far it never developed.
He was taken to an Old People's Home
Because he developed an ailment in his head
That became progressively worse, that poor man
And he was forced
To move into the Hillsboro Old People's Home.
But he did not improve
His face reflected his worsening condition
And there remained no choice for him
He went to the Hillsboro Hospital
He was there only a short time
When he was freed of his pain.

Andres Powolski, a long-term employee.
He typified longevity and indeed correctly so
Because while still quite a young man
Already as a nineteen-year-old
He came to the grandparents
And took a position there.
As the grandparents with many others
Had to prepare for their journey
The year was '76
And it probably was in June

The Petals of a Kansas Sunflower

Andres did not pass up the chance
To join the emigration.
His father had died shortly before
So there was nothing to hold him in Germany anymore.
When they came to America
The inspection of land was undertaken
Kansas had the best appeal for them.
Consequently, they decided to move there.
Andres had endured everything
That immigration brings with it.
I know this from asking questions
Or as one says, "I heard it said."
So I will skip this
And describe Andres as I saw him.
His figure was small and thin
But his nature was quite peace loving
His eyes were blue and his face somewhat pale
Earlier he had a full beard, but not later
His feet pointed outward and his legs were very thin
For that reason he did not need to join the military in Germany.
He played a lot with us children
He enjoyed holding us in his lap
However, whoever teased him too much
He threatened to put in a sack.
Andres was a faithful employee.
For him everything was always satisfactory
However, he talked to himself
In a continual, uninterrupted stream.
"Does Andres practice preaching?"
Asked a small boy once
And it cannot be denied
That one could get that impression
When one hears him talk
That went on continuously.
Andres took good care of the livestock
Hens, horses, pigs and cattle
He never fed them sparingly
Only he tended to feed them too early
Consequently, he was usually
Belligerent for a period
When he would be told: "The animals
Were really fed too early."
We had only two piglets
Or perhaps it was three,

So that we would not have a lot of work.
However, at least we had something to roast each year.
We also had some beef cattle
I believe there were four cows:
Pretty-face and Blue were two
Beauty and then also a Jersey.
We also had five horses at that time
I will now name them here
Molly, Lady, Prince, and Saul
And the really lazy Nellie.
But as the years passed
As we wanted to drive faster
Mother purchased "Tom" for that reason.
And that was the end of the peacefulness
Because he would really shy
When automobiles were still a long ways away.
And, that scared us so much
That we did not keep him very long.
We then purchased an auto
And there is nothing that can scare it.
Andres was truly happy about that
Because it also made things easier for him.
There was no more unhitching and hitching
He called it "driving in comfort."
For Andres it was a real aggravation
When he went to town with that old Saul
The horse was lame and Andres old
And sometimes it was also cold
The wagon had weak bones
And once it broke down together with him in it.
As he sat surrounded by grandmother's eggs
He had an accident that was not funny.
The wagon broke down with a loud noise
Andres fell forward and the eggs followed him.
Luckily nothing more happened
Than that Andres sat in scrambled eggs.
It is good that he was not made of eggshells
Otherwise he would have fallen apart.
This only happened once
Also, Andres was not really happy about it.
Indeed, it went better for him
When he walked to town.
However, he never went without telling us
"I want to have my face shaven"

The Petals of a Kansas Sunflower

He said this and then always added
"I just want to tell you that so you would know where I am."
However, going to town probably did him good?
His hat often sat a bit crooked
When he came back staggering
Or took steps 1 ¾ times the normal length
In the kitchen he would sit down
And out of the pot he poured the remainder of the coffee
If anyone came, he sat upright stiffly
And swallowed a cup of coffee in haste.
Claimed, however, the vanilla was only for refreshment
That the man in the little town served him
Consequently, each was happy
When he walked out of the door.
One time Andres was required
But for him it was truly awkward
To be summoned to El Dorado and appear in court.
However, it did not go badly for him
He thought now I will go to the "dark hole."
However, he was back the next day
He only had to tell
Where he was able to buy that
Which he usually bought
When he ever came to town.
However, that is why he was legally questioned.
He usually did not say much.
But let this be said additionally
Generally, he was very reliable.
He cleaned the chickenhouse
Sometimes twice in one week.
Naturally, it was worth a lot for us
That he valued the chickens so highly.
He also brought in the firewood
Because that needed to be constantly full.
Winter was a bad time for him
Then he shoveled when it was still snowing.
Or he sat near the warm oven
And read about the Kaiser in the newspaper
During harvest he also worked
Often beyond his capacity.
Because he wanted to do more
Than the boys could do.
And so two or three times a year
Because he was a Catholic

He would go to Newton for church.
He would have to hurry a lot
He washed himself in a great rush
And went to the train two hours ahead of time.
Andres caught a thief once
Who was stealing oats from us
Yet the punk wanted to fight
Rather than make it up.
He did not say a word about it then
However, after years it escaped him.
Once in the course of time
Came here and indeed from a distance
His brother's son from Cleveland
He had let us know already that he was coming.
He wanted to convince Andres
To come to Cleveland to live.
Brought many little bottles from the East
Gave some to Andres and also to Schmidt
But Andres stayed where he was
And stayed on about twelve years after that.

Figure 13
Andres Powolski (1848–1928) sitting on a kitchen chair brought from West Prussia near the kitchen stove in Grandfather Harder's kitchen. He is reading a German newspaper as he warms his feet. Photograph by Marie. Source: Author's file.

The Petals of a Kansas Sunflower

When Andres had been here fifty years
We celebrated his Jubilee
With supper and speeches
Which is the usual custom for something like that.
Andres was very touched
As Uncle described in his speech
How it was in those first years
When they had come from Germany
How they had gotten along
And Andres was always involved
And after that as Uncle
Led in singing German folksongs
Which Andres in melodic tone
Fondly sang as he worked.
That was indeed too much for Andres
Tears upon tears fell onto his beard.
He continued to sing after that
When he was alone as was his custom.
Quite particularly how easy and quick
His stooking also progressed then.
Andres was often sick
However, he always recovered.
Once he started to get sick
So bad that the doctor came
There was nothing else one could do
Except he had to submit to an operation.
In the later years, he also had
The flu several times every winter.
Then he lay in his small room in the barn
So all alone the whole day
However, he always seemed to be glad
When at mealtime, someone brought him a tray.
As year after year passed by
And Andres became an old man.
It happened at that time
That the "Bethel Old Folks Home" was dedicated.
Andres was happy about this
Settled himself into retirement there.
After lengthy consideration he purchased
With a portion of his assets
A place there to spend the rest of his life.
Wanted to be a "Newtonian" from then on.
The remainder of his assets
He gave to missions through "Regiers."

History as a Reference Point

Whenever we visited him, it was a great joy to him
But then he immediately began asking his questions:
"What is the mister doing?" "Where is the wife now?"
"And the little Susie?" "Are you already sowing wheat?"
Those were his questions in his own style.
Immediately, he began by wishing, "Have a safe trip home."
But as it often happens
Homesickness suddenly touched him.
Became quite weak and sick
He was like this for several weeks.
It has always been like this
Whoever wants to recover from homesickness
There is a sure cure
If he can go back home.
This was also true for Andres
He was completely healed by it.
On Friday, brother-in-law John went to get him
For two days, so he thought.
However, Andres had his own different thoughts
Than to stay for only one night.
"I will return on Monday"
He said with an introspective look—
And as he sat here with us on Saturday evening
He said halfway jokingly
"Well, now it starts over there already."
"What then?" "Well, only the bathing."
"They are completely too clean there for me."
Excessive cleanness was painful for him.
Was this then the real reason
Why he wanted to be here on a Saturday night?
On Monday he happily bade farewell
And did not pine for home from then on.
He was there nearly two years
When he suddenly became sick
And his time also ran out.
Pneumonia brought him to his grave.
He is resting here in the cemetery
Not far from the entry gate
And at his grave
Stands a simple gray stone.
On the gravestone it states correctly
A short inscription, "a faithful employee."
During the time that he served here
He was acquainted with five generations.

The Petals of a Kansas Sunflower

He served grandfather, father, child
And their growing children
He remained in one place a long time
No one stays that long anymore these days
For nearly sixty years is
Truly a long term.

However, I shall now come to the conclusion of
What I have undertaken to do.
I have somewhat refreshed my memory of
What already happened long ago
Because time rushes on relentlessly.
Gone are many who once were here.
Might everyone live so
That their remembrance remains a blessing.
1930

4

The Sparrows in the Fields

PERIODICALLY I MEET PEOPLE who visit Kansas and find the place very bare, monotonous, and monochromatic. "The horizon is visible aaaaall the way around." Some visitors express fear and insecurity, agoraphobia, i.e., the fear of openness or unencumbered exposure. In Kansas, standing flat-footed in the middle of the back forty, the visual image is measured in miles. There is no need for overlooks or observation decks, such as those on the Empire State Building, to create visual vantage points that allow you to see forever. Sometimes the wind will blow a cloud all the way from the far left, up and across the dome of the sky and out of sight below the horizon to the right. Summer thunderheads, dark blue clouds with pristine white edges, often billow up from the east/northeast and are visible early enough so that one can find shelter in the safety of the house before the storm strikes.

Mother was keenly aware of the elements in her environment. She saw the natural world of the prairies for she truly was a child of the plains. She was aware of the change in the angle of the sunlight as it progressively varied in different seasons. She instinctively measured the time to the next solstice by the position of the sun: at the winter solstice the sun set behind the elevator and at the summer solstice the sun set behind the cattle barn. The equinoxes of spring and fall occur when the sun sets halfway between the two. These celestial changes she observed while working in the house and glancing out the west windows. The changing seasons also brought a cyclical succession of flowers and birds into her viewing world.

During the time I was beginning elementary school, the field south of the farmhouse was planted with alfalfa. After supper in the coolness that a summer evening provides, my mother, some of my sisters, and I would occasionally sit on the house steps and watch the nighthawks fly over the field, periodically going into their gravity-defying, straight-down-towards-the-ground, bug-catching dives with a whirring sound as they bottomed out. From her reading one of my sisters shared, "the sound comes from the taut feathers of their partly spread wings. A sudden spreading of the wings slows down the descent and the bird easily sweeps itself into a graceful upward projectory to continue its apparently aimless wanderings." I did not see nighthawks on the farm during the 1960s or 1970s; with the use of less toxic chemical pesticides, these birds began returning annually in the 1990s when there were more bugs. Now, during the day, I occasionally see these nighthawks camouflaged, sitting parallel on the top of fence made of four-inch oilfield iron pipe or sitting on the dry, hard, tire tracks in the middle of sanded country roads.

In 1947 Mother wrote a poem about the birds that she had seen on the farm. This poem is written with a meter that mimics the movement of many birds, particularly those that scratch or hop around on the ground. Often, hopping is in three rapid successive, moves between scratching and pecking the earth. Some woodpeckers also have characteristic pecking patterns that ring from the trees and if put into words would have a two or three-part repeat with staccato simplicity. Here Mother uses many one-syllable words to create similar rhythm.

Our Feathered Friends

Birds are here
   With songs to cheer,
   Chirping all day long.

The mocking bird
   Can be heard,
   With its merry song.

Flocks of sparrows
   In the furrows
   Pecking at the peas.

The Sparrows in the Fields

High and low
   To and fro
      The oriole swings with ease.

Turtledove
   Is cooing in love
      With its little mate.

Nighthawks fly
   Towards the sky
      In the evening late.

Robin red breast
   Builds its nest
      Early in the spring.

Hark, Hark,
   The meadowlark
      Is perched on a post to sing.

Swallows soaring
   Their nest adoring
      Fastened to the eaves.

Thrashers rest
   In their nest
      Hidden in the leaves.

Far away
   Throughout the day
      Calls the Bob—Bobwhite.

Sound a quivering
   Sets me shivering
      Screech owl in the night.

Cute little fellow
   Warbler yellow
      Searching the bark for food.

Flicker spry
   Is hammering high
      In a happy mood.

The Petals of a Kansas Sunflower

Across the sky
   Wild geese fly
   In a pretty V.

Rain is nigh
   When cuckoos cry
   Hidden in a tree.

In hedges green
   Cardinals are seen
   Singing in a race.

With blue jay, kingbird
   Wren and cowbird
   Each one in his place.

In won't be long
   And summer is gone
   And with it the birds will leave.

No sweet song
   All day long
   When we gather the last sheaves.

Then hoarse and low
   Shrieks the crow
   Fall weather will it bring.

Cedar berries
   And snow flurries
   Will beckon little waxwing.

With a sigh
   We'll say good-bye
   To our feathered friends.

And we long
   For their song
   Till winter finally ends.

        —Marie Harder Epp
        May 7, 1947

These birds are still seen in season in this part of Kansas. Several summers back, I was sitting at dusk on the farm patio at the edge of several rows of shelterbelt trees, when I heard a three-part rapidly repeating soft sound, "chhh, chhh, chhh." The sound moved around and changed locations. The hair stood up on the back of my neck. It was sufficiently dark; I had no clue what creature was in the shadows. Was it friend or foe? Several days later, I looked up and saw the face of E.T. (the Extra-Terrestrial). I squinted and saw a four-inch, yellowish round ball, then further noticed in the shadows three more faces on low branches of different trees. With time I became aware of their guardians hovering nearby higher in the trees. I was watching baby screech owls. Their antics and sounds entertained me for several weeks.

On a Sunday morning in July, 1877, between 5 a.m. and 8 a.m., when Henry Hunsicker was riding the twelve miles from *Goldschaar* (Golden Plowshare), the Prussian Mennonite village about two and a half miles east of Newton to my great-grandfather Bernhard Harder's farm, he noted that as they rode along they occasionally disturbed flocks of prairie chickens. If the translation is accurate and the birds were indeed prairie chickens (prairie grouse) and not bobwhite quail, it is noteworthy. Although this area is within the original range of the prairie chicken, I have never seen one here in the wild. With the plowing of the grasslands, their habitat was destroyed. Tour buses now go into the Flint Hills thirty miles northeast to Cassoday where before daybreak during the months of March to early May the male prairie chickens can be heard booming. The sound travels up to two miles and entices females to join in courtship rituals. On the road leading into Cassoday there is a sign announcing, "Cassoday, The Prairie Chicken Capital of the World."

In the late 1950s in late autumn and through the winter, I would see a small group of about six shrikes, probably Loggerhead Shrikes, roosting in the red cedar trees that lined the driveway. As I walked the driveway, these birds would fly from tree to tree ahead of me. I have not seen these birds for the past twenty years.

During the summer months, individual Great Blue Herons are often seen flying over the farm in a southwesterly direction, stopping at creeks and farm ponds in their search for food, and then later in the day can be seen flying in a northeasterly direction. These herons congregate for nesting in rookeries in tall sycamore trees along the east branch of the Whitewater River in the Plum Grove area about six miles northeast of the farm.

Sometime after June 8, 1941, the night a tornado demolished the farm, Mother wrote a poem about two owls. The poem tells of the need for the pair of Great Horned Owls to find a new location to roost at night because their old haunt had been blown away. The birds by natural instinct flew out of harm's way. The pair was sufficiently regular in roosting on the *Speicher*, granary, that Mother refers to them with names.

Die Beiden Eulen

Der Ludwig und die Ludiwike,
(Das schönste grosse Eulenpaar)
Heut hört man ihr gekluck u. ihr gequicke
Noch gerade wie vor ein paar Jahr.
Der schöne Speicher flog von hinnen
Wo gern das Päärchen einstmal blieb
Nun nehmen sie ohn' viel besinnen
Mit unsern Dächern es für lieb.

—Marie Harder Epp

The Pair of Owls

Ludwig and Ludiwika,
That beautiful pair of large owls.
Today one hears their lively sounds
As one has for the past several years.
The lovely granary flew away from here
Where the pair once preferred to stay.
Without much ado, they have taken
To our other roofs by preference.

5

But God!

ON THE NIGHT OF June 8, 1941, having demolished my parents' farm, the tornado continued on its northeasterly course and destroyed the Jake Regier farm across the road. More details are included in appendix 3. Several minutes later it wiped out the farm of Uncle John Thiessen and Mother's late sister Aunt Helene, who had passed away two years earlier.

That Sunday began like any normal, rainy Sunday morning in the Thiessen home. Dark rain clouds moved across the sky bringing heavy rain and much lightning. After breakfast and between showers of rain, Susan and other siblings tried to go out and pick mulberries for their lunch after church, but the intensity of the lightning scared the would-be pickers back into the house. They went to church and then had a leisurely afternoon at home.

Another neighborhood lad, Walter Entz, who was ten-years-old at the time and lived about six miles south of the Thiessens, also went outside before church to help his father feed their farm animals. He recalls the intermittent rain and the wind blowing the clouds across the sky. What intrigued him was that below one of the clouds there was an appendage dangling down, flapping back and forth with the wind, and spinning in a counter-clockwise rotation. He pointed out this funny cloud to his father who simply blanched with apprehension. His father explained that it was the funnel cloud of a tornado. Fortunately, the funnel never touched the ground and was blown away in a northeasterly direction by the wind.

There was more threatening prairie weather in the evening, but the John Thiessen family went to bed as usual. After 10:30 they were awakened by several unusual sounding claps of thunder. Uncle John called upstairs for everyone to come downstairs until the storm was past. The family always congregated in the downstairs bedroom during severe storms. Grabbing their pillows and light blankets and coming downstairs, Bernard (age twenty-one) and Gilbert (age seventeen) lay down on the kitchen floor next to the bedroom door. Lydia (age twenty-two) and Susie (age nineteen), a.k.a. Susan, settled down on the floor of the downstairs bedroom shared by Uncle John and Herald (age nine). Dorothy (age thirteen) was visiting a cousin in Beatrice, Nebraska.

They were just barely settled down when the winds of the tornado made the weather stripping on a door screech with an ear-wrenching pitch and then there was a very loud roar. They felt the house give way to the force of the tornado's high-velocity winds.

In the words of Susan, "There was a moment of unawareness and then we were flying, like leaves in the autumn wind, among all the debris of the household furnishings." The repetitive lightning provided enough light for each family member to see different things. Susan remembers seeing the posts of her father's bedstead fly past. Lydia remembers the northeast corner of the house opening up and the lit kerosene lamp sailing out of the bedroom window. Bernard and Gilbert saw the joists in the ceiling come down on them. Then another moment of unawareness and it was all over. They were all lying on the muddy ground, each believing they were the only one alive and with no idea of where they were.

Miraculously, they were all alive, lying among the debris within one hundred fifty feet north and east of the location of the demolished house. But as they got over the shock of the event and began to look around, it was hard to get oriented. All the trees and buildings that would have been reference points were gone. As Uncle John came back to consciousness, he screamed with such heart-wrenching, desperate fear, "*Kinder, wo seid ihr alle*? Children! Where are you all?" that my cousins still have chills running down their spines when they think of it sixty years later. Uncle John then called each child by name and each answered except Bernard, who was only semi-conscious at first, having been hit by something on his head that created a gash, which was sutured after he got to the hospital. Also, he was pinned to the ground by a piece of chimney lying on his pajama sleeve; it later took six men to carry the chimney piece away. As Susan tried to jump up, she could not move. Since she had no feeling in her legs, she thought they were gone. In fact, she was paralyzed since several of her vertebrae had been crushed and her spinal cord severed. Miraculously, Susan had landed partway on a mattress and could be moved enough to get some relief from the pain until the ambulance arrived. The corner of what formerly had been the wall of a closet had landed on Herald's foot; his injury required suturing when he got to the hospital and he was admitted for several days. Lydia and Gilbert escaped with barely a scratch. Uncle John must have landed on his knees because after the adrenaline of the moment wore off, he needed crutches for a time as his knees healed.

After regrouping, Gilbert was sent to neighbors across the section to the southeast to get help. Upon returning, he reported that all of their own buildings, silo, and fences were demolished. Soon, men of the neighborhood began arriving after having seen the storm clouds, hearing the roar, and following the path of the storm. They brought the news about the other farms destroyed to the southwest. Assessing the devastation, it was found that the new Pontiac in the garage had only a few boards lying around it but hardly any damage. Wondering where the keys might be, Uncle John tried to visualize where the writing desk in which he always kept the keys might have landed. Suddenly, as the moonlight broke through the clouds, Uncle John saw the keys lying right on top of a pile of clothes that had been dumped out of a closet. No pieces of the writing desk were ever found.

Bernard and Gilbert started for Whitewater in the car to get the local doctor, Dr. Regier, because all telephone lines were down. En route they met someone who told them that Dr. Regier was already out on another call and suggested they go to Potwin to get Dr. Stalman. Someone called the ambulance and with time both Dr. Stalman and the ambulance were there. Susan was given a sedative to make it possible to move her to a stretcher. Uncle John rode with Susan in the ambulance and the rest of the family followed in the car. About one-fourth mile east of the driveway the family saw Fanny, their white horse, lying dead in the ditch with a two-by-four stuck straight into her side.

The family got to the Bethel Deaconess Hospital in Newton at 3:30 a.m., about four hours after the tornado struck. The deaconesses were there ready and waiting for them having been alerted by several other families who had already received medical care. Susan was admitted in critical condition; Bernard and Herald had their wounds sutured. Uncle John and Herald were hospitalized. A picture of Herald in bed with Lydia at his bedside appeared in the *Wichita Eagle* evening edition on June 9.

The Petals of a Kansas Sunflower

For Susan, the next morning seemed especially discouraging. Newspaper reporters came to take pictures. A picture of Susan lying in her hospital bed was also included in the *Wichita Eagle* evening edition on June 9. This same picture appeared in the weekly issue of the Whitewater *Independent* on Thursday, June 12, 1941 with the caption, "Pictured above is Susan Thiessen, 16 [19], who is in the Bethel Hospital at Newton suffering from probable broken back in the storm." The same picture was also printed in the weekly edition of *The Potwin Ledger* on June 12, 1941. Here the caption read:

> "Susan Thiessen, 16 [19], one of those injured in the recent tornado. 'The first thing we knew of the storm,' said Lydia Thiessen, sister of Susan, 'was when we heard a loud roar. One wall crashed in and the plaster fell, then the whole house collapsed and started to move. The rest seemed like a nightmare until we started digging out. The wreckage, with us in it, was blown about one hundred fifty yards. We all came out from under the debris not seriously injured except Susan. She was pinned under heavy timbers. After the timbers were lifted she was unable to get up.' She was taken to a hospital by friends. Five others were in the house when the storm struck."

Truly, Susan did not feel photogenic on that first morning after having been in medical care for several hours. There was the pain of her injuries, and her hair was an incredible mess of tangles embedded with mud from the ground where she landed and plaster from the crumbling walls of the house. Since Susan was so weak, a deaconess, Sister Kati, took the task of combing her hair as her personal project. She carefully and tenderly combed each small strand of hair until it combed smoothly. She would then let Susan rest before she would comb the next strand later or the next day. It took nearly a week for Sister Katie to complete this project, but for Susan it felt so good.

Following x-rays in the next several days, a specialist from Wichita was consulted and he suggested surgery. Surgery was performed on July 1, but in 1941 the prognosis after a spinal cord injury was not good. The doctors gave Susan two years of life expectancy. When my mother heard this prognosis, she simply said, "But God!" Whenever Mother relived hearing about Susan's prognosis, she always included her exclamation, "But God!" It is repeated in the poem to follow as well.

But God!

I feel Mother believed that in life there are some mysteries. While doctors may render prognoses, sometimes unexpected things happen. Mother had the capacity to feel that through prayer and support, life could be energized. For her nineteen-year-old niece Susan, Mother felt that surely God had other plans, and this major injury would not become a limiting factor, even if it rendered her a paraplegic.

Susan got much emotional support from family, relatives, and friends. Her father and her siblings visited Susan every day in the hospital, even as they were beginning to rebuild the farm. After several months, when Susan was beginning to recover, the family visited twice during the week and then again on Sunday afternoon. The family continued this routine until the new house was constructed and Susan was able to come home by ambulance on January 6, 1942.

During the seven months in the hospital, Susan had non-family visitors every day. During visiting hours on the first few Sundays, as many as thirty-five people came to encourage her. She got much mail and many cards. On one visit, a resourceful woman from the local church community gave Susan an apple salt-and-pepper set. Standing on her dresser, this set became a conversation piece. Susan mentioned to another friend that she would be interested in a salt-and-pepper set collection. When this friend returned on her next visit, she brought the second set with her. By 1986, Susan was finding enjoyment from her collection of 589 salt-and-pepper sets, mostly from gifts.

During Susan's hospital stay prior to Christmas in 1941, an anonymous friend gave the local minister $5.00 with the request that Susan purchase Christmas gifts for her family. After consulting with Susan, the Rev. and Mrs. J. C. Kaufman went to a local bookstore to purchase Susan's choices. For her father and Gilbert, Susan chose a wall motto for each, for Bernard a book, for Herald an Uncle Wiggly game, and for Dorothy a storybook. For Lydia, Mrs. Kaufman ordered pillowcases from a catalogue, which Susan embroidered on those days when the family did not visit. Mrs. Kaufman then crocheted an edging on the pillowcases. Shortly before Christmas, the Kaufmans came with wrapping paper and ribbons. The nurses hid the wrapped gifts until Christmas.

Most of the student nurses became friends with Susan during her extended stay in the hospital and at Christmas they put up a small tree on her dresser. Under the tree were all the gifts that friends sent for Susan.

The Petals of a Kansas Sunflower

Figure 14
Susan among her salt-and-pepper shaker collection.
Source: Susan Thiessen's file.

It was a tradition on Christmas Eve at the hospital for the deaconesses and the nurses to sing a cantata on the second floor for the patients who were well enough to attend and their guests. Uncle John and Susan's siblings were invited to accompany Susan who sat in a wheelchair. Following the concert, Uncle John and the siblings celebrated their family Christmas in Susan's room. Completing the family Christmas, they helped Susan open the forty-two gifts from friends. Hidden among these were Susan's gifts for her family. She truly surprised them all. The anonymous friend can take pride and comfort in knowing that this gift brought incredible joy and happiness to Susan and her family as they celebrated Christmas around her hospital bed on that Christmas Eve in 1941.

Prior to the tornado, the family Christmas celebration was always also on Christmas Eve and included lit candles on the Christmas tree, reading the Christmas story from Luke 2, and places set with gifts and treats for each child around a table in German fashion. The tornado forced many changes for Susan, but did not diminish the joy, excitement, and celebration that the Christmas season engendered.

With time Susan's father arranged for physical therapy and she spent some time in California. Uncle John also built the first handicap access ramp that I saw, as well as exercise bars for Susan to use. Since I was born after the tornado, I am not aware of the first years of Susan's recovery, except for two clippings from the Whitewater *Independent*. With a headline of "Miss Susie Thiessen Slowly Regaining Strength," the July 24, 1941, clipping read, "Friends of Miss Susie Thiessen who was so badly hurt during the recent tornado will be glad to learn that she is gradually regaining strength. She is still unable to use her legs but the sense of feeling is gradually returning to them. Otherwise she is gradually returning to normal." On April 5, 1942, the paper ran, "Miss Susie Thiessen, who was injured in the tornado of June 8 was able to be taken to the Emmaus Church Sunday evening where she sat in a wheel chair and enjoyed the Easter song service. This is the first time she has attended a church service since she was injured."

Susan completed high school at home by correspondence. She also graduated from Grace University, Omaha, Nebraska and inquired about career opportunities after the director of the "Go Ye" Mission from Tahlequah, Oklahoma gave a sermon in the local church. Arrangements were made for her to live with coworkers and she became a secretary in the "Go Ye" Mission offices. My mother kept in touch with her by letters.

After Susan worked there for twenty-five years, this accomplishment was celebrated on January 8, 1978. Mother wrote a poem for the occasion. Kathy Klaassen, Susan's niece read the poem. Recently, Susan celebrated her ninetieth birthday. She continues to live in our community and enjoys her exquisite salt-and-pepper shaker collection.

Figure 15
Susan's graduation picture from Grace University in 1949.
Source: Susan Thiessen's file.

Figure 16
Susan at her desk in the "Go Ye" Mission office.
Source: Susan Thiessen's file.

But God!

Susan's Twenty-fifth Anniversary with the "Go Ye" Mission
January 8, 1978

A day indeed outstanding we celebrate today,
    A day that calls for praises in a very unique way.
A day on which we are pausing, reflecting on past years
    With all their many blessings, anxieties and fears.
We are joining today with Susan in a time of special praise
    For truly unsearchable are God's mysterious ways.
On the 15th day of April in Nineteen-twenty-two,
    She started on life's journey as most of you here knew.
A sister and a brother rejoiced to see her come,
    For their love and admiration she instantly had won.
She enjoyed a carefree childhood, there was work and also play.
    She joined in all activities in a pleasant happy way.
Where the days and years had gone so soon, seemed like a mystery.
    Before she knew, the grade school years were also history.
Already as a teenager she liked to cook and bake.
    Was there sickness somewhere near, a cake she liked to take.
The household duties, just the same, with her sisters she would share
    And, through lingering illness, their Mother had tender care.
Then through God's sovereign leading sad changes came about.
    She could then but acknowledge: "God's ways are past finding out."
On the 8th of June in '41, within a minute's time
    A harsh wind crushed the lovely flower, being still in years of prime.
About the following days and weeks, we shall not here relate;
    She yielded to God's leading, though uncertain was the fate.
The life expectancy was brief, the future seemed so dim;
    Even the doctor's decision brought no encouragement from him.
But God! She was not forgotten. He saw her safely through.
    There were brighter days in coming, there was work for her to do.
The many friends and callers, made the hospital stay more bright.
    With friendly words and often gifts, she found them a delight.
This way the fine collection of salt-and-pepper shakers grew;
    Indeed a rare collection, excelled by very few.
Then finally after surgery and months of tender care
    The bed confinement ended with the use of the wheelchair.
With this change came confidence, as the future she would face.
    And hope giving way to action, was seemingly the case.
She acquired more education. In her handicapped state
    It was far beyond expectation that from Grace she could graduate.
When later opportunity for office work arose,
    It was more than she had ever thought or even could suppose

The Petals of a Kansas Sunflower

That with the "Go Ye" Mission, she would closely be involved.
>But now the future uncertainties were slowly being solved.

Still many questions crossed her mind, of fear and sometimes doubt.
>Was this the place of God's own choice and would her strength hold out?

She asked the Lord that in his grace, five years He would allow.
>And abundantly God answered, giving twenty-five years by now.

All through these years it wasn't just her office work alone
>But also in the Park Hill Church her influence is well known.

To Velma and to Ruby, much credit we here ascribe.
>They surround her with loving care from morn till eventide.

In the office too we find, where she works day by day
>That things are there arranged in the most convenient way.

Now thinking of the future, we commit you to God's care
>As again office responsibilities with others you will share.

May it be with anticipation that each new day you face,
>For the Lord is ever present with his sustaining grace.

Our prayers will go with you, may the future hold for you
>Days filled with joy and blessings, in all you're called to do.

—M.H.E.

6

In the Days before Hallmark Cards

It is hard to imagine a time when one could not just go and get a greeting card off an extended rack expressing the exact sentiment that one felt at that moment in time. But in 1929 when Mother began writing poetry, some of her first works were short poems that complemented gifts. Back then gift giving involved a bit of theater and fanfare. First, one had to shop for the gift in the local mercantile stores or order it from a mail order catalogue, which could take weeks to arrive. A social occasion was planned to set the proper ambience for the gift giving. Following normal community traditions, there would be a sit-down dinner. After the second seating for the children and the women who worked in the kitchen, including the hostess, the table would be cleared. Everyone congregated in the parlor or under the trees outside in the summertime, and the program would be initiated. There would be a rather formal beginning with the singing of a hymn, followed by speeches. Some words would be spoken prior to the presentation of a gift at a birthday or anniversary. On very special occasions, even the elder or a minister was invited and asked to share a few words.

Mother initiated her poetry writing with two short verses to accompany gifts as mentioned in chapter 1. The following year, there was a fruit shower for John T. Reimer and his new bride, Elsie. Mother's sister Mina had passed away in 1928 and John was remarrying. John and Mina had two young sons, John and Raymond. Mother wrote these poems as if my sisters Hildegard and Martha were giving these gifts. However, since Hildegard was twenty-two months old and Martha was three months old when this shower occurred, perhaps Mother attached these poems as notes to the gifts. Here the gifts were some soap and sugar. I do not know how the gift of soap relates to a fruit shower, but it seems not to have been critical with Mother's imagination. A fruit shower would have been a community effort to stock the pantry for Elsie, because she had not been around the previous summer to grow a garden and to preserve or can produce for the winter larder. A fruit shower in January would constitute sharing canned goods from one's own store of foods.

Zu John T. Reimers Fruit Shower, 17 Januar 1930

Nehmt von mir dem Marthalein
Die nicht mögt, die einzige sein
Die mit leeren Händen kam
Eines Päckchen Seife an.
Wohl jeder Seife brauchen kann
Führ ein Beispielchen noch an
Sollt's dem Onkel wohl passieren
Das vielleicht beim tractor schmieren
Was ja leicht kommen kann
Das er sich färbt die Hände an
Dann hat er und Tante auch
Wohl gern Seife im Gebrauch
Und die Jungens liebe Zeit
Werden wohl zur Sauberkeit
Wie es denn so ist bei Knaben
Öfters Seife nötig haben.
Darum nehmt's in liebe an
Und denkt an Martha dann u. wann.

For John T. Reimers' Fruit Shower, January 17, 1930

Take from me, the little Martha,
Who does not like to be the only one
Who came with empty hands,
Presents a little parcel of soap.
Truly, everyone can use soap.
Consider the example:
Should it happen to the uncle
That probably as he greases the tractor,
What can easily happen,
That he stains his hands.
Then he and auntie as well

In the Days before Hallmark Cards

Truly apply the soap gladly.
And the boys in this moment
Will truly be brought to reality.
As it is with boys then
They often have a need for soap.
For that reason, take this in love
And think of Martha now and then.

Für John & Elsies Fruit Shower, 17 Januar 1930

Wer süßt die Liebe wohl auch viel
Alles süßt sie nicht
Davon ist als Beispiel
Ein saueres Gericht
Habe es mir so bedacht
Dazu braucht es mehr
Und habe denn darum gebracht
Etwas Zucker her
Bitte nehmt ihn also hin
Wie's gespendet ward
Mit liebenden Sinn
Von klein Hildegard.

For John & Elsie's Fruit Shower, January 17, 1930

Even though love is truly very sweet
Not everything is sweet.
There is for example
A sour-like inclination.
Having thought this through,
What one needs more of
And have brought for that reason
A little sugar.
Please take this and use it
As if given
With a sense of great appreciation
From little Hildegard.

The Petals of a Kansas Sunflower

So far, the purpose and content of the following poem remains a mystery. My cousins do not recall what leadership activity resulted in a reward relating to food or a kitchen. The poem is rather cleverly constructed, so it will need to be appreciated for its word and thought construction, rather than any broader significance.

Für Schwager Hans Thiessen, 15 Mai 1932

Es kam noch einer her
  So vor ein paar Tagen
Nun Ihr wüßt ja wohl schon wer
  Brauch es schon nicht sagen
Und wir waren fast gerührt
  Als wir aus gefunden
Wer uns hatte zu geführt
  Einsen einer Kunden
Das kann doch nicht so um hin
  Bleiben unbeachtet
Und bald kam uns in dem Sinn
  Als wir noch gedachtet:
"Wie würd wohl als kleiner Lohn
  Sein ein schoner Küchen?
Und sogleich als Kommission
  Sollten's doch versuchen."
Also ist's dann auch geschehen
  Und beendet ist das Lied.
Wünschen: Bestes wohl ergehe
  Und guten Appetit.

For Brother-in-Law John Thiessen, May 15, 1932

It came to someone who is here,
  A few days ago.
You surely already know whom
  So it does not need to be stated here.
And we were pleased
  As we learned
Who has been a leader among us.
  One of our acquaintance.
Surely that can not
  Remain unnoticed

And soon it comes to our attention
>As we from memory:
"How surely will as a little reward
>A nice kitchen be?
And similar to this as commission
>One should expect."
It then also occurs
>And the song ends.
Our wish: best wishes
>And good appetite.

In her autobiographical book, Mother wrote about going by train from Whitewater to Elbing, a distance of seven miles, to visit her sister Justine who would pick her up at the train station with a horse and buggy and drive her to their farm west of Elbing. These visits occurred between 1914, the year of Justine's wedding, and 1919, the year that she passed away from influenza while still in the hospital having just given birth to her youngest daughter, Helen. Bertha, the eldest, Edna, and Helen were raised on the Elbing farm with the help of their Aunt Louise, John H. Regier's sister. A poem, included in chapter 12, was written for Helen to recite at Bertha's wedding and it expresses the warm camaraderie of these sisters as they grew up.

For Mother's niece Edna, the gift was a bath towel on the occasion of her fifteenth birthday. Also mentioned was the hard work these sisters did to maintain the household, thus the pertinence of a bath towel after a refreshing bath.

Für Edna zum Handtuch, 26 Mai 1932

Ist heiß der Tag, die Arbeit schwer
>*Das Wirken wird zur Last*
Und schwitzen tust du auch gar sehr
>*Und sehnest dich nach Rast.*
Wenn dann nach vollbrachter Tat
>*Eine Sonne schon verschwunden*
Und du im schönen kühlen Bad
>*Erquickung hast gefunden.*
Dann hoffe ich wird eins Handtuch doch
>*Recht nützlich sein dir*
Jetzt bitte grüß' die Biedere noch
>*Von Onkel Hans und mir.*

The Petals of a Kansas Sunflower

For Edna about the Towel, May 26, 1932

The day is hot, the work is difficult
    The work becomes a burden
And you also perspire a lot
    And you look forward to a rest
When finally the task is achieved.
    The sun has already vanished
And in a nice cool bath you
    Have found renewal.
Then I hope that a towel will
    Rightly be comfortable there.
Now greetings from us both
    From Uncle John and me.

Ernest Wiebe gave his wife a lid for her cooking pot. The occasion is obscure. It is very interesting to have expressed so clearly what Mother considered the role of the wife and her function. Pleasing her man with good food is the key to happiness, and this is not a burden, it is an extension of wifely affection.

Für Ernest Wiebe zu Deckel, April 1932

Kocht für den Mann die Frau das Essen
Denn darf sie ja nicht vergessen
Daß, der Deckel sei am Platz
Soll es schmecken ihrem Schatz
Alles wird dann gut geraten
Und viel saftiger ist der Braten
Wenn nicht fehlt dies eine Stück
Es erhöht ja auch das Glück
Denn freuen tut es stets den Mann,
Wenn schön sein Frauchen Kochen kann.
So bitte nehmt mit frohem Sinn
Einse kleine Gabe hin.

For Ernest Wiebe to the Lid, April 1932

As the wife cooks the food for her man
Then she should not forget
That the lid be in its place

If it is to taste good for her sweetheart.
All this will then be good advice
And the roast meat will be very juicy
If this one suggestion is not missed.
It also increases the probability of success.
It will surely please her man,
When his affectionate wife can cook well.
So please accept with a sense of happiness
A small gift.

Someone gave John Thiessen a comb box for Christmas. This would definitely solve the problem of the lost comb every time someone needed to look less than windblown living on the Kansas prairies.

Für John Thiessen zur Kammbox
24 Dezember 1932

Hier ist was für die Jungen
Sowohl wie fürs Ehepaar
Obzwar nicht sehr gelungen
Ist's pracktisch das nicht wahr?
Hing sie nur am Spiegel an
Zum täglichen Gebrauch
Für die Frau und ihren Mann
Und die sechs Kinder auch.

For John Thiessen about the Comb Box
December 24, 1932

Here is something for the youngsters
As well as for the married couple,
Indeed, it is not very fancy,
It is practical, is that not true?
Hang it on the mirror
For the daily preen
For the wife and her man
And also for the six children.

The Petals of a Kansas Sunflower

My father shared the same birth date with his niece Marilyn Wiebe. Here Mother writes a tender, affectionate verse in Father's voice for Marilyn's second birthday. The gift was doll house accessories. Unfortunately, she passed away six years later following complications of a ruptured appendix.

Für Marilyn Wiebe, 13 Januar 1933

Weil dein und mein Geburtstag ist
Und du ein kleines Mädchen bist
Möchte ich zum Geburtstag dir
Schenken dieses Tässchen hier
Koch für die Püppchen du nur Tee
Dann tut ihn ganz gewiß nichts weh
Und du als kleines Puppenmädchen
Ist noch dazu ein Butterbrötchen
So nimme in liebe sie dann hin
Von Onkel Hans' für Marilyn.

For Marilyn Wiebe, January 13, 1933

Since it is your and my birthdays
And since you are a little girl
I would like for your birthday
To give you these little cups here.
Make tea for the dolls as you do
Which you knowingly do with perfect innocence
And since you are a little doll yourself
Also, here is a little loaf of bread with butter
So accept this with love
For Marilyn from Uncle John.

Mother's papers also include one poem used for a bridal shower gift in 1987. Here she expresses the sentiment that the joy of cooking for one's husband supersedes the excitement of doing it with shiny new utensils. This is consistent with her definition of wifely priorities expressed earlier.

In the Days before Hallmark Cards

For Lisa Harder, June 27, 1987

What joy it will be
To cook for two
Using utensils all shiny
And new.

The meat is just right
The potatoes are done.
Cooking for hubby will
Really be fun.

7

For a Good Laugh

MOTHER LOVED A GOOD laugh and some of her poems reflect her lovely sense of humor. She grew up with people who enjoyed laughing. Her sister Helene was known for her contagious laughter, acknowledged by my grandmother (Helene Wiebe Harder) in a comment to my mother, "If we want to have a good laugh, we need to invite Helene." Helene's daughters, my cousins, inherited the gift of storytelling and laughter.

My father was not entirely without humor but, on the other hand, did not like unstructured, non-goal-oriented activity. Just having fun was not within his comfort zone. He once shared with Mother that he considered some of her early poems frivolous, with no eternal value. In his worldview, his only purpose on earth was to have dominion over God's creation and to work towards rewards in the next life. His humorless attitude of life, together with his lack of support and negative remarks, appear to have discouraged Mother from continuing to openly express the joys she found in life. After the first several years of writing, her poems were mostly project oriented, rather than expressing joy and wonder at the things she saw and sensed around her. Running a rural farm household with its enormous workload while bearing, feeding, and clothing eight children may also have been contributing factors. However, she could not easily be suppressed and continued to slip her humor in now and then, e.g., "Doughnuts."

Not only did Mother enjoy cooking, she also enjoyed eating, particularly donuts. Glazed or plain, all were a treat. She made raised donuts from scratch and the anticipation of this sweet treat was worth the half day of effort. It goes without saying that she grew up without a donut shop around the corner. The soft dough was mixed and then let to rise for an hour or so. On a floured breadboard she gently rolled out a wad of dough. First she would stamp out the outer dimension of the donut-to-be with a cookie cutter or a large-mouthed jar, snugly cutting as many as possible from the rolled dough. Collecting all the dough not included in the circles, she would put that back into her dough pan. With a smaller cutter she would cut the donut holes; these too were tossed back into the dough pan as donut holes were not in her repertoire of confectionaries. This procedure was repeated until all the dough was cut. The newly cut donuts were allowed to rest and rise again.

Doughnuts

> Doughnuts fresh and doughnuts brown
> Marie is sure to gobble them down.
> Some doughnuts are big and some are small
> There is no difference she loves them all.
> Doughnuts hot and doughnuts cold
> She even likes them one day old.
> So doughnuts here and doughnuts there
> She surely likes them everywhere.
> So long may she live and happy be
> Eating doughnuts with her family of three.
>
> —Marie Harder Epp

In the basement was the row of covered ceramic crocks filled with lard rendered on butchering day between the previous Christmas and New Year's. That was the time of the year when the ambient temperature in the detached garage chilled and preserved the carcass and meat during cutting at a safe temperature. Mother got enough lard so that the melted fat would fill her black cast-iron skillet with two inches of oil. To test for the proper temperature and to remove any undesirable flavors that may have accumulated in the lard in storage, Mother put paper thin slices of an Irish potato into the oil. When the potato slices were brown and crisp, the oil was hot enough for the twice-raised donuts to be gingerly nudged off the breadboard into the hot oil. The donuts were turned once to brown both sides evenly. As they were draining and cooling on a towel, Mother predictably broke a donut into sampling bites. She just could not resist, and if she also gave some to us children, there never was any guilt from "*naschen*," i.e., eating on the sly or nibbling secretly. Mother's face would light up and she would smile her biggest smile and say, "That was good eating."

"So long may she live and happy be / Eating doughnuts with her family of three." Since this was written in English and her family went down in size as children went away to college and got married, I make the assumption that Mother wrote this poem after I left for college and someone was home for a period of time.

When I left to go to college in the fall of 1960, Mother assumed my responsibility for milking the cow. Milking had become my responsibility when my older brother left to go to college. Every morning and evening, before and after school, I milked the Guernsey cow named Peach.

Being the youngest child, I represented the end of the labor pool. Mother gamely insisted that she would take over; she surely needed fresh milk and especially the cream for her cooking. But what her exuberance had not factored in was that during the fifteen to twenty years since she last sat on her milking stool, her knees had aged and become stiff. Milking was within the domain of woman's work and Mother had milked cows from early teenage years until her children were old enough to take on this chore.

The last night before I left for college, Mother came to the barn to milk. I had Peach in the stanchion with hobbles on her back legs to keep her from kicking over the milk bucket or taking any large steps. Sitting on her signature milking stool, Mother milked like a trooper and finished in good time. Peach stood motionless. But when Mother stood up from her milking stool, she just gasped and hunched over, grabbing the barn wall for support. Concerned, I asked, "Are you all right?"

Slowly Mother responded, "Just give me some time. My knees are not used to this anymore." Between her groans, she muttered, "They will slowly limber up if I keep doing this."

I left for college with this lingering image of Mother hunched over at the barn wall. When I checked back after a short time, Mother responded using an expression from Low German; she mumbled, "*Est mi nuscht*, it was nothing to me."

Figure 17
Marie's milking stool was a gift from Father after Mother's surgery in 1944. Marie carved the decorations. The legs are a recycled pitchfork handle with the leg on the right the top of the handle. The other milking stools were simply two pieces of two-by-four boards nailed into a "T." Source: Author's file.

The Petals of a Kansas Sunflower

Die Kuh ist Frisch

Die Kuh ist frisch, die Kuh ist frisch.
Bald gibt es mehr Milch für den Tisch
Die Katzen sehen auch ganz dünn
Mehr Milch ist ihnen ganz nach Sinn
Das Kalb ist rot mit weißen Kopf
Zum Market bestimmt, der arme Tropf.
Wer melkt die Kuh, ist jetzt die Frage
Die Antwort ist klar in unserer Lage.
Wir sind hier nur zu zweien da
So sag ich noch "Three cheers for Ma"

The Cow is Fresh

The cow is fresh, the cow is fresh.
Soon there will be more milk to drink.
The cats also look rather thin,
More milk is definitely on their minds.
The calf is red with a white head.
Destined for market this poor wretch.
Who milks the cow is now the question?
The answer is clear in our situation.
There are only two of us here
So, I will say, "Three cheers for Ma."

When a cow gives birth to a calf, in the vernacular this is referred to as "the cow is fresh," meaning that her milk production has begun anew. There is always excitement, since there is a new supply of milk for use in the kitchen and to drink during meals, which in German is expressed as more milk for the table. Every barn also has a cat pan into which some fresh milk is poured. The cats just hang around at milking time knowing they will be rewarded with the first fruits since they serve a major benefit for rodent control in and around the barn. The color of the red calf with a white head indicates that its sire was a meat-type Hereford and so the calf would be raised for selling or butchering as a meat animal.

Since only Mother and Father remained on the farm when I left, the milking was up to Mother, because Father, in a farm accident years earlier, lost the three longest fingers on his right hand and so could not squeeze the cow's teats for the milking action. "Three cheers for Ma." It was she or nobody. Within several years, they located a source of milk from another farm, so they only needed to pick up jars of milk without sitting on a milking stool to produce it and to test the flexibility of Mother's aging knees.

When my youngest sister Justina turned thirty, Mother wrote a poem on her birthday. She was two years older than I, but Justina was petite, especially when she stood next to me. I remember one visitor asking if Justina was a grandchild after Mother introduced me as her youngest child.

Oct 21, '70

Can it be our Teeny dear
    Has already come to her 30th year?
It seems to me like yesterday
    When she stirred up cookies in her own sweet way.
In studying the recipe some time was spent—
    A little of each to her "allspice" meant.
Not knowing what baking soda was about,
    Why worry further? Just leave it out.
With a little help the result was swell.
    We all enjoyed cookies for a spell.
Year after year has since rolled by.
    She, now, even tackles an apple pie.
        —Marie Epp

Mother recalled fondly the day Justina tried to make cookies while Mother was away. For allspice, Justina, as an eight to ten-year-old, used a little of a number of spices. Mother thought this was so inventive.

The name, allspice, originally did describe its flavor, which seems like a combination of nutmeg, clove, and cinnamon or ginger. Clove seems to dominate, with some cinnamon and a trace of nutmeg. There are peppery overtones. Allspice is used throughout most of the world but is particularly popular in European cooking. It is a predominant spice used in traditional West Prussian cooking. Mother used it routinely, but Justina must not have found it on the shelf.

Not knowing why baking soda was used in the recipe, Justina simply left it out. Fortunately, Mother got home while the cookie dough was still in the bowl and so she was able to doctor the dough into useable cookies. Justina's baking skills continued to develop as she aged up.

8

Request for Poems

PEOPLE FROM THE COMMUNITY would stop Mother in town, at church, or call on the party telephone line at number 96F4 and ask her to write a poem to help them celebrate an event. Often these requests were from the extended family of relatives who knew Mother could recall many everyday as well as celebratory events in their lives. The requests did not come with formal contracts or advanced payments, but Mother gave many community events special credence and honor with creative poems. She filled specific requests, writing something especially for them, something uniquely theirs. Such requested poems were read or recited at birthday celebrations, posthumous birthday remembrances, bridal showers, rehearsal dinners, wedding receptions, wedding anniversaries, church and school anniversaries, and bon voyage services for missionaries. In addition to local celebrations, the initial reading of some poems was in other states: California, Idaho, Nebraska, New York, Oklahoma, Pennsylvania, and South Dakota.

In the local religious community, lectures or sermons were routine. This communication technique uses words in an expository, linear mode. Music also became, with time, an integral component of worship and communication. In music, words are vocalized with expressive varieties. They can be vocalized softly or with volume over a large range of pitches from a low G by the men, and with effort and talent to a high C by the women; pronunciation of words can be drawn out or shortened to eliminate the routines of speech. Poems were not as common and put words into new sequences. The novelty of word sequences with different rhythms and rhymes that could recall events, paint images in one's imagination, or express an emotion with the economy of few words had special meaning. The uniqueness of each poem made it worthy of attention. Many of the poems reaffirmed the strengths of community bonds where joys and sorrows were shared jointly. Strong community bonds were the underpinning buttress for Mennonites in general and especially supportive during the early years of life among the tall grasses of the prairie.

Mother's relationship to the recipient is included with each poem partially to illustrate how the "Mennonite name game" is played. Mentioning the name of the recipient also draws attention to the interrelatedness of community members, where families tended to be large and the opportunities for intermarriage were great. Since the Mennonites in Europe lived in small self-contained villages, most people were related to each other but many continued to choose spouses from within their own villages. Consequently, familial relatedness is extensive. Here in America, if a fellow Mennonite asks your name, you immediately provide rather accurate information about your European and American origins and to whom you are related. This results in endless questions like, "were they your first or second cousin, or was he your second cousin once removed (of the next generation)?" The questions can go on ad infinitum including "now, was this on your mother's or your father's side?" These issues of relatedness were and are more than sheer entertainment; they are the threads of the fabric of Mennonite community, a community historically set apart.

Writing poems for others was volunteer work; Mother viewed her poems as a contribution to her community. She was a village poet, although she never used the term or perceived herself as such. Mother hoped that her poems would help people in her community gain a renewed perspective, feel rewarded, be honored, or they simply put a smile on their faces. She wanted to remind people that all good things in life come from the hands of God.

Mother was not the only poet in the community. There was another poet from the Plum Grove area, Helen Kopper, who is remembered for creating poems for her relatives. Several of Mother's cousins also wrote a few poems, but none of these wrote for community events, but rather focused on celebrations within their own families.

After receiving a request for a poem, Mother would conduct an informal interview with the person requesting the poem, asking what should be included. She would ask what events, experiences, and family activities were important or that they remembered. If a wedding poem was requested, Mother would ask where the couple grew up and went to school, how they met and courted, and what their plans were for the future. The more prolific the information provided, the longer the poem. It was from this collage of facts obtained through the interview or from Mother's own memory that the intimate core of a poem developed.

There was only one exception when Mother was paid for writing a poem—I saw the transaction as I bashfully peeked through a barely ajar door from an adjacent room. A local man asked Mother to write a poem for their twenty-fifth wedding anniversary. When he picked up the poem, he said, "I want to pay you $25, realizing that you have spent considerably more valued time than that."

Mother flashed into her refusal routine, "Oh, no, no. I cannot take money," but the man persisted and in the end she accepted the payment. This single event gave Mother a new sense of importance and created a new measure of value for her writing.

For most poets, after the final editing, the work is done, but not for Mother. Writing a poem was often only half the work. She then needed to arrange for its oral delivery. Often she would ask one of her children to memorize the poem and recite it at the social event. We all knew that our time was coming, we just did not know when. This was always high drama and a traumatic event. Her chosen reciter screeched, "Why me?" Through copious tears and begging, alternatives would be suggested—all the other sisters or brothers. "I am scared of so many people—I cannot speak loudly enough." Community weddings often involved receptions of 200-400 guests and there were no microphones. "I can never remember my lines."

Mother would calmly say, "I will be there to help you."

"What will my friends think if I make a fool of myself? Other children do not have to recite poems."

Mother reassured the reciter, "If the poem is well-memorized and delivered, people will be impressed." So she patiently listened over and over again while she did other household tasks until her selected reciter knew their lines.

In Mother's journal, most poems are identified by the person or event for which the poem was written. Also, normally noted is the name of the person who delivered the poem or whether one of Mother's children was uniquely chosen for appropriate impact and delivery to recite the poem. To get a perspective of time and the comparative ages of the reciters, the names of my siblings from oldest to youngest are Hildegard, Martha, Albert, Phebe, John E., Frieda, Justina, and then me.

Request for Poems

Figure 18
Marie's children and pool of potential poem reciters ca. 1945. The age spread was fourteen years. Photograph by Marie. Source: Author's file.

Mother never envisioned her poems in print, available for side-by-side comparison. She considered every poem a unique event and repeated lines particularly if she thought they were expressive or if she liked their rhyme or rhythm. In the unique setting of oral delivery, the impact of the total poem was important, not the individual lines.

Examples of lines that repeat in wedding poems that follow include "They grew to man and womanhood / not knowing of each other" and "For we see you here as husband and wife, / your ways from now on are one." Mother thought it noteworthy when people married strangers, i.e., people whom they had not known as children; she attended church and elementary school with my father and so was acquainted from childhood with the man she married. Also, for Mother, marriage was biblically defined based on Genesis 2:24, "Therefore shall a man leave his father and his mother, and shall cleave unto his wife: and they shall be one flesh." Mother would repeat "they are one flesh" whenever I, as a child, asked about marriage details.

Once while in the farmyard near the implement shed, Mother, some of my sisters, and I were standing in the shade of a maple tree watching sparrows flitter around in a neighboring elm tree, when to

109

The Petals of a Kansas Sunflower

our amazement two sparrows mated seven or eight times within a span of a minute or two in typical sparrow behavior. One of my sisters commented under her breath, "I guess they are now really one flesh."

Mother just shook her head thinking, "children."

The concept of one flesh is repeated three more times in the Holy Bible in Matthew 19:5, 1 Corinthians 6:16, and Ephesians 5:31. Since the King James version uses "one flesh," I checked *The Message: The Bible in Contemporary Language* for additional perspective on this idiom. Matthew 19 of this translation uses "one flesh," but the context is interesting; Jesus says, "Haven't you read in your Bible that the Creator originally made man and woman for each other, male and female? And because of this, a man leaves father and mother and is firmly bonded to his wife, becoming one flesh—no longer two bodies but one . . . Not everyone is mature enough to live a married life. It requires a certain aptitude and grace. Marriage isn't for everyone. Some, from birth seemingly, never give marriage a thought. Others never get asked—or accepted. And some decide not to get married for kingdom reasons. But if you're capable of growing into the largeness of marriage, do it." From 1 Corinthians 6:16, "There is more to sex than mere skin on skin. Sex is as much spiritual mystery as physical fact. As written in Scripture, 'The two become one' . . . So let people see God in and through your body." There is no doubt in my mind that Mother would have found poetic value in these contemporary language biblical passages.

9

Wedding Invitation

MOTHER PENNED THIS WEDDING invitation for a neighbor in 1956. There is no record of how it was formatted and mailed since only a handwritten copy has been found. That the event occurred is sure—I was there. I was sufficiently young that my only recollections are seeing Mr. Tannahill escort Margaret Ann down the aisle of the church, and then playing outside with other children after the service. This is the only wedding invitation Mother wrote.

Margaret Ann Tannahill's Wedding Invitation

Now listen folks! Please lend an ear
   Of a joyous occasion you shall hear;
At Grace Bible Church it will transpire,
   At which time your presence is much desired.
Margaret Ann, that day, will join her life
   To that of Dean Rensberger and become his wife.
For March 16th the date is set.
   The time 7 P.M., please don't forget.
Already her Mother and Daddy anticipate
   Seeing you on the mentioned date.

10

Polterabend

MOTHER ENTITLED TWO 1970S poems, "*Polterabend* (Nuptial Eve)." *Polterabend* is a German wedding tradition that dates back to sixteenth century. However, I believe that Mother was generically referring to any activity on the night before the wedding and quite possibly the dinner that followed the wedding rehearsal in the church. A 1970s rehearsal dinner was not a rigorously defined activity but rather reflected the imagination and planning of the hostess, often the bride's mother, since the dinner would be served locally in a home or in the church fellowship hall. Typical activities might include a sit-down dinner, a short after-dinner program with reminiscences, toasts, and perhaps poems, and generally a time to get acquainted and to visit with all members of the wedding party.

In Germany, *Polterabend*, now sometimes referred to as "Rumbling Evening," is an informal, traditional get-together of the young couple with friends, including those who might not have been included on the wedding guest list, who all bring pieces of porcelain and ceramics that are broken to make as much noise as possible. Dictated by the custom in each community, it was celebrated the evening before the wedding or perhaps a few days earlier. Since medieval times, the objective was to drive away evil spirits with loud noise—the louder, the more successful. The smaller the broken pieces of porcelain and ceramic, the more luck the couple is said to have. The couple then sweeps up the rubble and may keep shards as a memento to use as they choose, e.g., in a craft project to decorate a vase. Glass and mirrors are not allowed, since they are thought to bring bad luck. Food, drinking, and a good time are interspersed with breaking of more porcelain and the couple cleaning

Polterabend

up together. The whole event is comprehensively photographed for the nuptial pair's album of remembrances.

The Germanic Mennonites in West Prussia and their relatives in Russia retained the *Polterabend* evening, but created activity consistent with the more conservative mores of their community. The rumbling activity was eliminated and replaced with gift giving. Following the evening meal, gifts were presented to the bridal couple. These festivities probably included all the wedding guests since they would have arrived the day before the wedding in horse-drawn carriages. Other activities like the presentation of poems, songs, musical numbers, and skits followed the gifts. Visiting for the adults and games for the young people would end the evening.

This social activity normally took place in the barn hayloft or a big outbuilding like the machine shed, cleaned up for the event and decorated for the wedding activities the next day. Village churches in Europe as well as early churches on the United States prairie did not have kitchens or fellowship halls, so most early prairie wedding receptions were on the farm of the bride's parents in a cleaned up machine shed or barn, or perhaps in a newly constructed building. New construction of barns, granaries, and machine sheds in the community was often timed with wedding festivities.

Another regional German-American variation on *Polterabend* included "shivaree," a variation of "charivari," the French tradition of serenading newlyweds with loud and clanging noises. The "shivaree" is a noisy demonstration, e.g., a mock serenade with kettles and horns for a couple on their wedding night. In our community, the shivaree was several days after the wedding and in some communities, the shivaree included activity much like hazing for the young couple by their exuberant friends.

Although difficult to imagine now, my mother once organized her whole family to shivaree cousin Lydia and her husband Waldo shortly after their wedding. They lived on a neighboring farm less than a mile south of our farm. In the dark of night in the first weeks of September 1944, the whole family, Mother, Father, and all eight children, walked to Lydia's house equipped with old discarded pots, pans, and wooden spoons or sticks to make a ruckus under their bedroom window at the northwest corner of the house. After some fumbling to get the kerosene lamp lit, Lydia and Waldo came out of the house onto the porch

The Petals of a Kansas Sunflower

laughing, wondering who was making that awful noise. The older children shouted, "shivaree." We had a good laugh, said, "Good night," and started for home. As we crossed the railroad track between their house and ours, one of my brothers tried to frighten me by saying the train would run me down. Mother took my hand and responded matter-of-factly, "The trains for today are already gone." Lydia's wedding was on August 31, 1944 and I was just past my second birthday. I remember begging someone to carry me home, but do not recall who actually did. The poem for the wedding of Lydia and Waldo will appear in the next chapter.

The following two poems were used after rehearsal dinners on nuptial eves. In the first, three younger siblings shared in reciting segments of the poem. The ideas touched include losing a sister to marriage; or is it rather adding another brother? Woven into the poem is the presentation of gardening tools, which the newlyweds would surely need. The poem ends with a blessing.

Polterabend (Nuptial Eve)
For Sharon Busenitz and Brad Graber
July 1972

What about all the excitement
    That I see around tonight?
Is it true we're losing Sharon,
    And her wedding is in sight?
Will she too set up housekeeping?
    Cook for a husband as I hear?
Make a garden and then hoe it?—
    Weeds are sure to appear!
Please allow me to be helpful
    And accept this hoe from me.
And a rake I'm also bringing,
    Which is a necessity.

∽ ∽ ∽

Listen now! To what he's saying
    I cannot fully agree.
What to him seems rather serious
    Is a joyful thought to me.
It's not that we are losing Sharon—

> Another brother she brings in.
> It might seem we are the losers,
>   But at the end we surely win.
> With the tools that he is giving
>   Only the surface they can scratch
> Don't you see? For deeper digging
>   A spade would be a perfect match.

> They will surely want their garden
>   To be the best one on the block.
> And the seed that they are sowing
>   They will choose from hybrid stock.
> An advice!—for faster growing
>   And for plants that show some spunk,
> Let them take a basket of plant-food
>   From the barnyard in their trunk.
> Yet we know all is depending
>   On God's blessing from above.
> May he also bless their efforts
>   Together and with mutual love.

In the second poem, a younger brother expresses his appreciation for the friendship and camaraderie his older, marrying brother shared while still at home. In remembrance and with continued wish for interaction, the younger brother gives the marrying brother a ball and bat with the request that "when we'll come to see you, / Some time in playing can be spent." Mother reminds the younger brother that marriage will create other interests for his older brother. This poem too ends with a blessing.

Sammy was fourteen years old at the time he recited this poem, so Mother crafted this poem with the voice of a young adolescent.

The Petals of a Kansas Sunflower

Polterabend (Nuptial Eve)
For Clarence & Twila Busenitz
August 4, 1977
Recited by Sammy Busenitz

May I please have your attention?
   A few things I would like to say.
It's not a long speech I am making
   But kindly listen any way.
I want to thank you, precious brother,
   Since soon our home you plan to leave,
And in your own domain you'll settle
   For the title of husband you'll achieve.
I want to voice appreciation
   For being patient, kind and all
When I've been pestering you and begging
   To come with me for playing ball.
Then in the nights of storm and thunder
   Beside you in your bed I'd crawl,
Or even on the floor close to you
   I would not be afraid at all.
In appreciation for your kindness,
   This ball and bat I now present.
Hopefully, when we'll come to see you
   Some time in playing can be spent.
From now on everything is different,
   I thought I had first claim on you.
But since Twila came into the picture
   I see that I'll be sharing you.
Now in closing, my best wishes
   Are for you, and Twila, too.
In your married life together
   May God abundantly bless you.

11

Celebration of Marriage

IN THE SMALL, CLOSELY-KNIT rural religious community of the early twentieth century there were several core activities. Attending church regularly would be priority number one. Their God directed everything and through the study of God's words (The Holy Bible) one could develop an understanding or rationale for things that happened and why. The promises of God's love and care were a major comfort as the pioneers dealt with grasshoppers, jack rabbits, irregular weather patterns, sickness and death, low prices for commodities, slow modes of transportation, and isolation. For these hard-working Germans, the greatest gift God could give them was the ability to learn patience.

The elder and ministers set the moral and intellectual tenor in the community, if parishioners paid attention and did not sleep during the sermon. After six days of intense physical farm labor, it was difficult to focus on the content of a serious, philosophical lecture intended for one's betterment while sitting quietly relaxed on a warm church bench, even if the bench was hard and not sculptured to fit one's anatomy. But more importantly, there was a vital social aspect to attending weekly services; the church attendees were a community. Relatives and friends could get in touch and keep abreast of the happenings in neighboring households. Family groups could share a letter from relatives in Europe. Prior to about 1905 when telephones became common in every home, the women learned of the health of neighbors, budding courtships, pregnancies among newlyweds, recent births, and the health and illnesses of children. Also discussed by the womenfolk would be their kitchen gardens where they grew the yearlong supply of produce to eat immediately or to preserve, and the spring acquisition of baby chicks for meat and egg production. The number of quarts canned and the number of chicks in the coop lent bragging rights. Grandparents saw their grandchildren weekly and followed their development and maturation, even if there was only time for an acknowledging nod. Farmers exchanged views of the weather and its impending effect on the next harvest; the price of corn, wheat, cattle, and hogs was analyzed as they walked to the buggies or cars in the parking lot.

This community was a village within which to find one's identity and cultivate friendships. Mennonites have always cherished social activity. This is derived perhaps from the years of living in self-contained communities where minimal external contact was legislated in West Prussia and later practiced by choice. Above all, they were human beings craving communication and affection, even as they were viewed from outside their communities as perpetual immigrants with unique (peculiar) religious practices, habits, and languages.

The community was also the primary group from which spouses were chosen. While there was a lingering attitude for a young man to "find a wife" sometimes with the help of a parent or a busybody auntie, most found a friend first and then subsequently joined together in marriage. The interrelatedness of many of the recipients of Mother's poems is a reflection of the influence of the close-knit community on partnership choices and marriage.

The festivities of a wedding would qualify as another core activity. No other activity on the prairies lent itself as well to the strong emphasis on community. Weddings and wedding anniversaries were the activities that elicited grand celebrations. This was the opportunity to invite the whole community to your function, an act of friendship and an opportunity to repay favors. Relatives who lived a day's buggy ride away would surely use this opportunity to visit during the happy occasion and to keep in touch with everyone.

During the period from 1900 to 1930, when my mother and her three sisters married, excitement was initiated when a prospective groom asked his father to go to the home of a desired bride and ask her parents for her hand in marriage for the son. In no way did this imply that the prospective bride and groom were strangers; most were part of the same community and had been in Sunday school together, worshiped in church together, and may well have attended the same elementary schools. The pair had probably also participated together as teenagers in social activity at community functions, but now had grown older and felt the need for permanent bonding. If the response of the prospective bride was positive, the engagement was announced from the pulpit in church the next Sunday, since there were no Sunday service bulletins with announcements. That Sunday, many relatives and friends would be invited to the bride's home for an engagement dinner, the first of many social activities for the nuptial pair. Then most of the homes represented at the engagement dinner would individually invite the pair and the bride's parents for a congratulatory evening meal and visiting.

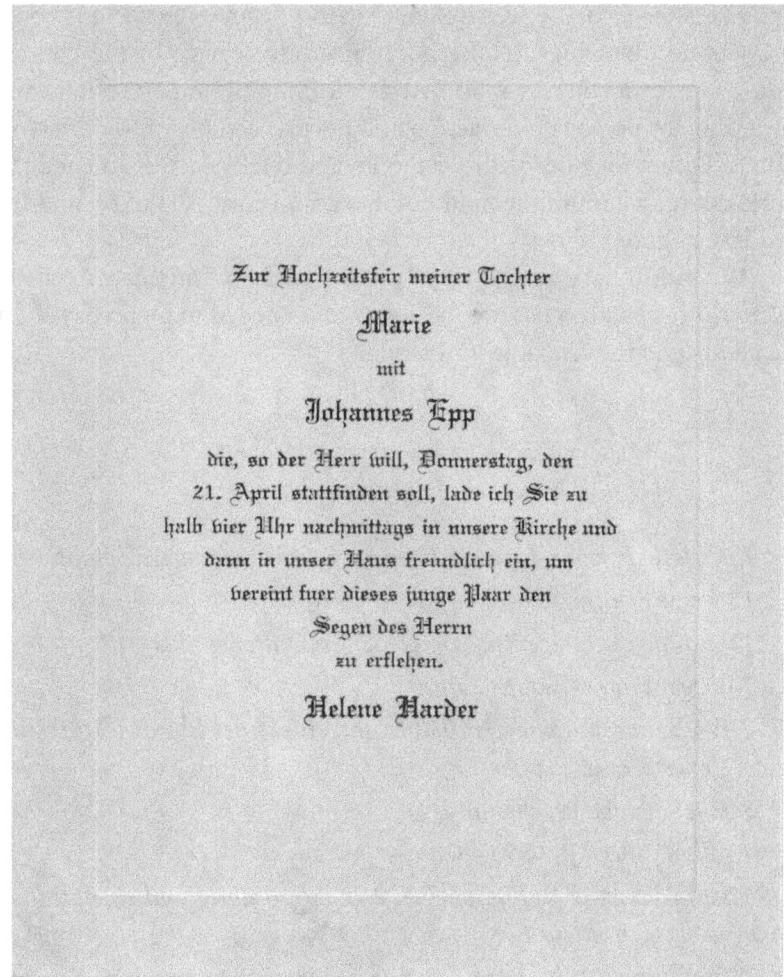

Figure 19
The 1927 invitation for my parents' wedding. "For the marriage of my daughter Marie with Johannes Epp that will occur on Thursday, April 21, the Lord willing, I happily invite you for 3:30 in the afternoon to our church and then at our house to implore the Lord's blessing on the union of this young pair. Helene Harder." Source: Author's file.

The wedding would follow shortly, but adequate time was needed to either construct a new barn or machine shed, or to clean out an existing structure. The weddings of my parents and mother's sisters were held mid-afternoon on a Thursday in the church with the reception following at the Harder farm.

The farm yard was cleaned up as adequate space was required for hitching posts to accommodate the many buggies with horses or to park cars. Food needed to be prepared for 200 to 400 guests that would come to celebrate following the afternoon wedding service in the church. Eating meals together as a family was meaningful human contact and rewarding for personal interaction and normal activity of wedding festivities. Eating together with neighbors and relatives strengthened the fabric defining community and became an integral part of Mennonite wedding culture.

When Mother's sister Minna got married on Thursday, April 19, 1923, Mother made a list of food items that needed to be prepared for the guests and the schedule for baking:

1923 Zu John Reimers Hochzeit
hatten wir folgendes gebacken

7 ½ Blechkuchen—*1 ganzer blieb über und eine Plate geschnittenes*

12 weiße Schichtkuchen—*4 ganzer über*

11 braune viereckige Kuchen—*bloß geschnittenes über*

7 Roggenbrote—*blieben 2 über*

25 Weizenbrote—*blieben 10 über und eine ganze Balge voll geschnittenes Brot blieb über*

3 gallone halbe Peaches und

4 gallone Sliced Peaches—*wurden gebraucht*

5 Schinken zu je 10 lb.—*blieben 2 ganze zu übrig und eine Schüssel voll geschnittenes*

8 Braten zu 12 lb. jeder,—*blieb ein halber über und eine Schüssel geschnittenes*

5 dz Makronen zum Haus—*waren genug*

1 bx Chocolate Queens—*blieben keine über*

1 bx andere Zuckerkuchen—*blieben wenig über*

Von 10 Eier Schaumkuchen—waren genug

3 Gallone Getrocknete Pflaume—waren gerade genug.

Montag dem 16 April nachmittag backte ich die braune viereckigen Kuchen. Dienstag backten wir ein paar Brote und die weiße Schichtkuchen. Mittwoch backten wir Brote und Blechkuchen, quellten Pflaume und Frau Brucks brat die Braten.

1923 For John Reimer's wedding we have baked the following:
Left over after the wedding meal

7 ½ Prussian Coffee (Sheet) Cakes—One complete cake remained left over and one plate of cut pieces.

12 White Layer Cakes—Four complete cakes remained.

11 Brown Four-cornered Cakes—Only cut pieces remained.

7 loaves Rye Bread—Two loaves left over.

25 loaves White Bread—Ten loaves left over. A complete sack of cut bread was left over.

3 gallons of Peach halves

and

4 gallons of Sliced Peaches—Were used

5 Hams to about 10 lbs each—Two complete hams left over with a plate full of cut slices.

8 Roasts to 12 lbs. each—A half left over and a plate of cut slices.

5 dozen Macaroons—Sufficient for the house.

1 box Chocolate Queens—None left over.

1 box Petit Four—Few remained.

Kisses (meringue) made from 10 eggs—These were enough.

3 gallons dried prunes—Was just exactly enough.

On Monday the 16th of April in the afternoon I baked the brown four-cornered cakes. On Tuesday we baked two kinds of bread and the white layer-cakes. On Wednesday we baked bread and coffee cake, soaked the prunes and Mrs. Brucks prepared the roasts.

The Petals of a Kansas Sunflower

The macaroons, chocolates, kisses, and petit fours were served only at the bridal table set up in the house. It is obvious there was ample food for everyone since there were copious leftovers. It was important to record the leftovers because the young people and the relatives who helped with preparations, set up, and clean up, as well as those who waited on the guests, were invited back to the bride's home for a meal to say thank you. This meal was a day or two later, but a local joke implied that the nuptial pair usually did not begin their conjugal lives until after all the tablecloths were washed.

Figure 20
Studio wedding picture of my parents John (1901–1995) and Marie Harder Epp (1903–1998) who married on April 21, 1927. Murphy Studio, Newton, KS. Source: Author's file.

Celebration of Marriage

Comforting the bereaved at funerals would involve the whole community and represented another core activity. When Mother wrote her autobiographical book, she lamented the loss of dear ones far more than she expressed the joy of marriages. Although weddings constituted community celebrations and called for unique complementary poems, funerals solicited only a few special poetic verses. A funeral poem is presented in chapter 16. More common, however, were posthumous birthday poems remembering influential people on the occasion of their one-hundredth birth dates. These will be presented in chapter 15.

Between 1936 and 1991, Mother wrote many poems that were recited or read at wedding receptions, indicating that the receptions were sufficiently formal to include presentations. Singing hymns and short sermons (toasts) were also included.

The wedding poems are presented in chronological sequence to capture the changes of traditions with time. Details about the people getting married, who recited the poem, etc., will be included to create a sense of community or village within which these poems found their initial recitation. The anniversary poems in the next two chapters will recount some very early weddings and will give additional insights into the changes in the traditions of marriage celebrations.

In Mother's journal there is a short poem that summarizes everything that she considered important in a wedding wish: happiness, prosperity, good health, no distractions from mutual affection, and a reliance on the divine. These themes are repeated over and over in her wedding poems. This poem is undated with no mention of when it was used, or if used at all. It was written in English, so it was probably written after the mid-1940s.

Just a Little Wish

We are wishing you much happiness
Prosperity and wealth
Enough of rain and sunshine
And every day good health
But just one wish is lacking
In the little rhyme above
That nothing ever may sever your love.
But just one more wish I'm adding here this day
May Jesus ever be with you and guide you all the way.

The Petals of a Kansas Sunflower

In 1935, my eight-year-old sister Hildegard recited a poem at the wedding of my father's youngest sister, Aunt Agnes. Mother wrote this poem with the voice of an eight-year-old. The wish or blessing here is "Much good fortune and happiness / That God's hand guides you / Throughout your married life / And that you are one in him / Joyfully as your pathway moves ahead." Hildegard then presented Aunt Agnes a cooking pot lid as a keepsake, because a successful cook is a pleasure to her husband.

Für Edward Regiers Hochzeit
12 Dezember 1935
von Hildegard vorgetragen

Liebes Tantchen heut zum Feste
Bring ich dir mein Wunsch aufs Beste
Dir und Onkel Edward beide
Wünsche ich: Viel Glück und Freude,
Das Euch leite Gotteshand
Immerdar im Ehestand,
Und Ihr beide eins in Ihm
Fröhlich Eurer Weg wegziehe.
Ein kleines Andenken bring ich hier
Tante für die Küche dir.
Ist es auch mir klein und schlicht
Doch recht pratisch denke ich nicht?
Einen Rat noch füg ich ein,
Schein ich auch dafür noch klein:
Kochst für dem Onkel du das Essen
Dann nicht du ja nicht vergessen
Daß der Deckel sei am Platz
Soll es schmecken deinem Schatz
Viel Besser wird es dann geraten
Und viel saftiger ist der Braten
Wenn nicht fehlt dies eine Stück
Ein bischen hilft es auch zum Glück
Denn freuen tut es stets den Mann
Wenn schön sein Frauchen kochen kann
So bitte nehmet in lieben dann
Diese kleinigkeit hier an.

Celebration of Marriage

For Edward Regiers' Wedding
December 12, 1935
Recited by Hildegard

Dear Auntie, at this celebration today
I bring you my best wishes
For both you and Uncle Edward
My wish: Much good fortune and happiness
That God's hand guides you
Throughout your married life
And that you are one in him
Joyfully as your pathway moves ahead.
I bring here a little keepsake
Auntie, for you for your kitchen.
For me also it is little and simple.
But rightly pretentious, I don't think so?
A suggestion I do want to give
Even though I appear too small for that:
When you cook meals for Uncle Ed
You should not forget
To have the lid in its place.
It should be tasty for your sweetheart.
The outcome will be much better
And the roast will be much more succulent,
Not a piece will be missed.
A little helps to bring good luck.
It will then constantly gladden your husband
If his little wife can cook nicely,
So then please accept with love
This little insignificant thing.

Mother wrote two poems for the wedding of her oldest niece Bertha Regier to Albert Busenitz. One was recited by my sister Phebe when she was four and a half years old and the other poem was recited by Helen, Bertha's younger sister, who was nineteen years old. The contrast in writing styles is noticeable immediately. The first poem is short, gentle, and sweet with Phebe giving Bertha a tablecloth and wishing that "the good luck of sunshine / be in your house constantly," sunshine signifying positive energy.

The first few lines of the second poem sound almost like a bishop's admonition, "Honor the Lord, dear sister, honor the Lord, dearly betrothed . . . " Since Mother put quotation marks around the first four lines, I assume that these are unidentified quotations. She then goes into a discussion of the adjustments inherent in setting up a new household because in so doing, one leaves the comforts of the home of one's parents. But Mother says that all the relatives are thinking of her and "the village" is willing to help, "and you can believe that in spirit, we will often be with you." Albert and Bertha set up a household on a farm ten miles north of my mother's farm and so Bertha lived in 1938 on the outskirts of the adjacent Elbing community. Mother compliments Bertha on her skills of housekeeping and farm life and ends the poem with a blessing and an admonition "so go with confidence and courage on your road, hand in hand, / Jesus leading you through life until you are up above in heaven."

Albert & Bertha zu Hochzeit, Erste Gedicht
16 März 1938
von Phebe vorgetragen

Es machte mir gar viel bedenken
Was ich sollt der Bertha schenken
Da fiel es mir plötzlich ein
Eine Decke würde pratisch sein
Wenn schön gedeckt den Tisch man sieht
Dann bekommt man schon Appetit
Noch meinen Wunsch zum heutigen Tage
Ich in wenig Worten sage
Mög des Glückes Sonnenschein
Stets in Eurem Hause sein.

For the Wedding of Albert & Bertha, Poem 1
March 16, 1938
Recited by Phebe

I have thought a lot about
What gift I should give to Bertha
Suddenly it came to me
A cloth would be very practical
When one sees a table with a nice covering
Then one develops a good appetite.

Yet my wish for you on today's event
I with few words will say
May the good luck of sunshine
Be in your house constantly.

Albert & Bertha zu Hochzeit, Zweite Gedicht
16 März 1938
von Helen Regier vorgetragen

"Grüß dich Gott, geliebte Schwester, Grüß dich Gott, geliebte Braut,
    Willst jetzt in der Ferne bauen dir ein Nestchen lieb und traut."
"Willst verlassen deine Lieben, ziehest aus dem Vaterhaus
    Gehst an des Geliebten Seite freudig in die Welt hinaus."
Schwer wird alles uns doch scheiden, fehlen wirst du uns hier sehr
    Doch wir hoffen das du oftmals kommest auf Besuch hier her.
Unsere Liebe dich begleitet bis ins neue Heim hinein.
    Und wir werden kannst es glauben oft im Geiste bei dir sein.
Wie wird man als junges Frauchen doch so gern dich schalten sehe
    Weiß gewißlich deinen Haushalt mustergültig vorzustehe.
Haben wir doch schon erfahren wie geschickt du dazu bist
    Wenn die Tante zur Erholung im Sommer in Colorado ist.
Ja so manche liebe Enrinnerung heut mir in Gedanken schwebt
    Die wir drei Schwestere hier gemeinsam mit einander haben verlebt.
Mutter liebe hast erfahren Bertha mir als du noch klein
    Doch welch ein Segen für uns alle, daß Taute konnte bei uns sein
Hat sie doch so treu geholfen uns zurecht zu jeder Zeit
    Was ja bei so vieler Arbeit oft ist keine Kleinigkeit.
Bertha gern hast du geholfen Warst überall du ja gewand
    Gingst auch außerhalb der Hause Papa gerne du zur Hand.
Doch nun wird er anders werden.—Lang sehntest du den Tag heran
    Wo gemeinsam ihr betreten konntet Eure Lebensbahn.
Heut nun ist der Tag gekommen wo am Traualter ihr stand
    Wo fürs ganze künftige Leben Herz und Herze sich verband.
Wir die in Liebe euch verbunden nehmen heut an Eurem Glücke teil
    Und wünschen euch für alle Stunden Gottes Segen, Glück und Heil.
Seht in Eurem Ehebündnis Jesu als der erste an
    Das Er gern, wie in Bethanien, bei Euch einkehr halten kann.
So zieht dann getrosten Mutter Eure Straße Hand in Hand
    Jesu führe Euch durchs Leben bis hinauf ins Vaterland.

The Petals of a Kansas Sunflower

For the Wedding of Albert & Bertha, Poem 2
March 16, 1938
Recited by Helen Regier

"Honor the Lord, dear sister, honor the Lord, dearly betrothed,
    Do you desire in the future to make a dear and beloved boudoir?"
"Will you forsake the love that you had in your parents' home?
    Do you go out into the world happily as a sweetheart?"
Surely the separation will be difficult for us all, you will miss all of us here very much
    However, we hope that you will come to visit those of us here often.
Our love continues as you settle into your new home
    And you can believe that in spirit, we will be with you often.
One would willingly direct you since you are a young wife
    You know surely that with your housekeeping you must set a standard.
We have already come to know how skillful you are at this
    Like when our aunt was in Colorado in summertime for recuperation.
Yes, so many lovely recollections are sweeping through my mind today
    That we three sisters here together with one another have experienced.
Bertha, you have expressed mother-like-love to me since you were small
    However, it was a blessing for us all when our aunt came to stay with us
She surely was a great help for us at that time
    Surely much work is often truly no small undertaking.
Bertha, you willingly helped because you were very skillful at many things
    Things also happening outside your father's house on which you enjoyed working.
But now, for him things will be different.—For a long time you have perceived the day coming
    Where you are able to step on to your life's pathway jointly.
Now today is the day when you have stood at the marriage altar
    Where for your whole future lives, your hearts and embraces are bound together.
We, who with affection today, recognize your fortunate participation in taking your wedding vows,
    And wish for you for all times God's blessings, good fortune, and health.
In your married life, see that Jesus is perceived as the most important
    That he gladly, as in Bethany, can commune with you
So go with confidence and courage on your life's highway, hand in hand,
    Jesus leading you through life until you are up above in heaven.

That same year, Mother wrote poems for two other weddings. The first was for my father's uncle Bernhard Regier who married Justine Busenitz. Justine was the oldest sister of Albert Busenitz whom we just met above. Bernhard was the youngest of twelve children born to the

Celebration of Marriage

Rev. Cornelius H. and Anna Regier and only nine years older than my father. My father's mother, Grandmother Epp, was the oldest daughter in that family and remembered in chapter 13. Cornelius and Anna Regier are honored with poems for their one hundredth birth dates in chapter 15.

This poem simply and briefly summarizes Mother's views of the marriage union and the attributes that she wishes for everyone in marriage, and here for this newly joined couple. After the good wishes and congratulations, Mother moves into divine guidance that brought this couple together and God's continued role in making their marriage happy. "He shielded you and wishes to sustain you in your home for a long time / Already like he governed our great-grandparents for many years. / Similar to a beautiful morning, the sun then in its magnificence / And from the beautiful blue sky, so hopefully you will merge towards laughter / Likewise, this day is a morning in the fortunes of your joined lives." She continues with the suggestion to rely on the Lord, "In later years think back to this time when he radiates over you / So on this wedding day, also take now from his hands / Think about what he would like to contribute here to your love."

Hildegard, the presenter, gives the bridal pair a blanket and ends the poem with a blessing, "may God be with you now and in the days ahead."

Für Onkel Bernhard & Tante Justine
27 Juli 1938
von Hildegard vorgetragen

Manch Glückwunsch wird Euch heute schon von Groß und Klein gebracht.
Auch ich sing' meinen Wunsch noch bei; sei er auch kurz gesagt.
Zum frohen Feste mögt' ich gern von Herzen gratulieren.
Der Herr der Euch bis her gebracht mög treu Euch weiter führen,
Er schirme Euch und mög' Euch lang in eurem Heim erhalten,
In dem ja schon so manches Jahr unser Urgroßeltern walten.
So wie an einem schönen Morgen, die Sonne dann in ihrer pracht
Und von dem schöne blauen Himmel, so hoffnungsvoll entgegen lacht.
So ist auch dieser Tag ein Morgen von dem gemeinsamen Lebensglück
Der hinüber strahlt in späteren Jahren denkt Ihr einmal daran zurück.
So nehmt an diesen Ehrentage jetzt auch noch von meinen Händen
Was ich zum Andenken Euch hier in Liebe mögte spenden.

The Petals of a Kansas Sunflower

> *Denn in einem Haushalt braucht es ja der Sachen mancherlei*
> *Und ich hoffe, daß die Decke Euch auch oft recht nützlich sei*
> *Und nun zum Schluß, da weiß nichts bessers ich zu sagen*
> *Als Gott mit Euch jetzt und in künftigen Tagen.*

For Uncle Bernhard & Aunt Justine
July 27, 1938
Presented by Hildegard

Many good wishes are brought to you today from people, big and small
I also sing my wishes to you which will be said shortly
At this happy celebration I gladly congratulate you from my heart.
The Lord who has brought you this far would truly like to guide you further
He shielded you and wishes to sustain you in your home for a long time
Already like he governed our great-grandparents for many years.
Similar to a beautiful morning, the sun then in its magnificence
And from the beautiful blue sky, so hopefully you will merge towards laughter
Likewise, this day is a morning in the fortunes of your joined lives
In later years think back to this time when he radiates over you
So on this wedding day, also take now from his hands
Think about what he would like to contribute here to your love.
Like in a household various things are surely used
And I hope, that the blanket is also often rightly useful for you
And now in conclusion, I do not know of anything better to say
Than may God be with you now and in the days ahead.

Again, the next poem has childish simplicity, since the reciter was seven years old. "Everything here today is so festive and beautiful / Also the both of you project such happiness / Today is indeed a happy day / About which everyone can be glad." Mother expresses the community's delight at the event of my father's cousin from the Newton community marrying a Busenitz girl who was a cousin to Albert and Justine Busenitz mentioned above.

The poem continues "And when dark hours in life come / That you may also then lift your outlook upwards / Because behind the clouds the sun constantly shines / Through cross to the crown, that is the way a union goes." This depicts Mother's visualized pathway to a successful marriage.

The poem ends with a gift of a tablecloth for the bride and a blessing, "And now yet I wish for you God's guidance / For your joined lives—for all times."

Celebration of Marriage

Zu Albert Entz & Frieda Busenitz Hochzeit
12 Januar 1939
von Albert vorgetragen

Wie ist hier heut alles so festlich und schön
  Auch ihr Beide tut ja so glüklich aussehen.
Es ist ja auch heute ein froher Tag
  An dem ein jeder sich freuen mag.
So dacht ich war es nicht ungeschickt
  Wenn mit einem Glückwunsch ich Euch beglükt.
Ganz kurz mich zu faßen, daß hab ich im Sinn
  Um lange zu reden zu klein ich noch bin.
Mög' die Zukunft des Glückes Sonnenschein hegen
  Doch nur an Gottes Segen ist alles gelegen.
Und kommen trübe Stunden im Leben
  Das auch dann noch oben der Blick ihr mögt heben
Denn hinter der Wolken die Sonne stets scheint
  Durch Kreuz zur Krone, so geh'es vereint.
Und nun zum Schluß—fast ich es vergaß
  Das dieses Packet ich euch überlaß.
Eine Tischdecke ist's was es enthält
  Ich hoffe, daß sie dem Bräutchen gefällt.
Auch hoff' ich der Bräutgam hat Freude daran
  Wenn sein Frauchen der Tisch schön decken kann.
Und nun wünsch ich Euch noch Gottes geleit
  Fürs gemeinsame Leben—Für alle zeit.

For the Albert Entz & Frieda Busenitz Wedding
January 12, 1939
Presented by Albert

Everything here today is so festive and beautiful,
  Also the both of you project such happiness.
Today is indeed a happy day
  About which everyone can be glad.
So I thought it would not be inappropriate
  If I would make you happy with a congratulations.
Shortly, I will take hold of what I have in mind,
  To give a long speech, I am too small for that.
May the future succeed to foster sunshine
  Since everything is predicated only on God's blessings

The Petals of a Kansas Sunflower

> And when dark hours in life come
> > That you may also then lift your outlook upwards
> Because behind the clouds the sun constantly shines.
> > Through cross to the crown, that is the way a union goes
> And now for the conclusion, I almost forgot,
> > That I present to you this package.
> What it contains is a tablecloth.
> > I hope that the new bride likes it.
> I also hope that the bridegroom has happiness at it
> > When his little bride can cover the table nicely.
> And also, I wish for you God's guidance
> > For your joined lives, for all times.

Although the next poem is one that focuses on the marriage of Waldo and Lydia, "In that you will soon as man and wife / Be joined officially," it must have been recited a day or two before the wedding. John Edwin was eight years old when he presented this poem, which begins with congratulations and a blessing, "The Lord who has brought you this far / May truly lead you further / He protects you and may he for a long time / Keep you in your home." John then presents Lydia with a collection of brushes. The poem ends with a whimsical discussion of the uses of brushes and not the typical benedictions of the poems presented at church receptions.

The wedding dress display guide developed for the 125th anniversary of the Emmaus Mennonite Church included this description of the wedding on Friday, August 31, 1944, at 6:00 p.m.:

> Waldo Klaassen and Lydia Thiessen were married on a pleasant Friday evening at the Emmaus Church. The Rev. J. C. Kaufman married them, using Joshua 24:15, "As for me and my house, we will serve the Lord", as the wedding text. Lydia wore a white floor-length dress that was purchased at a bridal shop in Wichita. The dress had a small train, but Lydia's dad, John Thiessen, thought the train was too extravagant, so the train was cut off and the dress rehemmed. The wedding colors were green and white. After the wedding ceremony, the guests ate a meal in the church basement. The wedding party and the guests then went to John Thiessen's home to visit. The family went back to church the next day (Saturday) to wash the dishes from the wedding meal and to clean the church. Waldo & Lydia spent their wedding night in a hotel in Newton. Due to Waldo needing to help with farm work, a honeymoon trip was postponed for several months.

Celebration of Marriage

Für Waldo & Lydia
31 August 1944
von John Edwin vorgetragen

Manch Glückwunsch würd Euch heute schon
  Von Gross und Klein gebracht
Auch ich füg meinen Wunsch noch bei
  Sei er auch kurz gesagt.
Zum frohen Feste mögte ich gern
  Von Herzen gratulieren
Der Herr der Euch bis hier gebracht
  Mög treu Euch weiter führen.
Er schirme Euch und mög euch lang
  In Eurem Heim erhalten
In dem Ihr bald als Man und Frau
  Gemeinsam werdet walten.
So nehmt an diesem Ehrentage
  Jetzt auch noch von meinen Händen
Was ich zum Andenken Euch
  Hier in Liebe mögte spenden
Den in einem Haushalt braucht es
  Ja der Sachen mancherlei
Und ich hoffe diese Gabe
  Möge Euch recht nützlich sein.
Seht ich bringe Euch hier Bürsten
  Gute Bürsten groß und klein
Bürsten jeder braucht ja Bürsten
  Starke, schwache, grob und fein
Eine hier zum Schuhe wichsen
  Eine weiche für den Hut
Habe ich nicht schön gewählet
  Sind die Bürsten nicht recht gut.
Eine Bürste für die Zähne
  Diese Bürste für das Haar
Diese feine für die Kleider
  Und hier die Scheierbürste gar.
Braucht die Bürsten nur recht fleißig
  Diesen Rat noch geb ich heut
Dann wird es bei Euch nicht fehlen
  An der schönsten Sauberkeit.

The Petals of a Kansas Sunflower

For Waldo & Lydia
August 31, 1944
Recited by John Edwin

Many good wishes have been brought to you
    Already today from big and small,
I also join my wish to these
    As I will say shortly.
For the happy celebration, I would like to
    Congratulate you from my heart.
May the Lord who has brought you this far
    Truly lead you further,
He protects you and may he for a long time
    Keep you in your home
In that you will soon as man and wife
    Be joined officially.
So take on your wedding day
    Now from my hands yet also
What I for a remembrance
    Here in love contribute to you.
As in any household, yes,
    Various things are used
And I hope this gift
    Might be right useful for you.
See, I bring you brushes here,
    Good brushes, large and small
Brushes, yes, everyone uses brushes
    Strong ones, weak ones, coarse and fine
One here to polish your shoes
    A soft one for your hat
Haven't I chosen well,
    Aren't the brushes quite good?
A brush for the teeth
    This brush for your hair
This fine one for your clothes
    And here is the polishing brush
Use the brushes right diligently
    This advice I still give you today,
Then you will not miss
    To achieve remarkable cleanliness.

Celebration of Marriage

Two years later, Mother wrote a poem for Father's nephew who was marrying Mother's cousin. This is the last of the wedding poems written and recited in German. Frieda was eight when she recited this poem.

Even during World War I, the English speaking rural community surrounding the local Mennonite community was more tolerant than many in adjacent towns. There was some anti-German sentiment as will be discussed in chapter 13, but the greatest contribution for the increased use of English was the attitude of the first and second generation of Mennonites born in America. Some saw no advantage in teaching their children "old-fashioned" German because all commerce and education was conducted in English. Not knowing German was perceived as being contemporary or American. The unique contributions of ethnic culture were elements for embarrassment during 1940s and 1950s and they only became cherished again later in the twentieth century. Ellis County, Kansas, home of many of Volga German descent, now prides itself in tourist advertisements as the "German Capital of Kansas."

The little anti-German sentiment that surfaced again during World War II also encouraged the integration of the English language into church and community activity. The replacement of horses with cars increased contact with other communities and battery-operated or electric radios increased access to state, national, and global news. These changes modulated the walls of exclusion of the fragmented village of immigrant Mennonites in Butler County. The concept of "a community set apart from the secular world" lost its vitality within the seductive freedoms that Kansas provided her citizens.

This poem is fascinating in that it consists of only three sentences in true Germanic fashion. It begins with compliments. "For you, who are such a lovely young couple / I bring you my best wishes / On this day, which is so nice for you / Never have you seen the likes of this . . ." The blessing follows: "May you at all times / Be constantly accompanied with the grace of God / May you be blessed by him / At all times throughout the year and in years to come / That also your future lifetime / Constantly remains full of happiness . . ." The poem ends with the presentation of a gift that is for use, somehow, in patching both socks and tires. No other clues about the gift are given. The patching of socks is definitely described as woman's work, while that of patching car tires is in the masculine realm. But Mother acknowledges a shift in attitude and notes that the demarcation lines between male and female work

The Petals of a Kansas Sunflower

activity was modulating. It was 1946 and the post World War II time period was filled with prosperity and many changes, even in the home and the rural church community.

Für Waldimar & Ester Wiebe
25 Juli 1946
von Frieda vorgetragen

Euch ihr liebes junges Paar
  Bring ich meinen Glückwunsch dar
An diesem Tag für Euch so schön
  Nie habt des gleichen Ihr gesehn
Nun auch wir sind hoch erfreut
  Wünschen Glück von Herzen heut.
Möge Euch zu allen Zeiten
  Gottes Gnade stets geleiten
Mög Er segnend bei Euch sein
  Alle Zeit Jahr aus, Jahr ein
Das auch die ferner Lebenzeit
  Stets bleibe voller Seligkeit
Euren eignen Hausstand wollt ihr gründen
  Manche Arbeit wird sich da schon finden
Bald werdet Ihrs merken an allen Seiten
  Das Leben besteht aus Kleinigkeiten
Doch der Stolz der Hausfrau wie wir meinen
  Ist treue üben auch im kleinen
Da sind Strümpfe ein nie endendes Problem
  Schön ausgebessert mag man die sehn
Um es zu erleuchtern dir
  Bitte nimm dies Päckcken hier.
Auch für dem Bräutgam ist was hier
  Bitte nehmt's nicht übel mir
Früher tat sich ja das flicken
  Nur für eine Hausfrau schicken
Tat es nur für Frauen passen
  Wollt der Mann sich nicht damit befassen
Doch wie wir alle sehen heut
  Hat dies geändert mit der Zeit
Soll daß Auto bleiben im gehen
  Und ein jedes Rat im drehen
Muß der Mann sich auch schon schicken
  Und einmal die Tires flicken.

Celebration of Marriage

For Waldimar & Ester Wiebe
July 25, 1946
Recited by Frieda

For you, who are such a lovely young couple
   I bring you my best wishes
On this day, which is so nice for you
   Never have you seen the likes of this
Now we too are also really pleased
   Wishing you today good fortune from our hearts.
May you at all times
   Be constantly accompanied with the grace of God
May you be blessed by him
   At all times throughout the year and in years to come
That also your future lifetime
   Constantly remains full of happiness
You want to establish your own household
   Already, you will find this to be some work
You will soon become aware that in all aspects
   That life endures with the mundane
However, what we mean is that the pride of the housewife
   Is also faithful about little things
There are stockings with never ending issues
   One likes to see them nicely darned
In an effort to assist you
   Please take this little package here.
There is also something here for the bridegroom
   Please do not think ill of me
Earlier you surely did the patching
   Only a housewife spends her time at this
This is fitting for a woman
   A man does not want to be involved with that
However, as we all see it today
   This is changing with time
The car needs to remain in running order
   And all advice applies
The man must already now be called
   And sometimes patch the tires.

With the change to English, Mother begins to compose poems using lines that, once written, were used again in other poems. Since the poems were recited orally at different venues with different sets of guests, Mother's efficiency in the creative crafting of her verses is admirable.

The Petals of a Kansas Sunflower

This poem begins with a few lines that will be used again. "A leaf has been turned in the book of your life / A new chapter has just begun / For now you are considered as husband and wife / Your ways from now on are one." Mother further admonishes Father's niece Olga Wiebe and her husband Gerhard Busenitz to rely on the divine. Frieda presents the gift of a guestbook: "Still blank are all the pages. / Later, you will find it to be true: / It brings to you sweet memories / Of those that called on you." Olga did use her guestbook. I remember one occasion when my parents and I were at her house for dinner, she had Mother and the other guests sign it. The poem ends with two lines that Mother will also use again, "May God be with you all the way; / May your love be pure and true."

For the Wedding of Gerhard & Olga Busenitz
May 31, 1947
Recited by Frieda

A leaf has been turned in the book of your lives
    A new chapter has just begun
For now you are considered as husband and wife
    Your ways from now on are one.
The path that together from now on you tread
    Lies unknown before you this day
It is like a book with pages unread
    That opens as you proceed on your way
As comes to your knowledge day after day
    You'll find as you journey along
Life has its dark days as they say
    And days full of praises and song.
Shall days for you be dark and dreary
    Or bright and sunny as on you glide
Shall you feel happy or feel weary
    You'll need the presence of a guide
So turn to God he is ever near
    Read in his Word each day
It will strengthen you throughout the year
    And encourage you on your way.
A guest book I have chosen,
    As a gift for you today
Which I hope will serve the purpose
    In its own specific way.

Celebration of Marriage

>Still blank are all the pages.
>>Later, you will find it to be true:
>
>It brings to you sweet memories
>>Of those that called on you.
>
>In closing may I briefly say
>>The wish that's mine for you—
>
>May God be with you all the way;
>>May your love be pure and true.

Ruby and Bernard Thiessen were married on my birthday in 1949, when I turned seven. Bernard was Mother's nephew, a son of her sister Helene and a brother to Susan (chapter 5) and Lydia mentioned above. Their wedding was in Omaha, so this meant a car trip of three hundred miles. I had never been out of the state of Kansas, so this was a big event. My parents sat in the front seat of the 1947 Chevy Fleetline with me sitting in the middle on the driveshaft hump. A number of sisters were in the backseat. It was hot and there was no bottled water, so Father would stop after several hours of going fifty-five miles per hour to get soda pop, or gas and pop. Fifty-five was the highest speed my father ever drove, because Mother would frantically grab the dashboard with white knuckles if he went any faster. The highways of 1949 predated our modern freeways and were not designed for higher speeds. At best the surface was macadam usually with potholes, or loose gravel or sand.

My mother was excited as we initiated this day-long journey. Her nephew Bernard was getting married. The sights and sounds through the windshield or open window on her right were also experiences that she savored. These were new and different from her daily life on Section 17, Milton Township, Butler County, Kansas. Her head was constantly moving from side to side to take in the new views that each further mile of travel brought into focus. The agricultural landscape riveted her attention.

After an hour of travel, I slouched down in my seat and asked, "*Sind wir bald da*? Will we be there soon?" Mother just roared with laughter and suggested that I look out of the window and then she began to point out the observations that she thought were fascinating. The trip no longer seemed utterly endless.

Justina recited a poem at the wedding reception. Although she was eight years old, she was very petite and the poem has childlike qualities. After the opening congratulations, the newlyweds were presented with a set of hand-embroidered tea towels and Bernard was teased, saying that surely he too will on occasion help with the dishes. The poem ends

The Petals of a Kansas Sunflower

with Justina simply asking them not to forget about their cousins and Aunt Marie.

For the Wedding of Bernard & Ruby
June 16, 1949

Best wishes to you Ruby.
Bernard, congratulations too.
I've brought with me a little gift
That I'll soon present to you.
It's towels, to wipe the dishes
That always will collect,
Which in your housekeeping, Ruby,
You'll find to be correct.
Perhaps, Bernard will help you
With this little daily task.
So will you please remember us
That's all that I will ask.

For the wedding of Louise Entz and Howard Wedel on October 10, 1951, their niece Marilyn congratulated her uncle and aunt and presented a kettle just right for two.

Wedding of Aunt Louise Entz & Uncle Howard Wedel
October 10, 1951
Recited by Marilyn Harder

Best wishes, Aunt Louise
Uncle Howard, congratulations too.
I've brought with me a little gift
That I'll soon give to you.
It is a little kettle
Just big enough for two
And love will add the seasoning
So you will find it to be true.

When my brother Albert got married in South Dakota in 1953, the trip was twice as long. I remember standing in the farm yard of his bride-to-be, Joann, and looking north, west, south, and east, trying to orient myself relative to my eleven years of living on Section 17 in

Kansas. It was beyond my understanding to be so far from home. The wheat harvest had been completed in Kansas by the middle of June, and yet in South Dakota the harvest had not even started at the end of July!

This time Mother stopped at my name as she went down the sibling list and it became my responsibility to recite a poem during the reception. I think Albert had personally requested a poem. The reception was tape recorded to add to my nervousness. The tape, if it still exists, will show that Mother was there to prompt me whenever I forgot my lines.

Mother begins by describing the bridal pair and mentioning that "They grew to man and womanhood / Not knowing of each other." Their date to the spring banquet of their first year at Grace University resulted in many letters being exchanged during the summer months. The poem ends with the phrase, "Your ways from now on are one" and the nuptial blessing.

The Wedding Poem
July 31, 1953

Since I was asked to speak tonight
   I think it's only fair
Just to review the past a bit
   A few thoughts with you to share.

Two babies born a long time ago
   Brought to their homes much joy.
One was a darling baby girl,
   The other a little boy.

The boy, with a mischievous smile,
   Was brown-eyed with light hair;
And dark hair with blue eyes the girl—
   A contrast, I declare.

In South Dakota lived the one,
   In Kansas lived the other.
They grew to man and womanhood
   Not knowing of each other.

One thing they had in common though,
   The urge for Christian training.

The Petals of a Kansas Sunflower

    Both came to Omaha to "Grace"
        To satisfy this yearning.

    Almost the whole first year went by;
        They just went on as any,
    But then the banquet came along;
        The changes then were many.

    Between these two something took place
        That no one can explain;
    But we have evidence tonight,
        The result is very plain.

    And, oh, the letters that were sent
        From Kansas and Dakota,
    And each one surely did his part
        In filling out their quota.

    Now for you on this happy occasion
        A new chapter has just begun.
    For we see you here as husband and wife,
        Your ways from now on are one.

    So I wish you God's richest blessing,
        May his presence with you abide,
    May he ever bless and keep you
        And be your constant guide.
          —Marie Harder Epp

On April 29, 1954, my father's nephew Elvin married Ann, who was a citizen of Holland. Ann had been working in the home of Elvin's parents, the Emil Wiebes, for a year in an MCC-sponsored trainee exchange program. The wedding was in Holland and included both a civil and a church ceremony. The formality of the ceremonies was fascinating for those of us who had never been outside our community. This poem was recited by Elvin's nephews at the reception in their honor held in the local church fellowship hall shortly after they returned to the local community.

Celebration of Marriage

Wedding Reception of Elvin and Ann Wiebe
Presented by Olga Busenitz's boys

On this very rare occasion
We have thoughts we'd like to share;
So that we have a chance to speak
Seems only just and fair.

∽

God has really undertaken
   In behalf of you two here,
In leading Aunt Ann to America,
   As a trainee for one year.

∽

As by Grandpa and by Grandma
   She worked for a while,
It was then that Uncle Elvin
   Was enchanted by her smile.

∽

And as again she left them,
   She still was on his mind.
In repeated corresponding
   Much enjoyment he would find.

∽

Some find a girl in their own church,
   Some go to a different state,
But here was one that traveled
   To Europe for a date.

∽

He went to Aunt Ann in Holland,
   To the land where the tulips are.
He crossed the big wide ocean
   Oh my, but that was far.

∽

I wish I could have seen him
   On that special wedding day,
With his gray gloves and high silk hat,
   He looked elegant they say.

∽

And Aunt Ann in her bridal clothes
   Was lovely all around.
Such a nice and handsome couple
   Has never yet been found.

∽

The Petals of a Kansas Sunflower

>We are happy now that you are back
>   And here with us to stay;
>Now may God richly bless you.
>   This is all I have to say.
>
>   ∽
>
>We are wishing you much happiness,
>   Prosperity and wealth.
>Enough of rain and sunshine
>   And every day good health.
>
>   ∽
>
>But first of all I wish you:
>   God's blessing from above,
>That he may guide and keep you
>   In his abiding love.

My brother's friend from Grace University, Eldon Wohlgemuth, got married to Jan Diller on August 28, 1958 in Bluffton, Ohio. On September 7, Eldon's parents here in our hometown of Whitewater organized a wedding reception for the newlyweds. Local relatives and friends who did not go to Ohio came to greet and congratulate the newlyweds. Mother was asked to write a poem, but there is no record of who recited or read the poem.

The poem begins with recollections of the memorable wedding day. "The wedding bells have just ceased ringing, / The candle light has faded away." Mother reminds them of divine guidance, "You marvel how the Lord has led you, / He caused the meeting of your ways." She also suggests that marriage "is like a book with pages unread / That open as you go on your way." She then closes the poem with two simple lines that take late adolescent idealism and project it forward to late adulthood for the attainment of a dream: "In closing I wish that the happiness / You wished for will come true."

For Eldon Wohlgemuths' Wedding Reception
September 7, 1958

>The wedding bells have just ceased ringing,
>   The candlelight has faded away.
>Fresh in your minds is the impression
>   Of your memorable wedding day.
>It was a day of special meaning
>   For now you are one—where you were two.

Celebration of Marriage

It was for you a God-given blessing
    Your hopes and wishes have come true.
You marvel how the Lord has led you,
    He caused the meeting of your ways.
Your friendship grew to fond affection
    And many were the happy days.
At Bluffton, Ohio lived the one
    In Kansas lived the other,
You grew to man and womanhood
    Not knowing of each other
One thing you had in common though
    The urge for Christian training
You came to Omaha to "Grace"
    To satisfy this yearning.
In course of years something took place
    That no one can explain.
But we have evidence today
    The fact is very plain.
A leaf had been turned in both of your lives,
    A new chapter has just begun.
For now you are considered husband and wife
    Your ways from now on are one.
The path that now together you tread
    Lies unknown before you this day,
It is like a book with pages unread
    That opens as you go on your way.
As day after day for you comes in view
    You'll find as you journey along
Life has its dark days as they say
    And days full of praises and song.
So whatever may be your portion
    The Lord Jesus will prove a friend;
He will bless and guide and keep you,
    Just trust him to the end.
In closing I wish that the happiness
    You wished for will come true.
And that together you will fill in life
    The place God has for you.
        —M.H.E.

The mother-of-the-bride, Alma Regier Dyck, requested the next poem. In 1933, Alma recited the poem Mother wrote to honor Alma's grandparents on their fiftieth wedding anniversary, as presented in chapter 13. Alma grew up in our community and helped Mother with the housework for a time when my sister Hildegard was born. The Dyck family moved to California and lived in Paso Robles at the time their daughter Marline got married. The groom, Larry, worked for a utility company and was transferred to a new assignment there; he attended the same church Marline's family attended and became acquainted with her.

This poem expresses excitement and a bit of theatrics. In Hollywood style, Mother even includes speaking cues, "(now address the couple)." The message for the newlyweds is Mother's reminder that "your ways from now on are one." The future is unknown and there will be joys and sorrows; but "the Lord Jesus will prove a friend; / He will bless and guide and keep you, / Just trust him to the end." The final wish is repeated from the previous poem, that "the happiness / You wished for will come true. / And that together you will fill in life / The place God has for you."

For Marline Dyck and Larry Lutz
May 2, 1959
Paso Robles, California

As days and months will come and go,
   You'll find it oft' to be the case;
(I'll even prove it to be true)
   That strange things really can take place.

From Compton came into this area
   Someone, soon spied by Marline's eye,
And this one too, soon was her target
   At ground work or on poles up high.

We all know too, she's good at aiming,
   The target she will seldom miss,
And what today we have before us
   Is evident enough, for this.

In Bible-school she acquired knowledge;
   Then agricultural training, to fill in.
And these combined will prove as assets
   As housewife duties now begin.

Celebration of Marriage

It's not that we give up a sister,
    But another brother she brings in.
It seems to others we are losing,
    But at the end we surely win.

Now wedding bells are gaily ringing,
    The candlelight is bright and fair.
A special day for Marline and Larry,
    The future seems without a care.

(now address the couple)

A leaf has been turned in both of your lives,
    A new chapter has just begun.
For now you are considered husband and wife
    Your ways from now on are one.

The path that now together you tread
    Lies unknown before you this day,
It is like a book with pages unread
    That opens as you go on your way.

As day after day for you comes into view
    You'll find as you journey along
Life has its dark days as they say
    And days full of praises and song.

So whatever may be your portion
    The Lord Jesus will prove a friend;
He will bless and guide and keep you,
    Just trust him to the end.

In closing I wish that the happiness
    You wished for will come true.
And that together you will fill in life
    The place God has for you.
        —M.H.E.

Mother's niece Edna married Martin Graber, a widower, when she was in her early forties. Edna, whom we met in chapter 6 when Mother and Father gave her a bath towel for her birthday, was a sister to Bertha. Bertha's youngest daughter recited this poem at the wedding reception.

The Petals of a Kansas Sunflower

Mother also baked the wedding cake for Edna. The base was square topped with three round tiers. The wedding colors were lavender and white, so Mother used white frosting on the cake and decorated it with white frosting piping. She then formed cattleya orchid flowers out of sheets of frosting and hand-painted them with lavender cake coloring. These were strategically placed on the white frosted cake. I always felt that this cake was one of the crowning achievements of Mother's cake decorating contributions to her daughters, nieces, and the community.

Edna Regier and Martin Graber Wedding
August 4, 1959
Recited by Verna Marie Busenitz

For many weeks we waited
    For the coming of this day;
And how I now enjoy it
    'Tis more than I can say.

Of course, our hearts are saddened
    To see Aunt Edna leave;
But she brings us Uncle Martin,
    So we'll call it gain, not grief.

Grandpa will be lonesome
    Left by himself from now,
But we'll try to keep him company
    And cheer him up somehow.

I am wishing you God's blessing
    Even in duties that are new,
And may you find real happiness
    With disappointments few.

As from now on you journey together
    May the Lord with you abide,
Strengthen, bless and keep you
    And be your constant guide.
        —M.H.E.

In the following poem, the bride's younger sibling presents a box of Tide® with the hope that this will ease the transition into the new home.

The bride's home chores apparently involved a lot of washing for the whole family. Highlighted are sibling friendships that "Just happy joyful moments in our memory will last." The poem ends with a blessing.

Della Busenitz and Brian Loewen Wedding
1973

I would like to add a present to the collection that I see,
   And may it be a token of love and harmony.
The frequent fuss and squabbles are now all in the past.
   Just happy joyful moments in our memory will last.
What fun we had when riding the tractor or the bike,
   Unloading milo, choring, doing errands or the like.
A special gift I'm bringing, a box of Tide® for you.
   I trust this tides you over from the old home to the new,
And that it will be washing Brian's clothing clean and white
   As you so often did to mine and they came out just right.
Well, here my poem is ending, just one more thing I'll share
   May the Lord richly bless you and keep you in his care.
—M.H.E.

The final four wedding poems were requested by Mother's grandsons. Not all grandsons thought to request poems for their weddings. Mother would be very proud that she was asked to write wedding poems for grandsons who have become professionals, as most of her grandchildren have done. Gregory is a certified public accountant; Steven has a master's degree in computer science and writes computer manuals in Silicon Valley; Michael is a National Merit Scholar and also works in the computer industry; and James is an attorney. The initial recitations of these poems were in Nebraska, California, Pennsylvania, and New York, respectively.

Mother begins the poem for Gregory and Caroline, "But that was not yet the end of the story / The half has not yet been told. / Here too, was a time of progressing / Just like a flower that slowly unfolds." I feel that Mother was referring to the rhythm of life and saw these young people in marriage as flower buds just beginning to open, in transition to full beauty. She then continues and recalls events that her grandsons had shared with her. She ends all four with a blessing and the last three with the identical "As from now on you travel together / May God with you abide, / Strengthen, bless and keep you / And be your constant guide."

The Petals of a Kansas Sunflower

In Mother's view, God controlled all aspects of the physical world. In marriage, it was God who brought people together, and allowed them to be attracted to each other, resulting in bond formation. Happiness was realized through God's constant presence and by discerning his leading. Through the pursuit of his guidance, marital bliss could be achieved and sustained for a lifetime.

The poem written in 1991 for James and Lisa was her final poem. She affectionately signed it, "Grandma Epp," the only time she used this signature. It seems so appropriate that she ended her writing, which spanned from 1929 to 1991, by writing for a member of her family, the family that she held so dear.

Gregory and Caroline Epp Wedding
April 21, 1984

But that was not yet the end of the story
    The half has not yet been told.
Here too, was a time of progressing
    Just like a flower that slowly unfolds.
We left the two on the country road,
    Both being out on their bikes.
Enjoying the out-of-doors and exercise,
    In this the two were alike.
In summer, leisurely, she said:
    "Why don't we two go west
To see the Colorado mountains
    And skiing at its best?"
It took but little persuasion,
    Come winter both were there.
And other friends were joining them
    This adventure with them to share.
But that was not as easy
    As in few words we just said.
There was planning, there was packing
    For housekeeping that lay ahead.
The day had come, she says, "Good-bye"
    And alone she travels west,
A month later Gregory does the same
    And joins up with the rest.
Caroline settled down in Breckenridge
    To ski through rough and rocky;

Celebration of Marriage

Through much heart searching and the grace of God
   Their friendship only prospered.
Being "Personnel Manager" in a clothing store,
   Kept Caroline busy all day.
And as a ski lift attendant
   Greg could his skill display.
This went on through the winter months,
   Then each in their car came back.
Greg left his car, and together
   To Colorado they retraced their track.
Before long Greg is getting restless,
   A breath of spring is in the air.
He suddenly felt a homeward pull
   Which didn't seem but fair,
On bicycles they started out,
   Greg and a friend, one day,
Via Nebraska, Iowa, and Missouri
   To Kansas on their way.
Greg found work in Wichita,
   And has since been there employed.
Caroline stayed in Breckenridge,
   Where a cool summer she enjoyed.
She now vividly recalls
   In taking a backward look,
Ma Bell played its toll
   On their pocketbook.
In the local church in Breckenridge,
   (Let us insert that here)
She worked with the junior high group
   During the entire year.
By now Greg was getting serious,
   And explained, by phone, one day:
"It's now your turn to follow!
   Why don't you come this way?"
That was what Caroline waited for . . .
   The mountains she left behind
And came to join Greg in Wichita
   Full contentment there to find.
This now was October '83,
   Caroline too had found employment.
They now spent their free moments together
   Which proved a great enjoyment.
After days of long working hours,
   They enjoyed running, biking, walking.

The Petals of a Kansas Sunflower

We know, and it's self understood,
    That this included talking.
They tried their hand at cooking,
    The specialty is pizza we hear.
And Carmel Rolls, Greg's favorite
    How fast they disappear.
Today we are here at the wedding,
    A new chapter has just begun.
We see them now as husband and wife
    Their ways from now on are one.
As they look into the future
    A light concern is shown
There are things that they are pondering
    For them today unknown.
The Huenefelds are close as a family,
    Each staying close to the home nest.
Greg and Caroline are wondering
    About acreage, adjacent to the rest.
No matter where they settle,
    We're sure that they will find
The hand of God will guide them,
    Wherever their path may wind.
        —M.H.E.

Steven and Kimberly Epp Wedding
December 28, 1985

Wedding bells and lighted candles
    Are the order of the day.
Congratulations and best wishes
    In abundance come your way.

And I too would like to join them,
    Wishing now God's best for you,
As your lives have been united
    And you are no longer two.

God has ways and means in leading
    Those he wants to join for life.
And your ways are now united,
    Seeing you as husband and wife.

Celebration of Marriage

Many years have gone before this;
   Childhood days with play and fun.
With many out-of-doors enjoyments
   Beneath the California sun.

His adolescent years Steve spent in Kansas;
   Included were his high school days.
Soon after these for him were ended,
   To California led his ways.

He sought for higher education,
   For a degree in Computer Science he aimed.
This, however, brought him lonely hours
   In the nice mobile home he claimed.

On coming home no dinner waited,
   Since living there all by himself.
The cabinet doors he then would open
   And check the food cans on the shelf.

This from now on will be different;
   The bachelor days he leaves behind.
The meal is waiting on the table
   Prepared for him by loving hands.

You will recall that in recent years
   There was a crossing of your ways,
And friendship soon was turned to love
   And that brings on this day.

But now Steve is confronted
   With an added responsibility—
The spiritual leader of the home
   From here on he will be.

And with Kim comes Joshua,
   An active little laddy.
This gives Steve a new degree—
   It's that of being daddy.

I'm wishing you God's blessing
   Even in duties that are new,
And may you find real happiness
   With disappointments few.

The Petals of a Kansas Sunflower

    As from now on you travel together
        May God with you abide,
    Strengthen, bless and keep you
        And be your constant guide.
          —M.H.E.

Michael and Corinne Cressman Wedding
June 27, 1987

Wedding bells and lighted candles
    Are the orders of the day,
Congratulations and best wishes
    In abundance come your way.

And we too would like to add ours
    Wishing now God's best for you,
As your lives have been united
    And you are no longer two.

God has ways and means of leading
    Those he wants to join for life
So your ways are now united,
    For you are husband and wife.

Remember that in recent years
    There was a crossing of your ways.
Friendship soon was turned to love
    Bringing in this special day.

Mike, now you are confronted
    With an added responsibility . . .
The spiritual leader of the home
    From here on you will be.

Cori, you too will be included
    In the changes taking place.
Plans, decisions and activities
    Now together you will face.

We're wishing you God's blessing
    Though duties may be new.
And may you find real happiness
    With disappointments few.

Celebration of Marriage

As from now on you travel together
  May God with you abide,
Strengthen, bless and keep you
  And be your constant guide.
      —M.H.E.

James and Lisa Epp Wedding
August 24, 1991

A festive air is prevailing, an atmosphere of praise;
Such as we find on the occasion of very special days.
The wedding bells are ringing, lit candles too we see,
James and Lisa are excited, what might their reason be?
God has a way of leading those that he will join for life.
In wisdom he is choosing them to make them husband and wife.
From far off Hong Kong comes the one, from New York state the other.
They grew to man and womanhood not knowing of each other.
At first their meetings were but casual, in honors class they were,
Quiet and unnoticed their friendship grew from there.
The week of orientation was helpful all the while;
Lisa found James handsome and with a pleasant smile.
Things the two have in common from time to time will show
Both becoming Christians at age five is interesting to know.
No date we have for Lisa, but it's real to her, you see
While James can relate his conversion to a date in history.
It was the Billy Graham Crusade Hong Kong Seventy-Five,
Which was a worldwide blessing by touching many lives.
Another thing in common is desiring higher learning,
Both came to Roberts Wesleyan to satisfy their yearning.
James first noticed Lisa in school their freshman year,
Delivering an honors class speech was a privilege to hear.
More pleasant grew their friendship as they do now recall,
As juniors, James asked Lisa to join him in racquetball.
Joining in activities the school was offering here,
Who's Who among American Students, their names both now appear.
A good cheerleader is Lisa and she does it with a will,
And the hope for skillful nursing is ever with her still.
They visited grandparents in Kansas and parents in Hong Kong, too,
Then a rather rare experience that comes to only a few.
Standing near Hong Kong harbor the marriage proposal was made,
At the same time the foundation for their future home was laid.
This being a new chapter that for them had just begun,

The Petals of a Kansas Sunflower

A new year just beginning the year of 1991.
What seems most important in life for the two?
For James it's serving the Lord in whatever they will do.
Lisa we see as ambitious, lending her helping hand
Preparing herself for whatever her busy life will demand.
As of yet it is unknown what the years will have in store.
God's presence always with you, you need not ask for more.
We are wishing you God's blessing even in duties that are new,
And may you find real happiness with disappointments few.
As from now on you travel together may God with you abide,
Strengthen, bless, and keep you and be your constant guide.
—Grandma Epp

12

Celebration of Sustained Bonding

ANNIVERSARIES OF WEDDINGS WERE traditionally celebrated as major achievements. This involved an evening church service followed by a supper reception with a program. Most anniversary poems in this chapter were read or recited aloud during the after-supper program. The evening concluded with hours of visiting.

In 1929, the fellowship hall (the church basement) in the third church building (see chapter 3) was completed by the local community. It became optional to use the church basement for the wedding reception rather than to go to a local farm where either a new building or a cleaned-out hayloft or machine shed was utilized. Initially some parishioners felt that the church building was a house of God and it was inappropriate to trivialize the space with social activity and meals in the basement. However, the convenience of having social activity in the basement of the church immediately following a formal religious service in the sanctuary soon prevailed. With the use of a church fellowship hall, church weddings began being held in the evenings. Evening services complemented the work schedules of the rural community. After dark, everyone was free to celebrate and visit.

In my childhood and youth when the church service was followed by a meal, the scent of coffee would permeate the sanctuary midway through the service. The reception committee would be making coffee in copper wash water vats by immersing muslin bags filled with coffee grounds into the boiling water. When the guests with stimulated appetites went downstairs, the coffee was ready.

There was good reason to celebrate wedding anniversaries. Divorce was contrary to the practiced biblical doctrines, so when young people got married, they knew their decision was irrevocable. There was no pre-marriage counseling about sex or money, so the Sunday morning hour-long sermons as well as the examples of their parents were their only guidance. Consequently, the gravity of their union encouraged the solving of marital disagreements with prayer, prayer, and more prayer rather than resorting to separation and divorce. Occasionally rumors were heard that an individual couple appeared not to be compatible and so they were in for a long life of unhappiness. Only in extremely rare cases would there be a divorce. In such cases, the church was silent but the community ostracized the pair with cold shoulders and raised chins. However, if either husband or wife ever remarried or if someone ever married a divorcee, they were immediately excommunicated from the church with no opportunity to participate in any church activity, not even singing in the choir. Even a public confession of transgression for conscience's sake in front of the voting members of the church did not solicit forgiveness (i.e., forgetting) or reinstate membership. Continued attendance at church was encouraged, because what better way to remind the erring couple of their guilt and sin.

It is very easy, as well as simplistic, to view prairie life of the nineteenth century as idyllic with only happy families and virtually no divorce. Outside the church community, territorial and state legislatures regularly granted divorces. Impotency, adultery, extreme cruelty, drunkenness, bigamy, and willful desertion of three years' duration were grounds for divorce. The new states and territories west of the Mississippi River had divorce codes that many considered very liberal. Within the Mennonite church communities, divorce was a religious and not a civil issue.

Fortunately, most young people made great choices and lived happy and productive lives within the community. The poems included in this chapter honor sustained marriages of seven to forty years. The next chapter is reserved for golden wedding anniversaries.

In the twenty-first century, the celebration of the twenty-fifth wedding anniversaries no longer routinely involves a church celebration. The opportunity to gather for an evening of praise and reminiscing is no longer cherished, because existing communication technologies and transportation methods no longer leave individual farm families isolated on a sea of prairie grass. Small private receptions in a home or family trips have become the choice of celebration.

From these anniversary poems we learn that sometimes in the early years, the wedding ceremony and the reception were both held on a parental farm. If the wedding ceremony was on a farm, the couple would sit in front of the group to listen to an hour or more of sermon before the elder or a minister would concede to unite them in marriage. The Jacob Thiessen wedding in the next chapter is an example.

Some couples got married after the Sunday morning church service. This was true for the wedding ceremony of the Henry Wiebes in 1925 who are remembered with poems later in this chapter. The bride and groom sat separately on decorated chairs at the front of the church on either side of the middle aisle that separated the men from the women. After being totally ignored during the morning service, the elder or a minister announced that the couple wanted to get married and forthwith married them. The Wiebe couple then went to the Epp farm for the reception in the hayloft of the horse barn.

Many brides wore dark wedding dresses prior to 1920. My grandmother Helene Harder wore a black dress sporting a short train on her wedding day, October 26, 1893. The dress is shown in figure 21. Mrs. Jake Thiessen wore a black dress in 1909 and carried the traditional wedding wreath. Mrs. Henry Wiebe in 1925 wore a brown silk dress. White wedding dresses began to appear after 1900 and with time became the norm. My mother in 1927 and her sisters before her all wore white dresses. Colored wedding dresses were subsequently used as church attire for as long as they fit; designed into the waistline of the skirts were possibilities for enlargement needed during the impending first pregnancy.

Jake Wiebe married my father's sister Agathe in 1926. Mother wrote a poem to commemorate the seventh anniversary. Vividly, the wedding ceremony is recalled. In this poem, after the ceremony in church on a Thursday, the couple arrived at home. "You came from the house to the barn." Grandfather Epp had seven daughters and the wedding receptions for the six that married were all held in the cleaned out hayloft of the horse barn. The loft was decorated with cedar boughs and flowers, kerosene lamps and lanterns were hung for lighting after it got dark, and meals were served, followed by another program with sermons and additional admonitions from male leaders within the church. The newly-married couple, together with other couples within the community whose engagement had been announced from the pulpit would sit at the head or special table. The older people would visit into the early morning hours and the children and young people would visit and play outside.

Figure 21
Wedding portrait of my grandparents, Bernhard Jr. (1864–1904) and Helene Wiebe (1864–1930) Harder, who married on October 26, 1893 in the home of Helene's parents in a double wedding ceremony together with John and Emilie Regier who are remembered in a poem in chapter 13. Grandmother's wedding dress was black with a short train. Tripp, Newton, KS. Source: Author's file.

Celebration of Sustained Bonding

Since Grandfather Epp did not want all the guests to go through the barn past the horses to get to the ladder for the loft, he built a portable set of steps that could be moved into position whenever there was a reception, so guests could get to the loft through a door from the outside of the barn. The newly married Jake Wiebes with "little steps" would have ascended this set of steps for their wedding reception.

The poem ends with the wish "That you with each other / Yet for a long, long time / May travel together."

Für Jake Wiebes
17 Juni 1933

Schon sieben sind's an Jahren,
  Weiß ich's doch ganz genau,
Als wir zur Kirche gefahren
  Zu Jacob Wiebes Trau.

Ich seh' sie in gedanken noch,
  Als wär's gestern erst geschehe,
Wie die beid' so Würdig doch
  Den Kirchengang rein gehe

Und auch noch später dann,
  Wie kleine Schritt sie nahmen,
Als, daß erstmal als Frau u. Mann
  Von Haus zum Stall sie kamen.

Und hatte ihre Gedanken gar
  Wohl einer können lesen,
Dann denk ich ist es nicht unwahr
  So ähnlich sind sie gewesen.

So wie unser Wunsch auch heut:
  Daß, Sie so mit einander
Ja noch lange lange Zeit
  Gemeinsam dürfen wandere.

The Petals of a Kansas Sunflower

>For Jake Wiebes
>June 17, 1933

>Already it is at the seventh year,
>>I know this exactly,
>Because we were at the church
>>For the Jacob Wiebes' wedding.

>I still see you absorbed in thought,
>>As if it only occurred yesterday,
>As you both were so worthy
>>To walk down the church aisle.

>And then also later,
>>How you took little steps,
>As, for the first time as wife and husband
>>You came from the house to the barn.

>And had all of your thoughts
>>Been able to be read,
>Then I think it is true
>>That you are like this.

>So our wish for you today:
>>That you with each other
>Yet for a long, long time
>>May travel together.

Five years after my parents got married and three years after Mother began writing poetry, she wrote the next poem for Father's oldest sister on the occasion of her twentieth wedding anniversary. This is the only poem with a personalized message. The message was that you have lectured me repeatedly on being frugal, and I have learned my lesson all too well; the occasion merits porcelain and it would be nice, but do not hate me for giving you in love some plain ceramics.

Being the only daughter-in-law with seven sisters was daunting for Mother, as already mentioned in chapter 1, and help and advice from her oldest sister-in-law was not always appreciated. The Harder family traditions that were enjoyed and cherished by Mother were challenged; their relaxed natures that included a lot of laughter and camaraderie were considered different and frivolous by the in-laws. Mother was a very gifted and creative person with soul, but perhaps with inadequate self-confidence. The rigidity of the discipline that Grandfather Epp enforced was excessive for Mother's spirit. After Grandfather Epp lectured Mother on her errant ways in raising her children, for several years her babies always seemed to have the sniffles that required her to stay home when family gatherings occurred. It took my father about sixty years to really fall in love with Mother and to appreciate her as a helpmate on whom he could depend. By then she had learned to ask his permission to do almost everything in her life. As an adult, if I telephoned Mother and said that I had arranged my airline tickets with a stopover in Wichita, Mother would say, "Just a minute, I'll ask Father." Pause. "Yes, Father said you may stop for a visit."

The challenge presented to my parents at marriage was that Mother grew up without brothers or the presence of a father in the household since her father passed away when she was eight months old and her mother never remarried. My father grew up with seven sisters doting on him and Grandfather Epp and catering to their every request or wish. Grandfather Epp knew what he wanted and when; he was not a relaxed man. Grandfather Epp is remembered for his regal deportment as he walked erectly into church; he was bald and late in life had a lovely fringe of white curly locks.

Anna as a sixteen-year-old took over the household at the death of my grandmother Epp in 1907. This included being mother to my father when he was a six-year-old child. When my parents married, Anna assumed the role of the mother-in-law. Her recurring theme indeed was frugality, because she thought the Harders were wealthy and spendthrifts. When my mother was in her 80s and had just removed the hulls from a basket of strawberries, she laughingly said, "My sisters-in-law could not have done a better job." In her waste container there was absolutely no red or white color showing, only the green from the hulls indicating that absolutely no fruit was wasted.

Whenever one of my older brothers had a need for superiority he would ask, "When did Melvin get his first spanking?" The solicited answer was, "When Aunt Anna and his parents gave Melvin his first bath." Apparently, after I was brought home from the hospital and the time came for my first home bath, my parents with Anna's ever-present assistance, gave me a swat on my behind to get me to relax sufficiently to fit into the basin of water. The feel of the water had made me stiffen and consequently I was too long for the basin. A sister who observed this event commented that she could not understand why it took three adults to give an eight-pound, one-week-old baby a bath, when this was the eighth baby in the family. Surely Mother and Father would have been proficient at bathing an infant through practice.

Anna's birthday was on January 1 and many New Year's evenings were spent celebrating her birthday at her house. Once as we arrived for the evening, I observed so clearly Anna's "Hello" to my father was said with the affection of a mother rather than that of a sister. Of course there were no hugs or even the shaking of hands, for Mennonites are not known for their tactile interactions, but it was the affection expressed in her voice that left a memory. When Mother was eighty-five years old, she wrote her autobiography, and included, "I think God, in his foresight had given Anna a nature that helped her. She liked to be a leader, as I learned to know her, and knew how to cope with situations."

Here are the poems Mother wrote per Anna's request for their twentieth and fortieth wedding anniversaries. In the next chapter, there are three poems to celebrate Anna's golden wedding anniversary; these poems express affection with congratulatory verses.

Für Herman A. Wiebes, 12 November 1932

"*Porzellan für den 20ten Hochzeitstag*"
   So haben wir gelesen,
Doch warum das wohl immer so sein mag
   Wie es schon öfters ist gewesen
Daß, gerad von dem daß paßt dazu
   Ist leider nichts vorhanden.
Doch ließ es uns gar keine Ruh
   Bis was anders wir dann fanden.
Porzellan ja mir daß Aug' erfreut
   Doch dies auch noch den Magen
So tut es euch ja wohl nicht leid
   Daß, zu bringen wir es wagen.
Und ist die Gabe auch ganz schlicht,
   Nicht kostbar wie Porzellan,
So bitte verachtet sie darum nicht
   Und nehmt sie in liebe an.

Celebration of Sustained Bonding

For Herman A. Wiebes, November 12, 1932

"Porcelain for the 20th wedding anniversary"
    This is what we have read.
However, it might have always been like this.
    This is often how it has been
That, whatever exactly fits an idiom like this
    Is unfortunately not presently at hand.
That surely gives us no comfort
    Until we find something else.
Porcelain, yes for me, pleases the eye
    Albeit, it also enhances dining pleasure
So surely you will not regret
    That, for this event we bring,
And the gift is also completely plain,
    Not costly as porcelain,
So, please do not despise it
    And accept it with affection.

Der Vierzigster
12 November 1952
von LeRoy & Carolyn Busenitz and Delbert Regier vorgetragen

Wunderbar ist Gottes Walten,
Wunderbar sein weiser Rat.
Wunderbar ist sein verhalten
Der euch treu geführet hat.
Wunderbar mit sein Erbarmen
Trägt Er euch schon 40 Jahr.
Und mit seinen Liebesarmen
Führte Er euch wunderbar.
Vierzig Jahre sind vergangen
Seit, als schönes junges Paar
Eure Herzen sich verbanden
Und ihr stand am Traualtar.
Bald belebten diese Räume
Eine frohe Kinderschar.
Unter Arbeit, Freud and Sorge
Schnell vergingen Jahr um Jahr.
Ach wie bald zog eins ums andere
In sein eig'ne Heim hinaus
Bis jetzt nur noch Tante Gladys

The Petals of a Kansas Sunflower

Ist allein bei Euch zu Haus
Doch der Kreis von euren Lieben
Immer grösser wurde er
Und wir kommen ja auch alle
Immer gerne zu euch her.
So sollt ihr nicht einsam werden,
Auch freuen wir uns schon der Zeit
Wenn wieder wir euch Wünsche bringen
Wenn mit Gold geschmückt ihr seid.

The Fortieth
November 12, 1952
Presented by LeRoy & Carolyn Busenitz and Delbert Regier

Wonderful is God's will,
Wonderful is his wise counsel,
Wonderful is his support,
Who has truly guided you.
Wonderful with his compassion
He already carried you for forty years
And with his loving arms
He has guided you wonderfully.
Forty years have passed
Since, as a lovely young pair
Your hearts were bound
And you stood at the marriage altar.
Soon this space was animated
With a troop of happy children.
Through work, joy and sorrow
Year after year passed by quickly
So shortly, one after another moved
Out into their own homes
Until currently only Aunt Gladys remains
Alone with you in your house
Yet the sphere of those that love you
Becomes increasingly larger
And we all continue to come
Always with increased preference to you here.
So you should not get lonesome,
Also we will enjoy the time
When again we will bring you good wishes
When you are adorned with gold.

Celebration of Sustained Bonding

The following two poems were written to commemorate the twenty-fifth and the thirtieth wedding anniversaries of neighbors. Mrs. Jacob J. Regier (Helene Harder) was Mother's cousin who grew up across the road from the farm.

Gustav Harder, Helene's father, was twenty years old in 1876 when the family came to America. After three years, he returned to Germany to look for a wife. He renewed acquaintance with Helene Kroeker and they were married on May 25, 1880. When they returned to America in August, they brought with them a large Fluegel grand piano, which had been a gift to Helene (Kroeker) on her sixteenth birthday. The young couple lived for a period with his parents until Gustav established a farm across the road to the east from his father's farm and the Harder cemetery. When the church was formally organized, in 1877, Gustav was chosen to be a chorister. In the absence of a musical instrument, the *Vorsänger* (chorister) needed to know the melody of each song and begin on the proper pitch. Their hymnal at this time was the *Gesangbuch ohne Noten* (songbook without notes) with only the words of the hymn printed. Gustav is remembered for his exceptionally clear voice. There were no musical instruments in the church until a pedal reed organ was added in 1908. Peter Thiessen, Christian Thierstein, and J. G. Regier were the organists, because only men were allowed at that time to participate in the worship service. Women were allowed to play the organ for Sunday school, however. When the church acquired a piano in 1926, there were no men who could play and so a concession was made to allow a woman to play the piano for the worship service.

In 1884, Gustav was ordained as a minister and in 1902, the elder of the group. The General Conference Mennonite Conference elected him to serve on the foreign mission board in 1890, and within three years he was chosen to be the treasurer of the board, holding that position until he passed away in 1923. Gustav was active in governance of Bethel College in North Newton, and from 1912 to 1918 served as a member of their board of directors. He also served for a time on the board of directors of the Bethel Deaconess Hospital. He farmed extensively using hired help to free him for his church activity. Approximately six hundred of Gustav's handwritten sermons in German are archived in Bethel College's Mennonite Library and Archives. On the Sundays that Elder Gustav Harder delivered a sermon, he would come to the dais from an adjacent room and would kneel beside the pulpit for a short, silent prayer. He would then stand up and routinely take a handkerchief from his pocket and lay it on the pulpit because he got so emotionally involved in his sermons that he would need to wipe his tears.

On May 25, 1905, Gustav and Helene (Kroeker) celebrated their silver wedding anniversary to which the entire local church congregation as well as the foreign mission board was invited. The celebration took place on their farm where an implement shed was cleared for the day. Four hundred people gathered to thank God for his graciousness to his children, the celebratory couple. Gustav is interred in the Harder cemetery beside his parents, wife, and other members of his immediate family.

When Jacob J. Regier married their daughter Helene Harder, Gustav and Helene (Kroeker) Harder built the newlyweds a large house three-quarters of a mile north of their farm. Jacob's parents built a large barn for them. The grandeur of the new farm was the talk of the town in the community. After an interval of twenty to thirty years, to create financial solvency during the Great Depression, this farm was sold to my father and the couple moved to the parental farm across the road from the original Harder farm.

The bridal house was very large and grand. When I was in the third grade and at a potluck dinner at the elementary school, someone asked Mother if the marble staircase was still in that house. What a public perception of the house! There never had been a marble staircase in the house, but the large parlor and living room did have area rugs on the floor. It was a very rainy day when the bridal couple held a housewarming reception after they had moved in; the story goes that the old men, not knowing or living with rugs on floors, unwittingly wiped the mud off their boots onto the carpets as they entered the house.

The Regiers were wonderful neighbors, and Mother expresses this appreciation in the second poem. Expressing affection was not readily done within the Germanic Mennonite community, so I consider these poems unique with more thoughtful emotional expressions than most of her other poems.

In the first poem for the twenty-fifth anniversary, Mother composed a poem with twenty-five verses, and in the second poem for the thirtieth anniversary there are thirty lines. Mother ends the second poem "I do not have the intention / Every five years to furnish a poem." Unfortunately, the tornado of June 8, 1941 demolished the Regier's home and farm the year before their thirty-fifth anniversary, and they moved to Newton and never rebuilt the farm. The tornado moved the house off the foundation and dropped it demolished in the garden.

Celebration of Sustained Bonding

Figure 22
Gustav (1856–1923) and Helene Kroeker Harder (1858–1919) in their silver wedding anniversary portrait in 1905. Source: Photo collection, Mennonite Library and Archives, North Newton.

Some of my siblings remember walking across the road to inspect the damage to the house and being able to walk in and play the Fluegel grand piano as it stood on a sloping floor. The Regier family went to

Newton for medical treatment during the night immediately after the tornado and within two months moved permanently. Our family lost wonderful neighbors. That area across from our driveway is now a grain field with no signs of a farm ever having been there. (See appendix 3 for more details.)

There are several passages that I would like to highlight. In the first poem, verses 3 and 4 express joy, romance, youthful excitement and thankfulness to God for making things happen: "Happy are the periods in life / When still with the full strength of youth / Two hearts find each other, / A God working for both. / And they with the promise of life / Commit themselves to fidelity until the grave, / Their hearts happily exalted / To him who has given everything." From verse 15, "Focusing on regrets and sorrow / At your home was rare," and from verse 17, "Here on earth, things alternate / Constantly, happiness versus sorrowfulness, / And we scarcely become either, / Time lapses so fast."

Apparently, the twenty-fifth anniversary celebration occurred in the same barn where the wedding reception was held. "The same circle of relatives / are rejoicing with you today." The blessing is in the twenty-fourth verse, "With his grace he wants / To constantly remain with you here / On life's pathways in the future / And guide you forever and ever."

Mother initiates the poem for the thirtieth wedding anniversary by reminding the listeners in the first six lines that the Regiers had invited them as guests for this festivity on Armistice Day. Playing with the number thirty, the end of the Thirty Years War indeed occurred on this very day, October 24, but in the year 1648. How and why did Mother remember these facts without the help of the Internet? The Thirty Years War (1618–1648) was pre-eminently a German war, but was also important for the history of the whole of Europe.

The next six lines are also noteworthy and compliment the celebratory pair: "Scarcely known to me is a house where it is like it is here / A married couple with their children so well loved as here / The man is the head of the household, the woman is a helpmate / And then happy children are the offspring. / So for you together the thirty years have passed quickly / Yet still you have remained a happy married couple."

After the discussion of the children's activity, the poem ends with "But I would like to take this heartfelt opportunity / It pleases us to have you as our neighbors / And wish as our parents who governed here before us / To constantly maintain true friendship as neighbors."

Celebration of Sustained Bonding

Zu Jacob J. Regiers Silberhochzeit
24 Oktober 1932

1.
Heut an diesem seltenen Feste
Wo noch fünfundzwanzig Jahr
In denen Gotteshand aufs beste
Euch geführt stets wunderbar.
2.
Und durch Gottes gnädigen Walten
Ein Sillbermyrte heut' Euch schmückt
Habt Ihr wohl schon angehalten
Und im Geist zurück geblickt.
3.
Froh sind im Leben die Stunden
Wenn noch voll Jugendkraft
Zwei Herzen sich gefunden
Ein Gott für einander schaft.
4.
Und sie in Lieb' geloben
Sich Trauen bis ans Grab
Die Herzen froh erhaben
Zu Dem der alles gab
5.
Und Grün der Hoffnung Zeichen
Schmückt dann ein solches Paar,
Die sich fürs Leben reichen
Die Hand am Traualtar.
6.
Wohl blicken dann die beide
Voll Hoffnung froh voraus,
Obwohl es gilt ein scheiden
Von liebem Elternhaus.
7.
So habt auch Ihr begonnen
Gemeinsam die Laufbahn
Der Eltern Segen genommen
Mit Euch auch dann fortan.
8.
Leichter schieds sichs von den Lieben
Bechen da du zogest aus
Da du in der Näh geblieben
Und recht oft konntest du nach Haus'.

The Petals of a Kansas Sunflower

9.
Mit Fleiß und frohen Triebe
Richtest ein dies Heim du traut,
Daß treue Eltern Liebe
So schön für Euch erbaut.
10.
So ist dann wohl verflossen
Für Euch manch schönes Jahr.
Viel Segnungen habt Ihr genossen
Und die Herzen sind dankbar.
11.
Doch nicht immer sonnig blos
War Euer Weg bis her
Auch Tage waren Euer Los
Ein lange trüb' und schwer.
12.
Denn es kam auch solche Zeit.
Ein bange Ihr durchlebt
Und wo in schwerer Krankheit
Ein teures Leben schwebt.
13.
Dann habt auch wohl Ihr Leide
Stets Gotteshand gespürt
Und sicher durch dem Leide
Hat seine Hand geführt
14.
So stimmt es Euch auch dieses mal
Voll Dank, Da Ihr dies Fest begeht
Da Ihr heut in voller Zahl
Die Kinder um Euch seht.
15.
Auch Leid und Trauer blieben
Von Eurem Heim nicht fern
Schon drei von Euren lieben
Eltern sind droben bei dem Herrn.
16.
Wohl hat Euch schwer betroffen
Das Auseinandergehe,
Doch steht der Christen Hoffen
Ja stets auch Wiedersehe.
17.
So wechselt hier auf Erden
Stets Freude ab mit Leid
Und kaum wir's eine werden,
So schnell verläuft die Zeit.

Celebration of Sustained Bonding

18.
So ist auch schnell vergangen
Für Euch hier Jahr um Jahr
Seit Ihr hier angefangen
Ist's ein Viertelhundert gar.

19.
Und zwar an selber Stelle
Wo im grünen Myrtenstatt,
Ihr einstmals über die Schwelle
In's Eheleben trat.

20.
Seit heut' zum zweitenmale
Ihr festlich geschmückt
Hier im selbigen Stalle
Recht fröhlich und beglückt.

21.
Derselbe Kreis Verwandten
Sich heute mit Euch freut
Doch unter den Onkeln und Tanten
Ist schon mancher nicht mehr heut.

22.
Schon manchem vermist Ihr heute sehr
Denn viele fehlen schon
Und herangewachsen ist seit her
Eine neue Generation.

23.
Doch Jesus ist geblieben
Wie gestern so auch heut
Und bleibt bei seinen Lieben
Ja bis in Ewigkeit.

24.
Er wolle mit seiner Gnade
Stets bleiben bei Euch hier
Auf weitere Lebenspfade
Euch leiten für und für.

25.
Und ist es sein Wille geben,
Daß um fünfundzwanzig Jahr
Ihr diesen Tag dürft verleben
Als Goldenes Jubelpaar.

The Petals of a Kansas Sunflower

For Jacob J. Regiers' Silver Wedding Anniversary
October 24, 1932

1.
Today, at this rare celebration
Where after twenty-five years
God's hand was at its best
As it steadily guided you wonderfully.
2.
And through God's merciful direction
Today, you are adorned with silver myrtle
You surely have already perceived this
And in spirit are reminiscing.
3.
Happy are the periods in life
When still with the full strength of youth
Two hearts find each other,
One God working for both.
4.
And they with the promise of life
Commit themselves to fidelity until the grave,
Their hearts happily exalted
To him who has given everything.
5.
And green, the sign of hope
That adorns such a pair,
Who for a lifetime reach
Their hands towards the marriage altar.
6.
Surely both looked
Ahead, full of joyous hope,
Although it required a separation
From the home of loving parents.
7.
Likewise, you too had your beginning
Jointly in this career path
You took the parental blessing
With you also then henceforth.
8.
Easily you negotiated yourself from this love
Though you lingered as you left.
However, you remained close by
And often rightly able to come home.

Celebration of Sustained Bonding

9.
Intentionally and with joyous inclination
The betrothed established this home
That faithful loving parents
Built for you so nicely.
10.
Truly, so it then transpired
Many beautiful years for you.
You have been involved with many blessings
And you have thankful hearts.
11.
However, it was not always sunny
Your path until now.
Also days were your destiny
That were long, dark, and difficult.
12.
For such times also came.
You lived through a crisis
And where in difficult sickness
A precious life was suspended.
13.
Then you truly had your sorrow
And God's hand seemed absent
But surely through the sorrow
His hand has led.
14.
And you will agree this time also,
You wish to be thankful, since you are celebrating
Because today you see a large number
Of children around you.
15.
Also, suffering and sadness
Were not kept far from your home.
Already three of your beloved
Parents are above with the Lord.
16.
Truly you have been heavily stricken
With the break up,
However, there exists the Christian hope
Yes, constant, also of meeting again.
17.
Here on earth, things alternate
Constantly, happiness versus sorrowfulness,
And we scarcely become either one,
Time lapses so fast.

The Petals of a Kansas Sunflower

18.
So it also quickly passed
Year after year for you here
Since you began here
A quarter of a century is done.
19.
And indeed at your place
Where in green myrtle status
Over the threshold you once
Trod into married life.
20.
Today, for the second time
You are festively adorned
Here in this very barn
Rightly joyous and blessed.
21.
The same circle of relatives
Are rejoicing with you today
Yet of the uncles and aunts
Many are not here today.
22.
Several you miss very much today
For many are already missing,
And growing up since then is
A new generation.
23.
However, Jesus has remained
As yesterday, so also today
And remains by his love
Yes, until into eternity.
24.
With his grace he wants
To constantly remain with you here
On life's pathways in the future
And guide you forever and ever.
25.
And if it is his will
That after twenty-five more years
You may pass through this day
As a golden jubilee pair.

Celebration of Sustained Bonding

Jake Regiers zum 30ten Hochzeitstag
24 Oktober 1937

Zum Fest des Waffenstillstands habt geladen Ihr uns heut!
Das ist ein groß Ereigniß worüber man sich freut.
Das beendet ist um heute der 30 jährige Krieg
Und in diesem Falle freuen sich alln an dem Sieg.
Es war ja nicht ein streiten von zweierlei Parteien
Es war ein Kämpfen, Wirken gemeinsam zu zweien
Kaum ist mir noch ein Haus bekannt wo es so ist wie hier
Ein Eltere mit den Kindern so liebewohl wie ihr
Der Mann ist Haupt des Hauses die Frau die Gehilfen sein.
Und dann frohe kinder die sind der Sonnenschein.
So ist euch schnell vergangen gemeinsam 30 Jahr
Doch seid ihr noch geblieben ein frohes Ehepaar.
Und kamen trübe Tage, kam Lehnhen dein Humor
Gleich der Sonne hielten Wolken, bald wieder hervor.
Zwei von den lieben Kindern verließen das Elternhaus
Zur Vorbereitung fürs Leben dazu traten sie hinaus.
Wilbert in California ein Prediger wird er sein
Und nimmt bald die Stelln der Großväter ein.
Im Hospital Elfriede wo sie mit lieber Hand
Schon manchen Schmerz der Menschheit so liebevoll verband.
Noch wissen wir nicht heute was gewählt die andere zwei
Doch kann ich so viel sagen was gutes wird es sein
So wünsch ich euch dann ferner noch Gottes Geleit
Der ja immer zur Segene so gern ist bereit
Ich mögt zum Schluß noch sagen: die Absicht hab ich nicht
Alle fünf Jahre zu liefere ein Gedicht.
Doch mögt ich hier noch nehmen die Gelegenheit wahr
Es freut uns euch zu haben als unsere Nachbar
Und wollen wie unsre Eltern, die vor uns hier walten
Stets treu Freundschaft als Nachbaren halten.

For Jake Regiers' Thirtieth Wedding Day
October 24, 1937

For the Festival of Armistice you have invited us today!
That is a great event about which one is happy.
The end of the Thirty-Year War was today
And in this case all are happy for this victory.

The Petals of a Kansas Sunflower

> It was not a dispute of two kinds of parties
> It was a dispute between two factions.
> Scarcely known to me is a house where it is like it is here
> A married couple with their children so well loved as here
> The man is the head of the household, the woman is a helpmate
> And then happy children are the sunshine.
> So for you together the thirty years have passed quickly
> Yet still you have remained a happy married couple
> And on gloomy days, your supporting humor came
> Soon reappearing similar to the sun from behind the clouds.
> Two of your lovely children left the house of their parents
> They left to prepare for life.
> Wilbert in California wants to become a preacher
> And soon have a career similar to his grandfather
> Elfriede, in the hospital where she with loving hands
> Affectionately bandages the many pains of mankind
> But today we do not know the career choices of the other two
> But I can say many things, but what good would it be
> So I wish you then further to God's guidance
> Who surely always blesses those who willingly prepare.
> In closing, I would still like to say: I do not have the intention
> Every five years to furnish a poem
> But I would like to take this heartfelt opportunity
> It pleases us to have you as our neighbors
> And wish as our parents who governed here before us
> To constantly maintain true friendship as neighbors.

For the twenty-fifth anniversary celebration of Father's sister Margarethe, Mother wrote a poem in English. It was 1944 and the period when English had become the dominant language. The poem was presented by the honoree's son, Elvin Roy.

In the celebration of an achievement like being married for twenty-five years, Mother assumes there has been or will be a review of the past, "Your thoughts will involuntarily / Go back to days gone by / . . . Your thoughts go back to childhood." The setting of the wedding date had been suspenseful, because the groom, Emil Wiebe, was waiting to hear whether he would be called into non-combatant military service. World War I was happening and indeed Emil was inducted, so the wedding did not occur until 1919 when he returned home. At the end of Emil's life, the local American Legion honored Emil with a flag-draped casket and a 21-gun salute at the Emmaus Mennonite Church cemetery.

The newlywed couple moved to a farm where, with time, they built a new beautiful home. Emil was known in the community for his farming ability. His cattle always garnered the highest premium prices on the market. "He has blessed you with material wealth." I think Mother was impressed that he drove a Buick to church, while his neighbors drove Chevys and Fords.

In this poem, as in many others, Mother draws attention to those who were at the wedding, but who have in the intervening time passed away. As grand as this celebration may have been, the circle of friends and relatives had regrettable gaps. A benediction ends the poem, "That in love we may to each other / And in love to God we may cling."

Emil Wiebes' Silver Wedding
October 30, 1944
Recited by Elvin Roy Wiebe

A special day has come to you
   Your hearts are full of praise
To God the heavenly Father
   Who kept you on life's ways.
"This is the day, which the Lord hath made
   Rejoice and be of cheer."
This is the thought that's ringing
   In your heart sweet and clear.
Your thoughts will involuntarily
   Go back to days gone by.
God showered you with kindness
   And blessings from on high.
Your thoughts go back to childhood
   To days you spent at school
To winters cold and summers hot
   And autumns fair and cool.
Your ways were two in those years
   They crossed from time to time
Till later they were united
   On a day for you sublime.
But before that day was dawning
   There was a time of suspense for all
For Papa had to leave for camp
   In answer to the nation's call.

The Petals of a Kansas Sunflower

> When finally those days were ended
>   Your wishes came all your way
> When your hearts and hands were united
>   Twenty-five years ago today.
> You moved to this farm in a little house
>   From where you never did roam
> Till in later years on the very same place
>   You built this beautiful home.
> You have always felt God's mercy
>   After sickness he restored you to health
> His kindness has shone upon you
>   He has blessed you with material wealth.
> For among the best in the county
>   Have been, Papa, your fattened steers
> That you have been sending to market
>   Repeatedly for years.
> You have also experienced sorrow
>   Since your green wedding day
> For several of your loved ones,
>   To their final rest, were laid away.
> Another day needs mentioning
>   That from others you set apart
> That is the day when Donald
>   Came into your house and heart.
> Now Donald had experiences as papa
>   The call came to him and he went
> So far away from home in California
>   The last few months he has spent.
> In closing I wish you God's presence
>   Whatever further years may bring
> That in love we may to each other
>   And in love to God we may cling.

In 1925, my father's sister Maria Epp married Heinrich Wiebe. Mother wrote a devotional poem to commemorate the twenty-fifth anniversary and a more historical poem for their fortieth wedding anniversary. The latter poem describes how on November 6, 1925, a Sunday morning, a roadster (carrying Henry and Maria) turned into the churchyard. Maria, wearing a brown silk dress, was married to Heinrich at the end of the morning worship service. The reception was "in a clean and garnished hayloft where the children could freely roam." As the cars moved from the church to Grandfather Epp's farm, it began to rain hard. Boards were laid down as sidewalks so the guests could walk from their cars to Grandfather Epp's steps to the hayloft. The poem recounts that the rains continued into the evening making a lot of noise on the barn roof.

In the lines, "You were called to walk dark valleys, when the death angel came in / And God in His sovereign wisdom took one up to be with him," Mother is referring to their daughter Marilyn who we met in chapter 6 when Father gave her dollhouse accessories for her second birthday.

The poem ends with the blessing, "Until then may God's own presence lead you on to higher ground. / May yours be the peace and gladness that alone in him is found."

Twenty-fifth Wedding Anniversary of Henry and Maria Wiebe
November 6, 1950
Recited by Justina and Melvin Epp

A quarter of a century you've walked life's way together,
Through joy and sorrow, loss and gain, and through all kinds of weather;
And as you've shared its pain and grief, as well as many a blessing,
You've found your gladness more complete, your sadness less distressing.
For love can tinge the darkest cloud with glints of heavenly sweetness,
And add to even our deepest joys a sense of rich completeness.
So on this silver wedding day life holds a fuller meaning
Than ever it did in bygone hours of wishful, empty dreaming.
Your Father's hand hath never failed in any time of trial,
And never when his help you've sought have you met stern denial.
Today with hearts still undismayed, you face the unknown morrow,
Strong in his might, and unafraid of turmoil, pain or sorrow.

Henry Wiebes' Fortieth Wedding Anniversary
October 29, 1965
Read by Frances Wiebe

Oft when we come to occasions, like the one we have today,
   It's hard to express our feelings or to know just what to say.
For many are the memories that are entering our mind,
   Of memorable experiences, that you two have left behind.

The Petals of a Kansas Sunflower

Now long ago, to both of you, are seeing your childhood days.
  Then slowly passed by months and years, with others planning your ways.
Then suddenly a change took place, just how, you never quite knew,
  But mutual was the attraction as both of you older grew.
It was on a Sunday morning in the fall of twenty-five,
  A roadster was approaching to turn into the churchyard drive.
There was Dad in his best attire and Mom in a brown silk dress.
  They were thought a handsome couple for no one would dare say less.
For the 6th day of November the wedding date was set.
  For you a day of thanksgiving that you never will forget.
The ceremony was at the church, the reception at the home
  In a clean and garnished hayloft where children could freely roam.
That morning dawned somewhat dreary, soon the sky was overcast.
  The rain held off for a while yet. But it started in at last
As lines of cars were coming from the church onto the place.
  Boards then were laid for sidewalks, a need that they had to face.
All evening lasted the downpour, beating on the barn roof loud,
  Where for the wedding reception then assembled was the crowd.

The house you moved to was not new. Yet to you it became dear.
  There together as a family we've spent many a happy year.
Months and years have passed by swiftly, there was always much to do.
  And for your life changed its aspect as four children joined you two.
You were called to walk dark valleys, when the death angel came in,
  And God in his sovereign wisdom took one up to be with him,
Life for you since then seemed different as this vacancy was there,
  But the one that never leaves you, kept you in his special care.
Forty years you now have journeyed, side by side, on life's pathway.
  Parents, brothers and two sisters left you since your wedding day.
We could mention many changes even in the family,
  Where two daughters now have joined you and the grandchildren we see.
Now the old house too has vanished with a new one in its place.
  And the woodstove and the oil-lamps also vanished in this case.
Let us look a little further in the area round about,
  Three new schools have been erected. Consolidation was worked out.
The present church and its addition and the parsonage as well,
  All were built since you were married. There was progress, we can tell.
Also in the line of farming what a progress there we see!
  Everywhere more speed and power for greater efficiency.
Over the whole globe are scattered our young people nowadays.
  Education, special service, and the like, calls them away.
And on you, our precious parents, years have left their marks of care.
  You would probably not admit it, yet we find them to be there.
And if now of late, dear Mother, you can scarcely get around,

Yet your hands can still be busy many things to do you've found.
Now I'm wishing you God's blessing as I bring this to a close.

I might, from here on, continue in ten years from now, who knows?
Until then may God's own presence lead you on to higher ground.

May yours be the peace and gladness that alone in him is found.

The next silver wedding anniversary poem is one of praise to God and thankfulness for his guidance and gracious care for twenty-five years. "Our celebrated pair is now / Gifted grace from the Lord."

There were no notes on the sheet of paper with this poem other than the title, a date, and that it was presented by a great-niece, Velma Busenitz. My parents, John and Marie (Harder) Epp, celebrated their twentieth wedding anniversary on April 8, 1952, so by deduction, this poem was presented that day at the reception following the evening church service. The poem is in German, and by 1952 most of her writings were in English.

The wedding date was actually April 21, 1927, but April 8 was chosen to coincide with school breaks for the children away at college. Approximately three hundred people were invited to the celebration. Included in the guest list were persons to whom my parents wanted to express appreciation for their help with the recovery effort following the tornado ten years earlier. There was a formal evening church service with scripture reading, prayers, a sermon, special music, and the singing of hymns. The special music was a male quartet singing the hymn, "My God and I," which was my mother's favorite hymn. This hymn was sung again at their fiftieth wedding anniversary and also at my mother's memorial service, but by that time, as we will see in chapter 22, she had written her own second and third stanzas.

A reception followed in the church basement with tables for the old people. Those who did not consider themselves old ate a lap supper. The menu consisted of sliced ham and cheese on homemade buns with a home-cured pickle on the side. I have no recollections of what the side dishes were but they probably included orange Jell-O with shredded carrots and pineapple tidbits, a dish that Mother favored. The crowning touch was the cherry tarts accompanied by a paper wrapped block of ice cream. Prior to the event, Mother, with the help of her niece Lydia, had baked from scratch about four hundred three-inch tart shells. On the day of the celebration these were carefully stacked in boxes and taken to the church where they were filled with cherry pie filling. Some tart shells were left over, so I continued to enjoy the celebratory event over the next several weeks.

The Petals of a Kansas Sunflower

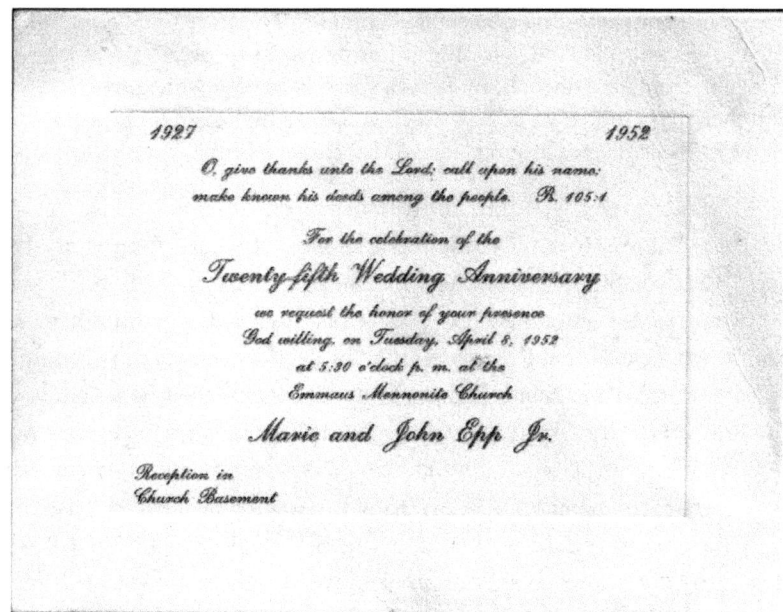

Figure 23
Twenty-fifth wedding anniversary celebration invitation of John and Marie Harder Epp for April 8, 1952. Source: Author's file.

Figure 24
Twenty-fifth wedding anniversary portrait of the John and Marie Harder Epp family. Back row L to R, Melvin, Phebe Ann, Albert, John Edwin, Frieda, Justina. Front row L to R, Hildegard, Mother, Father, Martha. Woodall, Newton, KS. Source: Author's file.

Celebration of Sustained Bonding

This poem was presented in German to reflect my parents' familiarity, comfort, and enjoyment of that language. The evening church service that preceded the reception and post-dinner program were in English to reflect the times.

Silberhochzeitsgedicht
8 April 1952
von Velma Busenitz vorgetragen

1.
Lieblich aus dem Alltagsleben
Hebt sich heut ein schöner Tag,
Manch Gebet wird sich erheben
Manch ein stiller dank wird wach.
Fünf und zwanzig Ehejahre—
Welche Zeit wenn man's bedenkt!—
Sind nun unserem Jubelpaare
Gnädig von dem Herrn geschenkt.
Einst vor fünfundzwanzig Jahren
Stiess das Schifflein von dem Strand—
Was habt Ihr denn stets erfahren?
Wars nicht Gottes treue Hand?
2.
Rückwärts schaut Ihr auf die Pfade
Wie der Herr Euch sanft geführt,
Rühmet nur von seiner Gnade,
Der Euch Euren Gang regiert;
Manche Freud durft Euch erblühen,
Manches Glück hat Euch gelacht
Segen von des Lebens Mühen
Heut wird lobend des gedacht.
Und wenn von des Lebensstürmen
Euer Schifflein wurd erfasst—
Fandet unter Gottes Schirmen
Ihr bei Ihm nicht sicher Rast?
3.
Mancher ist schon abgerufen
Aus der einst'gen Festesschar,
Der den Gruß Euch zugerufen
Euch dem neu verbundnen Paar.
Der vor fünfundzwanzig Jahren

The Petals of a Kansas Sunflower

Liebend Euch noch angeblickt
Jetzt schon lange heimgefahren,
Dieser Erde nun entrückt.
Ob sie kürzlich erst von hinnen,
Ob ihr Rasen lang schon grün—
Laßt Ihr nicht vor Euren Sinnen
Heut ihr Bild vorüberziehen?
4.
Kindeslieb darf Euch umgeben
Freunde stehen um Euch heut!—
Schöner Tag in Eurem Leben!
Ganz dem Lob und dank geweiht.
Ziehet denn in Gottes Namen
Rüstig weiter Eure Bahn,
Saget jetzt und allzeit; "Amen,
Grosses hat der Herr getan."
Bis Euch einst der Herr wird rufen
Selig zu Ihm heimzugeh'n
Was wird's sein an seinen Stufen
Gott im lichten Glanz zuseh'n.

Silver Wedding Anniversary Poem
April 8, 1952
Presented by Velma Busenitz

1.
Delight in everyday life
A wonderful day has arisen for you,
Many prayers have been raised up
Many a silent "thank you" has been awakened
Twenty-five married years
During which time when one remembers:
Our celebrated pair is now
Gifted grace from the Lord.
Once twenty-five years ago, you
Shoved the little vessel from the shore—
What have you learned constantly?
Was it not God's faithful hand?
2.
You looked backwards on the pathway
As the Lord gently led you
Glorified only by his grace

Celebration of Sustained Bonding

By which he completely governed you.
You thrived through some joy,
Some good fortune made you laugh,
Blessings from the troubles of life,
Today the thought is one of praise.
And when during the storms of life
Your little vessel was engulfed
You found protection with God.
Did you not securely rest through him?
3.
Some have already been called away
Those that were in the original group of celebrants
Who greeted you as you recall.
You, the newly united couple
Where twenty-five years ago
Your affection for each other was visible.
Now gone home a long time already
Now removed from this earth
But they just recently have gone
But their sward is already green for a long time—
Do you not let their reflections
In your mind's images march past you today?
4.
You are surrounded by filial love
Friends stand around you today!—
A very nice day in your lives!
Complete with praise and trumpets of thanks.
Draw then on God's name
Vigorously on your continued pathway.
Say now and at all times; "Amen,
Great things the Lord has done."
Until the time that the Lord calls you
Blissfully to go home to him,
Which will be at his bidding,
To look upon God in clear splendor.

When my oldest sister's parents-in-law celebrated their twenty-fifth wedding anniversary, they asked Mother for a poem. Mother gathered a lot of facts and began this poem describing a simpler time of Model T Fords and reading books on porch swings. Although the Alvin Goossens grew up and were married thirty-five miles northwest of us in the Alexanderwohl Mennonite Church community, as a young couple they moved to Colby in western Kansas to farm. This poem chronicles the family and their activities.

The Petals of a Kansas Sunflower

Hitherto the Lord Has Helped Us
For Alvin Goossen's Silver Wedding Anniversary
October 3, 1954
Read by Hildegard Epp Goossen

On this very special occasion, it should be only fair
   That we shall think of former years and see what happened there.
There are instances I shall relate, they are history today;
   Yet they lead to this occasion in a very unique way.

Let's start way back in 1926 on the eighteenth of July,
   God led from there on graciously, as no one would deny.
Southwest of Hillsboro that day, a young man in deep thought
   Was seemingly not satisfied, there was something that he sought.
In a Model T he started off. No one knew where he went;
   But he was looking forward to, —where the evening he would spend.
On a farm northwest of Hillsboro, he found upon approach
   A lovely lady young and fair, who sat reading on the porch;
The storybook was laid aside. In fellowship the time went by
   And he had found companionship that nine brothers couldn't supply.
Between these two something took place that no one can explain;
   But it led to an engagement day, then the evidence was plain.
Much prayer, however, went before, God's will they sought to do.
   He answered, led, and guided the decisions of these two.
Many happy memories are lingering with them still
   Of hours spent together and probably always will.
There are memories of planning, the future seemed so bright,
   Responsibilities and duties at that time seemed but light.
There are memories of how one day while going for a walk
   The seventeen-year locusts buzzed so loud they out-sounded every talk.
They may recall experiences that even weren't nice;
   But to the common routine of life, they add a little spice.
Quite absorbed in themselves, one day, as young people sometimes are
   They lost as they were traveling, a wheel from their car.

On October 4th in 1929 their wishes came all their way
   When their hands and hearts were united on this their wedding day.
The Alexanderwohl Mennonite Church was the scene of this great event.
   The church where oft' Sunday mornings, in worship they had spent.
The Reverend P. H. Unruh, the elder at that time
   Performed the wedding ceremony on this day for them sublime.
The text he chose from Isaiah, chapter 54, verse 10.
   Through the years this proved more precious than it seemed even then:

Celebration of Sustained Bonding

The promise of God's presence, though mountains be removed;
  That in mercy he'd look on them and faithful God has proved.
Parents, friends, and relatives came this event with them to share,
  Many prayers of good wishes for the two were offered there,
The hope of this young couple was high, their aim was one.
  They went to western Kansas there a new home they begun.
Northwest of Monument, Kansas, a little western town
  It was there they started farming and soon were settled down.
Together they shared experiences and blessings from on high;
  Both materially and spiritually as the dear Lord would supply.
A special high point came to them, on a cool November day;
  God entrusted them with a baby boy, who came with them to stay.
The following year God blessed again with a baby girl, who joined the three
  The family then seemed quite complete as far as they could see.
It would be difficult to find a sister and a brother
  Who have so much in common now as these had with each other.
Almost unnoticed years went by, God always saw them through
  He blessed with "rain and sunshine" as he alone can do.
Not always rosy was the path, there were steep and thorny places,
  Where God's ways to them were mystery and care showed in their faces.
1935 was such a year, then prices were but low
  And the high winds that swept the plains caused destructive dust to blow
Then as though this wasn't enough, —For God has wondrous ways
  The mother of the home took sick—was hospitalized thirty-one days.
There was serious surgery to go through, —it was a trying year;
  Again God's grace proved sufficient through all suspense and fear.
But just as after storm clouds the sun again appeared,
  So after trials and hardships again were better years.
As days and month again went by, there came a day of joy
  When to the family circle, God added a baby boy.
There was another day outstanding, that come a few years hence
  When a nice farm could be bought and home sweet home it's ever since.
But here too was no exception to the common course of life
  That after times of blessing come testings, trials and strife.
So when a little baby girl was entrusted to their care;
  For her life she had to struggle, for sickness was her share.
In answer to much prayer it was and the dear Lord's healing hand,
  That after seven weeks at the hospital, she joined the family band.
Life here has not at any length, gone on in the same routine,
  For joy would alternate with care, through the years that they have seen;
But through it all they felt God's love, he was their strength and guide
  Throughout the years that came and went, whatever would betide.
He led them on to pastures green; to the waters still and clear
  And on the stormy sea of life; "It is I," his voice they'd hear.

The Petals of a Kansas Sunflower

Their interests, however, go beyond their family and the home.
   They turn their eyes to foreign lands where refugees still roam.
And many are the parcels they have packed and sent abroad
   To clothe their needy brethren, to strengthen their faith in God.
In the year of 1947, they could lend a helping hand
   In bringing three young people across to this our blessed land,
These went to the State of Washington, where at present they are living.
   So in recent years there was a chance for oft and repeated giving;
Not only of material means but of time and interest we see
   And especially dear to their hearts is the work of the Gideons and MCC
In the activities of church and community, they take an active part
   And through the years endeared themselves to many a human heart.
They like to attend conferences and in traveling they find joy;
   Therefore for lasting memories, their movie camera they employ,
The many friends that visit and go in and out their door
   Have because of these pictures enjoyed it all the more.
Another one we could mention who of the family is a part;
   A daughter that came by marriage into their home and heart.
And later yet in the course of time, a grandchild came, a boy
   Thankful the grandparents claimed him and were overwhelmed with joy.

∽

Dear Parents, on this Silver Wedding day, your hearts are full of praise
   For they are filled with gratitude, you marvel at God's ways.
This is the day the Lord hath made, rejoice and be of cheer.
   This is the thought that is ringing in your heart sweet and clear
And as today you celebrate with friends from far and near
   You notice that some are missing that years ago were dear
Some of those that were present at your first wedding day
   Are gone, they were called to glory, for their eternal stay.
Today a younger generation is present in their stead.
   Still we see that God is gracious and wonderful he led
That Mother, you have your parents still with you this day
   For which our hearts are thankful in a very special way.
Today too you are thankful that your children love the Lord.
   In studying Paul is preparing for the ministry of his word.
Also Susie is preparing, mission work is on her heart,
   And Alva hopes that in God's work, he'll too, someday take part.
Your parental prayers for Elsie are that, she the place may fill,
   That God for her has chosen and be in the center of God's will.

∽

Celebration of Sustained Bonding

In closing we wish you God's blessing, may his presence with you abide
    That he may guard your footsteps and be your constant guide,
That he may direct in decisions, in the work of various kinds;
    That all you need and desire in him you ever find.
All our other wishes, we will just sum up in one
    That at the end of life's journey you will hear the Lord's, "Well done."

Alfred Regier requested a poem to celebrate his twenty-five years of marriage to Ione. Alfred was Mother's cousin and son of Johannes and Emilie Regier, whom we will meet in the next chapter. Ione was a public elementary school teacher at the one-room Pleasant Hill School located a mile west of the local church. Interestingly, Alfred was in the eighth-grade graduating class during Ione's first year of teaching there. She probably was the same age as Alfred since only a few hours of summer school instruction were necessary to get a teaching certificate in 1930. After Alfred completed his high school at Bethel Academy in North Newton, he came courting with exuberance. Every time he passed the school with car or wagons of hay, he would wave or honk the horn. Feeling guilty for being such a disturbance he stopped by to apologize. "He took again that road but stopped and on the schoolhouse door he knocked, / It was the first time that he knocked but not the last time that they talked. / We'll just pass by what then took place. It was the last year that she taught." They got married on Thanksgiving Day 1932. Since it was not proper for married women to teach school in the community during the 1930s, Ione gave up her position. They lived on a rented farm for the first several years. This was the time of the Great Depression when they got six cents per dozen of eggs and $5.25 per 100 weight for their fattened cattle in Kansas City.

The poem continues with a description of the family and family life. The tornado of June 8, 1941 did major damage to their farm, "Yet all members of the family were kept from serious harm." The family enjoyed traveling together. Mother reminds them of loved ones who have passed away, but here there is also joy expressed for the attendance of Ione's aged father and a little granddaughter at this anniversary celebration. The poem ends with a blessing that is repeated from the previous poem, but the meaningfulness remains since the repeated oral presentation of this blessing was separated by three hundred miles and three years of time, with no guests in common at these events.

The Petals of a Kansas Sunflower

Alfred Regiers' Silver Wedding
November 24, 1957

Today we have come together, in a very special way,
    To commemorate with these dear ones their anniversary day.
It is a day of thanksgiving for all that God has done;
    How he blessed and led and guided since this home was begun.
If over twenty-five years of married life, today they will take a look;
    Could they turn back the years like pages and read them in a book
They would find various experiences. Some already forgotten by now;
    Others are still vivid in memory; just like when they happened and how.

Let us go back even further, to their youth and childhood years,
    And see what helped and influenced in choosing their careers.
Both grew up in Christian homes, in church and Sunday-school.
    And this proved a special blessing as is the general rule.
Alfred was, as most here know, the fourth in a family of six
    And added to life's variation with his pranks and little tricks.
He wasn't to eat mulberries when little sister would see,
    But not long afterwards, the two were in the mulberry tree;
And when reproved he smugly said, "Why mother, she never found out,
    I always told her to close her eyes when I put one in my mouth."
But his very first ambition was, raising livestock on the moon
    Who knows it may yet happen and happen pretty soon.
Ione claims Oklahoma as the state where she first saw light;
    But two years later the family found that Kansas was all right.
At Burns, Kansas lived the one, near the Emmaus church the other,
    They grew to man and womanhood not knowing of each other.
Through the years she acquired training because teaching was her aim.
    This community later was happy among its teachers her to claim.
The Pleasant Hill board soon realized that in her a pearl they had found.
    With her pleasant and efficient way she was satisfactory all around.
Year after year she was hired back, their youngsters knowledge to impart;
    And through the years endeared herself to many a pupil's heart.
Maybe it's not out of place should I right here relate
    That, Alfred himself was among the first of her eighth-grade graduates.
On his father's farm Alfred worked, following his graduation
    From Bethel Academy, where he had gone for his high school education.
There was much work and one job was hauling the straw his Dad had bought;
    And with every load he'd pass the school in which Ione then taught.
A strange attraction had that school. He waved to the children that would look
    Or honked at them when in the car, every time that road he took.

Celebration of Sustained Bonding

That the teacher must be displeased with such interruptions, he could see.
  Therefore in this case the proper thing apologizing seemed to be.
He took again that road but stopped and on the schoolhouse door he knocked,
  It was the first time that he knocked but not the last time that they talked.
We'll just pass by what then took place. It was the last year that she taught.
  The wedding bells in November rang, for they had found just what they sought
Since six weeks before his wedding, Alfred is warning boys who date:
  "Don't stay out in the evening and your coming home is late,
A special word of warning to those that take their girl home afar
  You could fall asleep while driving and wreck your precious car."

Till Thanksgiving day their ways were two, from then on they were one.
  It was a real day of thankfulness for all that God had done.
In the depth of the Depression they rented a farm, and together they ventured out
  On record they have low prices such as today we know nothing about;
Six cents for eggs per dozen, nine cents for cream they could glean,
  For two and a half they sold their hogs, which today seems pretty lean.
And for the fattened steers they sold, I say, "Believe it or not."
  They were pleased that at the Kansas City market, five and a quarter they brought.

Even though somewhat hard the beginning, the years came quickly and went;
  They left the farm they had rented on which four years they spent.
On his father's farm they made their home. Alfred was by him employed;
  A busy homemaker was Ione, successful in whatever she tried,
Motherly and content about her work in the daily routine, she was seen;
  Even after the scope somewhat enlarged and three little Regiers came on the scene,
They gave them the best of training that a Christian home can afford.
  Now they are all members of Emmaus and are going on with the Lord.

An RN. degree Louvina owns. A strange experience in training she had—
  While she was working on the floors, in the kitchen worked a 1W lad.
While she ministered to the sick and had dreams and wishes—
  He in the kitchen, was vegetable boy and was washing dishes
Shall we leave it at that, having the story short and sweet?
  Today we are happy, Herman Miller, in the Regier family to meet.

Fremont has his eyes on Africa, where already he has been;
  To a greater desire for service he was challenged by what he has seen.
To help the African natives along the agricultural line,
  To find what fits for soil and location so starvation to decline.
After two years in the Congo, lending to missionaries a helping hand,
  To his fiancée he was returning, who was waiting in this land.
Sara Mae wasn't idle during the time he was away,
  She received a diploma in nursing just before their wedding day.

The Petals of a Kansas Sunflower

Now together they are planning, their hopes and ambitions they share,
  And she proves an ample help to him, as together they prepare.
When they think of African people, it is their foremost desire indeed;
  To minister not only to their physical, but also their spiritual need.

Donice the third of the children, studies toward her Bachelors degree,
  And prepares to be a teacher just as her mother used to be.
She likes to work with children, to them her heart goes out in love
  Which is indeed a blessing and given from above.

We are coming back to the honored couple, to see how they have fared
  In the years when joy and sorrow they with each other shared.
Alfred worked for his father eight years as farmhand
  And was a willing and efficient helper whatever the demand.
Since his father's death in '46 he has been farming on his own
  And through the years good management in farming he has shown.
Four years he had registered Short Horns. But later all through the years
  He found it satisfactory to feed commercial steers.
Even though tonight some gray hair we detect, yet both are still young at heart
  And in the church and community both take an active part.
Eight years as 4H leaders is indeed a record rare,
  To which they gave considerable time with skill and special care.
Also in church and Sunday school, year after year they both have served;
  Of their efficiency along that line a mentioning here is well deserved.
Ione in teaching the young mother's class, has seen many a familiar face
  Of former pupils through the years, or the wife of them in many a case.
Then again as capable leader of the junior group in Christian Endeavor
  There too, children of former pupils, among the juniors would be.
But this is not all they are doing, through the week we see a different side.
  This is the third year Alfred drives the bus and Ione cooks at Country Side
Ione with her cooking ability has gained herself much fame
  And to her home, in bygone days, the threshers gladly came.
She fixed for them fried chicken like no one else they knew
  And she found much satisfaction in cooking for the crew.

A sad experience in '41 showed them, that God overruled and kept
  When through this community and over their home a destructive tornado swept.
Even though much property damage was noticed throughout the farm,
  Yet all members of the family were kept from serious harm.
And so in the different experiences, they found it all along
  That the grace of God is sufficient and in the night he gives a song.
Even though Ione had operations and others a broken bone
  Yet no serious extended illness, within the family was known.

Celebration of Sustained Bonding

A very nice variation in life's everyday routine
    Was for them a trip to Colorado and all that they have seen.
The whole family together enjoyed the trip and needed vacation
    And together they admired the beauty and vastness of creation.
Another trip also a high point, was the one five years ago.
    At that time Louvina was in Chicago; in VS. work, you know.
This trip took them through Montana, Colorado, and Yellowstone Park, to see
    The enjoyment that it brought to all, will ever a cherished memory be.
Therefore it is with thankful hearts, that they celebrate this day;
    They are acknowledging the grace of God that brought them all the way.
When they think back to those present at their first wedding day,
    They find many of them called to glory to their eternal stay.

We think of Alfred's parents, Ione's mother and many others today,
    But we also see a new and younger generation that's pretty well on the way
Ione is happy that on this day they have with them her aged father.
    We'll not neglect to mention here also, Nancy Lee, the little granddaughter.
As to the future, they here can claim, that God who even clothes the grass
    Of all the good things he has promised, none will fail, all come to pass.

In closing we wish them God's blessing, may his presence with them abide
    That he may guard their footsteps and be their constant guide;
That he may direct in decisions, in the work of various kinds;
    That all they need and desire in him they ever find.
All our other wishes, we will just sum up in one
    That at the end of life's journey they will hear the Lord's "Well done."

    From the composition of the next poem, it appears that one of the children presented it to their parents at the celebration of their twenty-fifth wedding anniversary. Emma, Mrs. Willie Busenitz, was Mother's cousin and here twenty-five years of family life are gently honored. "The lovely day you're celebrating / Is different from all other days; / Ascending are your many prayers / Of joy and gratitude and praise."

    After my mother passed away in 1998, I began to realize that Emma and her two sisters, Frieda and Paula Wiebe, reminded me more of Mother than anyone else in the community. Their actions, words, and thought processes were so similar to Mother's, and their eyes sparkled. Frieda Wiebe once shared a story with me that during the time period of 1910 to 1925, when Grandmother Harder and her daughters would come to Whitewater to shop, they would stop in at the Wiebe home for a visit before driving their horse and buggy the two miles back to the farm. After 1916, this trip was made with a newfangled automobile. The Wiebe girls enjoyed visiting

The Petals of a Kansas Sunflower

and playing with my mother, because she would always have verbal riddles for them to solve.

Willie Busenitz Silver Wedding Anniversary
May, 1959

The lovely day you're celebrating
   Is different from all other days;
Ascending are your many prayers
   Of joy and gratitude and praise.
Now twenty-five years you are married
   Oh, how long that seems to me.
But in this our precious parents,
   The love of God you clearly see.
It's twenty-five years, since together
   In your little boat you left the shore;
Wasn't God's grace ever with you?
   Would you ever ask for more?

You look back along life's pathway
   Seeing that God leads and cares.
You will evermore be grateful
   How he overruled affairs.
Many joys and also sorrows,
   Success and failures, blessed your ways;
This is vivid in your memory
   As you think of bygone days.
Would on life's sea, tossed your vessel be,
   And winds would blow and hearts would quake;
Peace still was yours in the assurance
   That the Lord makes no mistake.

Loved ones that long have left you,
   Again today you seem to see.
Their words, their deeds, their faces
   Pass by in memory.
Your thoughts go back to childhood,
   How slow these years went by!
The winters cold, the summers hot,
   But now time seems to fly.
Your ways were two in those years;
   They crossed from time to time—

Till later they were united
   On a day for you sublime.

The farm that you moved to,
   Still is "Home Sweet Home" so dear.
And life was rich and meaningful
   As you toiled from year to year.
A group of healthy children
   Brought joy as well as care.
Today we all are with you
   This day with you to share.
We are wishing you God's blessing,
   May each day be filled with a song.
May the days the Lord still grants you
   Be many, happy and long.

That at the end of life's journey
   We all hear the Lord's "Well done."
And when we meet in glory
   There will not be missing a one.

The ebb and flow of life on a farm is chronicled in the next silver wedding anniversary poem written for one of Mother's close friends. The farm was newly constructed for them when they married; they lost a daughter when she was four years old, and they survived the June 8, 1941 tornado—"Then in a night, in minutes' time, / Demolished lay the farm. / It seemed in vain you'd labored there, / Yet to you there came no harm. / And through this all you will agree— / Life took on a fuller meaning. / You valued more each other's love." They were also very active in church work.

Gus and Edna Regier's Silver Wedding Anniversary
September 12, 1960

Can it be it's Silver Wedding
   For the two of you today?
And you came to this rare milestone
   As you journeyed on your way?
Five and twenty years passed swiftly
   As you traveled side by side.
Your experiences were many
   On life's ocean ebb and tide.

The Petals of a Kansas Sunflower

Calm seemed to be the ocean;
   And the sky was fair and blue
As your vessel left the harbor—
   Life seemed perfect then to you.
With the bloom of youth still on you,
   You had joined your hands and hearts;
Nothing really seemed to matter,
   Each of the other was a part.
To the farm, just then erected,
   You moved as husband and wife
And there you shared, through all these years,
   The experiences of life.
Many were the happy hours
   And the days that you could share,
But also hardships and some trials,
   You were called upon to bear.
For in the line of farming
   There are ups and downs to face,
Which through the years sufficiently,
   You found to be the case.
There were years of ease and plenty
   With new blessings every day,
Then years of drought and hardships
   With low prices all the way.
There were days that weren't pleasant
   With things hard to understand,
But still they were a blessing
   You took them from God's hand.
You stood one day with aching heart
   Beside a little grave;
God claimed again the little jewel
   That years earlier he gave.
Then in a night, in minutes' time,
   Demolished lay the farm.
It seemed in vain you'd labored there,
   Yet to you there came no harm.
And through this all you will agree—
   Life took on a fuller meaning,
You valued more each other's love,
   As on God you two were leaning.
Because of this you are assured
   God is still on the throne;
He never left nor forsook you;
   He is still caring for his own.

Celebration of Sustained Bonding

In C.E.F. and Sunday school
   You long took active part,
And through the years imparted truths
   To many a seeking heart.
Eternity will once reveal
   The souls that you can claim,
That stand with you before the throne,
   Redeemed in Jesus' name.
And mother's mind isn't idle,
   While her hands may busy be—
Long chapters of the Bible
   She has committed to memory.

Now after a quarter of a century
   That you have sailed together
In rain and sunshine, calm and storm,
   And in all kinds of weather,
Wonderful you find God's leading,
   Wonderful his love and care,
Wonderful the rich experiences
   That together you could share.
As you now resume your voyage,
   I'm wishing you Godspeed;
With the Lord still as your pilot,
   You should never suffer need.

The next poem was written for friends in the community and presented by one of their sons. Elvira (Regier) Klaassen was a sister to Gus Regier of the previous poem. "The purpose for this gathering, is to praise the Lord on high / For the years you had together, which unnoticed have gone by. / A quarter of a century, how long when still ahead; / But when it's passed it seems but brief, we've often heard it said. / Yes, the time has slipped by swiftly, months and years have come and gone. / And today you ask the question, 'Can it really be that long?'"

In this poem and in three subsequent ones in this chapter and two more times in the next chapter, the following lines are used: ". . . of your courtship now long past. / And to this there was the climax when the wedding came at last." Courtship, as Mother experienced it, was indeed a big event. Her courtship began when John Epp Sr. came to the Harder farm and asked Grandmother Harder for the hand of Marie in marriage for his son John. Mother's positive response put into action a sequence of activity. This included the preacher's announcement of the engagement from the pulpit followed with the engagement Sunday dinner, discussions of the arrangements for Father to move in with Mother and Grandmother and to operate the farm after the wedding, visits by Father to learn to know Mother as a life companion, numerous dinner invitations by relatives in the community to honor the newly engaged couple, planning the wedding with the cleaning out and decorating of a farm building, cutting by hand the grass and weeds from the farm yard, preparation of adequate food for three hundred people that probably included special butchering of an extra hog or steer, organizing relatives to help with food preparation and service at the reception, a photo shoot at a photographer in town, and more. After the wedding, there was the cleanup that included returning all the borrowed chairs and tables, removing the decorations and lanterns from the site, preservation of the leftover food, and bidding farewell to the overnight guests. Several days after the wedding all the people that helped to set up, clean up, and prepare and serve the food were invited back for an appreciation supper to eat the leftover food. By this time the tablecloths were washed, ironed, and stored, and the couple could move in together and get on with life and work together. Is it any wonder that the wedding seemed like a climax, and married life as a return to a relaxed life style?

Herman and Elvira Klaassen's Twenty-fifth Wedding Anniversary
November 19, 1963

Silver sprays and silver garlands decorate this special day.
    With a festive air pervading everything seems in array.
Friends and relatives assembled here with you to celebrate.
    Many plans and preparations for this day, you've made of late.
And the purpose for this gathering, is to praise the Lord on high
    For the years you had together, which unnoticed have gone by.
A quarter of a century, how long when still ahead;
    But when it's passed it seems but brief, we've often heard it said.
Yes, the time has slipped by swiftly; months and years have come and gone.
    And today you ask the question, "Can it really be that long?"
Many memories you cherish, of your courtship now long past.
    And to this there was the climax when the wedding came at last.
In the prime of life you promised loyal you would be and true
    And your love for one another never failed but rather grew.
Many were the happy hours and the days that you could share,

Celebration of Sustained Bonding

But some hardships and some trials you were called upon to bear.
So, even in everyday living there were ups and downs to face,
    Which through the years sufficiently you've found to be the case.
The first few years brought many a change when you often moved around,
    Near Brainerd, Walton and Burns, during those years you were found.
And now you're settled near Newton. The Lord has blessed your days;
    He has given you the best of health and prospered all your ways.
That we boys express our gratitude, to me, seems only fair—
    At whatever hour we'd come home, that Mother was always there.
In closing we say: "Best Wishes on your anniversary day."
    With all its pleasant memories of the years gone on their way.
May it prove a day of happiness, of special joy and pleasure,
    And may God's blessing give to you good things in fullest measure.

This is another poem for dear friends within the community. Elma was also Mother's cousin.

Elma (Regier) Busenitz together with Martha Thiessen were my first Sunday school teachers when I was four years old. Each Christmas, I get out the fold-out Christmas card of the nativity scene these two teachers gave me.

Edgar Busenitzs' Silver Wedding Anniversary
March 1, 1963
Presented by Viola Klingenburg

Today we have come together in a very special way,
    To commemorate with these dear ones their anniversary day.
It is a day of thanksgiving for all that God has done—
    How he blessed and led and guided since this home was begun.
If over the last twenty-five years today you will take a look,
    Could you turn back the years like pages and read them in a book?
There, you would find experiences, some already forgotten by now,
    Others still vivid in memory, just like when they happened and how.
In both of your family circles some loved ones have bid "adieu."
    They have gone before to glory and are waiting there for you.
In C.E.F. and Sunday school you long took active part
    And through the years imparted truths to many a seeking heart.
Eternity will once reveal the souls that you can claim
    Standing with you before the throne, redeemed in Jesus' name.
Through the years your home was open in kind hospitality.
    Some stayed a day, some longer, what'er the circumstance would be.

The Petals of a Kansas Sunflower

As you look back over the years some changes you can trace,
   And you don't need to go too far, it's right on the home place.
You stepped aside now, as it were, and a new house there we see;
   And your children and grandchildren are where you used to be.
For you life seemed an upward trend, through the years that have gone by.
   Soon a declining you may note that you wouldn't dare deny.
In closing we wish you God's blessing, may his presence with you abide;
   That he may guard your footsteps and be your constant guide,
That he may direct in decisions, in the work of various kind,
   That all you need and desire in him you ever find.
And all our other wishes we are summing up in one
   That at the end of life's journey you will hear the Lord's, "Well done."

Mother wrote two poems for Albert and Bertha Busenitz to celebrate their wedding in 1938; these are presented in the previous chapter. Twenty-five years later she honored them with a poem for their twenty-fifth wedding anniversary. "Many memories you cherish of your courtship now long past / And to this there was the climax when the wedding came at last. / In the prime of life you promised loyal you would be and true, / And your love for one another never failed but rather grew."

For Albert Busenitzs' Twenty-fifth Wedding Anniversary
March 16, 1963

Hitherto the Lord has helped you; hitherto the Lord has led.
   Graciously he has provided, by his hand you have been fed.
Constantly he was beside you in the cares and joys and fears.
   And today you can't but praise him, thinking over twenty-five years.
Yes, the time has slipped by swiftly. Months and years have come and gone.
   And today you ask the question, can it really be that long?
Many memories you cherish of your courtship now long past
   And to this there was the climax when the wedding came at last.
In the prime of life you promised loyal you would be and true,
   And your love for one another never failed but rather grew.
Many were the happy hours and the days that you could share,
   But also hardships and some trials you were called upon to bear.
Also in the line of farming, there are ups and downs to face.
   Which through the years sufficiently you found to be the case.

There were years of ease and plenty with new blessings every day.
   Then years of drought and hardships with low prices all the way.

Celebration of Sustained Bonding

There were days that weren't pleasant with things hard to understand.
  But still they were a blessing; you took them from God's hand.
At the time your family started, a double blessing came.
  The others followed one by one, all precious just the same.
Why childhood days went by so fast you never understood.
  Today some have already grown to man and womanhood.
So now the next generation already is present here.
  Together with many others that are close to you and dear.
In closing we say "Best Wishes" on your anniversary day.
  With all its pleasant memories of the years gone on their way.
May it prove a day of happiness, of special joy and pleasure.
  And may God's blessing give to you good things in fullest measure.

Waldo Harder was the son of Mother's cousin and grew up on a farm near Newton. My parents followed Waldo's career with interest because he began as a missionary to Native Americans in Arizona and then joined the Berean Academy staff as superintendent in 1946, where he worked closely with my father. Subsequently, Waldo left Berean for the mission field in the Congo and with time moved into the presidency of Grace Bible Institute (Grace University), Omaha, Nebraska. Since the Harders knew Mother very well, Waldo requested a poem for their twenty-fifth wedding anniversary.

Waldo Harders' Twenty-fifth Wedding Anniversary
August 28, 1965

Hitherto the Lord has helped you; hitherto the Lord has led.
  Graciously he has provided as life's pathway you tread.
Constantly he was beside you in the cares and joys and fears
  And today you can't but praise him, thinking over twenty-five years.
Yes, the time has slipped by swiftly. Months and years have come and gone.
  And today you ask the question, "Can it really be that long?"
Many memories you cherish of your courtship now long past
  And to this there was the climax when the wedding came at last.
In the prime of life you promised loyal you would be and true,
  And your love for one another never failed but rather grew.
Many were the happy hours and the days that you could share,
  But also hardships and some trials you were called upon to bear.
If over these twenty-five years today you could take a look,
  Could you turn back the years like pages and read them in a book?

The Petals of a Kansas Sunflower

There you would find experiences, some already forgotten by now.
    Others still vivid in memory, just like when they happened and how.
On farms not far from each other you spent your childhood days,
    The youngest in both families, —You chose to join your ways.
In early married life you felt that God was calling you.
    In the vineyard of our master there was work for you to do.
To the Arizona Mission field you gladly heeded the call,
    But you later came to Berean—in '46 in fall.
You gave your best to help along, this too is widely known.
    From Berean's small beginning it steadily has grown.
As you challenged the students to give to God their all,
    It seemed as though more vividly you again heard his call.
You pulled your stakes, as it were, and to the Congo you went
    Where together as a family many blessed years we spent.
Because of failing health it was that to the states you came
    And little did you realize that you would here remain.
It was to Grace's presidency that the Lord was calling you.
    Your faithfulness found its reward in greater work to do.
Once more we shall but briefly, glance over the years gone by
    Blessed and rich in experience, which you will verify.
God blessed your home with children, which brought both joy and care.
    Today we are here with you this special day to share.
One thing is quite outstanding and of interest to me
    That in different states, even continents, we joined the family.
In both your family circles some loved one bid "adieu."
    They have gone before to glory and are waiting there for you.
Sad were the days when God reached down and picked two little flowers
    That you thought he was giving you; but in those crucial hours
He took them up to higher ground, free from all sin and care,
    To blossom forth to God's own praise, most beautiful and fair.
How nice that both your mothers are present with you here
    Together with many others who came from far and near.
In closing I say, "Best Wishes, on your anniversary day,"
    With all its pleasant memories of years gone on their way.
May it prove a day of happiness of special joy and pleasure.
    And may God's blessing give to you good things in fullest measure.

—M.H.E.

For Father's niece Emilie Ruth and her husband Ben, Mother wrote this poem.

Celebration of Sustained Bonding

B. E. Busenitz Silver Wedding Anniversary
December 30, 1965
Recited by Phyllis & Judy Busenitz

Can it be it's Silver Wedding
    For the two of you today?
And you came to this rare milestone
    As you journeyed on your way?
Five and twenty years passed swiftly
    As you traveled side by side.
Your experiences were many
    On life's ocean ebb and tide.
Calm seemed to be the ocean;
    And the sky was fair and blue
As your vessel left the harbor—
    Life seem perfect then to you.
With the bloom of youth still on you,
    You had joined your hands and hearts.
Nothing really seemed to matter,
    Each of the other was a part.

Now after a quarter of a century
    That you have sailed together
In rain and sunshine, calm and storm,
    And in all kinds of weather,
Wonderful you find God's leading,
    Wonderful his love and care,
Wonderful the rich experiences
    That together you could share.
As you now resume your voyage,
    I'm wishing you God's best.
With the Lord still as your pilot,
    You should never be distressed.

—M.H.E.

Mother uses a new analogy for marriage and the family in this next poem. "The home is woven of fine threads / Much like an oriole's nest." "A child's bright eyes and happy smile" erase the stress of problems. "If God's abiding presence / Is hovering over it all, / The home will then fare safely."

The Petals of a Kansas Sunflower

Willard Thiessen Silver Wedding Anniversary
March 12, 1972

The Home

The home is woven of fine threads
    Much like an oriole's nest,
Where intelligence and unity
    Provide comfort, joy and rest.

It takes skill and ingenuity
    With patience, love and care
To weave the home-life carefully
    In which all family members share.

The Father's wise and thoughtful words
    Build the framework of the nest;
And Mother in her tender ways
    Is responsible for the rest.

And should they encounter problems,
    Even difficulties face,
A child's bright eyes and happy smile,
    These shadows help erase.

If God's abiding presence
    Is hovering over it all,
The home will then fare safely
    Whatever may befall.

—M.H.E.

Melvin Claassen, a cousin within the community, left farming for missionary work in Zaire. Mother chronicles the career and experiences of the family. This poem was read by one of their children and ends with the blessing "May the Lord bless and keep you and lead you on from here / That together as a family we yet have many a blessed year."

Celebration of Sustained Bonding

Melvin Claassens' Silver Wedding
August 14, 1977

Hitherto the Lord has helped you, hitherto the Lord has led.
   Graciously he has provided as life's pathway you have tread.
Constantly he was beside you in the cares and joys and fears,
   Today you can't but praise him, thinking over twenty-five years.
Yes, the time has slipped by swiftly; months and years have come and gone.
   So today you ask the question, "Can it really be that long?"
Many memories you cherish of your courtship, now long past.
   To this there was the climax when the wedding came at last.
In the prime of life you promised, loyal you would be and true.
   Your love for one another never failed but rather grew.
Many were the happy hours and the days that you could share,
   Also, hardships and some trials you were called upon to bear.
If over these twenty-five years, today you would take a look,
   If you turn back the years like pages and reread them as a book,
There you would find experiences, some already forgotten by now,
   Others still vivid in memory, just when they happened and how.

One of you lived in Mountain Lake—on the Kansas plains the other.
   You grew to man and womanhood not knowing of each other.
Mother with her teaching career, to Kansas felt led to go
   Where a handsome youth was farming, ten miles away, or so.
Many happy days soon followed—in meeting and in making plans.
   It seemed the mission field was beckoning to you with outstretched hands.
Daddy gave up farming and at G.B.I. enrolled.
   Receiving Bible training, for several years, I'm told.
Later the Lord led to Ithaca, for agricultural studies as well,
   This year proved very profitable, as I have heard you tell.
It prepared you for the mission field, to trust the Lord indeed,
   For has the Lord not promised that he will supply each need?
Then followed deputation, God provided without fail
   So that in March of '58 you were ready to set sail.
From New York you left by freighter—after saying the last "Good-bye,"
   To study French in Belgium—six months this would employ.
All this was complicated, since no longer you were just two,
   Vangie and Steve had joined you and were ages three and two.
You remember the frustrations, new language, new faces and all.
   So with anticipation you flew to Zaire that fall.
First impression of Kamayala lingers, the church steeple was first in view
   A beautiful station and dark, strange faces all looking alike to you.
But soon you loved these people, their welcome was warm and real.

The Petals of a Kansas Sunflower

    The Lord had called you to this work. This assurance you would feel.
Your first term, though enjoyable, came to a sudden brake
    When for political reasons you had to evacuate.
One year you spent in the homeland—a year at the "U" it was.
    You wondered at God's leading—why suddenly this pause?
When the request came to Daddy—the request to return alone
    The former Zaire Mission field was still in dangerous zone.
After nine months of separation, we joined Daddy in Zaire.
    In meantime James had joined us, his age was now one year.
You found neither peace nor safety, tribal conflicts still abound.
    So a safer place in the city for the women and children was found.
But to us another blessing came in April of '63
    When Ruthie joined the family—sweet, happy and carefree.
So with worries, work and blessings the years for you went by.
    You did your share of moving, which no one would deny.
And when because of unrest your moving was done by air,
    Some things you valued highly—you parted with right there,
Mother spent much time in teaching missionary children grades one to three.
    Also afternoon Bible and sewing classes, to women that were free.
Your work over the years has varied, it changed with every move.
    Along the agricultural line Daddy found much he could improve.
Then there was village evangelism and the work each day would bring.
    Jack-of-all-trades, we could call him, for many things depended on him.
Was it carpentry or mechanics or a new water system to be laid,
    Even a new airstrip came into being with axe, hoe, shovel and spade.
After the last furlough new doors opened as often is the rule,
    That of being houseparents to missionary children in school.
It was God's direct leading that to this work you could consent.
    This year proved one of the highlights that in mission work you spent.

We now have taken a backward look, gotten a bird's-eye view, as it were
    Of busy missionary life at home, as well as over there.
In loneliness and frustration, God proved faithful, kind and true.
    And times that seemed so difficult, turned into blessings for you.
The privilege of bringing to the benighted souls that grope—
    A life free of superstition and in death, eternal hope.
What joy it was when seeing a soul from sin set free
    And now on the way to heaven for all eternity.

May the Lord bless and keep you and lead you on from here
    That together as a family we yet have many a blessed year.

13

Celebration of the Golden Wedding Anniversary

A GOLDEN WEDDING ANNIVERSARY is still a very special event. When both spouses survive the fifty years, their children normally take on the responsibilities for the festivities within the local community.

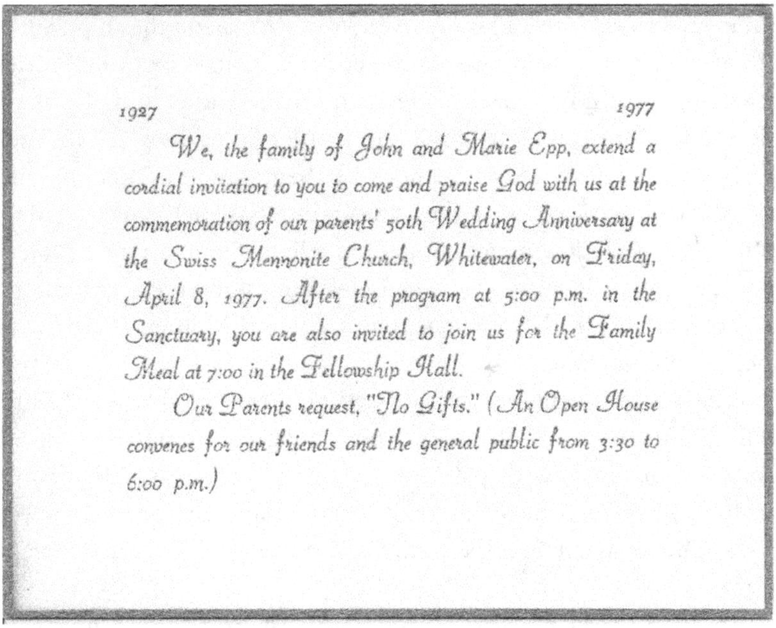

> 1927   1977
>
> We, the family of John and Marie Epp, extend a cordial invitation to you to come and praise God with us at the commemoration of our parents' 50th Wedding Anniversary at the Swiss Mennonite Church, Whitewater, on Friday, April 8, 1977. After the program at 5:00 p.m. in the Sanctuary, you are also invited to join us for the Family Meal at 7:00 in the Fellowship Hall.
>
> Our Parents request, "No Gifts." (An Open House convenes for our friends and the general public from 3:30 to 6:00 p.m.)

Figure 25
The golden wedding celebration invitation for John and Marie Harder Epp.
Source: Author's file.

The poems that Mother wrote for golden anniversaries are dated from 1933 to 1977, celebrating weddings that occurred fifty years earlier from 1883 to 1927. Life expectancies in the late 1800s and early 1900s make these events particularly noteworthy and very special. These poems are rich in descriptions of traditions and customs of an era that we presumptuously refer to as simpler. The poems tend to be lengthy, because Mother had so many things she wanted to review for each celebratory couple.

The poem entitled "For Uncle Gerhard Regiers' Golden Wedding" was presented on October 25, 1933. Gerhard Regier (1858–1935) was my mother's uncle by marriage to Catharine (1859–1938), my grandmother Harder's oldest sister. The presenter, Alma Regier, was their eldest granddaughter.

Gerhard was eighteen years old when he came to America in 1876 with his parents Gerhard (1822–1890) and Anna Ensz (1824–1904) Regier and seven, mostly younger, siblings. Gerhard was a large man, over six feet tall and at times exceeding three hundred pounds. The Regier family was one of the six original families that traveled together with my ancestral Harder family from West Prussia on the ship *SS Rhein* to New York and then directly to Halstead, Kansas by train "entirely because of faith and conscience / left friends and Fatherland." Gerhard's oldest sister, Marie, married Johannes Harder Sr. on May 26, 1876 just days before the newlyweds, together with their parents and siblings, immigrated to America. Due to the advance purchase of the tickets, Marie is still listed as "*Fräulein*" or young unmarried woman on the *SS Rhein's* passenger roster. Johannes was the oldest son of my great-grandfather Bernard Harder; in the next chapter is a poem Mother wrote for his ninetieth birthday.

The Regier family purchased Section 3, Milton Township, Butler County, three miles northeast of where my great-grandfather Harder purchased his land. Both patriarchs wanted high ground that would not flood since their farms in West Prussia had been prone to spring flooding being located on the lowlands between the Vistula and Nogat Rivers.

In 1883, Gerhard (Jr.) returned to West Prussia and married a childhood friend and cousin, Catharine Wiebe, on October 23 in her home in Gurken, near Heubuden. Two and a half weeks after their marriage, and with begrudging parental consent, the bridal pair initiated their journey to Kansas. The young couple lived with Gerhard's parents to help with the farm work because his father was ailing. At the same time they began construction of a new farm one mile north on the

Celebration of the Golden Wedding Anniversary

southeast quarter of Section 33, Fairmont Township and moved there on May 11, 1885. From the poem, "Then it happened, it really is true, / Grandfather, you accomplished / What you as a five-year-old already said / that you would like to build a house for grandmother." Apparently as children, playing together in West Prussia, Gerhard said to Catharine that someday he would build a house for her. This new farm fulfilled that promise. They were blessed with twelve children, eleven of whom lived to adulthood.

When the local church celebrated the one-hundredth anniversary of the arrival of the West Prussian Mennonites in America, they printed a history that included several talks given at the fiftieth celebration on July 5, 1926 by original members of the immigration group. Gerhard was asked in 1926 to reminisce about "Agriculture During Pioneer Days." I am going to share some of the passages he wrote, because the themes and activities complement the concepts that appear in Mother's poems.

> When our parents with children, relatives and friends, left the dear old home, they also left good economic conditions and moved to a country where these were unknown to them. In faith they went out and in the belief that it was God's will they established their farms here. In the past fifty years we have experienced that God has been with us and has blessed us beyond asking and comprehension—and for that we thank God!
>
> We arrived at Halstead, Kansas, on July 6, 1876, and from there did our land viewing, which resulted in our settling here in Butler County. We young people enjoyed all this. Whether the older people were always so happy about it is a question. But of my parents I cannot say that they ever regretted emigrating and settling here . . .
>
> After we had selected our land, we began working here in late August. Our first house was 8 x 16 feet. Six 2 x 4's eight feet long were set in the ground, then 1 by 6 boards were nailed on the sides, top and one end. The south end was left open for an entrance. Prairie hay was stacked over this frame, and the house was complete. With some hay inside for a bed, we slept as well as today on springs and mattresses.
>
> The land on which we settled is the section [one square mile or 640 acres] on which my brothers John and Gustav Regier now live. Here we spent the first night—my father, my two brothers and I.

The Petals of a Kansas Sunflower

After breakfast next morning, we prepared to look over our land. It seemed large to us, since in Germany such an area would have been occupied by ten or more families. It was rather foggy at first, and we could not see much; but the fog gradually disappeared. We had driven about half a mile when we saw two riders coming toward us. Horrors! They were naked, bows and arrows on their backs. We turned aside, they waved, we waved but kept driving sideways at a walk. They rode off, and we drove away. Later individual Indians passed by and stopped in, but were no longer a terror for us; nor did they ever trouble us . . .

Our time at first was taken up with hauling of stones and lumber. Of the buildings which were put up for the first six families, probably most are still standing . . . By Christmas all the families had moved in . . .

In May of this year [1877] our chief task was to bring the prairie under cultivation. This was not easy for us as new immigrants. We had to learn without teachers. We had to keep a hammer, a wrench and file always at hand. The plowshare would often get bent in cutting the tough prairie roots, and would need to be hammered straight again. The share had to be filed every round, and sharpened every half day.

The first wheat was sown in the fall of this year. Dairying and cattle raising had been started in spring. There was pasture enough, and we could make as much hay as we desired. It did not bring much, but it did not cost much. It gave us work, and that was good for us as new immigrants . . .

We lived economically, and money was not spent until it was on hand or until one was sure of it coming in. If one had to borrow, interest was two percent per month, equal to twenty-four percent per year. One had to figure carefully and either avoided borrowing or paid as soon as possible. The high rate of interest was a blessing for us so that we did not borrow recklessly, only to find ourselves unable to pay.

We used farm wagons to get to our meetings. Seats were made of planks laid on nail kegs, and we were just as happy as today in modern pews. Farm wagons took the place of modern automobiles, but they were somewhat slower. Economic conditions were very difficult at first. It took a long day to haul lumber from Newton or Peabody over the prairie roads. We had to learn patience. When we bought horses they did not understand our language and still less our whips. There were bridges only near the towns, and throwing down a few stones in the fords did not help much. Later there were small bridges and culverts. Then there generally was a mud hole on each side of the bridge. In July of 1877 I had to drive at night to summon a doctor, a round trip of thirty-eight miles across the prairie in five hours. That was a fast trip, and the horses were not overdriven . . .

I would like to say with regard to economic conditions: Ask Jesus to be with you, work and pray, plow under the morning dew, discriminate among those who come to collect money; then it will be well with our economic conditions, and we will continue to be able to help the needy.

Gerhard also wrote, "At that time, this region was literally a desert of high prairie grass. Only those who have experienced it know what it means to settle in a region of virgin prairie where there is no tree or houses." The first order of business after these pioneers purchased their land was to obtain building material to construct farm buildings. It took a long day to make a round-trip by horses and wagon to Peabody or Newton for supplies, which were fifteen and twenty miles away. Roads were non-graded paths through the grass and there were no bridges. Traveling at the rate of three to four miles per hour, with shopping time at the town of commerce, there was ample time for thunderstorms to occur after leaving home in the morning. The streams could flood, and in this poem, Mother mentions that going through streams with empty wagons was easy, but crossing a flooded stream with a wagon full of supplies created complications. Here the poem gives the example of the wagon driver carrying the whole load of supplies across the swollen stream one piece at a time, then driving the wagon through and reloading the wagon on the other side. This whole process was very time consuming.

The entire immigrant community became sensitized early to the dangers of crossing flooded creeks with supplies, when in May 1877 the two sons of the Rev. Peter Dyck family had a fatal accident. Peter (age twenty-two) and John (age twenty-three) went to El Dorado for another load of lumber. On their return trip they spent the night on a farm about ten miles from home because a thunderstorm passed through the area and lightning strikes had ignited prairie fires. Early the next morning they continued their homeward journey and had to cross the swollen Whitewater River at the ford about a mile southeast of the location of the former Plum Grove schoolhouse. Their wagon and load floated unmanageably and their screams were heard by a girl who was milking nearby, but help did not arrive in time. Both men drowned. The horses and wagon were found immediately, but the bodies of the two young men were found only two days later when the creek waters receded. On May 4, a funeral was held in the Dyck home and the two were laid to rest in a double grave on the open prairie on their parents' land. They were the first interments in what is now the Zion Mennonite Church Cemetery east of Elbing. The Peter Dycks and five of their children were among the first Prussian family immigrants who also came on the *SS Rhein*. The Dycks had purchased land six miles north of the Regier family and worshiped with the Emmaus Mennonite group until they formed their own Zion Mennonite Church group in the Elbing area in June 1883.

Mother continues the poem, "One experienced jointly pleasure and sorrow / And so fortunately year after year passed." Mentioned is the joy of having the noise of children in a home. With time the original home and barn were improved. Gerhard and his sons developed an award-winning dairy herd of Holstein Friesian cattle. One year at the Kansas Live Stock Show in Wichita, their four-year-old Regier Woodcraft Sadie 1024996 was named senior champion and grand champion winning over five of the leading show herds in the United States. The farm also developed systems for water and electricity utilization. Mother refers to this couple as leaders of the community. It is related that Gerhard also was influential in getting the cedar trees planted around the church and in rows through the parking lot. Mother then, in a general way, reviews their lives and points out that in 1933 their children and grandchildren numbered forty-five. The poem ends with the benediction that you "want the Lord your God as he has until now / To remain with you with his grace / As he promised forever and ever: / I will carry you into old age / And until you have become gray / I will constantly be your support / For every moment that you live."

Celebration of the Golden Wedding Anniversary

Zu Onkel Gerhard Regiers Goldenehochzeit
25 Oktober 1933
von Alma Regier vorgetragen

Liebe Großeltern zum Feste
　Wünsch' ich Gottes Segen Ihnen
Heut da so viel liebe Gäste
　Hier nun sind um ihn erscheinen.
An einem frohen Tag wie diesen
　Wo nach fünfzig lange Jahr
In den sich Gott stets treu erwiesen
　Liebend, segend mit ihnen war.
Und durch Gottes gnädiger Führung
　Dies goldene Fest sie feiere heut
Weilten die Gedanken wohl mit Rührung
　Auf die schon durch lebte Zeit.
In Deutschland sie zur großen Freude
　Einst das Licht der Welt erblickten
Und von klein an alle beide
　Der Urgroßeltern Herz beglückten.
Doch früh schon mussten sie erfahren
　Großmama der Trennung wehen
Denn es nicht als sie erst 5 Jahren
　Die liebe Mutter von ihnen gehe.
Drei noch jüngen Geschwister blieben
　Mutterlos zurück mit Ihnen dann
Doch die vielen Verwandten Lieben
　Nahmen sich ihnen freundlich an.
Bis der Herr in Lieb und Treue
　Noch seinem Rat es führte aus
Und eine liebende Mutter auch neue
　Zu ihnen brachte in das Haus.
Großpapa auch sie haben erfahren
　Viel interessantes an Freud und Mühe
Denn noch in den jünglings Jahren
　Mussten sie schon über den Ozean ziehe.
Mussten um Glauben und Gewissen gar
　Verlassen Freundschaft und Vaterland
Mussten vieles verlassen was lieb ihn war
　Und landeten an Amerikas freunden Strand.
Eltere und Geschwister kamen mit ihnen
　Sie siedelter auf weiter „Prairie" an
Wo unter Beschwerden und viel Mühe

The Petals of a Kansas Sunflower

Unsere Gemeinde ihnen anfang nahe.
Am Heuhaufen haben sie geschlafen
   Mit nur ganz einfacher Kost
Schnell verging die Zeit bei rastlosen Schafen
   Doch selten nur gabs zu der Zeit toast.
Sieben Jahr sind so verflossen
   Dann zog's zur alten Heimat sie zurück
Wo ihr Ehebündnis wurde geschlossen
   Gemeinsam zu teilen Leid und Glück.
Dann galt Großmama für sie das scheiden
   Von Geschwisterkreis und Elternhaus
Doch nach Amerika zogen sie beide
   Glücklich, auch übers Meer hinaus.
Dann wurde daß, auch wirklich wahr
   Großpapa sie führten aus
Was sie schon gesagt als erst 5 Jahr
   Sie wollen für Großmama bauen ein Haus.
Viele Beschwerden mancher Art
   Das Ansiedele mit sich bracht
Mit Pferde und Wagon galt's jede Fahrt
   Die man wohl damals macht.
Das Baumaterial wurde von weit
   Newton und Peabody gefahren
Und Wege gabs nicht zu die Zeit
   Auf Brücken nicht in den Jahren.
Mit dem leeren Wagon es noch besser ging
   Zu fahren durch die „Krücken"
Doch wenn inzwischen das Wasser zu steigen anfing
   Dann war es schlimm ohne Brücken.
Es musste dann die ganze Last
   Geladen von dem Wagon
Und dann von Fuhrman ohne Rast
   Zur andere Seit' getragen.
War hier auch alles klein und bescheiden
   Gegen wie es in Deutschland war
Sie trugen gemeinsam Freud und Leiden.
   Und glücklich verging so Jahr um Jahr
Es belebte eine frohe Kinderschaar
   Mit der Zeit das einst still Haus
Viel Arbeit stets vorhanden war
   Doch froh ging jedes ein und aus.
Eine Wirtschaft wurde erweitert dann
   Verbessert Haus und Stall
Eine schöne Herde Vieh man heut sehe kann

Celebration of the Golden Wedding Anniversary

Und gedeihe überall.
Wasserleitung haben sie seit Jahren
  Dazu elektrisches Licht
Auf dem Auto wird stets gefahren
  Legunmer konnt's sein ja nicht.
Sie Sahen unsere Gemeinde hier
  Gedein und auch schon entstehn
Und haben die dritte Kirche dafür
  In der Nähe bauen sehe.
Wohl eins der schächten Freuden Feste
  Feierten sie vor 25 Jahr
In Gegenwart viel lieber Gäste
  Als ihre Silberhochzeit war.
Es hatte Gottes treue Gnade
  Sie auch bis hierher gebracht
Sie auf ihrem Lebenpfade
  Treu behütet Tag und Nacht.
So ist dann noch verflossen
  Seither manch schönes Jahr
Viel Segnungen haben Sie genossen
  Und die Herzen sind dankbar.
Es zogen die Kinder eins nach dem andere
  Seither von Elterehause fort
Eins musste bis Wyoming wandere
  Dort zu gründen Heim und Haus.
Doch zwei sind zur Stützen noch geblieben
  In der Wirtschoft und am Herd
So wird noch alles wie einst betrieben
  Wie es Ihnen so traut und wert.
Auch Leid und Trauer blieben
  Von Ihrem Heim nicht ferne
Schon 4 von Ihren lieben
  Kinder, sind droben bei dem Herre.
Eins noch als eine Knospe zart
  Mussten Sie schon geben ab
Und noch drei mal es gefordert ward
  Zu stehe an Sarg und Grab,
Und diese drei in der besten Zeit
  Noch in voller Jugendkraft
So schnell nach schwerer Krankheit
  Von Tod dahin gerafft.
Doch der Herr war Ihre Stärke
  Er verließ Sie auch dann nicht

The Petals of a Kansas Sunflower

Er führt in seinem Werke
  Ja oft durch Nacht zum Licht.
Er gab Ihn das Geleite
  Durch Fünfzig lange Jahr
Und Ihr Kinder und Großkinder heute
  Zählen 45 Seelen gar.
Dies Freudenfest ist heute zwar
  Nicht allen vergönnt mit Ihnen zu Teilen
Doch mit ihren Gedancken gar
  Werden sie auch mit Ihnen weilen.
Auch Ihrem weitern Lebenpfade
  Wollen Gott der Herr wie er bishere
Bei Ihn bleiben mit seiner Gnade
  Wie er verheißen für und für:
Ich will dich tragen bis ins Alter
  Und bis du grau geworden bist
Ich will stets sein dein Erhalter
  Zu jeder Zeit und Lebensfrist.

For Uncle Gerhard Regiers' Golden Wedding
October 25, 1933
Presented by Alma Regier

Dear grandparents at this celebration
  I wish for you God's blessings.
Today there are many lovely guests
  Who are here because of you.
On a joyous day such as this one
  Where after fifty long years
Where God constantly remained true
  Lovingly, you were blessed.
And through God's merciful guidance
  You celebrate this golden anniversary today
Consecrated with thanks and praise
  As you have already done for a lifetime.
In Germany amidst great happiness
  You saw the first light of the world
And from childhood on, both of you
  Gladdened the hearts of your great-grandparents.
But early on you already needed to go to
  Grandmother, because of the void,

Celebration of the Golden Wedding Anniversary

You were only five years old
  When you lost your lovely mother.
Remaining also were three younger siblings.
  Motherless, you returned
However, to the embracing love of relatives
  Who took you in with friendship.
Until the Lord in love and faithfulness
  According to his counsel it happened
And a loving mother, also new,
  Was brought home to you.
Grandfather, you have also experienced
  Many interesting things with pleasure and pain.
Since while still as a teenager
  You already needed to move over the ocean
Entirely because of faith and conscience
  Left friends and Fatherland.
You had to leave much that was precious to you
  And landed on America's friendly shores.
Parents and siblings came with you
  And subsequently settled on the "prairie"
Where with difficulty and a lot of trouble
  You started our community near here.
At haystacks you have slept.
  With only completely simple food
Time passed quickly with relentless work.
  However, seldom does one notice the roar of time.
Seven years passed by this way
  Then you returned back to the old country
Where you took your marriage vows.
  Jointly, in part suffering and fortune
Then grandmother made possible the separation
  From the circle of siblings and parental home.
So, both of you moved to America
  Over the sea also with no misfortune.
Then it happened, it really is true,
  Grandfather, you accomplished
What you as a five-year-old already said
  That you would like to build a house for grandmother.
Many troubles of several kinds
  That settlement brought with it.
With horses and wagon every trip
  That one wanted to take, used them
The building materials were perilously obtained
  Over long distances from Newton and Peabody.

The Petals of a Kansas Sunflower

And the route was not determined at the time
   With no bridges in those years.
With an empty wagon the trip went easier
   To drive through the creeks
However, if before the return trip the water began to flood
   Then it was bad without bridges.
The whole load was required
   To be unloaded from the wagon
And then the wagoner without rest
   Carried it to the other side.
Everything here was small and unpretentious
   In contrast to how it was in Germany.
One experienced jointly pleasure and sorrow
   And so fortunately year after year passed.
Childrearing happily was revived
   With time in the once quiet house.
Constantly there was much work to be accomplished
   But happiness always comes and goes
Then a housekeeping project was expanded
   To improve the house and the barn.
Today one can see a beautiful herd of cattle
   And which are thriving overall.
For years you have already had a water system
   Additionally, electrical lights
You constantly drive with a car
   Surely, this is legendary
You see our community here
   Thriving, and also already originated
The third church for that reason
   Close by is visible.
Surely, per the rituals of happy festivals
   At one time you celebrated after twenty-five years
With many lovely guests, the reason being
   It was your silver wedding.
Because of God's true grace
   You have also been brought thus far
On your life's pathway,
   Truly guarded night and day.
So it has passed
   Since that time many lovely years
Many blessings you have known
   And your hearts are thankful.
The children moved one after another
   Away from their parents' house

Celebration of the Golden Wedding Anniversary

One moved all the way to Wyoming
    There to establish a house and home.
However, two remained supported
    In the household and at the hearth
So everything will yet be arranged
    To be beloved and worthy for you.
Also regrets and sorrows remained
    Not far off from your home
Already four of your lovely
    Children, are above with the Lord.
Once, sort of like a tender bud
    You already needed to give back
And three times also as a relative
    To stand at coffin and grave,
And these three in their prime
    Still in full youthful strength
So quickly after severe illness
    There snatched up by death.
Still the Lord was your strength
    He also did not forsake you
He guided in His workings
    So often through nights into the light
He accompanied you
    Through fifty long years
And today your children and grandchildren
    Even number forty-five persons
This celebration today is indeed happy
    You do not share everything experienced with them
However, surely you were thankful
    They will stay with you
On your continued life's pathways
    Want the Lord your God as he has until now
To remain with you with his grace
    As he promised forever and ever:
I will carry you into old age
    And until you have become gray
I will constantly be your support
    For every moment that you live.

After an interval of ten years, Mother wrote a poem for the fiftieth wedding anniversary of Gerhard Regier's brother Johannes, a.k.a., John. John (1867–1945) married Emilie Wiebe (1872–1944) on October 26, 1893. The ceremony was a double wedding occurring in the brides' home; the other couple were my grandparents, Bernhard Harder Jr. and

Helene Wiebe (see figure 21). The brides' father was so glad that Helene was finally marrying since she was twenty-nine years old; her sister Emilie was twenty. The wedding text was "Seek ye first the Kingdom of God and His righteousness; and all these things shall be added to you" (Matthew 6:33).

This was the second marriage for Bernhard Harder Jr. On November 7, 1887, he married his first cousin Justine Bergmann in the home of the late Elder Gerhard Penner in Beatrice, Nebraska, together with another couple of first cousins from the Kansas community, Heinrich Wiebe and Margarete Regier. (Margarete is a sister of Gerhard and John Regier.) Officiating was one of the Beatrice ministers. Kansas laws forbade the marriage of first cousins, so the two couples took the train from Brainerd, Kansas to Beatrice, Nebraska. Accompanying them were Great-grandmother Justine Bergmann Harder, Bernhard's two older brothers John and Gustav, Justine Bergmann's father Jacob, and Margarete Regier's mother and a brother. Prior to the wedding ceremony the entourage visited friends and relatives, and the young couples returned to Kansas the next day. The rest of the group returned to Kansas after a week of visiting. Unfortunately, the young Justine Bergmann Harder passed away on March 29, 1889, after a lengthy illness and is interred in the Harder cemetery. For the next four years, Bernhard moved back into his parents' house until he married my grandmother, Helene Wiebe.

For her Uncle John and Aunt Emilie Regier, Mother wrote a poem of praise and thanksgiving rather than reviewing history. Emilie was a sister to Catharine of the previous poem, i.e., brothers married sisters. John and Emilie Regier's daughter Marie J. Regier served as a missionary in China under the General Conference Mennonites from 1926 to 1941. During World War II, she was imprisoned in a Japanese concentration camp. Later she served in Paraguay and Taiwan, retiring in 1962. Their son Alfred requested a poem for their twenty-fifth wedding anniversary included in the previous chapter.

John Regier expressed his lifelong interest in education by supporting educational institutions. He served the church actively, including being on the library committee. For business, he wanted the best cattle obtainable and became widely known as an expert stockman raising registered Shorthorns. His mantra in business was "honesty and fairness is the best policy."

Emilie relived the celebration of their fiftieth wedding anniversary many times during the next year, because it brought her much joy. She

Celebration of the Golden Wedding Anniversary

died a year later on November 18, 1944, and John died shortly thereafter on May 18, 1945.

Goldenehochzeit von Onkel Johannes und Tante Emilie
26 Oktober 1943
von Phebe Ann vorgetragen

Wunderbar ist Gottes Walten
Wunderbar sein weiser Rat;
Wunderbar ist sein Verhalten,
Der Euch treu geführet hat.

Wunderbar mit sein Erbarmen
Trägt er Euch schon 50 Jahr
Und mit seinen Liebesarmen
Führte er Euch wunderbar.

Fünfzig Jahr ein halb Jahrhundert
Habt gemeinsam ihr durchlebt
Heut ihr Gottestreu bewundert
Die euch leitet stärkt und hebt.

Das im Kreis von Euren Lieben
Diesen Tag ihr feiert heut
Zwar sind nicht alle Euch geblieben
Und eins in China gar so weit.

Als einst mit grüner Myrt' geschmücket
Gestanden ihr am Traualtar
Da stand zur selben Zeit beglücket
Noch neben Euch ein Andres Paar.

Doch lange schon nach Gottes walten
Zogen ein sie in ein besseres Land
Ihr bliebt den Euren noch erhalten
Und pilgert dankbar Hand in Hand,

Manch Jahr der Herr Euch mög noch schenken
Des fröhlichen beisammen sein
Bis zum Himmel sich die Schritte lenken
Um ewig bei dem Herrn zu sein.

The Petals of a Kansas Sunflower

Golden Wedding Anniversary of Uncle Johannes and Aunt Emilie
October 26, 1943
Recited by Phebe Ann

Wonderful is God's will,
Wonderful is his wise counsel,
Wonderful is his support,
Who has truly guided you.

Wonderful with his compassion
He already carried you for fifty years
And with his loving arms
He has guided you wonderfully.

Fifty years is a half of a century
Through which you have jointly lived.
Today your God: truly admirable,
That he has given you strength and energy.

In the circle of your loved ones
You celebrate this day today.
Indeed, not all of yours have stayed
And one is far away in China.

Once you were adorned with green myrtle
As you stood at the marriage altar.
There stood at the same time
Yet another blessed pair next to you.

Already for a long time according to God's will
You have moved towards a better land.
You positioned yourselves so that you could attain
And pilgrimage thankfully, hand in hand.

May the Lord give you many years yet
That you may joyfully be together
Until your steps are guided to heaven
To be with the Lord for eternity.

On June 15, 1950, the local newspaper, *The Independent* (Whitewater, Kansas), printed the poem Mother wrote for the fiftieth wedding anniversary of Bernhard W. (a.k.a., B. W.) and Minna Harder,

Celebration of the Golden Wedding Anniversary

together with a lengthy description of the golden wedding celebration. Single copies of the newspaper at the time were five cents each or $2.00 per year. The paper reported that approximately five hundred people gathered to honor the Rev. and Mrs. Harder in the church where he had ministered for thirty years. The church service on that Wednesday night began with a traditional wedding processional march as the bride and groom of fifty years were ushered in by two grandsons. The three sermons that followed were interspersed with musical presentations. B. W. then gave a response and "spoke of the golden years of this half century that has passed as being the golden opportunity to attend at the instruction of the most wonderful schoolmaster—experience." B. W. and Minna, together with their two sons and their wives, and the evening speakers formed a receiving line as the guests went to the church basement for supper. Following supper there were two readings in German by children, three toasts, two songs including one sung by the members of B. W.'s 1916 parochial school class (my father was a participant), and the reading of the poem my mother wrote.

Bernhard W. Harder was born on July 30, 1877, the first surviving baby born within the West Prussian community of new immigrants of 1876. His parents, John and Marie (Regier) Harder spent their honeymoon on the *SS Rhein*. Marie Regier was the oldest sister of Gerhard and John Regier whom Mother honored with poems above.

B.W. married Minna Wiebe on June 7, 1900. Minna was a daughter of the large Jacob Wiebe family who came to America in 1890 when Minna was twelve years old. Since these Wiebe siblings were my mother's uncles and aunts many requested personalized poems written by their niece.

B.W. was what we would now call an intellectual, and a community and church leader. He was an educator and conducted German school for the children of the German community for several weeks after the public school ended in spring. In 1889, the public school term in Kansas was three months long. By 1903 it was increased to five months, and by 1909 to seven months. When my mother completed the eighth grade in Brainerd during the school year 1917–18, the school term was eight months long, ending around April 17. That was also the first year that Brainerd had two teachers, with Mary Hawes teaching the upper grades in the second floor classroom and Agnes Schmidt instructing the lower grades on the first floor in the original limestone two-story school building used from 1886–1929. There were forty-five enrolled that year. A picture of the school building is in chapter 17, figure 37. By 1930, the school term ended during the last week in April.

Figure 26
The Rev. B. W. (1877–1970) and Minna (1878–1951) Harder on their twenty-fifth wedding anniversary in 1925. Murphy, Newton, KS. Source: Author's file

Celebration of the Golden Wedding Anniversary

Mother recalls that for several years she and her sisters did not go to Brainerd Public School, but rather went to a small wooden frame building one and one-fourth miles south of the farm, where one year B. W. was the teacher. The following year Miss Katie Friesen from Burrton taught. She was mentioned in the poem "Reminiscences on the Past" in chapter 3. The next year Henry Thiessen taught, but that session was closed in February because a number of the pupils contracted chicken pox and whooping cough. The curriculum in this elementary German immersion school was similar to the public school, but with the addition of instruction in Bible.

Later, in addition to the end of the school term German Bible school, B. W. conducted a one-room advanced parochial school in the community. This school building was located a half mile west of the local church. His German school emphasized general education and religion with total immersion in the German language. My father attended this school in 1916 after he completed the eighth grade in Brainerd; he received advanced placement in language and Bible at Hesston Academy where he was enrolled for one year several years later.

B. W. was active in the local church and was elected as a lay minister from 1902 to 1923 and a lay elder from 1923 to 1939. In the church organization there was one ordained elder who was responsible for baptisms, to serve communion, and to ordain new lay ministers. Additionally, there were several ordained lay ministers, known as teachers, who could preach, perform daily duties as needed in the congregation, and conduct marriage rituals. These ministers were usually considered ordained for life and rotated giving sermons on Sunday mornings and at special events.

To further his own education, B. W. attended Bethel Academy, North Newton, Kansas for high school and subsequently, Emporia State College, Emporia, Kansas. Some in the community thought additional education was totally unnecessary. B. W.'s father, John Harder Sr., also had his doubts of its necessity, but "did not hold him back," i.e., did not forbid or discourage him from going. One of his grandfathers was less encouraging and is recorded saying, "If you would give your son a good whipping, he would forget these ideas of higher education." B. W. felt that to minister more effectively he also needed seminary training. In 1910, he together with his family, went to Dayton, Ohio, where for eight months he attended classes at the Reformed Seminary and then transferred to Moody Bible Institute in Chicago for an additional four months. Later he took a refresher course at the Bible Institute of Los Angeles.

The Petals of a Kansas Sunflower

It was during the period they were in Ohio that their two-year-old daughter, Linda Marie, became sick and died in 1911. B. W. also had two sons. Their names were John Schiller Harder and Bernhard Goethe Harder reflecting the appreciation B. W. had for the writings of the classical German poets. When his first granddaughter was born in 1931, he pronounced that she would be named Linda Marie.

During World War I, expressions of patriotism for many in the non-Mennonite community included purchasing war bonds and displaying the American flag. In Whitewater alone, $251,650 of bonds were sold through the bank; this was six and a quarter times over the suggested subscription. In one issue of *The Independent* all of pages two and three were used to advertise the bond drive with the caption "The business men of Whitewater gave up their ad space in the June 7, 1917 issue for a bond advertisement." The ad read "Business Men of Whitewater Do their Bit! Not a Slacker in the Whole Crowd." The third offering of Liberty bonds begin on April 6, 1918.

The Independent suggested that buying Liberty War Bonds was not an act of charity, rather it provided a badge to flaunt:

> When you buy United State Liberty War Bonds you are not giving away anything. Your act of purchasing is not an act of charity. Whatever money you have you possess because you have lived and worked in the glorious United States. Today the United States needs ready money to help win the war, to provide food, clothing and transportation for our soldier boys. So our government says to you: "Loan us $50 or $100, or whatever amount you like, and we will pay you 3 ½ per cent annual interest (Payment every June 15 and Dec. 15), and in addition to that we will pay you back the entire amount you lent us. Also, if the interest rate on our bonds goes up, we will advance your interest to the highest rate.
>
> That's the fair, square proposition. You can't lose. The United State helped you get what you have, and it is both patriotism and good business on your part to loan the government some of your money now . . .
>
> Every man, woman and child who buys a Liberty bond will be given a government button to wear. This badge of honor will be a sign to the world that its wearer believes in the United States, in freedom, in manhood, in righteousness, and has shown his faith by his works . . .

Celebration of the Golden Wedding Anniversary

Liberty bonds created a philosophical dilemma as well as disagreement among the Mennonites. They were very loyal to the United States government and were personally thankful for its economy and personal and political freedoms. They had no problems paying the taxes that the government imposed, because the teachings of Jesus taught to comply with governmental obligations (Matthew 22:15–22; Mark 12:13–17; and Luke 20:19–26). War bonds were presented as a volitional act, and many chose not to purchase bonds that by design supported a war effort. The advertisement above, which tried to create a moral obligation to purchase war bonds, did not resonate well with pious Mennonites. Many who purchased war bonds donated them to their churches, the Red Cross, or the mission outreach of the church, because they did not want to profit through collection of interest from a war effort. Given a choice, most would rather contribute directly to humanitarian and disaster relief efforts. Some Mennonites were forcibly coerced through neighborly scorn, intimidation, threats, and physical harm until they bought war bonds. Franz Busenitz from Whitewater defiantly bought a $50 Liberty War Bond and posted it in the window of his house.

Simply being good neighbors was a basic tenent of the religious conviction for the Mennonites; this benevolence had been fostered for the previous fifty years since they came to America in 1876. The bond issue jeopardized overt neighborliness.

Unlike some other ministers, B. W. encouraged members of the local Mennonite community to buy bonds. The encouragement may have been rather subtle since some of the parishioners who sat through his sermon were not aware of this encouragement to purchase bonds.

In 1918, there was a patriotic rally in Whitewater highlighting both the bond and the American flag issues that triggered mob action against the local Mennonite Church leaders.

As B. W. and his sons were roofing a chicken house that morning, a disgruntled former farmhand-turned-soldier who lived several miles east and who had formerly been employed by B. W., had stopped by to ask B. W. if he had a flag. The soldier explained that he was en route to the patriotic rally at the American Legion in Whitewater. B. W. sensed trouble and immediately dispatched his son John S. to go to town to purchase a flag, while B. W. and son Bernhard G. (B. G.) continued working on the chicken house roof. It wasn't long before B. G. noticed a row of cars coming from Whitewater like a funeral procession over the hill past his grandfather's farm along the sand road. B. W. and B. G. quickly went into the house to get the tar off their hands and B. W. went out and faced the mob in front of his farmhouse. B. G. watched, standing at the side of the house. Many members of the mob had no advanced knowledge of where they were going; the "patriotic" disgruntled farmhand-turned-soldier had simply said to the energized rally, "just follow me." Some members of the mob, when they realized where they were, wished that they had not followed so readily.

B. W. insisted that he had nothing against the American flag and did not protest when the mob asked him to nail a flag, which the mob provided, to the wood of the entry archway to the front porch. Since the flag was nailed into place, there was some discussion of proper flag display protocol for nighttime or rain, but the "hot heads" simply said to just leave it up. Sensing that the mob was still energized with anger, B. W. proposed that they join him in singing the patriotic hymn "America." He led the singing with his loudest voice and together the group sang the first verse. The level of anger seemed to subside a bit, so B. W. continued by singing the second verse, the third verse, and then the fourth one as well. Members of the "patriotic" group did not know the words of the last three verses and began to shuffle their feet and saunter back to their cars. The Whitewater patriots were embarrassed that they had been "out-Americanized" by a German Mennonite American. The mob then drove a mile and a quarter west and a mile and a quarter north to Elder Gustav Harder's farm, which was located across the road from the Harder cemetery and the farm where my mother lived. Gustav also told the mob that he had nothing against the American flag and that he had purchased some war bonds. Unable to vent their anger with causes for violence, the mob dispersed. Such patriotic acts as displaying a flag, singing a patriotic song, and purchasing a few war bonds for charity helped amalgamate the Anabaptist and American sets of values.

The Whitewater business leaders, however, fearing a potential Mennonite boycott of their establishments, signed an apology on April 27, 1918 to the Mennonite community. It was signed by twelve community leaders including two bankers, the *Independent* editor, the Methodist preacher, the butcher and others, and appeared in the local newspaper, *The Independent,* on May 2:

Celebration of the Golden Wedding Anniversary

"That the People May Know"

We the undersigned fathers and mothers being all the fathers and the mothers living in Whitewater having enlisted sons in the army and navy, by this express our deep sorrow that some of our most patriotic and loyal citizens have been humiliated by a number of persons visiting their homes and nailing up the American flag on their residences or having them do it, the same being demonstrations charging disloyalty and sympathy with Germany and her cause, under the wrong impression that these citizens were disloyal to this government. While it is not our purpose to shield any person of whatever nationality who is disloyal, yet we think it is due the public to know that Jacob J. Regier is one who not only purchased Liberty Bonds but went from home to home advising others to do so and wrote a strong article for a German newspaper advocating the purchase of Liberty Bonds. Not only this but that Mr. Regier has in season and out of season shown in many ways his loyalty to this government and his abhorrence for the course Germany has pursued. Rev. B. W. Harder and Rev. Gustav Harder have not only purchased Liberty Bonds but the church of which they have charge sent thirteen hundred dollars to the Red Cross before a cent was raised by any other church in this part of the country, and Rev. B. W. Harder in response to the request made by Secretary McAdoo and his representatives to the Ministers of the United States preached a sermon Sunday the 21st advising the members of his congregation to purchase Liberty Bonds.

The father of Rev. B. W. Harder, John Harder and his sons refuse to be referred to as Germans but pointedly remind any one who speaks of them as Germans that they are Americans and have no use for Germany or her cause. Mr. Harder has been from Germany forty years and says he has written back but once in thirty years, that he came from there to get away from the Kaiser and militarism, that he has made his money and raised his family here and loves this country.

Patriotism as well as Christianity is taught in this old gentleman's home and he with the others we have mentioned have been, in our judgment, wrongfully humiliated by the demonstration to which we have referred.

It might be well to mention that not infrequently the most disloyal persons make the most profuse display of flags and other outward appearance, while these venerable people while living beautiful lives have never at any time indulged in outward display of any kind, but have no objection whatever to displaying flags if it is the sentiment of the people it should be done. We wish to add that many, and we hope all, who visited these homes on the occasion mentioned sincerely regret the occurrence.

Signed this 27th day of April, 1918.

L. M. Page
P. J. Hershey
Chas. Liptrap
Jas. A. Thompson
J. B. Guiney
C. A. Neiman
Fred Breising
E. Davis
G. B Hanstine
J. D. Joseph
W. O Moore
Mrs. Alexander

The men mentioned in this apology were all uncles or cousins of my mother and on various occasions recipients of personalized poems. B. W. is admired in the next poem.

There were examples of Kansas communities where the "patriotic activists" alienated the resident Mennonites who preferred not to purchase war bonds. Nightriders tarred and feathered some of their Mennonite neighbors, shaved their heads, burned their buggies, and humiliated them for their religious conviction of pacifism. Fortunately, non-Mennonite friends interceded in some altercations and no deaths resulted from these incidents in Kansas. However, the Mennonites in some communities reacted by realigning their economical associations by removing bank deposits as well as their business activity to more hospitable neighboring towns; the economic and emotional impact of these boycotts on the economy of the few overzealous "patriotic" communities was still evident fifty years later.

During this period of World War I, the United States Congress passed an espionage law that made it illegal to discourage participation in the war effort. The law was applied against several Mennonite and Amish leaders who recommended that their congregations not buy war bonds. The first case occurred in West Virginia, but the second litigated case occurred in Dodge City, Kansas. Manasses E. Bontrager, an Old Order Amish bishop of Dodge City wrote a letter arguing against participation in the war effort including the purchase of war bonds. The letter was printed on May 15, 1918 in *The Weekly Budget*, an unofficial Amish/Mennonite newspaper edited by Samuel H. Miller. Both men were fined $500 and court costs.

Mennonite institutions of higher education also suffered at the hands of patriotic activists. At Hesston College there was a flag display altercation, at Tabor College in Hillsboro the main building burned with suspicion of arson, and at Bethel College in North Newton yellow paint graffiti was applied to some buildings. Bethel College even dropped German from the foreign language curriculum for a time.

It is fair to note, however, that the patriotic fervor in 1917–18 was not exclusively anti-(German) Mennonite. In Wichita, street popcorn vendors were harassed for not displaying flags by a crowd of fifteen hundred people on April 17, 1918; the vendors were Jewish rather than Mennonite and timely police protection avoided a possible hanging. At the Domestic Laundry on East Douglas in Wichita, the eighty-five employees, mostly women, collectively pronounced that they would "not stand for a slacker in their crew," and threatened to ride three fellow employees on a rail from the laundry to Main Street if they refused to kiss Old Glory.

Early in the twentieth century, as Kansas and America matured in democratic governance and focused on new forms of foreign and domestic policies, ethnicities were viewed with fear as potential elements for political and social disharmony. The internment of West Coast persons of Japanese descent during the 1940s is another example. With national maturation, in the latter years of the past century, personal ethnic individualism again has become an element of pride. For Kansas Anabaptists, martyrdom is currently not the avenue necessary to express faith as it was in Holland in the late sixteenth century for my ancestors. Mennonites continue to express their philosophic views of Christian love and pacifism through church outreach, social programs like disaster relief, participation with Christian Peacekeeper Teams, and humanitarian outreach through the Mennonite Central Committee (MCC). Also, they use participation in political demonstrations, in protest and peace marches, and in their right to vote. My mother contemplated these issues and ended her poem "In Butler County on the Farm" in chapter 2 with the lines, "Then we see the farmer thankful (now retiring for the night) / For the blessings that God gave him, and for freedom—still his right."

It is of interest to examine the prevailing attitudes of the Mennonite immigrants who came to the grasslands of Kansas expressly for the right to practice their religion and pacifism. In the local community, no one was involved in the Spanish American War at the turn of the century (1898–99). However, in the sister community of Prussian Mennonites in Newton, one of their members volunteered and served in the Philippines; he was summarily excommunicated from the church. The church released a statement that Mennonites were grateful for their country but they preferred nonresistance and encouraged "international arbitration." In 1905, their disgraced soldier sought readmission to church membership and was reinstated in June. Several months later the church adopted guidelines for church membership of former combatants. Within twenty years in America, religious principles of nonresistance were beginning to be modulated with the inculcation of American culture. During World War I, young men of the local church were drafted and some served as noncombatants. Emil Wiebe is an example where his marriage was delayed until his period of military obligation was fulfilled as mentioned in chapter 12. Some of the young men after their military service did not return to the church community. Stories abounded of noncombatants being severely harangued by other combatant draftees, especially those of Anabaptist faith who wore beards or home-spun garments. Gerlof D. Homan has reviewed this period of American Mennonite history in his book, *American Mennonites and the Great War 1914-1918*. Having come to America where they were fortunate to live in a country at peace for nearly forty years, the church and its young men were not prepared for national involvement in war. The changes in the Kansas militia laws, lobbied into action by the railroad in 1874 to entice Mennonite immigrants to Kansas, offered military exemptions for state activities, but did not extend to national war efforts. Many Mennonite leaders interacted with government officials, but the different Mennonite groups did not speak with one unifying voice. Learning from the lessons of World War I, immediately after that war the Mennonites with government approval developed programs for pacifists in the event of another war.

Celebration of the Golden Wedding Anniversary

During World War II, the local young men who were drafted either enrolled in alternative service programs administered for the government by Mennonite organizations, or military service with a few enlisting in the navy. By the 1940s, there were fewer cultural differences that identified the Mennonite communities, and the antagonism from the American public was minimal. The challenge to be both Mennonite and patriotic no longer seemed like an insurmountable issue.

This next poem begins with a description of the marriage of B. W. Harder and Minna Wiebe. The poem is written with the cadence and rhythm similar to Henry Wadsworth Longfellow's poem "Paul Revere's Ride." Mother memorized that poem possibly as she walked or rode a buggy to and from school, and continued to quote it even when she was in a nursing home and over ninety years old. B. W. and Minna were known for their gregarious natures and friendships within and outside the local community.

Their wedding, the twenty-fifth wedding anniversary, and the fiftieth anniversary celebrations included their many friends and relatives, and involved groups of three hundred to five hundred people. Mentioned in the poem is that for the twenty-fifth wedding anniversary there was a tent set up in the farmyard. Between 1890 and 1930, a tent was sometimes used if there were no new farm buildings available or if there was no building of adequate size that could be prepared for the occasion. The celebratory meal of homemade foods was served in the tent.

During the final thirty years of B. W.'s life, he suffered from heart problems. Once, when I was a preschooler and accompanied my mother to the local mercantile in Brainerd, we met B. W. He told his cousin, my mother, that he would soon be dying; his heart was so weak, etc. My mother with a glint in her eye looked up at him and said, "*Es sterbt ja nicht so leicht*. It is just not that easy to die." This conversation was in the mid-1940s during the time of penny postcards and five-cent loaves of bread. His health, however, did not deter him from climbing down into the seventy-foot hand-dug well to accomplish some repairs or from covering the roof of his barn with sheets of tin. He did not like heights and when asked how he covered the ends of the roof that stick out from the barn, he replied simply that he had done that work at night.

After Minna died in 1951, B. W. lived by himself for a period and did all his own cooking, including baking bread. He loved to tell the story that once he forgot the bread in the oven and it charred. In disgust he threw the inedible loaf out of the back door; as bad luck would have it, the charred loaf hit a chicken and killed it. With time he got bored living alone on the farm in retirement, so for a number of years he drove to Wichita and audited college courses in psychology, geology, and other subjects at Wichita State University.

When I entered elementary school, it became the responsibility of my sister and me to take handcrafted invitations to him for the school Christmas program and the end-of-year program because he lived between the school and our home. He was always so thankful for the invitations and would engage us in conversation. He often did attend our programs of singing, readings, skits, and plays.

Golden Years
Mrs. John Epp, Jr.
June 7, 1950
Recited by Elna Jane Harder

In 1900 the seventh of June,
Hot was the day at the hour of noon,
But many the heat were not aware,
A general excitement seemed in the air.
Preparations were made to attend a feast,
All wanted to go, to say the least.
Along the dusty road that day
A buggy with horses was speeding away.
The driver, a young man in his best attire.
The buggy shining, the horses afire.
And brand new harnesses gave the whole affair
A stately appearance and an elegant air;
Hurriedly the church it passed,
Stopping one mile north at a farm at last
Where he found a lovely maiden young and fair
In great excitement waiting there.
Soon many a carriage and buggy drove in.
What a joyous occasion it must have been
But what was the stir and excitement about?
In just a few seconds you shall find out.
It was the day that made husband and wife
Of two dear people, joining their hearts and life.
It was B. W. Harder, our Grandfather here

Celebration of the Golden Wedding Anniversary

With Minna Wiebe, Grandma so dear.
That God's blessing forever on you should descend,
Were the wishes of parents, relatives and friends.
Your hopes were high, your thoughts were one
So another home was soon begun.
It was in Brainerd, in the little town,
That you started housekeeping and settled down.
But it was within the very first year
That to your farm, you moved from there.
A mile south of Brainerd, on that very place,
You had experiences of God's love and grace.
Happy days would change with the days of care
And even dark valleys were your share.
As you are looking back to these days, you see
God's grace was sufficient and always shall be.
So you labored and toiled, as farmers will,
You planted, reaped, and raised livestock with skill.
And after a few years, so I am told,
A new convenient home replaced the old,
But the work on the farm was not all,
Soon to the ministry came a call.
Then behind the pulpit Grandpa was seen
In the church, where the first infant he'd been.
Besides the farm work and the preaching
Grandpa was active in Bible school teaching.
And many of those, that were present here
Have been his pupil at least one year.
Midst work and contentment days went fast
And years have come and years have passed.
Two boys were committed into your care,
Who faithfully helped and did their share.
The greatest joy that perhaps you knew
Was when a baby girl was given to you.
Soon Grandfather, you keenly felt a need
For further studying to which you gave most heed.
You took your family, left your farm here,
To go to Chicago and Dayton for a year.
And with you, memories linger still,
Of city life, and perhaps always will,
The Great Gardener there your darling found,
And transplanted her to heavenly ground.
So hopes would alternate with fears
And joys would sometimes change to tears.
The Lord has been your strength and guide

The Petals of a Kansas Sunflower

Whatever came whate'er betide.
He led, when roses bloomed along the way,
And guided through the darkest day.
But years have not gone by unheeded
They left their mark on you indeed
Placing wrinkles in the youthful face
And in the hair a silver trace.
Grandma, you too had busy days,
Your time was occupied in different ways.
Still many today, an appreciation feel
For kind hospitality and a splendid meal.
Flowers were your joy and pleasant to behold,
How many they have cheered is left untold.
Later many a parcel packed by your hand
Has cheered needy ones in a foreign land.
Today your friends and nieces testify
It has been a pleasure and also a joy
Just to have with you a friendly chat,
Just to talk of this, and a talk of that.
But we shouldn't forget to mention the day
That was so outstanding in many a way.
When the whole Emmaus congregation
Joined others in hearty congratulations
For the twenty-fifth milestone was set that day,
In your pilgrimage, on the life's highway.
It was a beautiful day, for having the feast,
Golden and majestic the sun rose in the east.
After, yet earlier at break of dawn,
You were awakened by strains of a song.
Close relatives as well as the choir, you know
Had come with best wishes and gifts to bestow.
The service that afternoon was sublime,
Many dear old ministers spoke at the time
Who no longer are with us this day
But have gone to glory, and were laid away.
The church was beautiful to behold
With a great abundance of flowers, I am told.
On the farm in a tent, as some will recall,
A most bountiful meal was served to all.
Life has not gone on this same routine,
Many changes since were experienced and seen.
Your two sons have left your parental care
And two new homes were started there.
They reared their families in a God-blessed way

Celebration of the Golden Wedding Anniversary

And are joining with you in praises today.
In looking back today, ten years,
There were long weeks of suspense and fears,
Which Grandma, were weeks in the hospital for you
With a serious operation, for you to go through.
Thirty-six years as minister and elder Grandpa served;
After this time a change was well deserved.
A heart ailment has kept you long on guard,
Doctors say, "Take it easy, don't work too hard."
You have since moved to Great-grandfather's place
Which was "moving home," in Grandpa's case
Even though failing health, you had to heed,
You did outstanding work indeed.
You painted the house, tin covered the barn,
Descended the well, and all without harm.
So on this special day of joy and praise
We marvel at God's wondrous ways.
And if this day you should by chance
Pause for a moment and take a glance
At the picture, that in such a unique way
Was taken fifty years ago on your wedding day.
You'll find many a person once so dear
No longer toils and labors here;
But they have gone to their reward,
Some sooner, some later, without regard.
And those that understood you best
Have left you lonely and gone to rest.
But God is with you and shall always be
Even beyond this Golden Jubilee.
His promise; "At evening there shall be light
With life's setting sun, in radiance bright."
May God your strength and comfort be
In the coming days until eternity.
  —Mrs. John Epp Jr.

Anniversaries, for Mother, were a time for reflection. "As though a curtain lifted / The past is brought in view / The happy days and hours / Which long ago you knew. / Loved ones that long have left you / Again you seem to see; / Old songs, old friends, old places / Pass by in memory." On the day of this wedding, December 18, 1902, the guests arrived "on sleds in snow," but by the time the guests left later in the day it had warmed up and the guests "traveled home in mud." The poem was presented by a granddaughter.

The Petals of a Kansas Sunflower

Mrs. Ed Claassen was my father's cousin. Their son Kurt and his family spent many years in India as missionaries. Another son, Melvin, who requested a poem to help celebrate their twenty-fifth wedding anniversary in chapter 12, worked on agricultural projects and education in the Congo.

In the late 1940s or early 1950s, when people still visited each other in their homes within the community, the Claassens invited my parents and me, and perhaps some of my sisters, for dinner one evening in late fall. There were other guests as well. What left a lasting impression was that in one of the south windows there was a large Christmas cactus in full bloom. Never having seen one before, I was mesmerized by the beautiful, delicate pink flowers. I pulled up a chair and while the others visited, I gazed at this spectacular plant.

For Ed Claassens' Golden Wedding Anniversary
December 18, 1952
Presented by Wynona Claassen

There are days that are outstanding
   Times of special joy and praise
When hearts are filled with gratitude
   And we marvel at God's ways.
And such a time has come to you
   This day; Our Grandparents dear
As now today you celebrate
   With friends from far and near.
This is the day, which the Lord hath made
   Rejoice and be of cheer.
This is the thought that's ringing
   In your hearts sweet and clear.
Your thoughts will involuntarily
   Go back to days gone by
God showered you with kindness
   And blessings from on high.
There is joy as well as sorrow
   Mingled in your thoughts today
As on this fiftieth milestone
   You linger on your way.
As though a curtain lifted
   The past is brought in view

Celebration of the Golden Wedding Anniversary

The happy days and hours
    Which long ago you knew.
Loved ones that long have left you
    Again you seem to see;
Old songs, old friends, old places
    Pass by in memory.
Your thoughts go back to childhood
    To days you spent at school
To winters cold and summers hot
    And autumns fair and cool.
Your ways were two in those years
    They crossed from time to time
Till later they were united
    On a day for you sublime.
It was a mild day in December
    We are told by those who know
And guests that traveled home in mud
    Had come on sleds in snow.
The farm that you moved to
    Still is "home, sweet home" so dear
The Lord has richly blessed you
    As you toiled from year to year.
A group of healthy children
    Brought joy as well as care
Again they all are with you
    This day with you to share.
All too soon they've left you
    As their own homes they start
Each time it brought new sadness
    When one from home did part.
But yet you are rejoicing
    That they had part in bringing light
To the Hindus in far off India,
    Still in heathendom and night.
Grandpa, in church and Sunday school
    You still take active part
And through the years, endeared yourself
    To many a human heart.
Of your many and rich experiences
    Your grandchildren like to hear
Which as years have come and gone
    Become to you more dear.
Three times this day you have observed
    In green, in silver, now in gold

The Petals of a Kansas Sunflower

> The next time that you celebrate
>   It's diamonds we are told.
> So I'm wishing you God's blessing
>   As you are journeying along
> Till you join with those in glory
>   In their triumphant song.

Jacob E. Thiessen was a brother to Mrs. Ed Claassen and both were children of *Tante Thiessen*, my father's aunt. Jacob married Marie Renatha Wiebe on November 23, 1909.

After an introduction, the anniversary poem presented by a granddaughter, describes wedding preparations. "To the day that found you busy / At the earliest morning's glow. / For more time and work was needed / In the horse and buggy days / With arrangements for a wedding, / In the good old-fashion ways." Relatives and friend came from near and far, "'Til there were long rows of buggies / No one coming in a car." The bride wore a black wedding dress and carried a traditional wedding wreath made of red cedar and embellished with either fall flowers or paper flowers. The ceremony was in a newly built granary that was decorated with the only native Kansas evergreen, red cedar. Coal-oil lamps were hung for illumination.

The couple sat through a sermon and then was united with a simple ceremony. After the ceremony the chairs were moved aside to allow the setting up of long tables for the wedding supper. The adults visited and the children played late into the night. Then "after a few days of relaxing / You moved as husband and wife / to a farm newly constructed, / Sharing the experiences of life."

Mother debated with herself and us children whether to include her editorial comments "Here time has brought some changes— / Today it's over soon / They are in and out together / and then the honeymoon." The older generation had problems dealing with the change from wedding receptions serving full suppers to cake-and-punch receptions, especially if it was an evening wedding and the drive to the wedding was over the dinner hour.

Life on the farm is reviewed, including the tornado of June 8, 1941, which demolished their farm but no family members were injured. Jake grew peaches in the garden and was proud of his good horses. "When you were in the prime of life / And time seemed to fly past." Mother discusses growing old and ends the poem with a benediction, "I wish for both of you / That as life's sun is setting / The sky is radiant and bright, / May thus the evening of your life / Be flooded with heavenly light. / Amen."

For J. E. Thiessens' Golden Anniversary
November 23, 1959
Recited by Lillian Thiessen

On this day of golden glimmer
The best wishes shall be yours,
And today with you we praise him,
Who forever more endures.
It is through God's love and mercy
That this day you celebrate
And a new song of thanksgiving
In your heart it will create.
Fifty years have gone by swiftly
Since together you set sail
Through the storm as well as sunshine,
God has guided without fail.
All your children and grandchildren
And a host of friends as well,
Now are joining in the praises,
Which in words are hard to tell.

Today, perhaps, your thoughts will wander
Back to fifty years ago;
To the day that found you busy
At the earliest morning's glow.
For more time and work was needed
In the horse and buggy days
With arrangements for a wedding,
In the good old-fashion ways.
Many relatives assembled,
Friends came in from near and far
Till there were long rows of buggies
No one coming in a car.
And a new erected granary
All adorned with evergreen
Was indeed a unique setting
For the solemn wedding scene.
Hanging coal-oil lamps illumined

The Petals of a Kansas Sunflower

At the time the space beneath,
There the bride in black was lovely
With the traditional wedding wreath.
The groom indeed was handsome—
He wouldn't admit it I fear,
Being in his best attire
Wearing a homemade boutonniere.
Though simple the ceremony
It was beautiful at that
Preceded by a sermon
Through which the couple sat.
Here time has brought some changes—
Today it's over soon
They are in and out together
And then the honeymoon.
The Ceremony being over,
The chairs were pushed away,
And soon another setting—
Long tables in array.
The waiters then got busy
And spread a delicious feast
Of which each one had plenty
And more, to say the least.
In those days the wedding lasted
Till twelve or even one;
The older people visited,
The young ones had their fun.
After a few days of relaxing
You moved as husband and wife
To a farm newly constructed,
Sharing the experiences of life.
And there each time you left the house
The church was in full view
With its steeple pointing upward,
Pointing you heavenward anew.
And on that farm you since have lived,
You built, you planted trees,
Some recall what luscious peaches
Were picked from some of these.
A few years thus passed swiftly by,
Then life too took on more meaning
As a son and daughter join you
And then on you were leaning.
You too saw life's reality

Celebration of the Golden Wedding Anniversary

As sickness entered in,
These days were trying days for you,
As such have always been.
But they also brought a blessing
That you wouldn't want to miss
For God was very near to you
And blessed you through all this.
Sad was the day when God reached down
And picked the little flower
That you thought he had given you.
But in that crucial hour
He took her up to higher ground,
Free from all sin and care.
She blossoms forth to God's own praise,
More beautiful and fair.
Grandma, you had days of sickness
When the hours seemed, oh so long,
But you too had the experience
That God knows and gives a song.
And I think we here should mention,
Grandpa too had his good share,
When he fell, and badly injured
Requiring hospital care.
After five long months were over
And he could come home at last
Not to work or take things over
But still coming in a cast.
Then too, came days outstanding,
Days of special joy to you,
When the family group grew larger.
Through the years it was by two.
So under varied experiences
The years would come and go,
For work was always plentiful
As every one will know.
Caring for livestock takes much time,
With milking yet beside,
And there was fieldwork to be done
But good horses were your pride.
There was a morning when you saw
That demolished lay the farm,
But yet in this you thanked the Lord—
To the family came no harm.
And so as months and years went by,

The Petals of a Kansas Sunflower

You both scarcely understood,
How empty seemed the house to you
When one day you realized
They all had left. You were alone.
Even though not too surprised
You saw it come. You want it thus.
You were satisfied. You knew
Each one had found a place in life
And by it the family grew.
Three daughters came in course of time;
Came into your home and heart.
Aunt Martha left for the "Go Ye,"
Where she took an active part.
Once more we want to turn our thoughts
To incidents of the past.
When you were in the prime of life
And time seemed to fly past.
It was then you built a house
For your parents in your yard,
That you would be their help and stay
When their days were getting hard.
You then were in the best of years,
You reached the summit since.
That there is now a downward trend
You will be easy to convince.
Now you moved in the little house
And slowly you give in,
Your children filling now the place
Where you so long had been.
You celebrated this day before
In green, in silver, now in gold.
And as you think of bygone days
Many changes you behold.
Of the good old aunts and uncles,
All but a few without regard
As well as both of your parents
Have gone to their reward.
A new and young generation
Is coming to take their place,
And in the audience tonight
You see many a new face.
But you still have each other,
It's God's leading all the way
And we too want to praise him

Celebration of the Golden Wedding Anniversary

On your golden wedding day.
Grandpa for you, I'm sure,
Grandma is still sunny and fair.
And Grandma do you notice,
How white is Grandpa's hair?
But as I am now closing,
I wish for both of you
That as life's sun is setting
The sky is radiant and bright,
May thus the evening of your life
Be flooded with heavenly light.
Amen.

In the following three poems, different grandchildren laud their grandparents with praise and thanks. Recalled are activities the grandparents shared with their grandchildren, stories told, and memories created. The concepts are simple and just right for delivery by grandchildren.

Herman A. Wiebes' Golden Wedding
November 27, 1962

I.

Can it be it's the Golden Wedding
    For the two of you today?
And you reached the golden milestone
    As you journey on your way?
It is through God's love and mercy
    That this day you celebrate.
And a new song of thanksgiving
    In your hearts it will create.

Fifty years have gone by swiftly
    Since together you set sail.
Through the storm as well as sunshine
    God has guided without fail.
All your children and grandchildren
    And a host of friends as well—
Now are joining in the praises
    Which in words are hard to tell.

The Petals of a Kansas Sunflower

Three times this day you have observed:
    In green, in silver, now in gold
And many a fond memory
    You cherish and still hold.
You fondly think of dear ones
    That left you through the years—
Of parents, brothers, sisters
    And others that were dear.

God blessed your home with children
    They brought both joy and care.
Again they all are with you
    This day with you to share.
But one by one they've left you
    As their own homes they did start.
Each time it brought new sadness
    When one from home did part.

We grandchildren like to listen
    When, Grandpa, in your jolly way,
You tell us how, as a little boy,
    In Germany you would play.
And many are the incidents
    Still vivid in your mind
Of friends, of home and garden
    That the family left behind.

A privilege, at that time rare,
    Was yours as a young man—
A trip to Europe and to see
    The old home place again.
You did however often think
    Of Kansas, and with yearning
Your thoughts were with a maiden fair
    Who longed for your returning.

Many are the happy hours
    And days that you could share.
But also hardships and some trials
    You were called upon to bear.
Even in everyday affairs
    Often changes come and go,
Which through the years sufficiently
    You have also learned to know.

Celebration of the Golden Wedding Anniversary

God gave you both the best of health,
    Even though your hair turned gray.
Your work reached out beyond the home
    In many a different way.
Your influence was keenly felt
    In church and Sunday school
And longer Grandpa here could teach
    Than is the average rule.

And as we are now closing
    We wish for both of you
That as life's sun is sinking
    You may find this to be true:
Just as the sun is setting
    The evening sky is bright.
May thus the evening of your lives
    Bring peace and heavenly light.

II.

We are quite young as you can see
    But yet we do our part.
So we will give the little piece
    That we have learned by heart.

We join with you in praises here
    For all that God has done
That he has kept you to this day
    And blessed us everyone.

We thank him for the birds that sing
    And flowers along the way
For brothers, sisters, parents dear
    And blessings every day.

We thank him for the sun that shines
    And for the rain he sends
For food and clothing that we have
    And blessings without end.

We thank him for our grandparents, too
    On this Golden Wedding day,
That he has given health and strength
    And kept them to this day.

The Petals of a Kansas Sunflower

III.

For many weeks we've waited
    For the coming of this day.
And how we now enjoy it
    Is more than I can say.

For a very special reason
    I'm standing here today
To wish you God's richest blessing
    In a very heartfelt way.

We always like to visit
    With both of you, you know.
We all like Grandma's cookies,
    And watch her flowers grow.

Some times she's busy quilting
    And Grandpa sits and reads.
Sometimes they both are working
    Since there are other needs.

Whatever they are doing
    I like to be around.
To me they're the best grandparents
    That ever have been found.

Willie Harder (1895–1971) was my mother's cousin, who in midlife moved his family in 1941 to Idaho from Kansas to be near his wife's family. Some in the community still remember the family packing their farm household into boxcars on the railroad siding in Brainerd and shipping it to their new home near Aberdeen, Idaho. Also put into boxcars and shipped was a dismantled house inherited by Mrs. Harder (Catherine Wiebe Harder) from her parents in 1935. The house was a large two-story structure, but initially built in 1885 as a four-room house with two rooms on the main floor and two rooms upstairs with the stairs to the upper floor on the outside of the building. After a number of years the house was enlarged and was considered one of the grandest houses in the town of Brainerd. The wood loaded into railroad cars would be used in building their new home in Idaho.

Celebration of the Golden Wedding Anniversary

The "Wedding Dress Display Guide" developed for the 125th anniversary of the Emmaus Mennonite Church included this description of the Thursday, May 31, 1917 wedding at 4:00 p.m.:

> Willie Harder and Catharine Wiebe invited the whole church to their wedding at Emmaus. The bridal couple came in together to the front of the church and sat on the two dining room chairs festively decorated for them. They sat there during the lengthy wedding sermon, and then stood together in front of the pastor for the marriage ceremony. A church wedding was a very solemn event. Afterwards, the reception was held at the bride's home, where supper was served. The bridal couple and their parents, as well as other engaged couples, sat at the decorated table. The loft was decorated with garlands of cedar and flowers. The oldest and honored guests were served first, then a younger generation, then the children, and finally the waiters and waitresses. After the eating, there was a program with messages by other ministers, poems tailored to fit the occasion recited by children and relatives, and singing, of course. Then followed an evening of visiting for the adults and games by the young people and children. Emmaus people believed in enjoying a long evening!

The poem mentions the wedding reception in a barn hayloft in Brainerd, a loft large enough to accommodate all the guests. "In the prime of life you promised loyal you would be and true, / And your love to one another never failed but rather grew." Their daughter, Wilma, worked as a missionary in Morocco for many years. When the Willie Harders celebrated their fiftieth wedding anniversary, they nostalgically asked their Kansas cousin, my mother, to create a poem.

For Willie Harders' Golden Wedding Anniversary
May 11, 1967

Hitherto the Lord has helped you; hitherto the Lord has led.
    Graciously he has provided as life's pathway you have tread.
Constantly he was beside you in the cares and joys and fears
    And today you can't but praise him, thinking over fifty years.
Yes, the time has slipped by swiftly. Months and years have come and gone.
    And today you ask the question, "Can it really be that long?"
Many memories you cherish of your courtship now long past
    And to this there was the climax when the wedding came at last.
In the little town of Brainerd, in the hayloft, you'll recall

The Petals of a Kansas Sunflower

Guests then gathered for the reception, there was ample room for all.
In the prime of life you promised loyal you would be and true,
   And your love for one another never failed but rather grew.
Many were the happy hours and the days that you could share,
   But also hardships and some trials you noticed here and there.
If over these fifty years again you could take a look,
   Could you turn back the years like pages and read them in a book?
There you would find experiences, some already forgotten by now.
   Others still vivid in memory, just when they happened and how.
You first farmed in Kansas—there raised chickens and fed steers,
   And almost thus unnoticed slipped by the months and years.
There too, five children joined you and also went to school,
   Then there came some changes as so often is the rule.
You pulled stakes, as it were, and to Idaho you went
   Where together as a family many happy years you spent.
But since there were more changes, again you are but two.
   For the children all have "flown the coop," as they all like to do.
And their influence as far as Africa is felt
   Where one, in Christian service for many years has dwelt.
You celebrated this day before in green, in silver, now in gold
   And when again you celebrate it's diamonds we are told
We regret, that not in person we are enjoying with you the day,
   But our thoughts and good wishes to you will find their way.
And now we wish you God's blessing. May his presence with you abide
   To guard your every footstep and be your constant guide.
All our other wishes we are summing up in one,
   That at the end of life's journey you will hear the Lord's "Well done."

A young grandson recited this next poem to honor his grandparents. John Schiller Harder (1901–1993), my mother's cousin, married my father's sister Emilie (1899–1992) on Wednesday, June 8, 1927 at 4:00 p.m. at the Emmaus Mennonite Church. The "Wedding Dress Display Guide" developed for the 125th anniversary of the church included this description:

> Emilie Epp chose to have her wedding gown made by a lady seamstress in Whitewater. She explained to the seamstress just how the gown was to be fashioned. The total cost of construction was $7.00. For the wedding, the bride wore a real wreath of myrtle leaves and small white flowers in her hair. The two diamond shaped pins on the gown were also worn on the wedding day. The low belt line was typical of the 1920s fashion . . . Rev. B. W. Harder, father of the groom, officiated . . . Following

the service, a time of eating and fellowship took place upstairs in the [Grandfather Epp's] barn . . .

A new farm was built prior to the wedding and was ready for the newlyweds on their wedding day. With the completion of the newly built house and barn, and all the arrangements for the wedding day celebration and feast for probably two hundred to three hundred people in Grandfather Epp's hayloft, the wedding day may well have felt like a major climax. Their second child and first daughter was named Linda Marie.

J. S. Harders' Golden Wedding Anniversary
June 28, 1977
Recited by Stanley Harder

On this day with golden glitter, the best of wishes shall be yours,
   And today with you we praise him, who forevermore endures.
It is through God's love and mercy that this day you celebrate,
   And a new song of thanksgiving in your heart it will create.
Now your children and grandchildren, and a host of friends as well,
   Here are joining in the praises, which in words are hard to tell.
Fifty years have slipped by swiftly. Months and years have come and gone.
   And today you ask the question: "Can it really be that long?"
Many memories you cherish of your courtship, now long past.
   And to this there was the climax when the wedding came at last.
Now in those days, —a honeymoon was not for everyone.
   With settling in the newly built farm, your lifework had begun.
At tilling the soil and milking cows, our grandpa soon was seen.
   While housework, chickens and the garden, for grandma became routine.
You also took an active part in church and Sunday school,
   And this continued through the years, which not always is the rule.
With one son and with two daughters through the years your home was blessed,
   And how long ago those years now seem when these were still in the nest,
And long ago it also seems since from the coop they have flown,
   To be active in God's vineyard and in places of their own.
The two of you still carry on; you seem as young as ever.
   Your interests in the Mission fields through the years diminished never.
And letters of encouragement you still find time to write;
   For those at the receiving end it makes the day more bright.
Three times this day you have celebrated—in green, in silver, now in gold.
   And next time when you celebrate, it's diamonds we are told.
I didn't have the intention to speak to you this long.

The Petals of a Kansas Sunflower

I trust you have enjoyed it and didn't find it wrong.
But since so many good wishes were brought to you today,
I, your youngest grandson, just couldn't stay away.

Theodore "Ted" D. Nickel, a high school teacher at Berean Academy, and his wife Rose Ann asked Mother for a poem that their three children could recite for Ted's parents' golden wedding anniversary. Mother was unacquainted with his parents since they lived in Mountain Lake, Minnesota. The poem is undated, but was written between 1947 and 1955, the years the Nickels were at Berean Academy.

Golden Wedding Anniversary of Ted Nickel's Parents

For many weeks we waited
  For the coming of this day,
And how we now enjoy it
  Is more than I can say.

∽ ∽ ∽

You celebrated this day before
  In green, in silver, now in gold.
And as you think of bygone days,
  Many changes you behold.
Grandpa, you were good at teaching,
  In farming you too had success.
Grandma always was beside you
  Helping you without distress.

∽ ∽ ∽

Many were the happy hours
  And the days that you could share.
But also hardships and some trials
  You were called upon to bear.
In the days that lie before you
  May God be your constant guide.
May he guard and bless your footsteps
  As in him you shall abide.

At the celebration to remember the day, fifty years earlier on March 6, 1890, that my grandfather John Epp Sr. married my grandmother, Anna Regier, my two oldest sisters recited the following devotional poem. March 6 was also Grandmother Epp's birthday. Anna was born in 1869 in West Prussia and immigrated to America with her parents, grandparents, other relatives, and friends on the ship the *SS Main* on June 6, 1880. Her parents, Cornelius and Anna Regier, and family settled in the Elbing area near relatives who had come several years earlier. Anna was the first of five daughters born in succession with the sixth child being a boy. Since her brother was a young child when they immigrated, Anna assisted with some of the farm work.

Figure 27
Anna Regier (1869–1907), my grandmother and second wife of John Epp Sr., pictured prior to her marriage on March 6, 1890. Author's file.

My father told the story that his mother as a teenager had been asked one morning to take a team of horses and plow a field. She was admonished to complete at least ten rounds, i.e., plowing from one end of the field to the other and then back to the starting end, before lunch. Anna was back on the farmyard by midmorning. When asked why she was back so early, she replied that she had already completed her ten rounds; no doubt, she was sent back to the field. Father also related that what Grandmother hated most about plowing was the feel of snakes slithering over her feet. She walked barefoot while plowing to conserve shoe leather. Before she was nineteen, she had also taught three years at a German elementary school for Mennonite children in their area.

John and Anna Epp had nine children: seven daughters and two sons. These were hardy children and all survived to adulthood, seven of them living into their nineties. Unfortunately, Grandmother passed away on September 15, 1907 after giving birth to the youngest daughter. Since there were telephones in homes already by that time, her parents, Cornelius and Anna Regier, were notified in rural Elbing eight miles away and, using a buggy, were at her side before Grandmother Epp passed away.

Figure 28
John Epp Sr. (1862–1943), my grandfather. Murphy, Newton, KS. Author's file.

Celebration of the Golden Wedding Anniversary

Grandfather Epp, a.k.a, Johannes, and affectionately referred to as "Papa" in this poem, had more life experiences by the time he married Anna Regier at age twenty-eight than most of us will have in a lifetime. He was born in West Prussia on a farm in Schönhorst on May 20, 1862. The farm consisted of only about one-fourth of a United States section of land. The land there was much more productive than that of the Kansas prairies; the climate was not so extreme and dry spells were unknown.

From ages six to eight, he attended the village school in Schönhorst. In 1870, his parents Peter (1825–1895) and Agnethe Andres (1849–1875) Epp sold their farm and moved to Halbstädt (Molotschna Colony) in southern Russia to secure a better political future for their son Johannes. The Mennonites in West Prussia had lost their privilege of exemption from military service in 1867 when a national conscription law was passed. Unfortunately, during the summer of their first year in Russia, compulsory military service was also introduced in Russia, negating the perpetual privilege granted to the Mennonites by Czarina Catherine the Great. A ten-year period for emigration was granted and an alternative military service in forestry service was negotiated. Although alternative service was introduced for the Russian Mennonites, it was perceived that new immigrants were not granted this privilege, so the Peter Epp family remained Prussian citizens and lived on a travel passport in Russia. From age eight to fifteen, Johannes attended government schools in Halbstädt. During the years, 1875–78, A. B. Peters was a classmate of Johannes at the *Halbstädter Centralschule* and they became intimate friends. A. B. Peters later wrote that Johannes "was a faithful student of God's grace who, to the delight of his teachers, was endowed with exemplary obedience and was a model of diligence. He had a congenial and winsome personality by which he found the favor of his fellow classmates."

His mother, Agnethe, passed away on January 12, 1875, five years after the family moved to Russia, when Johannes was thirteen years old. Among her last words were, "The Lord Jesus will guide you."

Between 1875 and 1882, lawlessness became so prevalent in Russia, that the Mennonites began to fear for their lives. In spring of 1882, Peter told his twenty-year-old son Johannes, who was approaching the military draft age, that "Now you will have to go to America." Since the family had retained their West Prussian passports, if they returned to West Prussia, Johannes would be subject to conscription there.

Figure 29
Peter (1825–1895) and Agnethe Epp (1824–1875), parents of John Epp Sr. and my great-grandparents. Author's file.

The Epps truly enjoyed Russia, so reluctantly, Johannes, together with a cousin his age, immigrated to Beatrice, Nebraska and lived there with an uncle. The understanding was that after Johannes would be beyond the draft age in Russia and had become an American citizen, he would return to Russia on an American passport. One serious consideration at that time was that a United States passport was canceled if a citizen was out of the country for more than two years. Circumstances intervened, however. During the winter of 1882, Johannes received a letter from his father stating that his property in Russia was up for sale. In 1873, Peter had purchased a collective Hutterite farm at Scheromet, fifty-five miles northeast of Halbstädt, as these thirteen families prepared to immigrate to South Dakota in 1874. The collective farm included a windmill to grind grain, a blacksmith shop as well as kilns for brick and roof tile production, and 568 acres of land. The Epp family moved to Scheromet in 1874 and Johannes boarded with relatives in Halbstädt during the school terms.

Peter sold his farm and businesses in Scheromet in 1883, and he, together with Johannes' only sibling, Agnethe (*Tante Thiessen*), her husband Heinrich Thiessen, and their son Peter joined Johannes in Nebraska. Feeling that the immigrants in Beatrice were trying to recreate their European existence rather than incorporating the realities of an American prairie lifestyle, and maybe also because the land prices were lower in Kansas, Peter and Johannes relocated and purchased a farm in the local Kansas West Prussian Mennonite community one mile east of the location of Great-grandfather Harder's farm. On August 12, 1884, John, as his name appears on the Butler County land deeds, bought 320 acres. This was the west half of Section 15, Milton Township. The land was purchased from the Heinrich Penner family for $7,000, with a $1,000 mortgage. Allegedly, the $1,000 was borrowed from my great-grandfather Harder.

In the fall of that year on December 8, 1884, Johannes married Margarethe Toews. In 1886 a fire destroyed their Prussian-style house/barn unit; the animals in the barn were saved and Margarethe was carried out of the house on a mattress with a one-week-old baby. A few other items were also saved. Then finally, in the words of Papa himself, "And so, after a few years, the heavenly Gardener found her ripe for transplanting to a better location. On April 4, 1888, he called her home. Through the joyousness that the Lord gave her in death, death lost a good measure of its sting for me. The Lord gave us three children. Two already preceded their mother in death, and the last one soon followed her. In 1890 the Lord gave me in Anna Regier, a faithful life's companion."

Prior to his death on April 16, 1943, Papa asked that he be buried in his shirtsleeves so that his suit could be sent to needy Canadian immigrants who had just come from Russia. He will always be remembered as the person who contributed $500 to the Mennonite Central

Committee (MCC) for a tractor-plow unit that initiated the first MCC development project to assist relatives suffering through a devastating drought in southern Russia where Papa had spent his childhood.

A. B. Peters, Johannes's schoolmate in southern Russia, who relocated to Canada, published a tribute in the *Christlicher Bundesbote*, September 1943, when he learned of Papa's death. During a period of famine in southern Russia from 1915–30, Papa sent as many as ten packages of food items to the Peters. This was a major contribution toward their survival. In 1924, Peters received notice from Moscow that his travel permit from Canada had arrived and that the expenses for the trip for the entire family had been paid. After arriving in Canada, Peters wrote Papa and asked how much he owed, including interest? Papa answered, "We won't even speak of interest and we won't consider any personal debt; that is extended to you as a gift." Peters concludes his tribute with the phrase: "Truly, the righteous are held in everlasting remembrance."

Here, then, is the poem my mother wrote for her father-in-law, Johannes (John) Epp Sr.

Für Papa's Goldenerhockzeitstag
6 März 1940
von Hildegard and Martha vorgetragen

Es eilt die Zeit so schnell dahin es reiht sich Tag an Tag
  Und werden Jahre dann daraus ehe man es recht merken mag
Doch immer wieder Gotteshand und seine Lieb' man spürt
  Wenn auf verborgenen Wege er seine Kinder führt.
Oft führt er sie durch grüne und sonnenlichte Auen,
  Daß sie nur seine Güte und Lieb' und Langmut schauen
Doch kommen auch wohl Zeiten wo rauh der Weg und scheint
  Daß müd eintritte werde und auch das Auge weint.
Und ist es auch ein Kreuze oder Last die er Auflegt
  Der Herr ist dann stets nahe er hebt, er stärkt, er trägt.
Und ruft er unsere Lieben zu sich in Himmelshöhe
  Und einsam will es werden und wir allein dastehe
So ist er und doch nahe der stets und helfen kann
  Es geh' durch Freud und Leiden doch immer Himmel an
So ist es ja nur Liebe und nur dies Ziel Er sieht
  Das näher immer näher zu sich sein Kinder er zieht.

Celebration of the Golden Wedding Anniversary

Und so hast du es Großpapa ja auch wohl schon erfahren
   In deinem ganzen Leben stets, daß jetzt schon reich an Fahren
Und sind wir nur geladen heut zu einem besonderen Fest
   Und heut in Gedanken du vorüber ziehen läßt
So manches aus der Vergangenheit, daß unvergeßlich blieb
   So manche Erinnerung die dir noch so teuer und so lieb.
Um Großmama's Geburtstag heut, zu seiner, sind wir hier
   Im näherem Familienkreis zum Andenken an ihr
Dann sind es ja wohl heute gerade 50 Jahr
   Daß du zum zweiten male auch standest am Traualter.
Ein feiner goldener schimmer das heutige Fest umzieht
   Es zeigt von Gottes Gnade und seine Treu und Güt.
Und bricht der Lebensabend nun bald für dich herein
   Mög' dir dann auch umleuchten wie goldener Abendschein
Die Liebe deiner Kinder und möge Gotteshand
   Dich schützen und dich führen bis zu dem goldenen Strand.

For Papa's Golden Wedding Anniversary Day
March 6, 1940
Given by Hildegard and Martha

Time hurriedly passes so quickly as in succession day after day
   And it may then be years before one may perceive it.
However, time and again God's hand and his love can be traced
   As he leads his children in hidden ways.
Often he leads one through green and sunlit meadows
   So that one only observes his goodness and love and patience.
However, times truly came when the way appears rough
   Because each step was tiring and the eyes have tears,
And it is also a cross or a burden that he applies.
   The Lord is then constantly near, he lifts, he strengthens, he carries.
And he calls our loved ones to himself in heaven above
   And it becomes lonesome and we stand here alone.
He is like this and yet is constantly near and can help.
   Going heavenward is always, however, through joy and suffering.
Yes, so it is that he only sees our love and only our aspirations
   As nearer, always nearer to him he draws his children.
And yes, surely you have also already experienced this, grandpapa.
   In your whole life that already has been rich with experiences
And since we have been invited today to a special festivity
   And today in thankfulness you draw from the burdensome past.

The Petals of a Kansas Sunflower

Some of the events of the past remained unforgettable,
  Some remembrances that you still have are so beloved and so dear.
Because of Grandmama's birthday we are here today and have come back.
  We think about her in this closely drawn family circle,
Because truly, it is exactly fifty years today
  That you also stood at the marriage altar for the second time.
A fine golden glimmer surrounds today's celebration.
  It shows God's grace and his faithfulness and goodness.
And now life brings you to its twilight soon.
  May you then have shining around you also, similar to a golden sunset,
The love of your children and God's willing hand,
  To shield you and to guide you until you reach that golden shore.

14

Celebration of Birthdays

LIFE AND LONGEVITY WERE envisioned as divinely granted gifts or privileges, and therefore worthy of recognition and celebration. Birthday poems were used to honor the longevity of special people. But really, birthday celebrations were another good reason to gather in groups for social interaction. For use at such occasions, Mother penned a Happy Birthday song that is metered to be sung with the melody of the hymn, "What a Friend We Have in Jesus."

Happy Birthday Song

We wish you a happy birthday;
May your future days be bright,
May the love of God's sweet sunlight,
Fill your life with heavenly light.
May God's presence ever cheer you
May his blessings be your store.
Happy birthday greetings to you
And we wish you many more.

For the sixtieth birthday of Christian Thierstein, Mother wrote a poem of celebration. Christ married my grandfather Bernhard Harder Jr.'s cousin Margarethe Bergmann. Mores of the community dictated that Mother address persons older than she prefaced with "uncle" or "aunt."

The Petals of a Kansas Sunflower

Zu Geburtstag von Onkel Christ Thierstein
17 Dezember 1930

Heute, lieber Onkel Christ
Da ja dein Geburtstag ist
Möchten wir nun alle hier
Bringen unsere Glückwunsch dir
Gottesgnade mit dir war
Nun schon 60 lange Jahre'
Und Er trug zu jeder Zeit
Väterlich durch Freud mit Leid
Er umgab dich mit viel Liebe
Und wir sichten seit du Triebe
Unsere Wünsche dir zu bringen
Und ein Lied für dich zu singen.
Lang schon sind wir ja bekannt
Schon als noch im Deutschenland
Hast du uns doch oft beglückt
Durch Packete die du geschickt
Lange haben wir gewart'
Endlich kam die Ozeanfahrt
Und nu sind wir alle da
Bei dir in Amerika
Gott mage dir Gesundheit schenken
Jeden Unfall von dir lenken
In aller deine Stärke sein
Und seinen Frieden dir verleihen
Das wir uns noch lange freue
Des fröhlichen bei Sonnenschein.

For the Birthday of Uncle Christ Thierstein
December 17, 1930

Today, dear Uncle Christ,
Is indeed your birthday.
All of us here would like
To bring you our congratulations.
God's grace has been with you
Now already for sixty long years
And he carried you at all times
Fatherly through joy with sorrow

Celebration of Birthdays

> He surrounded you with much love
> Since you were young and we observed this.
> Our congratulations we bring for you
> And a song for you to sing,
> We have been acquainted for a long time.
> Already in Germany
> You have often been fortunate.
> Through the packing that you undertook
> Long we have anticipated
> At last the ocean voyage materialized
> And now we are all together
> With you in America.
> May God grant you good health,
> Deflect every accident away from you,
> May you with all your stamina
> And with his peace that he imparts,
> That we may have joy for a long time
> That gladness remains ensconced with sunshine.

The next two poems were written in German to reflect the comfort of the honored elderly persons when most poems by that time were written in English.

In 1944, John Harder Sr. was honored with a special celebration for his ninetieth birthday and Mother was asked to furnish a poem.

Mother's uncle John Harder Sr. (known as Johannes when he was younger) was twenty-two years old when he married Maria Regier just three weeks before they immigrated to America in 1876. Together they had six children before Maria passed away in 1888 of what was described as rheumatic fever. One year later, John married Maria's sister Katharina Regier (1865–1931) who became the stepmother to her sister's six children, ranging in age from two-and-a-half to twelve. Over the next six years, Katharina had three children of her own. Katharina died at the age of sixty-five on January 8, 1931.

Realizing that she was near the end of her life, Katharina requested that John's seventy-seventh birthday celebration should occur as usual, and according to the old German custom, regardless of her health status. On January 11, Katharina's funeral was held in the afternoon, and in the evening they celebrated John's ninetieth birthday. Supper was served to 144 people not counting children three years old and younger.

Figure 30
Wedding portrait of John Harder Sr. (1854–1946) and Marie Regier (1853–1888) shortly after they arrived in Kansas. Tripp Photographer, Newton, Kansas. Source: Author's file.

Because John's birthday was on January 11, the family customarily gathered for his birthday and combined the event with the family's

Celebration of Birthdays

Christmas celebration. A granddaughter shared that "After we congratulated him and gave him a kiss, he handed each one a silver dollar. This was *special*. We sang our grace at the table before the meal was served. He had a devotional with songs—his favorites in German out of the *Gesangbuch mit Noten* (Songbook with Notes)."

Following the introduction in this poem, there is a reiteration of divine guidance, "Your trust in God is without waver / You cling to that, which his Word says / An extended treasury of experiences / That years have brought to you / Constantly filling you with a sense of God's keeping." There is a brief review of historical highlights and a conclusion describing the support in old age of friends and the strength of the Lord. "The circle of friends is worthy of you / Who will constantly stand with you / Those who wait on the Lord / He will give them new strength / As with eagle's wings you ascend / Where your steps are guided also."

Zu Onkel John Harders 90sten Geburtstag
11 Januar 1944
von Phebe Ann vorgetragen

Es trug der Herr auf liebes Armen
Grossonkel dich ein weiters Jahr
Gnadenreich und mit Erbarmen
Er dir fühlbar nahe war.
So sind nun schon hingezogen
Für dich 90 lange Jahr'
Oft ist die Zeit wohl schier geflogen
Dann wieder langsam es auch war.
Wechselhaft war ja dein Leben
Freude gab es da auch Leid
Vorwärts stets war dein bestreben
Getrosten Mutes alle Zeit.
Versäumst in Freuden nicht das danken
Warst auch in Trauer nicht verzagt.
Dein Gottvertrauen ist ohne wanken
Hältst dich an dem daß sein Wort sagt.
Einen reichen Schatz an Erfahrung
Die Jahre dir haben gebracht
Stets fühltest du Gottes Bewahrung
Was auch immer du durch gemacht.
Die Jahre der Jugend und Kinderheit

The Petals of a Kansas Sunflower

Hast in Deutschland du verlebt
Bis wegen Glaubensfreiheit
Eine neue Heimat wurde erstrebt.
Dann galt es auszuwandern
Unter Ereignissen mancher Art
Und dann mit vielen Andern
Die lange Ozean Fahrt.
O! Welch ein Packen gab es da
Von Sachen gross und klein
Bei den Indianern in Amerika
Konnte Alles ja brauchbar sein.
Im stürmischen Kansas auch grassiger Au
Ein neues Heim entstand
Für Viehzucht und für Ackerbau
Schien sich zu eiginen hier das Land.
Von manchen Erlebnis kannst du heut
Grossonkel uns jetzt noch sagen
Kaum Wege gab es zu der Zeit
Auch Brücken nicht in den Tagen.
Viel Veränderung gab es schon seitdem
Man merkt es über all
Es wurde verbessert und bequem
Was doch gut schien dazu mal.
Und verliessen dich im Lauf der Zeiten
So mancher der lieb dir war
Gab es Veränderungen nach allen Seiten
Und weiß schon wurde das Haar.
So bist du dennoch jung geblieben
Dein Trost und Freude war
Im Kreise deiner Lieben
Die Kinder und Enkelschaar.
Und einsam wurde es nicht für dich
Wie wir hier heute sehn
Der Kreis der Freunde erweitert sich
Die stets noch dir bei stehn.
Die auf dem Herrn harren
Will neue Kraft er schenken
Wie mit Adlersflügel sie auffahren
Wohin auch sie die Schritte lenken.

Celebration of Birthdays

For Uncle John Harder's Ninetieth Birthday
January 11, 1944
Recited by Phebe Ann

The Lord carried you with his loving arms
Great-uncle, for many extended years.
Rich in grace and with compassion
He was perceptibly near you
So drawn out now already
Ninety long years for you.
Well, time often almost flies
Then it again slows down.
Yes, changes depict your life
With joy; there was also suffering.
Constantly your endeavors moved forward
Confidently courageous at all times.
In happiness, you have not neglected to be thankful.
When sorrowful, you also were not despondent
Your trust in God is without waver
You cling to that, which his Word says.
An extended treasury of experiences
That many years have brought to you
Constantly filling you with a sense of God's keeping
Giving comfort in whatever you did.
The years of youth and childhood
You spent in Germany
Until because of religious freedom
A new homeland was sought
That resulted in emigration
With events of many kinds
And then with many others
Crossed the large ocean.
Oh! Such packing that occurred
Of things large and small
Among the Indians in America
Everything could be useful.
In stormy Kansas, also, oh so grassy
To give rise to a new home
For stock-farming and for agriculture
The land here appeared right for ownership
Of many events you could today
Still tell us now, great-uncle
There were few roads at that time

The Petals of a Kansas Sunflower

> Also, no bridges in those days
> There have been many changes since then
> One notices it overall
> It did improve and become more convenient
> The good of it was noteworthy
> And it kept you in the passage of time
> Many things precious to you
> Things changed continuously
> And the hair would become white
> Through this you have remained young
> Your consolation and joy were
> The circle of your loved ones
> The children and grandchildren
> And it did not become lonesome for you
> As we can see here today
> The circle of friends is worthy of you
> Who will constantly stand with you
> Those who wait on the Lord
> He will give them new strength
> As with eagle's wings you ascend
> Where your steps are guided also.

When Mother's aunt Marie (Wiebe) Dyck (1862–1950) celebrated her eighty-fifth birthday, my sister Phebe Ann recited another poem. Aunt Marie was a sister to our grandmother, Helene (Wiebe) Harder. The Jacob Wiebe family with their ten children immigrated to the U.S. in 1890, staying with the Gerhard and Anna (Ensz) Regier family until a house was built. The Gerhard Regiers immigrated with the first group in 1876 and Anna (Ensz) Regier was a sister to the late, first Mrs. Jacob Wiebe (Renathe Ensz), the mother of the first four siblings including my grandmother.

The poem begins with congratulations and thankfulness to God for guidance, "That you today in such an advanced age / Are still well and are with us here." Mother recalls that Aunt Marie was born in Germany (West Prussia) and then participated in packing: "Oh, what a packing was involved / Of items large and small / On Kansas' wide prairie / Surely everything could be useful . . . And already in the next year / You moved into your own home / And with diligence and thriftiness / There was progress and success."

Six years after the Dyck's twenty-fifth wedding anniversary, Herman Dyck, passed away and "your loved ones stood by you / with

Celebration of Birthdays

advice and action." Other relatives who passed away are remembered. The poem closes with the blessing, "I wish / For you in closing that God accompany you, / That he continues to remain with you / As he has remained with you until today."

Für Geburtstag von Tante Herman Dyck
25 April 1947
von Phebe Ann vorgetragen

Meinen Glückwunsch zum Geburtstag
   Bring ich Grosstante Dir
Danken Gott der ja so gnädig
   Dich geleitet hat bis hier
Der so freundlick dich behütet
   In so langer Lebensfrist
Das du heut im hohen Alter
   Noch gesund hier bei uns bist.
Ja auch du rühmst Gottesgnade
   Die ja jeden Morgen neu
Und du hast es oft erfahren
   Der Herr ist Liebevoll und treu.
Und an einem Tag wie diesen
   Von besonderer Festlichkeit
Gehn ja wohl die Gedanken
   Zurück in die Vergangenheit
Die frühsten Erinnerungen gehn
   Zurück ins Deutschland
Wo in Eurem Heim in Leske
   Einst deine Wiege Stand.
Doch schon 2 Jahre später
   Wurde die Mutter euch genommen
Doch habt durch Gottesgnade
   Ihr wieder Ersatz bekommen
Auch die Jahre der Jugend and Kindheit
   Verlebst du in Deutschenland
Doch löste durch die Auswanderung
   Sich da manch Freundschaftsband.
Noch erinnerst du dich jener Zeit
   Es gab Arbeit mancher Art
Und dann mit vielen andern
   Die lange Ozeanfahrt.

The Petals of a Kansas Sunflower

O! Welch ein packen gab es da
  Von Sachen groß und klein
Auf Kansas weiter prairie
  Konnte ja alles brauchbar sein.
Und schon im nächsten Jahre
  Zogst Du ins eigene Heim
Und unter fleiß und Sparsamkeit
  War fortschritt und gedeihen.
So ist dann schnell vergangen
  Für Euch da Jahr um Jahr
Bis dann in 1916
  Die Silberhochzeit war.
Doch schon 6 Jahre später
  Wurde einsamer dein Pfad
Doch stehn deine Lieben
  Dir bei mit Rat und Tat
Auf ein wechselhaftes Leben
  Blickst heute du zurück
Es wechseln trübbe Tage
  Mit Tage voller Glück.
Schon hat in schwerer Krankheit
  Dein Leben in Gefahr geschwebt
Doch die Geschwister die dir am nächsten
  Hast du lang schon überlebt.
Der Anfang dieses Jahres
  Brachte neue Trauerzeit
Um ein treues Glied der Familie
  Noch vermissen wir sie heut.
Und nun Grosstante wünsch ich
  Zum Schluß dir Gottesgeleit
Das er ferner bei dir bleibe
  Wie Er blieb bei dir bis heut.

For the Birthday of Mrs. Herman Dyck
April 25, 1947
Recited by Phebe Ann

My best wishes for your birthday
  I bring to you, Great-aunt,
Yes, thanking God who so graciously
  Has accompanied you until now

Celebration of Birthdays

Who has taken pleasure in guarding you
    For such a long lifetime
That you today in such an advanced age
    Are still well and are with us here.
Yes, you also praise God for his grace
    That is renewed every morning
And you have often heard
    The Lord is full of love and truth.
And in a day such as this one
    With specific festivity
Your thoughts surely go
    Back to the former life
Of your earliest recollections
    Back in Germany
Where in your home in Leske
    Once your cradle stood
However, already two years later
    Your mother was taken from you
However, through God's grace you have
    Again experienced compensation
Also the years of your youth and childhood
    You lived in Germany
Through the emigration you untied
    Yourself from the many bonds of friendship
You still reminisce about that time
    There was work of many kinds
And then with many others
    You crossed the wide ocean.
Oh, the packing that was involved
    Of items large and small
On Kansas's wide prairie
    Surely everything could be useful.
And already in the next year
    You moved into your own home
And with diligence and thriftiness
    There was progress and success.
So it then passed quickly
    For you, year after year
Until when in 1916
    It was your silver wedding anniversary.
However, after only six more years
    Your path became lonely
However, your loved ones stood by you
    With advice and action

The Petals of a Kansas Sunflower

>Upon a life of enforced change
>>You glance back today
>
>It oscillated from dreary days
>>To days full of happiness.
>
>Already during severe illness
>>Your beloved was carried far away
>
>However, the siblings that were next to you
>>You have already long outlived
>
>At the beginning of this year
>>Brought a new time of mourning
>
>Because of a faithful member of the family
>>We still miss her today.
>
>And now great-aunt, I wish
>>For you in closing that God accompany you,
>
>That he continues to remain with you
>>As he has remained with you until today.

My aunt Helen Ruth Epp was a very special person. She was gregarious, loving, and very helpful with counsel and kind deeds to many, many people. She functioned as a surrogate grandmother in my father's family, since Grandmother Epp passed away in 1907 when my father was six years old.

Each of us grandchildren received a gift of a little red children's chair from Aunt Helen Ruth at the Christmas following our fourth birthdays. She would invite her nieces and nephews to spend weeks at her house during the summer. She was thin with impeccable posture, had a sense of precision, and had the Victorian style of organization—a place for everything and everything in its place. Every December 26, for the Epp Christmas celebration, her candy dishes, which were liberally set out, consisted of candy corn, orange gumdrop slices, and vanilla chocolates.

Aunt Helen Ruth obtained more education than any of her siblings, in spite of her father's feeling that education was of minimal value for rural living and farming, although he himself was an avid reader. His childhood bouts of "Egyptian eye disease" resulted in uncompleted school work, making it impossible to write final exams and complete his education. Consequently, formal education beyond elementary levels did not seem important to him. Aunt Helen Ruth negotiated with Grandfather Epp that, if he would let her finish high school at Hesston Academy and nurse's training at the Bethel Deaconess Hospital, she would later return to the farm to take care of him in his old age, as well as live with her unmarried brother, Cornie, who was a wonderful, gentle man but who suffered from clinical depression most of his life.

After finishing high school, Aunt Helen Ruth worked for a time in Mountain Lake, Minnesota. She returned to Newton and completed her nurse's training at the Bethel Deaconess Hospital in 1926. Her greatest desire was to be a missionary nurse in India, but Grandfather Epp convinced her that she was not good enough. There are long discussions in her diary about her desire to go to India and her feelings of inadequacy. On June 11, 1939, she was ordained and joined the deaconess order at the Bethel Deaconess Hospital, Newton, Kansas.

The deaconess cause was first promoted by David Goertz at the Western District Conference of the General Conference Mennonite Conference in 1890. In 1903, the directors of Bethel College applied for a state charter authorizing a deaconess motherhouse as an adjunct of Bethel College. Two years later in 1905, the society became independent.

A deaconess was described as a servant of the church, who in the spirit of Jesus Christ and for his sake, spent her whole time serving those who were sick or poor or morally in danger. She not only nursed them, but took care of them as a Christian, in order that they might be saved through faith in Jesus Christ. The Bethel deaconess movement declined as members grew old and no new members joined. The last surviving deaconess moved into the Bethel Home for the Aged in 1986.

After six years of working in Newton, Aunt Helen Ruth returned to the farm, working thirty days a year at the hospital to fulfill her requirements to remain with the order, and continued to wear her dress habit to church on Sundays. Her dream was to return to deaconess duties full time, but by the time Uncle Cornie entered a nursing home, she was so old that she could only deliver flowers to patients' rooms and had trouble remembering room numbers at that.

When Aunt Helen Ruth turned fifty years old, her siblings celebrated her birthday at the home of her sister Margarethe and Emil Wiebe on April 20, 1948. Mother furnished a poem for the festivity.

The Petals of a Kansas Sunflower

Figure 31
Sister Helen Ruth Epp (1898–1986) was ordained as a deaconess on June 11, 1939.
Ordination photo. Murphy, Newton. Source: Photo Collection, Mennonite Library
and Archives, North Newton.

Celebration of Birthdays

For Sister Helen Ruth's Fiftieth Birthday

In a farm home near Brainerd,
    Fifty years ago today;
A sweet, dark-haired baby
    Was welcomed there to stay.

She was so weak and helpless
    Only seeking care and love
And it was freely given
    This precious gift from above.

Three sisters and one brother
    Were happy as could be
And in the early training
    Helped very faithfully.

She had a happy childhood;
    Always helping with a will,
And many a precious memory
    Is lingering with her still.

Yet young, there were experiences
    That probably no one understood,
And without the loving care of a mother
    She grew to womanhood.

There were added responsibilities,
    As for the younger ones to care.
A task that with her sisters
    She lovingly did share.

The circle soon grew wider,
    As from grandparents came a call
Or maybe aunts or cousins
    She gladly helped them all.

Again the circle widened,
    When she left for Mountain Lake;
There active part in nursing
    The weak and sick, to take.

The Petals of a Kansas Sunflower

A desire for full-time service,
    As with the sick she dealt
For our dear Lord and Master
    Was then more keenly felt.

Having a good preparation
    From Hesston Bible School
She entered Bethel Hospital
    And Nurses Training School.

On June 11, 1939
    She was ordained as Deaconess;
A work that for six long years
    She served with joy and readiness.

Then again she left the work
    That was precious to her heart
And in housekeeping at home
    Again took active part.

Hers was the joy of nursing
    Her father with tender love
Till he was called to glory
    To his reward above.

Though not in her chosen field
    She is laboring today.
Many for advice and treatment
    To her door have found their way.

Also in church and Sunday school
    She takes an active part.
And has endeared herself
    To many a human heart.

And many are the parcels,
    She packs and sends abroad
To clothe our needy brethren,
    To strengthen their faith in God.

And on this special occasion
    I believe to say in truth
That all our Best Wishes
    Go to Sister Helen Ruth.

Several years later, to celebrate Aunt Helen Ruth's twenty-fifth anniversary in nursing, the deaconesses invited some of her relatives for a dinner in the basement fellowship hall of the First Mennonite Church in Newton on September 28, 1951. Mother wrote a poem for the occasion. One of my sisters recited the poem.

In her life of service to others, Aunt Helen Ruth was a role model for all her nieces. Of the fourteen, four are also RNs, three have master's degrees, three are involved in full time church work, three have been school teachers, four were homemakers on farms, one worked as a secretary, and one was employed as a seamstress.

Twenty-fifth Anniversary of Nursing for Aunt Helen Ruth
September 28, 1951

There are days that are outstanding;
    Times of special joy and praise
In which we pause just for a moment
    As we marvel at God's ways.
And such a time has come to you
    In whose honor we are here;
As in the vineyard of our Lord
    You toiled from year to year.
A quarter of a century
    Has passed, the record shows—
Since as your work the nursing
    Of the weak and sick you chose.
To a milestone you are coming
    On the highway of life these days
On which the light is falling
    In lovely silver rays.
Our Lord and Savior is with you always;
    Gives courage and patience and strength for the day.
He will not forget you, nor fail you, nor grieve.
    He will not forsake you, he never will leave.
His grace is sufficient—we walk not alone
    As the day so the strength that he gives his own.

Delora Busenitz recited a short granddaughterly poem for the seventieth birthday of her grandmother, Mrs. Gerhard Busenitz (Marie Sudermann Busenitz). Delora is the daughter of Olga and Gerhard

Busenitz for whom Mother wrote a wedding poem in 1947. Marie Busenitz was born on October 28, 1889 and passed away on April 18, 1982, so Delora was able to enjoy the smile of her grandmother for another twenty-three years after reciting this poem.

Delora Busenitz for her Grandmother's Birthday
November 1959

Grandma dear, I'm coming
   With a special wish your way,
Because it's in your honor
   That we celebrate this day.

We thank the Lord for keeping
   You with us all these years;
Through happiness and sunshine,
   Through sorrow and through tears,

We pray that you'll be with us
   For yet a long, long while;
And we can come and visit you
   And see your pleasant smile.
      —M.H.E.

For the eightieth birthday of Mrs. Eduard Harder (Marie Wilhelmine Entz Harder), Mother wrote a poem that was presented by Priscilla, a granddaughter. She was the daughter of Waldo Harder (chapter 13). Eduard was my mother's cousin, son of John Harder Sr., for whom the first poem in this chapter was written.

Priscilla recalls the role of grandparents, since she and her family spent many years in Africa in what was then known as Congo. During periodic trips back to the home community, Grandmother's home became very special because many treasures were stored there.

In the Eduard Harder farmyard next to their house near Newton, Ed had set up a merry-go-round from an abandoned elementary school. This was a special merry-go-round with eight seats, each with a handle that, when pulled towards you, would make the merry-go-round move clockwise. The faster you pulled, the faster the merry-go-round would go. Eduard had this toy for his grandchildren, but whenever he had

Celebration of Birthdays

guests, all the men would ride his merry-go-round. As a child, I was included in these rides.

A lingering memory of Mrs. Harder is from 1947. My father was busy helping with the construction of Berean Academy (chapter 17), and I, as a five-year-old, was assigned the task of watering the newly planted plugs of sod. As she drove by in her white, four-door Plymouth she rolled down the window and encouraged me by saying with a smile, "Give them a good drink."

Mrs. Ed Harder's Eightieth Birthday
February 6, 1968
Presented by Priscilla

Grandma dear, I am bringing best wishes to you here.
   We praise the Lord for keeping you with us many a year.
In fact, today it's eighty. Oh, can it really be?
   You seem the same dear Grandma, you've always been to me.
What changes you have witnessed! From horse and buggy days
   To fast and modern living, and more convenient ways.
Many rich experiences the past has brought to you.
   Through many blessed days you've come, but through some sad ones too.
Happy was your family life, three sons have been your pride.
   And fast the years were passing with Grandpa at your side.
But since there were some changes, your boys are "on their own,"
   Grandpa was called to glory, this leaves you oft alone.
But still the Lord can use you in many different ways.
   By visiting the shut-ins, you shorten their long days.
Or with your nimble fingers you stitch quilts neat and nice,
   Useful and beautiful and of a costly price.
We as a family often recall the Mission field.
   How very dear Grandparents are was plainly then revealed.
For, those things we could not take would then fall to their care.
   Returning, we would find them just as we left them there.
We'll equally be sharing. (The reward is sure enough.)
   If being in the battle or staying with the stuff.
Another thing I'll mention is Christmas day with you.
   Each year it is a blessing, enjoyable and new.
Your kind hospitality I'll also mention here,
   Of which we take advantage repeatedly each year.
And then the little extras, you are giving to each guest.

The Petals of a Kansas Sunflower

    You have the toys for the children, adults relax and rest.
And talking here of "extras" brings heart cookies to mind,
    That an engaged young couple in their honor, would find.
Oh, how we do love letters signed, Grandma, with your name.
    (Though Grandpa's were oft longer) They're precious just the same.
There is more that I could mention but maybe this will do,
    To show that we do respect a Grandma just like you.

    Soon all of us are leaving and you are left alone.
    But God is still abiding, he does not forsake his own.
And should your strength be failing, you still can intercede
    For children and grandchildren, and for their every need.
May God's strong hand uphold you as days pass one by one.
    And when life's toil is over, you'll hear his kind, "Well done."

    In chapter 13, I mentioned the ministerial organization in the local church from 1878 to 1939, i.e., one lay elder and numerous lay ministers. When B. W. Harder resigned in January, 1939, the congregation of the local church passed a resolution to adopt the one paid minister system. On March 26, 1939, the Rev. John C. Kaufman was invited to become the minister, the first minister who had not been a lay member of the congregation prior to his election. In August, 1948 he was followed by the Rev. Walter H. Dyck. Both the Rev. Kaufman and the Rev. Dyck were fluent in German and included a fifteen-minute sermonette in German as well as a German hymn in the Sunday morning worship service. In December, 1954, the Rev. L. R. Amstutz, who was not fluent in German, was invited to become the minister. The German sermonette was dropped and only a German hymn remained. With time the hymn, too, was eliminated. Most of the young people from the third-immigrant generation, and especially the fourth generation, no longer knew German.

    Rev. Amstutz served the community for twenty years. After he had been in the community for fifteen years, Mother's dear friend Frieda Harder organized a celebration for his fifty-fourth birthday after a Wednesday night church service, and requested a poem. Mother begins the poem by noting that even preachers have birthdays, special days on which to honor them. She recalls his move from Minnesota to Kansas and refers to the different climates in summer with the high temperatures, the hot winds, and inevitable drought conditions. But she tells that during the fifteen years of his service, 139 people were added to the church rolls through baptism, 268 new babies were born to members, 115 couples got married, and 53 funerals were conducted. The poem ends with a benediction requesting the Lord's protection and guidance for Pastor Amstutz and a lengthy continuation of his services.

To open my eighth grade year at Brainerd Elementary, the teachers, Alma Classen (Mrs. Roy Regier) and Ann Jost (Mrs. Arlo Voth), invited Rev. Amstutz to give a devotional convocation in the two-room country schoolhouse. On the first Friday, nineteen students gathered in the basement of the school and Rev. Amstutz talked about hoarfrost, a natural wonder that is aesthetically very beautiful. I had never heard the word before nor had I paid attention to the phenomenon. Sensitized to its reality, now once every two or three years, when the humidity is very high, the temperature drops just below freezing and everything is covered with white crystals, I think back to the day when hoarfrost entered my consciousness. On those occasions when everything, even the smallest twigs on the trees, is covered with crystals, Kansas is enchanting, and before the sun warms the air, truly a winter wonderland.

Fifty-fourth Birthday of Rev. Amstutz
February 17, 1971

Though days may pass by in routine,
    Still one is our special day
Where more attention we enjoy,
    More love is coming our way.

The pastor too has come that far,
    Here we have his day of days.
So now today, this Wednesday night,
    We unite our hearts in praise.

The God that guided Abraham
    From Ur, up to Canaan's land,
Has also led and guided him
    With his tender, loving hand.

He came to us from Mountain Lake
    To the windy Kansas plains,
Where farmers still are on the job
    And oft' sparse can be the rains.

The Petals of a Kansas Sunflower

    They'll recall the warm reception
        That July had for them in store.
    Even if that was a hot day,
        They found there were many more.

    In the fifteen years he served us,
        We saw changes here and there.
    More Bible study, more witnessing
        And progress everywhere.

    One hundred thirty-nine were added
        By baptism to our group.
    And two hundred sixty-eight new voices
        We heard by cooing or a whoop.

    One hundred fifteen times, this aisle,
        Walked a young man with his bride.
    Fifty-three of our loved ones
        Their armors have laid aside.

    Now today we thank our Pastor
        That he guided us along,
    To dedication and service
        Still encouraging us on.

    That in peace we live with others,
        Separated from the world.
    In love and faith and devotion,
        Read and meditate God's word.

    He could pass the fiftieth milestone,
        This year it will be by four.
    And we as a congregation
        Are wishing him many more!

    May the dear Lord bless and keep him
        And watch over him, we pray,
    That together, in the future,
        We have many a blessed day.

    Ten years later, Frieda Harder wanted to honor the seventieth birthday of her husband Walter. Walter was a son of my mother's cousin and grandson of John Harder Sr. whom we met in the first poem in this

Celebration of Birthdays

chapter. Mother reviews Walter's childhood, how he went into farming and got married. Two children, Marilyn and Wesley, joined the family. In time Marilyn and her husband Marvin left the grandchildren in the care of Walter and Frieda, while Marvin was working on his master's degree. Mother reminds Walter of his wonderful parents and siblings and ends the poem with a blessing.

For Walter Harder's Birthday
October 4, 1981
Presented by Marilyn Harder Kaufman

A birthday comes but once a year, we enjoy them—I would say.
We like to pause and then reflect on happenings on that day.
And all along the clock moves onward, seconds, minutes and days go by;
But on God who never changes we at all times can rely.
And today for you it's seventy; seventy years have come and gone,
Still with God as your companion, fearlessly you travel on.
What happens in one's first few years is not easy to recall;
The loving care of a mother is overshadowing all.
So Dad, your first recollections, still vivid with you today
Are the happy days of childhood with excitements every day.
A group of twelve active children of course can have much fun;
But there was also much to do from morn till setting sun.
We know you had the honor of being the fourth in line;
For a sister and two brothers another baby boy was fine.
I wonder if when older you added to work some joy,
Taking monotony from the job with a few pranks that you would try.
After school days for you were over, the days for studying had passed
You decided to get married and farm on your own at last.
Farming for you held enjoyments, the Lord blessed the work of your hands.
After a few years you sensed a vacancy but unable to supply the demand.
This is where I stepped into the picture, a little girl, homeless and alone,
I thank the Lord for guiding me into the love of a Christian home.
I felt sheltered and protected, and security I had never had;
Also the love and care of parents and that I could call you "Dad."
Sometime later Wesley joined us, and with his smile and happy way,
He found his way into our hearts and there are memories here to stay.
We two enjoyed the twilight hours when the work for the day was done;
Sitting on the screened-in porch together hearing of incidents we thought
    were fun.
Then I remember our working together, when in my teens I hauled wheat for you

And commending me, that even in wet years I managed to drive right through.
Then the Sunday evening playtime, when no evening service that day;
In summer the outdoors was pleasant and in winter inside we would play.
This summer our children stayed with you "vacationing" as we would say;
They thoroughly enjoyed the farm life and you showing interest and enjoyed
    their play.
And we, without further worry, spent the summer in the South Land;
And later when returning, Marvin had his master's degree in hand.
There are more things I could mention but let it suffice with two;
For me, Grandpa and Grandma Harder were precious and the uncles and
    aunts are too.
I thank you, Dad, that you taught me to be punctual, already at an early date,
I can not remember that ever at any time you were late.
Now may the Lord bless and keep you and lead you on from here;
That together as a family we may still have many blessed years.

—M.H.E.

Sewing circles in the Mennonite churches, a support activity open to women, were an extension of the increased interest in missions during 1850 to 1875. The Rev. Edward Wüst was influential in organizing women's missionary sewing societies in 1853 among the Mennonites in Russia. When they immigrated to America, the women used sewing circles, beginning in the 1890s, as another opportunity to get together and visit while their hands were busy sewing for charity.

In the handout of the program for a 1978 women's fall fellowship program, Mother contributed the following poem entitled "Pattern for Living." The program does not identify the church or the organization that sponsored this fellowship.

Pattern for Living

Life to us, even though mysterious,
    "Is God's precious gift," we say.
He has made us, he will keep us,
    He will guide us day by day.

As we enter on life's journey
    God has a pattern for our life.
It may be one of ease and plenty
    Or one of hardship, pain, and strife.

Celebration of Birthdays

God works daily on the pattern,
   It takes a lifetime to complete.
He makes alterations, he makes changes
   Till his approval it will meet.

The design he weaves is for a purpose.
   To know him and to make him known.
By reading his Word and meditation
   New truths by him to us are shown.

He made us. We are the material.
   Our length of days is in his hands.
They may be short, they may be longer
   Just as his sovereign will commands.

With heat and pressure we are able
   Deep wrinkles and creases to remove.
In our life too, there may be wrinkles
   Of which the Lord does not approve.

Life's pattern may not always suit us
   With its denials and discipline,
But only joy and peace are ours
   When to God's leading we give in.

There also may be extra corners
   His loving hand need cut away.
Pride, stubbornness, conceit, and envy
   Our selfish nature will betray.

Let's gather in all evil yearnings
   And ease them in to fit God's way.
Troubles and trials smooth out neatly
   When Bible teachings we obey.

We enjoy the love of fellow Christians,
   A smile, a handshake when in distress,
It adds beauty to life, like lace and ruffles
   Will enhance an otherwise plain dress.

Now let us think just for a moment
   On material requirements we need.

The Petals of a Kansas Sunflower

> If love and joy and peace are ours
>   From many irritations we are freed.
>
> And as contacts are made with others
>   In our activities throughout the day,
> It's long-suffering, gentleness, and goodness
>   That smoothes the roughness of the way.
>
> Toward God we too have obligations
>   That easily are minimized.
> Faith, meekness, also self-control
>   Are worthy to be emphasized.
>
> We find in sewing we need notions
>   That are essential for success.
> Also in our daily living
>   We find needs as we progress.
>
> We look for elasticity and variety,
>   A sense of humor, a hearty laugh,
> Lip zipper, interfacing of forbearance
>   And backbone stiffening, to say the half.
>
> Measurements are our last consideration,
>   What will the width of understanding be?
> And what the length of our patience?
>   Any depth in our love do we see?
>   —M.H.E.

On May 8, 1975, Mother was asked to lead the devotional at an afternoon sewing circle at a local church. Her theme was birthdays and I will conclude this chapter with Mother's thoughts on this topic.

> As we today, in particular, want to honor one that is near and dear to all of us and since only a week ago she reached another milestone in that she added another year to the life that God has given her, I thought it wouldn't be out of place just to think on birthdays for a few minutes.
>
> There is one thing we all have in common. We all had parents and we all came into this world in the same way. We were a

helpless little bundle that depended entirely upon someone else for our well-being; to feed us, to keep us warm, or whatever the needs were.

The first few years of our life are erased from our memory, even though there are those that will remember incidents that happened when they were rather small. My father died at the age of thirty-nine when I was eight months old. How much later this was I do not know, but I remember sitting on my mother's lap wiping the tears from her cheeks.

The years up to four go by very slowly. Oh yes, once in a while there is a birthday and we are told that now we could hold up four fingers instead of three, if we were too bashful to speak, when someone would ask us how old we were.

After five it was apparent that we were getting restless, we needed something to keep us busy. And besides, we lost a few of our front teeth and this was a sure sign that we were ready for school. So when fall came, there was a new first-grader.

From then on years went by a little faster. Every new school year saw us a year older and before we realized it, we were teenagers and there was a year called sweet sixteen.

Also during these years we became concerned about our spiritual life. The instruction at home and in church and Sunday school was doing its work. Our foremost desire was to give our heart and life to the Lord, to read his Word and live a life pleasing unto him. We were baptized and added to the membership of the church.

At the age of eighteen to twenty or maybe earlier, we began to wonder: "Will I ever get married?" We have an ideal one picked. In my case he was square shouldered with brown eyes. Then came a day when their ways no longer crossed but ran alongside of each other as the two were united in marriage and set up housekeeping. With God's blessing and much work and activities, years went by swiftly as one little one after another came to join the family.

But birthdays keep on coming—it's thirty, then forty, and before we realize it, the fiftieth, and one of the children might be saying in surprise: "Fifty, well, then you are an antique."

It seems the summit has been reached, the declining has begun. The steps are slower and more careful. How soon ten more

The Petals of a Kansas Sunflower

milestones are passed and it is sixty and seventy. It seems time is flying; we would like to hang on to the years and we realize the songwriter is correct, "We are going down the valley one by one."

But who is afraid of birthdays? They don't count. It's life that counts and life is more exciting, more fulfilling as years go by . . .

15

Remembering Special People on Their Birth Dates

AT THAT TIME THERE was no TV blaring 24/7, no shopping at boutique strip malls, nor an Internet to blog one's opinion, views, or outlook, but early in the twentieth century within the local community of church and relatives there was a *gemütlichkeit* (an inner comfort and peace) in perpetuating pleasant memories. Effort was made to cultivate familial contact to reinforce the interconnectedness or bonding of relatives.

A celebration was organized to remember and to think about Great-grandmother Harder on the anniversary of her one-hundredth birthday. The event was held at the farm of son-in-law John H. Regier located west of Elbing.

Mother fondly reminisced that when she was a child she would walk across the farmyard to the other house to comb her grandmother's hair. Grandmother's hair was rather thin by then, but this gave Mother a reason to visit nearly every day. Mother was thirteen when her grandmother passed away.

Justine (Bergmann) Harder was born on July 6, 1834 in Leske, West Prussia to Dietrich and Justine (Claassen) Bergmann. She became the third wife of Bernhard Harder Sr. whom we learned to know in chapter 3. After the Harders arrived in Kansas in 1876, Justine, together with the other immigrant women, remained in Halstead in or near the homes of relatives until the first building, the *Speicher* or granary, was built on the farm. That autumn she moved the family into the granary until the house was completed the next July 1877.

The house had large rooms and a dark hallway, and was built with many West Prussian residential features. The kitchen was a lean-to on the north, preventing the heat of cooking on a wood-fired stove to warm

Figure 32
Justine Bergmann Harder (1834–1916) ca. 1885. Her white headpiece is a "Haube" worn on formal occasions and always in church. Baldwin Photos, Wichita. Source: Author's file.

the house in summertime. Food would have been carried from the kitchen through the dark hall into the living room or the summer room for mealtimes. Justine grew houseplants in the flower room and my mother specifically mentions lovely cyclamen. The parlor and the summer room were connected with a double door that could be opened when entertaining large numbers of guests or family members.

The Dutch ceramic tile stove brought from West Prussia was assembled in the house but with time was found to be less efficient in generating heat than an American cast-iron potbelly stove and thus

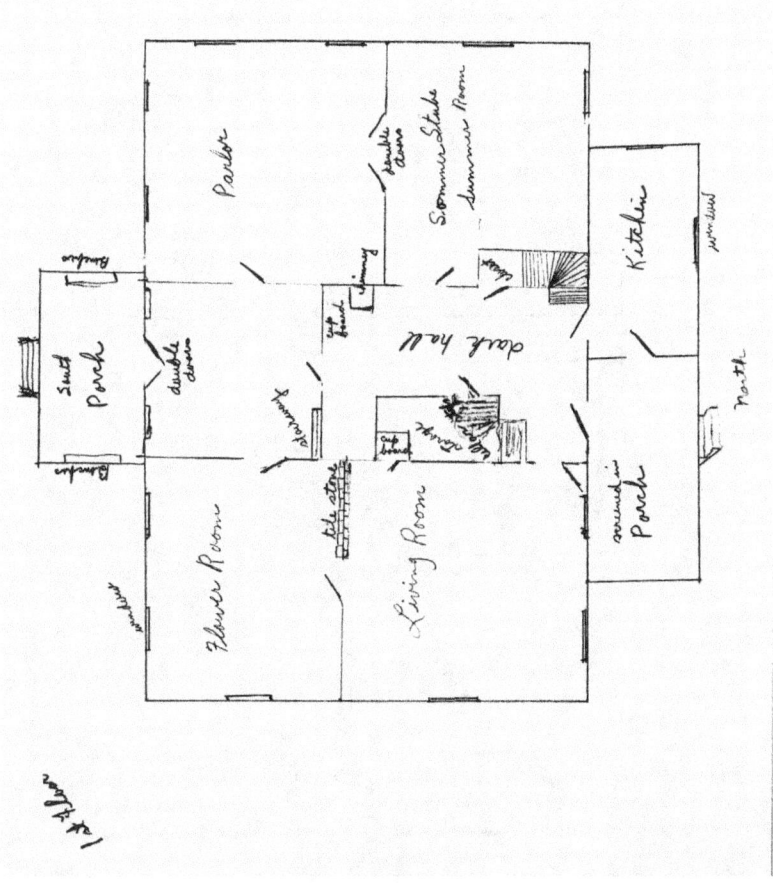

Figure 33a
Floor plan of the Bernhard Harder house of 1877, first floor.
Drawing by Marie. Source: Author's file.

was not used. However, the tile stove remained in place until the house was dismantled in 1927 when the tile stove was disassembled and never reassembled in another house. An example of a similar ceramic tile stove is presented in figure 71 on page 70 in *Mennonite Furniture*.

The second floor had bedrooms, storage areas, and the maid's quarters. Mother labeled one room, "the secret room," and to this day, none of Justine's granddaughters or great-granddaughters knows what was stored in that room, only that Great-grandmother forbade their entry into that room.

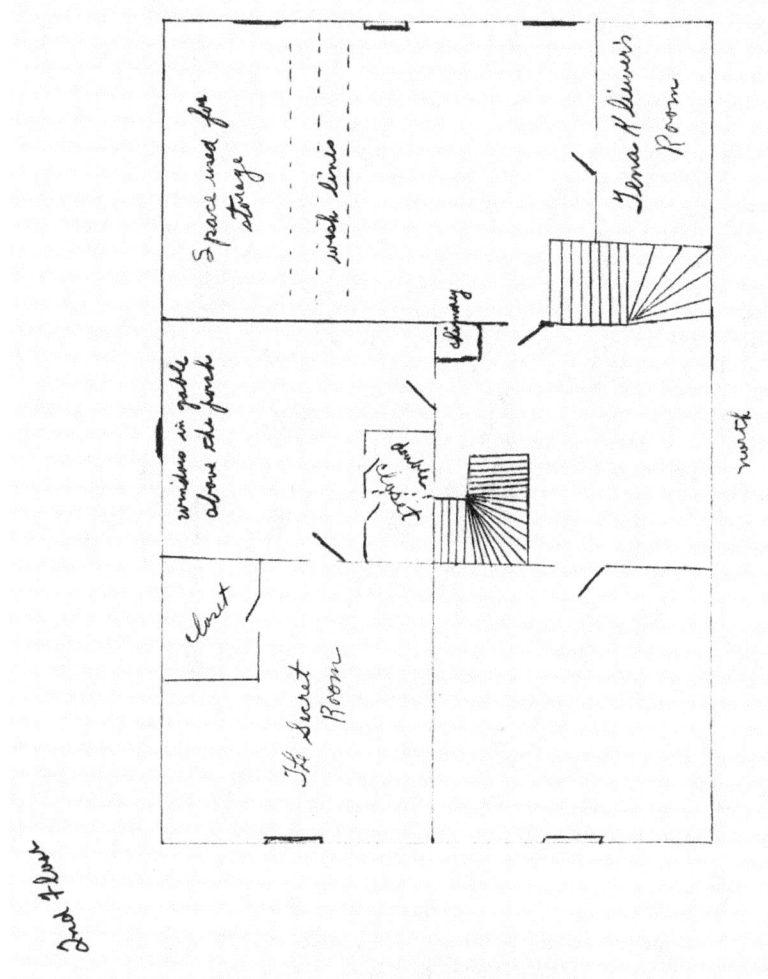

Figure 33b
Floor plan of the Bernhard Harder house of 1877, second or upper floor.
Drawing by Marie. Source: Author's file.

The house was surrounded with a picket fence. On the north side, which faced the farmyard, there was a gate sufficiently large enough to allow buggies to enter to take people and guests to the front south door. The arch joining the gateposts had the word *Willkommen* (Welcome) painted on it and a ship anchor on either end of the word. The welcome sign signified the congenial atmosphere that visitors would experience and the anchors were a reminder of their West Prussian heritage between the Vistula and Nogat Rivers. The arch has survived the tornado and other storms as well. The guests were welcomed through the south, double entry doors and ushered into the parlor.

Figure 34
The farmyard with Marie's sisters Helene Thiessen in white and Minna. The picket fence on the right surrounded Great-grandfather Harder's house. The *Speicher* is on the left with Grandfather Bernhard Harder Jr.'s house in center. Photo taken between 1920 and 1927. Photograph by Marie. Source: Author's file.

Justine enjoyed entertaining. She was also a lover of animals and once had two dogs named Fido and Hector; these dogs were bathed before social events and a ribbon was tied around their necks. At another time she had a dog, Moritz. When she fed her cats she was concerned that each get their fair share, and if one became greedy, she refereed the situation with her wooden spoon.

As the matriarch of the Harder family in America, she is remembered especially for her New Year's celebrations, and the celebration of her birthday in July. Her food preparations were noteworthy with fried chicken and ice cream being particularly memorable. She died in 1916, so her ice cream was an exceptionally novel treat when she served it on the prairies of Kansas over one hundred years ago. The ice cream was homemade with the eggs, milk, and cream produced on the farm. Ice would have been available from the towns of Brainerd or Whitewater located two miles east and west of the Harder farm. The *Walnut Valley Times* on August 28, 1885 printed a list of businesses in the new town of Brainerd founded on May 25,1885; a Mr. St. Clair had an ice cream and confectionery store. Also, an ice house was established in about 1888 in Whitewater by the owner of the first butcher shop, who cut and stored natural ice from the creek and ponds each winter. When I was a toddler, Mother continued to treat us children with ice cream made in her grandmother's hand-cranked ice cream maker.

After everyone had eaten their fill at Justine's celebrations, songs of thanksgiving were sung by all guests, and Gustav Harder, the preacher in the family and a stepson, often shared some devotional thoughts. Mother enjoyed listening to her Uncle Gustav. The grandchildren would recite poems or make little speeches of congratulations. At the New Year's festivities, Justine would give each grandchild a *Reichsthaler* when they personally greeted her. A *Reichsthaler* is any of a number of silver coins issued by various German states between the fifteenth and the nineteenth centuries and is equivalent to about a dollar.

During the summer celebrations at Great-grandmother's house, the guests preferred to sit outside in the cool of a quiet summer evening, when the wind usually calms down. South of the house, there was a beautiful garden patterned after Great-grandfather's beloved garden in West Prussia. Mother drew the layout of this garden from memory since no photos of the garden have been found, and included the diagram in her book, *Lest We Forget*.

Walking south from the house, one came to the garden gate incorporated in the picket fence and flanked by large cedar trees. Proceeding between the cedars on a broad gravel pathway, one became aware of vegetables on the right and flowers on the left. The vegetable patch was sufficiently large enough to supply the family with all their potatoes and vegetables for the year. The vegetables were bordered with a trimmed, twelve-inch hedge. Irrigation water was available within this enclosure, the water pumped by windmill from a well west of the garden. The water would have been hand-carried to the plants by a maid. Just beyond the vegetables was *eine Laube*, an arbor or bower, with three walls of trimmed, maple seedlings hedge and a bench for guests to use to relax. This arbor was the most visually exposed and no doubt was the first choice by the parents of courting children. Arbors functioned as places for relaxation, private conversations, and romantic getaways.

Remembering Special People on Their Birth Dates

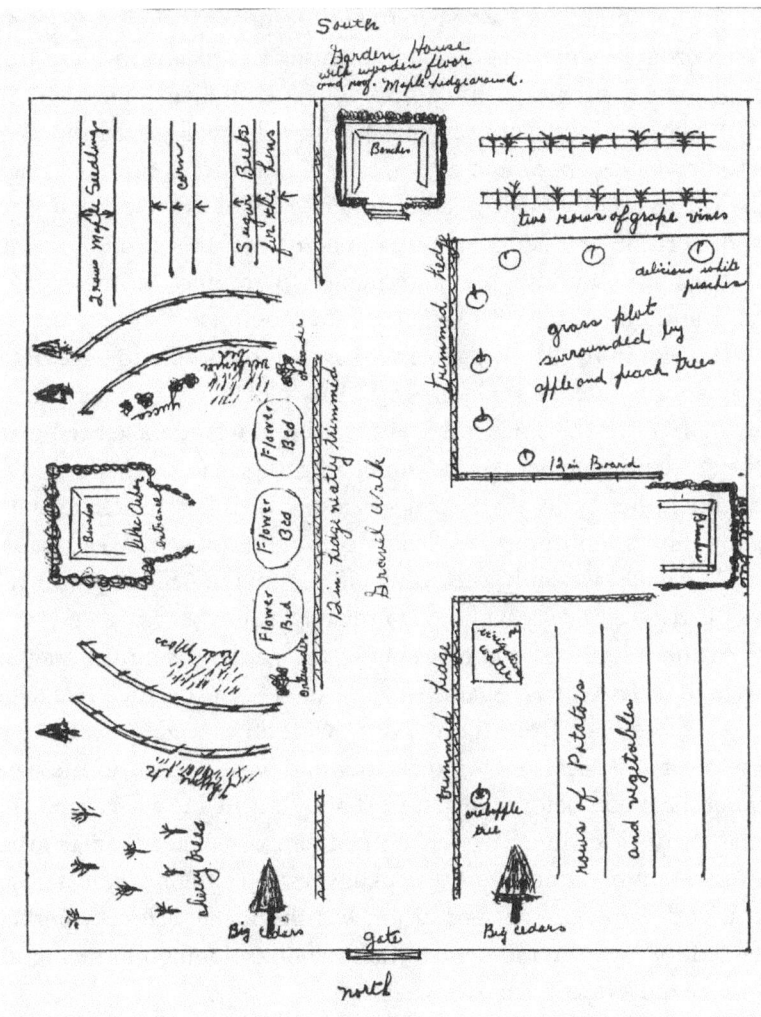

Figure 35
Drawing of the garden created by my great-grandfather south of his house, patterned after his beloved garden in Gurken, West Prussia. Drawing by Marie. Source: Author's file.

Continuing down the path, on the west side was a grass plot surrounded by apple and peach trees. Specifically mentioned were the delicious white peaches. There was a trimmed hedge along the central walkway, but the northern side of that plot was bounded by a twelve-inch board, no doubt removable to allow a horse and mower into the area to groom the grass.

Further south there were two rows of grape vines. My great-grandparents brought wine-making equipment and bottles with them from West Prussia to provide their communion and medicinal needs.

At the south end of the central walkway was a garden house. It sported a wooden floor and a roof, but the walls were trimmed maple hedges. This arbor was all-weather, and one could use it in the full sun of summertime or when it rained. I imagine that this structure would have been used by my great-grandfather to conduct business or my great-grandmother to serve *Vesper*, an afternoon tea.

The plot in the southeast corner had two rows of maple seedlings, presumably for hedge replacements. This plot also was reserved for growing feed for the chickens. The sugar beets would have been given to the chickens, one per day, in wintertime to provide something fresh to augment their grain diet. Corn was also grown for chicken feed, but not for human consumption. Prior to immigrating, in West Prussia corn (*Zea mays*) was only a curiosity plant from the Americas grown in flower beds as a novelty with no commercial value.

In the middle on the east side of the garden, were the fragrant flowers in orderly beds. Again, a twelve-inch high trimmed hedge delineated these beds from the walkway with an oleander at each end. These oleanders were not winter hardy and were carried to the basement of the house before the first frost and returned to the garden after the last frost of spring. Two fence-lined pathways led to a lilac arbor. Flowers mentioned next to these pathways were thymes, moss roses, yucca, and verbena. The lilac arbor was the most secluded, perhaps intended for intimate moments; when the lilac bloomed in spring, the fragrance must have been overwhelming.

Mother drew eight cherry trees in the northeast plot. These trees would have been standard sizes, also indicating the size and space needed by this garden.

The challenges for Great-grandfather, which all the West Prussian pioneers learned quickly, were that the rains did not come on a timely basis, the winds could be relentless, and the temperatures brutal in both summer and winter. The fluctuations in temperature on a daily basis far exceeded those of coastal areas in northern Europe. Yet the pioneers adjusted their techniques and were successful gardeners, reveling in the joy that gardening provides.

The obituary of Great-grandmother Harder mentions that in 1902 she underwent an invasive surgery. Indeed, she had a lump on her breast, but since her attending physician had scheduled a trip to the Middle East, the surgery was postponed for two months. In time the surgery was performed in the farmhouse. For a year and a half all appeared well, but after that period the growth reappeared and the medical opinion was that the malady was beyond treatment. She bore her pain and suffering with patience, and in 1916 Great-grandmother passed away and was interred in the Harder cemetery at the end of the farm driveway beside her husband of thirty-seven years, Bernhard Harder (1811–1900), her son Bernhard (1864–1904), her mother Justine (Claassen, Bergmann) Penner (1797–1884), and her brother Jacob Bergmann (1831–1909).

By the time Justine's one-hundredth birthday poem was read by Lydia in 1934 "everything changed with time," and she had been buried in the Harder cemetery at the end of the farm driveway for eighteen years. It had been about twenty years since the family had gathered to formally honor Justine. The garden area had been plowed and put to other uses, since maintaining the garden took an immense amount of time and labor. The original house had been disassembled in 1926–27 and reassembled on a new farm set up by Mother's sister Helene and her husband John Thiessen about a mile northeast of the original farm. The relocated house was demolished by the tornado of June 8, 1941 with Susan, her father, and her siblings in it as recounted in chapter 5.

Mother reminds the listeners that those who had already passed away each contributed to the collective Harder heritage. She mentions that on July 6, 1934, the family included 108 people. The poem ends with a reminder of how the presence of the divine sustained the family and how his presence and guidance will continue into the future.

Zu Großmutters Erinnerungs 100ste Geburtstag
6 Juli 1934
Von Lydia Thiessen vorgelesen

Es wurde schon vor ein paar Wochen
Der Wunsch wohl mehrmals ausgesprochen
Hier auf diesem seltenen Feste
Zu der erschienen lieben Gäste

The Petals of a Kansas Sunflower

Einige Erinnerungen wieder zu gehen
Aus Großmutters bewegtem Leben
Ihr zum Andenken sind wir hier
Denn ihren 100sten Geburtstag feiern wir
Wer sieht nicht noch vor Augen klar
Wie es einst in Großmutters Hause war?
Wer sieht nicht noch die Räume alle
Die sonnige Zimmer, die dunkle Halle
Wo Großmutter so gerne feierte Feste
Und oftmals bewirtete ein grossteil Gäste.
Viel Freude sie fand am Gastfreundschaft über
Was uns ja noch allen im Gedächtnis geblieben
Der Neujahr's Feier wir erinnern uns noch
Wie gut schmeckte stet das Abendbrot doch
Was alle Nachkommen und Verwandten
Stets mit Vergnügen anerkannten
Denn Hühnerbraten Großmutter zu bereiten verstand
Wie wohl sonst keiner hier im Land.
So einen eigenen Geschmack der immer hatte
Das kam von der reichlichen Zutate
Und waren alle gesätiget dann
Die Abendandacht bald begann
Zu Anfang ein Danklied wurde gesungen
Und war die letzte Strophe verklungen
O. Gustav Harder das Wort oft nahm
Und eine schöne Festrede hielt als dann
Wie wir sie alle zu hören lieben
Und unvergeßlich manchem geblieben.
Von den Kleinen Gedicht wurden vorgetragen
Größre Kinder kamen ihren Glückwunsch sagen:
Das Gottessegen zum neuen Jahr
Auch wieder ihr Wunsch für Großmutter war
Dann diese jedem damit beglückt
Daß Sie einen Taler in die Hand ihn drückt.
Denn in der heißen Sommerszeit
Mit einem andern Fest sie uns erfreut—
Ihr Geburtstag—Wer erinnert sich nicht daran
Und froh erschein wohl jederman
Auch dann war alles schön geplant
Das hat ein jeder wohl erkannt
Denn mit ice cream, damals was seltneres wie heute
Sie Gross and Klein sehr gern erfreute
Wohl gerne man dann draussen saß
Und denn schönen Abend so genau

Remembering Special People on Their Birth Dates

Gern ging man durch den schönen Garten
Der hatte so viel Eigenarten
Wie man jetzt wohl weit und breit
Es nirgends findet zu diesen Zeit
Wohl erinnern wir uns des Gartens noch
Wie schön es da nach Blumen roch
Am Eingang desselben am breiten Steig
Zwei Zedern breiteten ihr Gezweig
Weiter den Steig wir schreiten hinau
Noch einmal den Garten zu sehn an
Zur linken Blumen, zur rechten Gemüse
Weiter nach hinten eine kleine Wiese
Da standen Obstbäume, dahinter der Wein
In zwei langen schön gehaltenen Reihen
Auch gab es zwei Lauben, ein Gartenhaus
Froh gingen wir Kinder drin ein and aus
Und wo einst war ein leerer Raum
Stand dann ein schöner Apfelbaum
Viel verschiedene Blumen waren da vorhanden
Daneben die großen Oleander standen
Verbenia, Meerviole und Thymian
Waren stets schön zu sehe an
Im Hause die Alpenveilchen eine ganze Zahl
Waren doch immer die schönsten von all.
Doch alles verändert sich mit der Zeit
So gehört auch dies zur Vergangenheit
Das Haus ist weg, der Garten verschwunden
Der Platz hat für andres Verwertung gefunden
Nur einige Bäume stehn noch heut
Gerade wie damals zu der Zeit.
Heut sind es wohl an 20 Jahren
Als das letzte mal wir beisammen waren
Viel hat sich verändert in dieser Zeit
Viel hat jeder erfahren an Freud und Leid.
Es gingen schon von uns viele der Lieben
Und Einsam ist mancher zurück geblieben
Doch auch manchen Neuen kann man mit zählen
So zählt die Harder Familie heut 108 Seelen

Gottes Väterliches walten
Hat uns bis hierher erhalten
Er bleibt bei uns an jeder Ort
Wie Er's verheißen in seiner Wort.

The Petals of a Kansas Sunflower

Remembering Grandmother on her One-hundredth Birth Date
July 6, 1934
Read by Lydia Thiessen

It has already been a few weeks
Since the desire was mentioned several times
Here at this solemn celebration
To highlight for our lovely guests
To individually reminisce again
About grandmother's active life.
We are here to think about her
Since we are celebrating her one-hundredth birthday.
Who can not still clearly with mind's eye remember
How it once was in grandmother's house?
Who does not remember all the space,
The sunny rooms, the dark halls
Where grandmother eagerly celebrated festivities
And often entertained many guests.
They were very happy with the hospitality,
Which all remain in our memories.
The New Year's celebrations we still call to mind,
How good the evening meal always tasted,
Which all the descendants and relatives
Constantly acknowledged with pleasure.
Grandmother really understood how to fry chicken
Like no one else here in this country.
So whatever one's personal tastes are
It came from the abundance of ingredients
And then when all were satiated
The evening prayers would soon begin.
To begin, a song of thanksgiving was sung
And when the last phrase faded,
Uncle Gustav Harder often took the Bible
And gave a nice festive speech.
How we all loved to hear him
And some remained unforgettable.
From the little ones, poems were recited
Larger children came to say their best wishes:
That God's blessings for the new year
Was again their wish for grandmother.
Then everyone was happy
That she pressed into each hand a *Reichsthaler*.
During the hot summertime
She gladdened us with another celebration—

Remembering Special People on Their Birth Dates

Her birthday—who does not remember that
And everyone appeared happy.
Also, everything was so nicely planned
Surely that was recognized by everyone.
Then with ice cream, at that time much more rare than today,
The adults and children enjoyed it very much.
One truly preferred to sit outside then
And with a perfectly lovely evening
With pleasure one would walk through the beautiful garden
Which had so many unique features.
How surely far and wide
Nowhere does one find a garden like this anymore
How well we still remember that garden
How nicely it was scented with flowers.
The same was true at the entrance with a wide path
Two cedars extended their broad branches
Further on the path we proceed suddenly to
A view of the garden.
On the left were the flowers, on the right the vegetables
A little further to the back
There stood fruit trees, behind that the grapes
In two nice long bounded rows.
Also there were two arbours and a garden house
Happily we children went in and out of them
And where once was an empty space
Now stood a nice apple tree.
Many different flowers were planted there
Near where the large oleanders stood
Verbena, scented stocks, and thymes
Which were constantly nice to look at.
In the house there were many cyclamens
Which were however always the loveliest of all.
Everything changed with time, however,
So this also belongs to a former life.
The house is gone, the garden disappeared
The place has been converted to other uses.
Only individual trees still stand today
Exactly as they were at that time.
Today it is truly about twenty years
Since that last time that we were assembled
Much has changed during this time.
Everyone has come to know much about joy and sorrow
Many loved ones have already left us
And some of those who have remained behind are lonesome.

However, some new ones are also included
So the number in the Harder family today is one hundred eight persons.
God's fatherly governing directives
Have sustained us until now
He remains with us in every place
As he promised in his Word.

My father's maternal grandparents, Cornelius H. Regier (1842–1928) and Anna (Regier) Regier (1845–1920) are eulogized in the next two poems. Their oldest daughter Anna (1869–1907) was my grandmother Epp. Mother's sister Justine (1895–1919) married one of their sons, i.e., one of Anna's younger brothers, John H. Regier (1886–1974) on April 2, 1914.

Cornelius Regier was a farmer, teacher, and minister. Cornelius loved to write and so his journals provided his family with many facts and his reactions to events depicting his life. His father was Bernhard R. Regier Jr. (1810–1893), stepson of Great-grandfather Bernhard Harder by marriage to widow Anna (Peters) Regier on October 9, 1832 (see appendix 1). In 1836 Bernhard R. Regier Jr. was elected a minister in the Heubuden Mennonite Church in West Prussia; his interests were missions, Bible societies, and prohibition, and he was considered somewhat conservative by some in that congregation. When the family immigrated to American in 1880, Bernhard joined the ministerial staff of the newly organized First Mennonite Church in Newton and served there from 1880 until his death in 1893. He was known as a gifted minister. Cornelius Regier's mother was Marie Harder Regier (1812–1844), the first wife of Bernhard R. Regier Jr. and the only sister of my great-grandfather Bernard Harder as also mentioned in appendix 1.

When Cornelius and Anna Regier married in 1867, they inherited the parental homestead near Marienburg, West Prussia, according to the tradition of the time that the eldest son inherited the whole farm. Cornelius had an older brother Bernhard, who died at age sixteen of blood poisoning, most likely caused by a smallpox vaccination. The fertile farm was less than eighty acres but supported the family well. In 1880, Cornelius sold the farm for a good price in preparation for immigrating to America together with their six children. They were passengers on the ship, *SS Main*, leaving Bremen on June 6, 1880, arriving New York on June 18, 1880, there transferring to a train and arriving in

Peabody, Kansas on June 22, 1880. It was just assumed that they would settle near Elbing, the home of Anna's brother who immigrated with the first group in 1876. They lived with Anna's brother Bernhard Regier and family for six months until they found a homestead nearby. On their newly purchased farm was a log cabin into which the family moved while their new house was being constructed.

Figure 36
Fiftieth wedding anniversary photo of Cornelius H. Regier (1842–1928) and Anna (Regier) Regier (1845–1920), my great-grandparents. McDaniel, Newton, Kansas. Source: Author's file.

Immigration was not an exhilarating event for this family, but was undertaken to achieve a better life of religious and political freedoms for their children. Leaving the grave of their firstborn son, also named Bernhard, who died in 1868 as a six-month-old baby, was emotionally traumatic: "The gloomiest time that they lived through." Cornelius was not in the best of health himself and had recurring health problems. He considered going into business rather than farming because in 1880, of his six children, the oldest five were girls, with the son, Cornelius, just a toddler. But after six months in America, he purchased the farm that was operated with hired help and his daughters. In chapter 13, I mentioned the oldest daughter's (my grandmother Epp) involvement in field work. In America Cornelius and Anna had five additional children, including three sons who eventually took over the farming activity.

In 1885, Cornelius was elected a lay minister in the newly formed (1883) Zion Mennonite Church in Elbing to serve the community of immigrants in that area. He was ordained in 1885 by his father, the Rev. Bernhard R. Regier Jr. in the Emmaus Mennonite Church where the family attended up to that time. Emmaus was seven and a half miles from Cornelius' farm and travel time by horse and buggy took more than an hour. In addition to the driving distance involved, another reason mentioned for forming a local church was that in summertime, when the Elbing group was returning home and driving north with horse and buggy over dusty roads, it became almost unbearable with the dust from the slow south wind hovering over the buggies. Driving by the hour into the cold north wind in wintertime would also seem stressful. With time, Cornelius was elected to the lay elder position of the Zion Mennonite Church in Elbing, and retired from that ministry after thirty-six years.

Zu Großpapas 100sten Geburtstag
16 Oktober 1942
Von Bertha Busenitz vorgelesen

Wenn wir in Sprüche lesen Kapitel zehn Vers sieben
  Da werden wir dann finden es steht da so geschrieben:
Das Andenken der Gerechten im Segen Bleibet hier
  Daß gilt ja auch noch heute für uns, daß wissen wir.
Drum zu einer Gedächnisfeier ladete man uns heute ein

Remembering Special People on Their Birth Dates

So sind nun hier erschienen, Verwandte groß und klein.
Froh sind wir hergekommen denn gerne feiern wir
 Den Geburtstag des Großvaters, Cornelius H. Regier.
Von früher so manches Ereignis und noch erhalten blieb
 Durch Großvaters Aufzeugungen die gerne er einst schrieb
In Deutschland war er Geboren, war heut' nun 100 Jahr
 Wo ja von drei Söhnen der mitlere er war.
Seine Mutter Marie Harder im Verzeichnis lesen wir
 Sein Vater wie auch Großvater hieß beid' Bernhard Regier.
Früh hat Großvater erfahren, daß ernst dies Leben war
 Schon verlor er seine Mutter da er nur erst zwei Jahr.
Doch schon ein Jahr später der Herr in Lieb und Treue
 Ihm eine zweite Mutter geschenket hat aufs neue.
Die Schulbildung hat, wie wir wissen, Großvater von Deutschland her
 Doch fiel ihm das lernen wohl immer etwas schwer.
Mit der Gansfeder hat er geschrieben , die der Lehrer selber schnitzt;
 Wie anders heut wo von Kindern die "Fountain Pen" wird benützt
Drei weitere Jahr hat, in der Lateinschule er verbracht
 Und später ein Reise, zur Schweiz, er hat gemacht.
Von 25 Jahren er im Ehestand eintrat
 Und wohnte in dem Grundstück, daß sein Großvater gekauft einst hat.
Doch mussten sie, wie auch so viele andere
 Nach 13 Jahre schon, sich rüsten zum Auswandern.
Dies war für sie wie wir in der Aufzeugung lesen
 Die trübste Zeit, die sie durchlebt, gewesen
Das Grab des ältesten Kindes und sacht vieles was ihn lieb
 Sie mussten es verlassen, zurück es alles blieb.
Und dann hier angekommen wie schwer der Anfang war
 Doch wohnten bei Verwandte, sie das erste halbe Jahr.
Die letzte Zeit in Deutschland auch hier noch Anfänglich
 War Großvater nicht wohl; ja öfters etwas kränklich
So, daß in Erwägung wohl immer wieder kam
 Ob lieber als ein Bauer er würde Geschäftsmann;
Jedoch solche Pläne zur Ausführung nicht kamen
 Da die Großeltern, auch anraten, diese "Farm" übernahmen.
Hier bietet die erste Zeit, ein Blockhaus die Wohnungsräume.
 Dann waren auch auf diesem Platz viel schöne Obstbäume,
Etwas spatter wurde dann, dies Haus hier aufgebaut—
 Mit wenigen Veränderungen, wie man er heute schaut.
Beim Ansiedeln zu Anfang, viel Arbeit sich da bot
 Doch Gott gab seinen Segen, sie litten einmals Not.
Und waren da auch Jahre, wo die Preise nur gering,
 So doch durch Fleiß und Sparsamkeit es immer vorwärts ging.
Im Winter, oft drei Monat, lehrt Großvater Schule hier

The Petals of a Kansas Sunflower

Es blieben dann einige Schüler, stets bei ihm in Quartier
Als Großvater 41, noch mehr Arbeit er bekam
Er ward gewählt als Prediger, welches er ja auch annahm.
So ward er dann, in "Emmaus," als Prediger ordeniert
Und hat mehr als 30 Jahr, als Ältester, die Zions Gemeinde geführt.
Im Sommer musste dann, oft während den trockensten Zeiten
Großvater des Nachts, für den Sonntag sich vorbereiten.
Da, als schon Silberfäden durch zogen der Großeltere dunkeles Haar
Ein dankfest sie dann feierten, die Silberhochzeit zwar.
Im Kreise von Verwandten brachten Gott sie Preis and Ehr'
Der so liebreich sie erhalten, und treu geführt bisher.
Doch es für denn Großeltern, auch trübe Stunden gab
Davon legen auf dem Kirchhof, die Gräber, ein stilles Zeugnis ab.
5 ihrer lieben Kinder geleiteten sie zum Grab,
2 noch als zarte Knospen da rief der Herr sie ab.
Zwei in den besten Jahren, in voller Jugendkraft
So schnell nach schwerer Krankheit vom Tod da sie gerafft.
Dann eine, schon als Mutter, der verlust war O so groß!
Es wurden ihre Kinder ja dadurch Mutterlos.
Schnell sind im Wechsel vergangen, der Großeltern, Jahr um Jahr
Bis gebeugt die Haltung wurde und grau schon ward das Haar.
Oft hat Großvater gelitten an Rheumatismus ja
Er fuhr dann nach Missouri und suchte Liederung da
Dazu kam noch das Leiden, das rechte Aug' erblindet
Auch wurde er daran operirt, da er sich öfter entzündet
Als sich die schwächen des Alters, immer mehr zu zeigen begonnen
Dann die beiden jüngsten Onkeln, die Farm übernahmen.
So wie ja gegen Abend die Sonne zum Untergang sich neigt
Und dann mit ihren Strahlen alles goldig überleucht;
So war am Lebensabend das goldene Hochzeitsfest
Eine ganz besondere Gnade, sie vergoldete der Lebensrest
Als letzte Arbeit, wie wir wissen, die Großvater niederlegt
War Gotteswort verkündigen, was so lange er gepflegt
Gerne Erinnern wir des uns heute noch, in Gedächtnis uns noch steht
Wie ja so ernst und feierlich, Großvaters Predigt und Gebet.
Der Herr trug ihn ins Alter bis 85 Jahr
Bis müd die Schritte wurden und er ergraut schon war
Dann ging er ein in Frieden zur ewigen Seligkeit
Die Gott ja seine Kinder in Liebe hält bereit
Wenn wir heut die Glieder in Großvatersfamilie zählen
So sind den wir da leben sind 79 Seelen.
Elf sind nicht mehr hienieden sie gingen schon voran
Schon landeten sie in Frieden im oberen Kanaan.

Remembering Special People on Their Birth Dates

For Grandpapa's One-hundredth Birthday
October 16, 1942
Read by Bertha Busenitz

When we read Proverbs chapter ten verse seven
   We will then find there, that it says as written:
The memory of the righteous remains a blessing here
   Yes, that is still guidance for us today, this we know.
Consequently, we have been invited today to a celebration of remembrance
   So we are on track here now with relatives large and small.
Gladly we have come here because we eagerly celebrate
   The birthday of our grandfather, Cornelius H. Regier.
Some happenings from earlier times still remain as recollections
   Through grandfather's written records because he enjoyed writing these down
He was born in Germany, today it is now one hundred years
   Yes, where he was the middle one of three sons.
We read in the records that his mother was Maria Harder,
   His father, like his grandfather, were both named Bernhard Regier.
Early on, grandfather come to know the seriousness of life
   When he was only two years old, he already lost his mother.
But only one year later, the Lord in love and faithfulness
   Gave him a new, second mother.
As we know, grandfather received his education in Germany
   However, learning for him was always truly a bit difficult
With a goose quill he wrote, which the teacher himself whittled.
   In contrast, today the children would have utilized a "fountain pen."
He studied three additional years in the Latin School
   And later he took a trip to Switzerland.
For the twenty-five years, since he got married,
   He lived on the plot of land that his grandfather had once purchased
However, they had to, like so many others also
   After thirteen years already, begin to prepare themselves for the emigration.
This was for them, as we read in his writings
   The gloomiest time that they lived through that we know
The grave of the eldest child said a lot about the affection he received
   They had to leave it, it all stayed behind
And then to arrive here, how difficult the beginning was
   They lived with relatives for the first half year.
During the final period in Germany and also here at the beginning
   Grandfather was not well, yes, often somewhat sickly
So that in surges it truly always came again
   Rather than be a farmer, he would became a businessman
However, such a plan did not materialize

The Petals of a Kansas Sunflower

    Since the grandparents, upon advice, took over this farm.
Existing here at the beginning was a log house for the dwelling space
    There were also many lovely fruit trees on this place
Somewhat later this house would then be constructed here—
    With few changes as one observes it today.
At the beginning of the colonization, there was a lot of work to do.
    However, God gave his blessings, at times hard to determine
And there were years also, where the rewards were small,
    So through industriousness and thrift, things always moved ahead.
In winter for three months, grandfather taught school here
    Several students always boarded with them.
At forty-one, grandfather took on still more work
    He was selected to be the minister, which he took on also
So he was then ordained as minister at Emmaus
    And as elder, led the Zion congregation for more than thirty years
In summer during the busy times,
    Grandfather would prepare himself for Sunday during the nighttime
Then, as silver threads already drew through the dark hair of the grandparents
    A festival of thanks was celebrated, and that was their silver wedding anniversary
In the circle of relatives, they brought praise and honor to God
    Who so richly held them in his love and truly guided them this far
However, there were also times of gloom for the grandparents
    Silent indications of this are the graves which lie in the cemetery
Five of their loving children they laid into graves.
    Two already as tender buds as if the Lord called them
Two in their best years, in full youthful strength
    So quickly after severe illness were they called by death
Then one, already a mother, whose loss was oh so great!
    Through this her children were now motherless.
For the grandparents, year by year passed quickly as if waxed
    Until their posture became stooped and their hair already turned gray.
Often grandfather had bouts of rheumatism.
    He then still drove to Missouri and looked for relief there
In addition came the suffering also, the right eye was going blind
    Also, he was operated on because of it, since he was frequently infected.
As the weakness of old age became ever more apparent begrudgingly
    Then the two youngest uncles took over the farm,
Yes, just like the sun as towards evening it declines towards its setting
    And then with its rays cast a golden glow on everything
This is the way the golden wedding anniversary was at the evening of their lives
    A very special grace, their gilded life's rest.
The last activity, as we know, that grandfather laid down
    Was giving forth God's words, which for so long he turned out so well
Gladly we still remember today what still stands in our memory

Yes, how earnestly and solemnly grandfather preached and prayed.
The Lord carried him to the old age of eighty-five years
   Until his step became tired and he already was hoary with age
Then he entered into peace to everlasting happiness
   That God holds prepared in love for his children
When we count today the members in grandfather's family
   We are seventy-nine persons, which are living
Eleven are no longer with us, they have gone ahead already
   Already they have landed in peace over in the Promised Land.

In the poem that honors Anna Regier on the one-hundredth anniversary of her birth date, Mother projects forward the implication of the decision to immigrate to America. "It was for them the gloomiest time that they lived through / However, but what a blessing for their descendents who did not experience it." Mother reminds the listeners that because of the choices made between 1870 and 1890 by their grandparents, by the end of July, 1945, World War II had not destroyed their lives. "We are thankful today for God's protection and kindness / And His magnificent grace, —already to the fifth generation, / Will bless us here in part through our great-grandparents." The poem ends with a prayer of supplication and benediction for those present, "God, also give us for the future health, prosperity, and salvation."

Gedichte Aufgesagt für Anna Regier am 29 Juli 1945
Bei Phebe Ann vorgetragen

Feste feiern wie wir wissen ist ein schöner alter Brauch.
Schon feierten ihre Feste die Israelieten auch.
Sie feierten zum Andenken an dem das Gott getan
Wie Er auf wunderbarer Weiße, sie gebracht noch Kanaan.
Wir feiern Kirchlichefeste, sie kommen jedes Jahr
Und zeugen uns von Liebe and Güte wunderbar
Von Weihnacht bis zu Pfingsten sie alle sind ja schön
Man kann da immer wieder den Heilsplan Gottes sehn.
Dann giebt's Familienfeste auch diese sind viel wert
Denn wenn einem Familiengliede die besondere Gnad erfährt
Und ein neues "Ebenezer" setzt auf der Lebensbahn
Dann fühlt zum Dank erhöhen sich, sicher jederman.
Dann giebt's Feste des Andenkens, ein besonders Fest wie heut.
Wo zu Urgrossmutter's Andenken geladen sind die Leut,
Denn Hundert Jahre sind es da sie das Licht der Welt erblickt

The Petals of a Kansas Sunflower

Und damals in Westpreussen, Ein Elternpaar beglückt.
Ja, hundert Jahre sind es. O! Welch eine lange Zeit!
Viel hat sich auch geändert seit dem schon weit und breit.
Die alte Heimat zu verlassen wurde den Urgrosseltern schwere
Als mit andern sie sich entschossen zum Auswandern hierher.
In Urgrossvaters Aufzeugnung da ist es noch zu lesen
Es war für sie die trübste Zeit die sie durch lebt gewesen,
Doch aber Welch ein Segen für den Nachkommen draußentstand
Das die Urgrosseltern entschlossen, zu ziehe in dies Land.
Wie wenig hat vom Kriege gemerkt man hier bisher
Dagegen in Europa Zerstörung rings umher
Von den Söhnen unseres Landes fiel eine ungeheuere Zahl
Man zwang zum Kriegsdienst nicht die unsern, man lies sie freie Wahl
Die Städte unsers Landes, keine Bombe darauf fiel
Doch trafen sie in Europa die Unschuldigen so viel.
Wir haben reichlich Speise, ein jeder hat sein Brot
Dagegen in Europa da droht die Hungersnot.
Wie dankbar sind wir heute für Gottes Schutz und Güt,
Und seine grosse Gnade,—Schon bis ins fünfte Glied
Wurde durch den Urgrosseltern uns Segen hier zu teil
Gott gebe uns auch ferner Gesundheit, Glück und Heil.

A poem recited for Anna Regier on July 29, 1945
Presented by Phebe Ann

As we know, to celebrate festivities is a nice old custom
Already, the Israelites celebrated their festivals also.
They celebrated to remind themselves of what God had done
How he, with wonderful wisdom, brought them to Canaan.
We celebrate church festivals, they come every year
And engender a sense of wonderful love and kindness
From Christmas until Whitsuntide (Pentecost), they are all truly nice.
One can always see again in the festivals, God's plan of salvation.
Then there are family festivals, which are also of great worth
When a family member experiences a particular favor
And a new "Ebenezer" is put onto the path of life
Surely everyone then feels like giving thanks.
Then it gives festivals of remembrance, specifically a festival like here today.
Where to great-grandmother's remembrance the people are invited.
Since it is one hundred years since she became aware of the light of the world.
And at that time in West Prussia, blessed her parents
Yes, it is one hundred years. Oh! What a long time!

Remembering Special People on Their Birth Dates

Much has been altered far and wide since then already
To leave the old home was very difficult for the great-grandparents
As with others they decided to emigrate and come here
In great-grandfather's journal it is there to read
It was for them the gloomiest time that they lived through
However, but what a blessing for their descendents who did not experience it,
That the great-grandparents resolved to move to this country.
How little one notices the war from here until now
In contrast, in Europe destruction was everywhere
Of the sons of our country, a vast number fell
One became involved in the war cause, not because it was ours,
    one exercised free choice.
No bombs fell upon the towns of our country
However, in Europe the bombs hit many that were innocent
We have abundant food, everyone has his bread
In contrast, in Europe there is a threat of famine
We are thankful today for God's protection and kindness
And His magnificent grace—already to the fifth generation—
Will bless us here in part through our great-grandparents.
God, also give us for the future health, prosperity, and salvation.

Abraham Entz was born on November 27, 1844 near Marienburg, West Prussia; he married Marie Busenitz on July 10, 1873, and moved to a homestead called *Litsewitz*. The national conscription law of 1867 abolished military exemptions, and since they had five sons within the first seven years of marriage, the need to seek a new country where they could practice their religious conviction of pacifism encouraged them to sell their farm. In 1882, the family boarded the ship *SS Donau* for America. After three weeks on the Atlantic Ocean, they arrived in New York and boarded the Santa Fe Railroad for Peabody, Kansas.

In Peabody they were greeted by the Rev. and Mrs. Peter Dyck. Mrs. Dyck was Abraham's mother by a previous marriage. The Dycks immigrated in 1876 and settled near Elbing, and they were the couple who lost their two sons within the first year when the young men tried to cross a flooded river near Plum Grove. In 1883, Abraham purchased a farm with fruit trees and a vineyard three miles east of Newton. For many years, Abraham made all the wine used for communion in the First Mennonite Church in Newton where they attended.

After arriving in Kansas, three more children were added to the Abraham Entz family, including Marie Wilhelmine, for whom Mother wrote a poem for her eightieth birthday in the previous chapter. She married Eduard Harder and they adopted a daughter, Katherine, who married Mother's cousin's son, Gustav Harder. It was their two oldest children, Kenneth and Luella, who recited this poem at the remembrance celebration of Abraham Entz. Although they were too young to have met him, they learned to know him from the recollections their mother shared; he passed away October 15, 1924.

Mother ends this poem with "Let us foster these recollections / So the memory of great-grandfather remains a blessing." Mother repeats here again, that when one remembers the good and kind deeds of someone we knew, the memory provides happiness and favorable thoughts.

Für Onkel Abraham Entz 100sten Geburtstag
27 November 1944
von Kenneth & Luella Harder vorgetragen

Zu einem ganz besondern Feste
Sind gekommen wir als Gäste.
Wir feiern den Geburtstag ja,
Unsers lieben Urgroßpapa.
Doch ist er heut nicht mehr hienieden
Ging ein zur Ewiger Ruh in Frieden
Wo er jetzt im Himmelslicht
Jesus schaut von Angesicht.
Etwas klein sind noch wir beide
Hatten daher nicht die Freude
Ihn zu sehen ihn zu lieben.
Uns ist keine Erinnerung an ihn geblieben.
Uns hat die Mama aber gesagt
Da wir nach den u. jenes gefragt
Es war wunderschön die Weihnachtsfeier
Eine Erinnerung ihr noch lieb und teuer.
Alle wurden reichlich bedacht
Jedem eine Freud' gemacht
Ein jeder ist mit reichen Spenden
Heimgekehrt mit vollen Händen.
Doch alles dies ist lange her
War es dann auch schön gar sehr.
Lasst uns die Erinnerung pflegen.
Urgroßvaters Andenken bleibt ein Segen.

Remembering Special People on Their Birth Dates

For Uncle Abraham Entz's One-hundredth Birth Date
November 27, 1944
Presented by Kenneth & Luella Harder

For a completely special celebration
We have gathered as guests.
Yes, we celebrate the birthday
Of our beloved great-grandfather.
But today, he is no longer here below.
He has gone to his eternal rest in peace
Where he now is in heaven's light
Observing Jesus with esteem.
Both of us are still rather small
Consequently, we did not have the joy
Of seeing him, of loving him.
For us there is no remembrance of him that remains
But our mother said to us
When we asked about this uncle,
The Christmas celebrations were wonderfully nice,
A remembrance that you would love and cherish.
Everyone would be abundantly considered.
Each one was made happy.
Each one was presented a gift
Returning home with full hands.
All this was long ago, however,
When it was so very nice.
Let us foster these recollections
So the memory of great-grandfather remains a blessing.

16

Honoring the Patriarch

SAYING GOODBYE TO A patriarch after a long, productive career leaves an incredible vacuum within a family and the community. The headwaters for guidance and stability over many years have just evaporated. Organizations whose guiding influence has now disappeared begin to look around for new leaders to take up the vacated leadership roles.

The Rev. Abraham J. Dyck (1888–1959) was the third elder of the Hoffnungsau Mennonite Church near Inman, Kansas. He was born on a farm in the Hoffnungsau area, became an incessant reader, and was fascinated by nature, particularly flowers. In 1906 he enrolled at Bethel Academy in North Newton and by 1908 began his eight-year teaching career in western Kansas. He married Margaret Schmidt during this period and they were blessed with six children. He was invited to become a minister in his home church at Hoffnungsau in 1914 and shortly purchased a farm in the area. In 1925 he was ordained as an elder in the church and continued to fill that position until 1945. The Rev. Dyck is a fine example of the self-supporting lay ministers who were traditionally called out of the congregation during the first fifty to seventy-five years after the Mennonite migration began in 1874, a pattern of ministry that perpetuated European traditions.

Rev. Dyck was born into the third generation of Mennonites in America. His parents and grandparents were from the Prussian Mennonites of the Alexanderwohl church and village of southern Russia. He was born in America and it was his generation that began to reap the rewards of the immigration. My mother, who was of the same generation, also experienced the Americanization of our local church community with its changes in language, modes of transportation, the use of musical instruments and songbooks, and opportunities for communication. Some of the rewards of immigration were vividly expressed in

Honoring the Patriarch

the previous chapter in the poem recited on July 29, 1945 to honor the memory of Anna Regier.

As a minister, the Rev. Dyck's concerns focused on the smooth continued adaptation to American culture while still sustaining the basic principles of the Anabaptist ancestors. His broadminded approach envisioned changes as new opportunities with greater responsibilities, and he expedited the transition from German to English as the language of the worship service. He looked for the good in everyone and in every organization.

Rev. Dyck was an excellent leader. His twenty year tenure as elder is remembered for his excellent judgment, his logic, his approach to situations, and the methods he used to resolve disputes and church problems. His leadership skills were also respected as he worked with church and community organizations that included the General Conference (Mennonite), the Western District Conference of the General Conference, the boards of the Bethel Deaconess Hospital (Newton) and Bethesda Hospital (Goessel), the Inman Home for the Aged, and the Bethel College Board from 1939 to 1958. He passed away on May 5, 1959.

Two of his daughters married brothers within our local Emmaus church community. Bertha Dyck married Herman Toevs, and Rosella Dyck married Kenneth Toevs. When Rev. Dyck passed away, Bertha Toevs asked Mother for a poem in honor of her father. Since Inman and Buhler are about fifty to sixty miles west of Whitewater and he was not a relative, Mother had not been personally acquainted with him, so she asked Bertha to describe her father.

This poem was printed in the memorial handout as well as read during the memorial service.

In Memory of my Father
May 21, 1959

The voyage now is over, he reached the golden shore;
  His earthly tasks are finished; we hear his voice no more.
His memory still is vivid in blessings left behind,
  Words of advice and comfort still linger in our mind.

The Petals of a Kansas Sunflower

Three score and ten, God gave him in years of usefulness,
   His humble, faithful servant who would not ask for less
Than to be guided by the Spirit, submitting to God's will,
   To be molded by the Master for greater service still.

He left his loved ones lonely; the missing will be long.
   By faith they look to Jesus and in the night he gives a song.
Is there one like he was, burdened for the home, the church, the lost,
   And pleading for Christian workers who are willing to pay the "cost"?

So now there comes the challenge to each and every one.
   Arise! Continue building, there is yet much to be done
In the work God's faithful servant began and now laid down.
   The task is great, the standard high, but then—the victor's crown.

17

The Mission of Parochial Education

MY PARENTS WERE DETERMINED that the education of their children should reflect the religious perspective of their own deep commitments to Anabaptism and evangelical Christianity. They knew by heart the adage in Proverbs 22:6, "Point your kids in the right direction—when they're old they won't be lost." Pointing in the right direction took much commitment, thought, and effort.

All eight of us children attended grades one through eight in the Brainerd School, District No. 33, Butler County, the same school where my parents also obtained some of their elementary education. Although this was a public school, most of the board members during my lifetime were from the local Mennonite church, and the majority of the teachers hired were also of Mennonite heritage. The school opened in 1886 as a one-room school with grades one to eight. County records show that in 1902–3 and 1903–4 there was one teacher and fifty-seven and fifty-eight students enrolled, respectively. Beginning with the school year 1917–18, when my mother was there for her eighth grade, two teachers were employed. My father had completed the eighth grade a year or two earlier. During my elementary education, there were one or two teachers depending on the number of students enrolled. The school continued to hold classes for seventy-nine years and was consolidated into Unified District No. 206 after the 1964–65 school year.

A local public high school was established in Whitewater in 1900, but secular education did not appeal to my parents. Information outside of a biblical context was considered potentially dangerous and frightening, i.e., "modernistic." One sign of modernism was visualized by the image of a bejeweled bossy wife with bobbed hair and painted lips created in one of the books my father kept on his writing desk that was authored by the early twentieth-century itinerant, Bible-thumping orator, John R. Rice. There was always the fear that knowledge and a global outlook might divert a child's attention from the conservative views of religion that formed the core of my parents' existence, and which were so very personal for my mother.

Figure 37
Souvenir postcard for the September 22, 2001, Brainerd School Reunion. Brainerd School, District 33, Butler County, Kansas held its first classes in 1886 in the limestone building shown in the upper photograph. In the lower left corner is the Presbyterian church constructed on Horner Street in 1885. The Christmas and end-of-year programs of the school were held in the church to provide space for the whole community. The brick schoolhouse in the lower photo was used beginning in 1929. From 1936 until 1956, either my siblings or I attended school there. Photo sources: www.rootinaround.com/Brainerd and Brainerd Robin, September 29, 1948, No. 1. Author's file. Used with permission.

One option for private high school education was Hesston Academy in the town of Hesston about thirty miles west of the Harder farm. My father attended Hesston Academy from 1920–21 where he boarded, traveling by train from Brainerd to Hesston and back whenever he returned to his father's farm. His favorite teacher was Melvin Landis who taught history and Bible from 1911 to 1928; when my parents had to come up with a name for me, their third son and eighth child, my father reached back into his fond memories of adolescence and named me after his revered high school teacher. My oldest sister completed high school there in 1947, boarding at the school also. Hesston Academy became Hesston College in 1965 and now offers a two-year junior college program. The high school education program was given to the city of Hesston.

Another option for a local parochial high school education was Bethel Academy in North Newton, Kansas about twenty-three miles away, where my mother completed her ninth grade in 1919–20. Bethel Academy was converted into Bethel College in the spring of 1946. Both Hesston Academy and Bethel Academy were run under the auspices of Mennonite churches.

A group of laymen from the local Mennonite churches in Newton, Elbing, and Whitewater were concerned with the lack of options for parochial education after the closing of Bethel Academy and in 1946 decided to start a new Christian high school. Berean Academy began classes in the fall of 1946 with sixteen freshmen and sophomores and two instructors in the basement of Zion Mennonite Church in Elbing. By the second year of instruction, the school became a fully accredited high school. This meant that the education of the first graduating class of 1948 was recognized by the state of Kansas. One of the first promotional publications explained the reason for the school this way: "Berean Academy was founded in answer to a burden of prayer that young people might have the opportunity for Christian high school training in a spiritual atmosphere." In May, 1947, it was decided to expand the curriculum into a four-year high school. The Berean Academy *Catalog 1946–47* stated that "the purpose of Berean Academy is to give a systematic and thorough knowledge of the Word of God, to offer a well-rounded and scholastic high school education, to train Christian workers, to foster and promote Mennonite ideals and principles, and to provide a spiritual environment leading to a personal Christian experience with the Lord Jesus Christ and thorough consecration to him." In the 1950s, the school's governing Christian layman's association became nondenominational amid much dissension, and in the 1970s, the traditionally Mennonite distinctions were removed from the doctrinal statement. By August, 1975, the seventh and eighth grades were added, and in 1984, the fifth and sixth grades were included. Since 1991, the school has offered education from kindergarten through the twelfth grade.

My father actively participated in the initial planning that created Berean Academy, was a member of the original board of trustees, and remained on the board for thirteen years. He was very dedicated to this project, spending many days volunteering and helping with the construction of the physical plant. My mother helped in her own way by encouraging Father in his roles, being a prayer partner, and working with the food service providing lunch meals during 1948 to 1950. She was active with the ladies auxiliary.

My sister Martha was in the first graduating class of Berean Academy in 1948. She was homeschooled using the correspondence curriculum from the American School for her freshman year, attended Bethel Academy for her sophomore year during its last year of operation in 1945–1946 because they accepted the correspondence credits, and boarded at Hesston Academy for her junior year. She attended Berean Academy for her senior year and gave the valedictorian speech during the first commencement.

Composing speeches was never one of Martha's favorite activities. As she struggled with writer's block while composing her valedictory speech, Mother encouraged her with a Low German phrase, "*Frei von Läwa wajch*; just let it flow freely from your liver." Mother wrote a poem in the form of a prayer with which Martha ended her speech. This poem was reproduced later in a school publication.

Prayer for Berean Academy
May 28, 1948
Composed by Mrs. John Epp Jr. and delivered as part of the valedictory address by her daughter Miss Martha Louise Epp at the Berean Academy Commencement Exercises

May Berean 'ere continue as in the Bible told,
    Where Scripture is searched daily as Bereans did of old:
And that it may be founded on Jesus Christ alone,
    Who is the true foundation and only cornerstone.

May Berean have Directors who give themselves to prayer,
    Who search the Scriptures daily, uphold them day by day;
In all its enterprises a helping hand will lend,
    And find in Christ, our Savior, a counselor and a friend.

The Mission of Parochial Education

May Berean have instructors who hear the call of youth,
    Who search the Scriptures daily for wisdom and for truth.
To lead these young souls upward, though trials it may hold,
    And help to shape these vessels while easy yet to mold.

May Berean have the students with longing to do right,
    Who search the Scriptures daily for guidance and for light,
In all that shall confront them, in each decision too,
    Their lives be led by doing what God would have them do.

May homes be represented by students in the school
    Where Scripture is searched daily and kept as God's given rule;
That all respective parents who have their children come
    May feel the Christian influence of Berean in the home.

That all may stand behind it, (In unity is strength)
    And thus it may continue through days and years in length
And all those interested put shoulders to the wheel,
    Support in fullest measure as God shall give them zeal.

May all the happy moments that at Berean we spend,
    Be used in life's experience a steadiness to lend.
Though different traits and natures are represented here,
    May each one find God's calling for him in future years.

May Berean be a lighthouse that sends its rays abroad
    To those in heathen darkness to point the way to God.
May his name be exalted, be praised and honored more
    Because our dear Berean has opened wide its door.

Among my mother's papers was a poem that she dated February 22, 1956 with the note that it was my sister Justina's sophomore year poem for English class at Berean Academy, written with Mother's help.

Untitled

Dark is the night the wind is howling;
    Jack Frost is painting the window pane.
Tomorrow morning it's down to zero;
    Already now this fact is plain.

The Petals of a Kansas Sunflower

> Within the living room I'm sitting;
>   It's getting late, I should retire.
> But still I stay, it seems so cozy
>   Within the warmth of the fire.
>
> I finally have the needed courage
>   And upstairs to bed I go.
> Still increasing, the wind is blowing
>   Against the window, sleet and snow.
>
> Sound asleep, I soon was resting
>   In the warm and cozy bed,
> With the blankets all around me,
>   Even covering up my head.
>
> In Dreamland's garden I am wandering;
>   Oh, what beauty, free from harm.
> Then all at once a lion starts roaring
>   And I awake, it's the alarm.
>
> Yes, I know the night is over;
>   A few more minutes I shall rest.
> Oh, the comfort in the morning
>   When the bed seems at its best.
>
> How annoying when at that moment
>   From downstairs a voice will ask,
> "Didn't your alarm go off this morning?
>   It's getting late to do your tasks."
>
> Steadily the clock moves onward;
>   Oh, the hurry and the fuss.
> Just to find a little later
>   That the snow had stalled the bus.
>   —Justina Epp/Marie Harder Epp

The poem that I submitted two years later during my sophomore year was also among her papers. The instructor read aloud each of the poems submitted by class members. After he read mine, he looked at me inquisitively and inquired, "Did you have help writing this?" I shrugged my shoulders. He continued, "Did your mother help you?"

I answered, "A little bit."

He then said, "Because your mother helped you, I will give you an A-. However, wouldn't it be wonderful if all parents were as helpful with their children's homework assignments?"

Zaccheus

There was a man of Jericho,
    Zaccheus was his name;
Chief among the publicans,
    Which robbed him of his fame.

In spite of all his wealth and gold
    Christ Jesus he must see;
To overcome his short stature
    He climbed into a tree.

And there well hid among the leaves
    He sat upon a branch;
To see the Lord was his desire
    And now this was his chance.

A throng is now approaching,
    He held his breath in awe,
Could this be the Messiah,
    The Savior that he saw?

The procession now is halted,
    The Lord steps to the tree;
His eyes meet those of Zaccheus
    In love and sympathy.

And from the Master's lips he hears
    Words that sound strange but sweet;
In haste Zaccheus leaves the tree
    And at his house they meet.

The Savior and the sinner
    Are meeting face to face;
And this is an example
    Of a sinner saved by grace.
        —Melvin D. Epp/Marie Harder Epp

The Petals of a Kansas Sunflower

Mother was aware that many schools had school songs, so she composed one in 1969 that she felt would be appropriate for Berean Academy. I am not aware if she ever submitted the song to Berean administration, or if this was just an afternoon project for diversion, but I know the song was never adopted. The words are metered to be sung to the tune of "I've Anchored in Jesus." It is a song of thanksgiving rather than a rallying cry to create school loyalty or athletic fervor; from Mother's perspective, she probably would not agree with me. The school mascot became the Warrior during the 1950s and in 1959 the yearbook was renamed *The Warrior* from *The Gateway*. Mother's concept of a warrior was drawn from Ephesians 6 where Christian life was likened to a type of warfare between good versus evil and challenges each of us "to put on the whole armor of God." This is the warrior that Mother would have solicited with her school song.

In the 1993 artistic rendition of the mascot, the warrior is a Native American of chieftain status with a three eagle-feathered hairpiece. The women's teams became "squaws," and more recently "lady warriors." The biblical, peace-loving warrior that Mother perceived morphed conceptually into a combatant equipped with bludgeoning tomahawks, going on surreptitious raids, and exuding brutal warring forces.

Berean Academy School Song
April 1969
(Tune: I've Anchored in Jesus)

1.
We, students of Berean, our voices now we raise
To God our heavenly Father, in reverence and praise,
We thank him that he gave us Bere'n Academy,
To train us for his service efficiently.

Chorus:
Berean, Berean, God's word we daily read.
   To teach us and guide, in this dark world of need.
Berean, Berean, a lighthouse here indeed,
   All glory be to God forever.

2.
In answer to much planning, foundations here were laid,
That we could have the training, for which our parents prayed,
That our faith would be anchored on Christ and Christ alone,
Who is the Rock of Ages and cornerstone.

3.
The harvest fields are ready, the reapers are but few,
The Lord still calls for workers, He calls for me and you.
So let us answer quickly, "Lord here am I, send me,
I'll labor in the harvest joyfully."

—Marie Epp

For the twentieth and the twenty-fifth anniversary of the founding of Berean Academy, Mother wrote commemorative poems. The first poem was read at a booster banquet on February 15, 1966. Since the second poem expands on the first, I will only include the twenty-fifth anniversary poem, which was written in 1971. She reviews the founding of the school and building details, ending the poem by repeating the closing lines from the poem she wrote for Martha in 1948, "May His name be exalted, be praised and honored more / Because Berean Academy has opened wide its doors." Mother liked these lines because, as the doors to Berean Academy opened wide, she supported her husband as he put his energies into a project that she herself wholeheartedly supported and that she felt would be a positive contribution to the maturation and development of her own children.

Berean Academy
1946-1971

"With God all things are possible." This calls for joy and praise.
   "Great things have small beginnings," another well-known phrase;
And as we look at Berean, both statements we find true,
   So let us review its history, though briefly, here for you.
It started with a vision that, at the time, some brethren had;
   As it became more vivid, to action it soon led.
Seeing our young people going on through their high school years
   Without any Bible training, this created worry and fears.
Could they find and fill the place God had for them in life?
   And find their way through world's unrest, temptation, fear and strife?

The Petals of a Kansas Sunflower

Who would heed the call of the heathen crying out of endless night?
    Who would take up the gospel torch and bring them hope and light?
Also, there is work at home in church and Sunday school,
    Too often a lack of workers seems to be the general rule.
Does not the work of tomorrow rest on the youth of today?
    The need was Christian training and this without delay,
But where to start on such a task, the work seemed all too great.
    And more obstacles were encountered than we shall here relate.
Repeatedly groups met for prayer, God's will and guidance to implore
    And step by step he guided and opened many a door.
Of course, it took much planning; where to locate, where to start,
    Keen was the general interest. Many took an active part.
There was the mutual encouragement that in '46 in fall
    A Christian high school should be started, if possible at all.
Nine able men were elected as Board members to serve
    And an honorable mention, today they well deserve.
Time is never at a standstill; days go by in steady pace.
    The summer passed by swiftly as is the usual case.
As September was approaching and a new school year, you know,
    Berean too opened its doors—now twenty-five years ago.
In the Zion Church's basement we saw this nucleus appear;
    Sixteen students and two teachers met there the first school year.
All the while there was discussion and activity began,
    Monthly prayer sessions lent stability to each plan.
God seemed to lead directly here in Elbing to locate,
    Temptations larger cities bring, this would eliminate.
A donation of ten acres was gratefully received;
    So of a large expenditure the Board was thus relieved.
Next was the building program and carefully it was planned.
    It took prayerful designing with limited funds on hand.
The Board was led to consider, in seeking out God's will,
    School buildings then no more in use, located at Oil Hill.
The decision was to move them in, and this without delay;
    And as East and West buildings we remember them to this day.
But all this took much longer than they thought it might;
    For the moving of a building is never done overnight.
So there was ample time to work, voluntary labor was at hand,
    Forms were built, foundations made or whatever the demand.
It would have simplified the task had the east building smaller been,
    But now they had to cut it and in three sections brought it in.
For the Superintendent's dwelling another schoolhouse was found.
    This also was remodeled after being moved onto this ground.
Water was quite a problem. Several test wells first they tried;
    They proved inferior and insufficient a whole school to supply.

The Mission of Parochial Education

From a well beyond the campus, the water was piped in
    And, with the aid of a water softener, an adequate supply has been.
With the changing to city water, a great need could be met;
    For this is an improvement that no one will regret.
Then landscaping was also done and plans for this were drawn
    And what is now the parking lot was once a pretty lawn.
Now this has been a bird's eye view of what has gone before.
    Just briefly we have touched on things, we could have said much more.
As now we see Berean and over the campus we glance,
    Year after year brought changes; there is progress and advance.
Already a step in advancement the second school year brought;
    Grades eleven and twelve were added, to ninth and tenth then taught.
This called for more equipment, more teachers and more grace,
    It increased the student body considerably in this case.
The financial need was thus increased as has been year by year.
    The blessing of the Lord causes growth, we saw this also here.
Soon dormitories were needed, a cook, a dining hall—
    Met were the increasing demands and classes resumed each fall.
When we used to assemble, some here will well recall
    How crowded the East building was with the overflow in the hall.
Since many come to meetings and ball games as a rule
    A new auditorium seemed a real need for the school.
Again we saw God working as so often heretofore,
    The auditorium, though not complete, was first used in '54
And this at the Commencement, but without privilege or rank
    Twenty-three proud seniors came marching in on planks.
Then later the new classrooms; what a blessing they have been
    Since from scattered and crowded quarters the students could move in.
Eight houses were acquired in which the faculty now dwell.
    The new Superintendent's house filled a great need as well.
Still other needed improvements in recent years were made;
    With a growing student body they could not be delayed.
To a new and modern building the West Building gave way;
    More classrooms and equipment are thus in use today.
There we also find the Chapel with its prayerful atmosphere;
    And daily the students gather for spiritual uplift here.
The athletic field is also new and so a twelve member Board.
    And as student body to an all-time high has soared
An increased curriculum was needed on their behalf;
    This also called for an increase in faculty and staff.
Now on another project our eyes are focused on.
    It is with mixed feeling that we see the East building is gone.
Whoever would have guessed it—for twenty-five years it served!

The Petals of a Kansas Sunflower

    With present regulations a replacement it deserved.
Again we saw God working in a most amazing way;
    So plans for a modern building are reality today.
As in the days of Moses people gave with willing heart,
    Here also was a willingness to take an active part.
When of $250,000 the first mention was made
    It seemed a heavy burden on the constituency was laid;
But now only months later, the work could here begin
    For in gifts and pledges more then the mentioned sum came in.

In closing let us praise the Lord, for his guidance, for his love,
    For his kindness and his blessings that he gave Berean from above.
We thank him for our Alumni, though scattered they may be
    In foreign fields and homeland, to the islands of the sea;
For among them are doctors, nurses, preachers, missionaries, too,
    Farmers, housewives, teachers, to mention only a few.
May Berean remain a lighthouse that sends its rays abroad
    To those that are in darkness to point the way to God;
May his name be exalted, be praised and honored more
    Because Berean Academy has opened wide its door.
        —M.H.E.

    For a father and son banquet in 1981, Mother was asked to write a welcome poem. She reviews the role that she feels a father plays, and the division of labor between fathers, wives, and children is expressed. The diversity among fathers is observed, but the uniqueness that masculinity is expressed in fathers and sons is not very well depicted (masculine conversations and fellowship are hardly "sweet," but it rhymed).

Father and Son Banquet
Berean Academy
February 21, 1981

    We are so glad that you have come.
        We welcome each and everyone.
    The older and the younger, too,
        So that means everyone of you.

    Many homes are represented here,
        And wide the range in age of year.

The Mission of Parochial Education

This banquet honors fathers and sons
   No matter how old or even how young.
We see some here that are mere lads
   In course of time they'll too be dads.

Please excuse, but for easier rhyme
   We are substituting "dad" for "father" sometimes.

Father, in the home has a prominent place,
   His is respect and honor in every case.
The Bible, which gives guidelines for life,
   Requests children's obedience and submission of wife.
His family's welfare is close to his heart.
   Also, spiritual leadership is his part.
Still other responsibilities will come his way
   And this goes on day after day.
Some may weigh heavily, some may seem small,
   There is no way out but to cope with them all.
Children love too when dad finds time for them all
   Giving rides on the tractor or maybe playing ball.
In good condition the car has to be,
   Another of dad's responsibilities.
The wife is in a hurry, into the car she will hop
   And is on her way to town to shop.
He also complies to ma's wants and wishes
   And might even sometimes do the dishes.

Seeing these dads here today
   No two are alike in any way.
Some dads are stout, some dads are lean,
   Then there are those just in-between.
Some dads are short, some dads are tall
   It makes no difference after all.
Some are the jolly type and others more sincere,
   And that makes up this group that's represented here.
It matters not what shape or size
   Or any difference otherwise,
But that your fellowship is sweet
   As around these tables you now meet.
That everything you will find just right
   And being here is a delight.
We say again: "We are glad you have come!"
   And may God bless you everyone.

      —M.H.E.

The Petals of a Kansas Sunflower

My father initiated an outreach project through Berean Academy to explore the possibility of establishing a mission Sunday school in the Wichita area. After organizing daily summer Vacation Bible Schools for several years, beginning in 1952, a church was launched in Wichita named Berean Bible Church. My parents were active leaders in this church and for many years drove to Wichita several times a week to keep the church going. The church property was located at 29th Street North and Hydraulic, and after thirteen years the land was purchased by eminent domain for the highway project referred to as the Canal Route, Interstate 135. The church moved to a new location but closed its doors seven years later due to declining attendance. For the third anniversary of the church, Mother wrote this poem in which she contrasts foreign mission projects with those of local mission projects and focuses on reasons for an outreach church.

Anniversary of the Berean Bible Church
June 5, 1955

When we look around about us
    There's a need on every hand;
Not a need for food and shelter
    As perhaps in foreign lands—
With us it's not a lack of money;
    Ease and comfort here we see.
Different here from heathen countries
    Where people die in misery.

What then is the need? It keenly
    Presents itself in different ways
As we meet and talk with people
    Or just observe them through the days.
It's that they are so indifferent,
    Not realizing they are lost.
Life seems just for fun and frolic
    Getting the best at any cost.

Sunday in so many cases
    Is not the Lord's Day any more;
It's the day to do the washing,
    Mow the lawn, or a similar chore.

The Mission of Parochial Education

There's no knowledge of salvation;
   The doubtful future is faced with fear.
That strait the gate, the way but narrow—
   For such things they have no ear.

Could we point to us as Christians
   Finding even there a need?
Is it not Christ's call for laborers
   That we are so slow to heed?
Oh, we like to make excuses—
   "I'm not called," let others go,
And the "go ye" in Christ's commission
   To obey we are but slow.

Or we sometimes feel like Moses
   Thinking we don't qualify,
But to us, God, too, gives the promise
   That our needs he will supply.
And we hear him ask the question,
   "What is that in your hand?"
It's God's Word—his free salvation,
   To "Give it forth" is his command.

Today as we pause for a moment
   Looking unto God in praise
Thanking him that he was with us,
   Blessing us in different ways.
Our attendance slowly increased;
   In the beginning we had three,
Now for Sunday School each Sunday
   Five nice classes we can see.

Let us fix our eyes on Jesus,
   To do his will be our concern
Should we ever get discouraged
   From the prophets we can learn—
Little result for faithful labor;
   Yet watchman God calls us to be,
The purpose that his Word accomplished
   Will be revealed in eternity.

18

Encouraging Missionaries as They Say Goodbye

AFTER THE IMMIGRANT FAMILIES became comfortable and settled as pioneer farmers on the grassy plains of Kansas, they began to look toward people outside their immediate community. Consistent with their views of the teachings of Jesus, they wanted to share, not only material goods, but also their belief in God.

In 1920, the Mennonite Central Committee (MCC) was organized to address the most crucial needs of suffering people around the globe. The post–World War I period had left Europe devastated. In Russia, the czarist government had collapsed, and revolutions and counter-revolutions had ensued, leaving the social and economic infrastructure in turmoil. Amid the political chaos during 1920 to 1922, there was a devastating drought in the southern Russia. Among the many suffering people were relatives of the Mennonites in the United States, and these concerns took on an immediate personal element. More information about the relief efforts of the MCC during this period is included in appendix 1.

The pioneers of the local church also wanted to share their religious faith with people of different ethnic backgrounds and in other countries. Alfred and Agnes Wiebe were ordained in 1911 as the first missionaries from the local church under the auspices of the General Conference Mennonite's Mission Board to work among Native Americans in Montana. Marie J. (Regier, Frantz) Jansen worked in China from 1926 to 1941, and in Paraguay and Taiwan before she retired in 1962.

In each of the three poems in this chapter, Mother uses the word "vineyard" to conceptualize mission work, e.g., "In the vineyard of our Master, yet much work needs to be done." This analogy is derived from parables that Jesus taught including the one from Matthew 20:1, "For the kingdom of heaven is like a landowner who went out early in the morning to hire men to work in his vineyard."

In 1940, before Lester and Agnes (Harder) Wuthrich left for China, there was a farewell, and Mother wrote a poem that was recited by a seven-year-old nephew. After two years in China when a Japanese invasion appeared inevitable, the mission board transferred the Wuthrichs to the Philippines to continue language studies. However, the Japanese also invaded the Philippines and the Wuthrichs were placed in an internment camp for a number of years where they survived starvation because Filipinos threw food over the prison fence. They were released and able to come home in 1945, returning briefly to China in 1948, but soon left permanently because of the communist takeover. They continued missionary service in the mountainous regions of Kentucky working for the Scripture Memory Mountain Mission.

Agnes grew up in the local Emmaus Mennonite Church community, but changed her membership after marriage to that of her husband's, the Swiss Mennonite Church, in an adjacent community just to the west.

Farewell to Uncle Lester and Aunt Agnes
August, 1940
Presented by Kenneth Roy Harder

> Dear Uncle Lester, Aunt Agnes too!
> It's just a few words I'll say to you;
> My heart is so full I could say a lot,
> But since I'm small I better not.
> It surely saddened my little heart
> When my Mother told me, that soon you'll part
> From us for China away so far;
> Where many, many heathen are.
> Since the Lord calls you as I hear
> I will not keep you nor interfere
> But wish you God's blessing for every day
> While you work in his vineyard so far away.

During a ten-year period in the late 40s and early 50s, Dr. and Mrs. Mann were the directors of Child Evangelism Fellowship, Inc. for the state of Kansas. My parents were acquainted with the Manns and supported their work. When the Manns were appointed directors of a ten-state region in 1956, Mother provided this poem for their farewell.

Dr. & Mrs. Mann's Farewell
August 30, 1956

In the vineyard of our Master there is work for everyone.
    Still the call goes out for laborers; all are wanted, old and young.
He wants those that would be willing to give forth the gospel news,
    It's free salvation; all can have it; yet so many still refuse.

In our towns and in our cities, almost everywhere we go
    We can see some happy children in their play run to and fro.
We can hear their happy laughter, free from care their eyes are bright
    Some have all they ever ask for. All, but not the gospel light.
Parents find much joy in giving to their children a lot of toys;
    But all this is for a season; soon will vanish fun and joys.
Of things that are of lasting value they deprive their little hearts;
    In bringing them up in the admonition of our Lord, they have no part.

Tonight, therefore, we are grateful for the Child Evangelism Fellowship
    On the youngsters of our country it has loosened Satan's grip.
Many are today the children that have come into the fold
    Through a camp or a Good News Club—where of Jesus they were told
And that a heart all black and sinful through his blood is made all white
    Then on golden streets in heaven they shall walk in heavenly light.

Today, however, we came together to bid farewell to our friends;
    To wish them God-speed and God's blessing,
        as to another field he sends.
They gave ten years of faithful service to the children of our state;
    Of long hours of planning and much hardship,
        I'm sure they could relate.
Faithful laborers as we see here, is in a way here repaid:
    That a greater field of service at their threshold God has laid.
In one state God found them faithful; now ten states on them rely.
    Let us claim for them the promise that their needs God will supply;

Encouraging Missionaries as They Say Goodbye

That God's grace will be sufficient in the hardships of "the new;"
    That they find a fruitful service and their disappointments few;
That new friends are there to greet them as the old ones stay behind
    And that in God our heavenly Father
        an ever present help they'll find.

As Lois (Roth) Clinesmith was preparing to leave for further French language study in France in 1957, Mother wrote this poem to encourage her on her way. In 1950, Lois went to Morocco with the Gospel Missionary Union, now known as Avant. She had come home on furlough, a vacation period before additional language training, and in 1958, she returned to Morocco to continue her mission service. Lois, too, was from the Swiss Mennonite Church community.

For Lois Roth's Farewell
September 1, 1957

In the vineyard of our Master, yet much work needs to be done
    Calling to us out of darkness, there are poor souls, old and young.
Millions still are seeking, groping in the darkness of the night;
    Knowing nothing of the blessing and the peace of heavenly light.

Today there comes to us the challenge, as we look across the sea,
    To the souls in heathen darkness, ever longing to be free
From the chains of superstition that for years has held them bound
    In the clutch of Satan worship, where no peace and joy is found.

That someone would be faithful, as to heed the Lord's command;
    Going out to spread the tidings—going to the foreign land.
To the people lost and hopeless, even there some soul to glean
    For the blood of Christ our Savior, makes the vilest sinner clean.

And our sister heard the crying of those longing to be free.
    Gladly she has given the answer, "Here I am Lord, do send me."
One full term of faithful service, she has rendered to the Lord,
    Going forth in his own power—giving forth the precious word.

Then after years of faithful service, the needed furlough finally came
    To the homeland her steps then turning—but to find it not the same

The Petals of a Kansas Sunflower

Oh, there were the parents, brothers and the friends, they all are dear,
    But the love for her work had deepened—deepened with each passing year.

Now again we find her ready, stepping out in faith once more;
    Leaning on the arms of Jesus, looking out to Africa's shore.
And we would in no wise hinder, wishing her God-speed instead.
    Thanking him that he is "able" and that faithfully he led.

Even though the extent of darkness is well known to her by now,
    Still the love of God compels her, others too his love to show.
And God's prose she may claim here, he who even clothes the grass
    All the good things he has promised, not one fails, all come to pass.

Unto God's care we shall commit her, as again she bids farewell
    Knowing she is a chosen vessel, going forth good news to tell.
We are wishing her God's blessing for each step along the way
    And our prayers shall surround her as she labors day by day.

—M.H.E.

19

A Commercial Jingle, i.e., Song

BY THE MID TO late 1940s, Kansas State University had a very active program in plant breeding to improve the crops that farmers were growing. This program continues to the present time, both at the university and by private seed companies. University professors or private companies develop new varieties and produce the initial pure lots of seeds; these are called Foundation Class seeds. Foundation Class seeds are controlled by the developer of a variety and are not generally an item of commerce. Initial lots of seed are normally very small and need to be multiplied in volume for commercial use. Within the state of Kansas, the Kansas Crop Improvement Association (KCIA) maintains a "limited generation system" of certified seed classes and manages a seed certification service that verifies the genetic purity of the seeds during the increase and maintenance stages.

The Foundation seeds are provided to certified growers to grow the first increase—the Registered Class of seeds. These are then provided to other certified growers who grow Registered Class seeds into commercial volumes of Certified Class seeds. Regulations governing the production of certified seeds include the pre-usage cleaning of planting and harvesting equipment and storage bins; planting on ground that meets the KCIA requirements; rouging of off-type plants; and weed control prior to a mandatory field inspection by KCIA personnel. Seeds need to be conditioned at an approved facility, samples sent to the KCIA laboratory for analysis, and then seed lots must be properly labeled and registered to sell with appropriate authority. The KCIA is involved in every step of seed increase. When a farmer buys Kansas Certified Seed, he can be confident that the seed has high genetic purity, high physical quality, high germination, is free of noxious weed seeds, and has maximum yield potential.

The price of certified seeds is considerably higher, providing farmers an opportunity to create a profitable sideline business by growing and marketing certified seeds. In our community, three Claassen brothers, Walter, Herbert, and Arnold, grew certified seeds on their Golden Rule Farms. Two additional Claassen brothers, Paul and Carl, also grew certified seed increases. During the 1940s the new varieties Pawnee wheat, Buffalo alfalfa, and Madrid yellow sweet clover were grown under certification for seed increase.

The rate of release of new varieties was relatively slow during the 1940s and 1950s. After the enactment of The Plant Variety Protection Act of 1970, most of the work in developing new varieties was undertaken by private seed companies rather than the university. This act provided protection of the intellectual property rights of the owner. Consequently, many varieties are now available to the farmer.

At some point the subject of certified seeds caught Mother's attention and she wrote this advertising song. It is undated with no clarifying notes to indicate who requested it or when it was used. I do remember, though, that my father grew a demonstration plot of various cultivars on the west 80 of the northwest quarter of Section 16 sometime between 1944 to 1947; in late summer there was a field day for the community to observe these demonstration plots. This song may well have been part of that field day. Mother got her facts straight, and hopefully this song helped promote the use of Kansas Certified Seed.

Kansas Certified Seed
(Tune: Nellie Gray)

1. When you make your plans for sowing, and you have prepared your field,
   Be sure to choose some Certified Seed.
   For it will not disappoint you, you will have a perfect yield.
   Hurrah for Kansas Certified Seed.

2. Certified Seed with high germination, sow it and you'll see it grow
   And you shall not be in want of feed.
   So be wise all you farmers when your seed you're going to sow.
   Let it be Kansas Certified Seed.

A Commercial Jingle, i.e., Song

Chorus:
    Oh, grow Certified Seed.
    You will reap more grain and feed.
    And the seed for a better price you'll always sell
    For it germinates so well
    And your crop will have less weeds,
    So hurrah for Kansas Certified Seed.

20

The Celebration of Christmas

When I reflect on childhood, the Christmas season seems to be a primary recollection. Christmas involved our home, the school community, and the church community. The days between Thanksgiving and New Year were special with unique activities and foods, including peppernuts, without which Christmas simply would not have happened.

On Christmas day there was a church service in the morning and the children's Sunday school program in the evening, with another church service the morning of December 26. Derived from the Dutch Mennonite tradition, the early celebration of Christmas involved three days of consecutive church services while Easter and Pentecost each consisted of two days. Shortly after coming to America, the local Mennonite church limited the Christmas celebration to two services. Easter and Pentecost activities were reduced to a single Sunday service.

The children's program at church always began with a young child reciting a welcome, and when I was five years old, my Sunday school teachers pointed at me after consulting with Mother and said, "Melvin, you will give the welcome." There was no escape. Why me when there were others who were not as bashful as I? For the first five years of my life, I spent my time in the upstairs storage room whenever there was a stranger in the house, anyone other than my parents and siblings. My first recollection of being a dinner guest was at an uncle's house and seated beside my mother, I was so bashfully frightened that I put my head on my mother's lap as we were being seated and promptly fell asleep. I do recall my mother saying, "I think he is afraid of Waldo," one of my cousins. The next day, as my siblings raved about the pigs-in-a-blanket my aunt had served, I realized that my fears had prevented me from enjoying a delectable dinner.

The Celebration of Christmas

For the program welcome, with my mother's help, I memorized my lines. My oldest sister encouraged me to practice speaking very loudly, undoubtedly afraid that I would embarrass her in front of her peers since there was no sound amplification system in the church at that time. I can vividly remember going up the steps on the right side of the stage and not quite making it to the middle of the stage before I began reciting my welcome with whatever volume I could muster. I do not remember the words, but it must have been the first of the two welcome poems that Mother wrote. One memento of that early childhood lesson is a sixty-year-old Christmas card signed on the back "From your Sunday school teachers, Martha Thiessen and Elma Busenitz," that I include among the treasured decorations of our house every Christmas season. It is a three-dimensional foldout of the nativity in a stable.

Welcome

There is something in my heart today
And this is what I'd like to say,
"A joyful Christmas everyone,
We are so glad that you have come
To hear us children both large and small
And may God bless you one and all."

Welcome Poem, 1967
Presented by Nancy Regier

It's wonderful to gather in honor of our Lord
And celebrate his birthday, according to God's word.
So I say a hearty welcome to each and every one.
We appreciate your presence, we're happy you have come.
We'll give our recitations and sing the songs of praise
In worship and in gratitude, to him our voices we'll raise.
We trust you'll gain a blessing not only while you're here
But may the Christmas spirit be yours in the coming year.

As the children left the church after the program, the ushers, with the help of the Sunday school committee, would give each child a "*Tütchen.*" These were small brown paper sacks typically containing an orange or an apple, hard candy, and unshelled nuts and peanuts. For rural farm children prior to about 1950, these *Tütchen* were a major treat and pure ambrosia. Even today, the local church continues to treat children with *Tütchen* after each year's Christmas program by the children.

In the elementary school, the Christmas program was held on a Friday night in mid-December. This was a time when the community could see the workings of the local school. There was no parent/teacher association, and no volunteer involvement of mothers, so this program served to show the success of the school year. All fall, woodworking craft projects involved making gifts for our mothers, and art projects created invitations for the program that were passed out in the community. The program itself consisted of readings, plays, and group songs. After the program there would be a potluck dinner while the adults visited and the children played.

In the traditional German custom, the Christmas celebration at home when I was a child was on the evening of December 24. For several months Mother shopped in El Dorado, Newton, and Wichita whenever Father went to these towns on business. My father considered gasoline a precious, costly commodity and frugality dictated that the car would not be taken just for shopping. Mother always had a very special gift for each of her children, which she hid in the upstairs storage room closets until the twenty-fourth.

Right after Thanksgiving, Mother began her baking frenzy of Christmas goodies. However, her batch of peppernut dough was mixed before Thanksgiving and put into the unheated upstairs storeroom to age before initiating the baking in early December. Mixing this dough took physical strength because the volume to be mixed and kneaded filled a large crockery bread-mixing bowl. When the time came to bake the peppernuts, Mother would take a piece of dough, roll it out to one-fourth-inch thick, cut one-inch circles of dough with her inherited peppernut cutter, and stack these cut peppernuts onto greased and floured baking sheets. We children would sit and arrange them in rows. Mother cut fast enough to keep at least three children going simultaneously.

The peppernut cutter was a unique piece of antique kitchen equipment, handed down from my grandmother or great-grandmother. It was fabricated by a local tinsmith and was a circular cone one-inch-wide at the bottom with sides that tapered out slightly, about three inches long. This allowed Mother to repeatedly cut peppernuts until there were

The Celebration of Christmas

Figure 38
Marie's inherited prized peppernut cutter constructed of sheet metal, 2.5 inch long with tapered sides, bottom hole 1 inch across and top 1.5 inches. Private collection.
Source: Author's file.

twenty to twenty-five inside the cone. By inverting the cutter, the peppernuts all fell out. The cutter was quick and when making enough peppernuts for ten people to snack on during the month of December, it was a prized kitchen tool.

There are many recipes for peppernuts and every family has their own ancestral version. Mother alternated between two traditional recipes, one from her mother, Helene Wiebe Harder (1864–1930), and another from her cousin, Justine Harder Reimer (1894–1980), Mrs. Gus Reimer.

The Petals of a Kansas Sunflower

Grandmother Harder's Peppernuts

1 cup Sugar
1 cup Shortening
1 cup Cream
1 ½ cup Dark Karo Syrup
1 tsp Baking Soda
1 tsp Baking Powder
½ tsp allspice
½ tsp ginger
½ tsp cloves
½ tsp ground anise
4 to 6 cups flour

Justine Harder Reimer's Peppernuts

1 cup Syrup or Honey
1//2 cup Sugar
1 cup Shortening
1 cup Buttermilk or Sour Cream
½ tsp Salt
1 tsp Cocoa
½ tsp Cinnamon
½ tsp Ground Anise
¼ tsp Nutmeg
¼ tsp Cloves
¼ tsp Allspice
Enough flour for a stiff dough

Of course, there were no mixing instructions included. It was assumed that every cook would know that one creams the sugar and shortening until fluffy; adds the liquids, i.e., the cream, syrup, honey, buttermilk or sour cream; mixes in the dry ingredients; and finally kneads the dough with enough flour to make it very stiff. The dough was allowed to rest overnight or up to two weeks to let the spices and flavors blend, and then rolled out, cut and baked at 350 degrees to 375 degrees Fahrenheit for seven to ten minutes. Baking time was a personal preference; the flavor and texture of the peppernuts changed with the degree of brownness. Peppernuts were hard and dry, and endured being carried in pockets after school while doing the evening chores.

If, by chance, the peppernuts stuck together while baking, they became very special. If one took hold of one of a pair of attached peppernuts and offered the other to someone else, whoever said, "*Verliebchen*" first after the two broke apart, was entitled to a wish. It was a fun game and no one was ever too disappointed since there were enough attached pairs to do it again and secretly, we all understood that in our divinely guided world, wishes did not come true anyway unless one was self-reliant. In our family, the word connoted "good luck" or "with a little love."

At the time of her prime, Mother would also bake ten to twelve different kinds of cookies that would be served at the conclusion of meals. The German tradition is known for its Christmas cookies and Mother upheld that tradition.

Figure 39
Springerle cookie rolling pin. The images clockwise from upper left are Billy goat, bread basket, cat, church, buck, flower, stag, fronds, ram, poinsettia, dragon fly, and holly. This rolling pin was brought along from West Prussia in 1876. Private collection. Source: Author's file.

Springerle cookies are among the most famous traditional German Christmas cookies and also utilized an inherited, carved rolling pin to imprint a design on the top of the cookies. Mother's *Springerle* rolling pin had been brought along from West Prussia when the family immigrated in 1876. Recipes for this anise cookie are included in many cookbooks and a generic version is presented here.

Springerle (Anise) Cookies

3 ½ to 4 cups sifted all-purpose or cake flour
1 teaspoon baking powder
½ teaspoon salt
4 eggs
2 to 2 ¼ cups granulated sugar
1 tablespoon butter
1 teaspoon grated lemon rind or lemon extract, or 1 teaspoon ground anise seeds or 4-10 drops anise oil
2 to 3 tablespoons anise seeds

Sift together the flour, baking powder, and salt. Place the eggs, butter, sugar, and lemon or anise flavoring in a bowl and beat about thirty minutes; beat in the flour mixture, one half cup at a time. Cover the dough and chill overnight.

Roll the dough to one-half to five-eighths inch thickness on a surface generously spread with flour. Flour the chilled *Springerle* rolling pin and roll slowly over the dough, pressing firmly and evenly to leave clear designs. Cut the cookies apart. Sprinkle greased cookie sheets with anise seeds and transfer the cookies to the sheets. Alternatively, sprinkle the anise seeds on the cookies. Let stand overnight, uncovered, at room temperature. Preheat oven to 375ºF but immediately turn down to 300ºF as the cookies are placed in the oven to help set the designs. Bake for about fifteen minutes until very light yellow, but not brown, and thoroughly dried. Keep cookies in an airtight canister for 2 to 3 weeks. To soften, put a cut apple in canister a day or so before serving.

On the morning of December 24, the doors to the parlor and the vestibule that led to the parlor were closed. This gave privacy as Mother made her trips to the upstairs storeroom where the gifts were stored. She spent the entire day decorating and organizing the room for the family celebration in the evening. After supper, the girls washed the dishes as fast as possible, and Christmas was ready to begin.

We children would line up in pairs by age—sometimes the oldest first and sometimes the youngest. We would stand and impatiently wait for Mother to open the door through which we could then see, in unbelievable grandeur, a five-foot-tall decorated artificial Christmas tree lit with burning candles.

All the leaves had been put into the round table that normally stood in the corner of the parlor to extend it out to seat ten people. The table was covered with a white linen tablecloth and eight places were arranged, each with a pile of items; these too were arranged in order from oldest to youngest. We found our places and just stood and looked in awe at the tree in the middle of the table while the candles burned for ten to fifteen minutes. The Christmas celebration was very special; it truly was enchanting.

After the candles were extinguished and another light source was provided, we could examine our presents. I only remember the toys, the Lincoln logs, ceramic building blocks, and a barn with many animals, but there surely were books and items of clothing as well. At each person's place, there was also a twelve-inch soup dish filled with candy, cookies, nuts, dates, an apple or an orange, and always, homemade peanut brittle. However, the crowning touch in each plate of goodies was several pieces of Mother's handmade marzipan. Most of the pieces were shaped into two-inch logs or one-inch round buttons, but on every plate there was one four-inch flat marzipan heart with the center filled with red jam. I feel that this marzipan heart showed in art form the affection and esteem Mother had for each of us, expressing with her culinary skills an emotion that in a German Mennonite community was so often assumed, but seldom articulated. After the excitement of the presents subsided, my father would lead us from memory in the recitation of the second chapter of Luke and several songs, both in English and German. Finally, it was time to sample the candy.

Several years ago, I tried to recreate Mother's marzipan as a unique Christmas gift for special friends. In Mother's recipe the instructions were absent, but an acceptable marzipan was created when I took equal amounts by volume of shelled, blanched, dried, ground almonds and powdered sugar. After mixing well, some vanilla and rose extract were added and then just enough water drops until the mixture held shape. I molded short ropes or flat buttons three-quarters-inch thick and placed the pieces under a broiler to gently brown the top surface and allow the pieces to dry a bit. When cooled, a little powdered sugar frosting was drizzled over the marzipan.

This traditional celebration lasted until I was nine or ten years old. Only two sisters and I were home for Christmas that year and only a small tree with electric lights stood on a corner table in the dining room. I have few recollections of that Christmas. However, when my father insisted that I stand with him and my two sisters to sing a Christmas carol, I remember bursting into uncontrollable sobs. I was the youngest child and had not aged sufficiently to emotionally forgo the traditional Christmas celebration, sensing that a wonderful, enchanting era had closed and I was not yet ready.

In 1937, Mother entered this poem into her journal. It truly expresses the wonder and beauty of Christmas that Mother tried to create for her children.

Zu Weihnachten

Hell leuchtet heut die Kerzen
In jedem Haus und Raum
Wo frohe Kinderherzen
Sich freuen am Weihnachtsbaum
Doch heller noch wir sehen
Heut leuchtet einen Stern
Und mit den Weisen gehen
Noch Betlehem wir gern
Auf eine Gabe wir geben
Dem Christuskind wir heut
Das unser Herz und leben
Auf neu Ihm sei geweiht.

Froh singen heute wieder
Voll dankbarkeit und Freud
Die schöne Weihnachtslieder
Die ganze Christenheit
Es kam zu uns Armen
In dieser heiligen Nacht
Voll Liebe und Erbarmen
Der Sünder selig macht.

The Celebration of Christmas

Ein frohes Weihnachtskinde
Die den Hirten war zu teil
Aus Heiligen Engelmunde
Sie bringet auch uns Heil.
Es kam zu uns auf Erden
Von hohen Himmelsthron
Denn wir selig werden
Der heilige Gottessohn.

Darum singet heute wieder
Voll dankbarkeit und Freud
Die schöne Weihnachtslieder
Die ganze Menschenheit.

For Christmas

Today, the candles are brightly lit
In every house and room
Where hearts of children are gladdened
Pleased by the Christmas tree.
But we see something brighter yet,
Today, a star sheds light
And we go with the wise men
 Gladly to Bethlehem
To give a gift
To the Christ child today,
That our hearts and lives
Are consecrated anew to him.

Today, happily victorious again,
Full of thankfulness and joy,
The beautiful Christmas songs
From all of Christendom
Come to us, the needy,
 In this holy night
Full of love and with a show of mercy
To make the sinner one in Christ.

A happy Christmas child,
That the shepherds would impart
Out of holy angelic voices
They brought us salvation also,

The Petals of a Kansas Sunflower

It came to us on earth
From heaven's throne on high
For we will be blessed
Because of the holiness of God's son.

Consequently we sing again today,
Full of thankfulness and joy,
The lovely Christmas songs
For all of mankind.

21

The Art of Saying Grace

I HAVE OFTEN PONDERED the phrase from the Lord's Prayer, "Give us this day our daily bread" or "Keep us alive with three square meals," depending upon the Bible translation. When Jesus said these words two thousand years ago, as recorded in Matthew 6:11, obtaining food was a major activity on a daily basis. The constancy of the food supply was marginal, seasonal, and governed by the dietary laws recorded in Leviticus. Convection or microwave ovens were unknown. There was no refrigeration for extended preservation; salt, fermentation, and dehydration were used as storage methods.

Agricultural advances have contributed to increased production of food and have extended the seasons of availability, and new technologies have prolonged storage. In rural temperate zones, food sufficiencies are tied to self-reliant slaughter and food preservation (drying, canning, or freezing) and commercial distribution systems. So why do we continue to implore the Divine to "Keep us alive with three square meals?"

My Anabaptist forefathers placed no value on self-reliance and felt that all good things were a gift from God. The sunshine, the rain, the fertile soil, and the harvest were gifts, and humans, as recipients, were beholden to the creator who provided the environment for food production. Self-reliance was practiced in the act of taking or gathering what was gifted for use. Consequently, eating meals was an integral part of the religious experience, a repetitious act that constantly reminded them of their divine provider. Making prayer a part of dining was consistent with their rigorous fervor to follow after Jesus through the application of his teachings.

When a friend from *The Wichita Eagle* called a week before Thanksgiving in 2003 and asked what traditions I would be following in my home for Thanksgiving, I replied, "My wife prepares cold, marinated Brussels sprouts, I will make sweet potato pudding flavored with Jack Daniel's bourbon, and we will all say a grace that my late mother wrote." I sensed that saying a favorite grace as a tradition fascinated my friend, and she said she would call back. For that Thanksgiving issue of the newspaper, the front page carried her article and a small 1919 portrait of Mother with the caption, "Marie Harder Epp was a farmer and poet outside Whitewater who wrote three 'table graces.' Her son Melvin uses his favorite one as grace before the Thanksgiving meal at his home." Together with the stories of several other families, the article was titled, "Giving Thanks by Saying Grace: Prayers of Gratitude."

> . . . Marie Harder Epp was a poet who lived on a farm outside Whitewater for most of the last century. She recorded history, marked weddings and anniversaries, and expressed her thoughts in verse from 1930 to 1997 [1929 to 1991].
>
> Toward the end of her life, she wrote three "table graces," and this one is Melvin's favorite.
>
> Each Thanksgiving, as members of his family and their guests sit down at the table of his house just east of the old farm, he asks them to say the grace together, in an echo of Lincoln's call to speak in one voice, with one heart.
>
> "By saying a grace in unison, everyone's involved around the whole table," Melvin Epp says, "and it doesn't matter if you're a stranger at my table or familiar with my mother or my family—everyone can enjoy it because it's a beautiful little poem and it expresses what they're grateful for at that moment in time . . ."

Several friends, who read *The Wichita Eagle*, later related that they had enjoyed this grace so much that they too had used it to initiate their own Thanksgiving dinners that year. This grace can also be sung to the tune of the hymn, "What a Friend We Have in Jesus" following the old tradition of singing the grace when guests are present and the meal is celebratory.

Table Grace I

Lord, your hand of love and mercy
Spreads a table for us now
Hear our praise and adoration
As in thanks our heads we bow.

You have given more than needed
Through the years that we have known,
And we ever shall adore Thee
For the kindness you have shown.

—Marie Harder Epp

Saying grace at mealtime was an integral part of partaking of food. Following the traditions that my parents learned at their parents' tables, a grace of blessing was said at the beginning of each meal. A typical blessing might have been *Komm, Herr Jesu, sei unser Gast und segne was Du uns bescheret hast. Amen.* (Come, Lord Jesus, be Thou our guest and bless what you have provided for us. Amen.) An alternative blessing was *Segne Vater diese Speise, uns zur Kraft und Dir zum Preise. Mach uns hier in dieser Zeit fertig für die Ewigkeit. Amen.* (Heavenly Father, bless this food for our strength with which we praise you. Make us ready here now for eternity. Amen.)

At the conclusion of the meal in our home, everyone remained at the table for the grace of thanksgiving. Meals were truly quality family time. A typical thanksgiving grace would have been *Danket dem Herrn denn Er ist freundlich und Seine Guete waehret ewiglich. Amen.* (Thank the Lord since He is kind and His goodness continues eternally. Amen.) Or *Dank Dem Herrn für Seine Gaben, die wir von Dir empfangen haben. Wir bitten Dir als unsern Herrn, Du wolst uns immer bescheren. Amen.* (Thank the Lord for his gifts, which we have received from you. We request that you as our Lord will want to continue to provide for us. Amen.) Or *Alle Guten Gaben, Alles was wir haben, Kommt von Dir O Herr, Dank sei Dir dafür. Amen.* (All good gifts, everything that we have, comes from you, Oh Lord, we thank you for this. Amen.)

The saying of these graces aloud was assigned to a child and passed down through the ranks as the children grew old enough. As time passed in America, the blessing grace and the thanksgiving grace were combined into one grace that was said at the beginning of each meal.

The Petals of a Kansas Sunflower

Table Grace II

Lord, we thank you for these blessings
That your hands so freely give,
Let us honor, praise and serve thee
Every moment that we live.
—Marie Harder Epp

Table Grace III

The cattle on a thousand hills,
The sparrow in the tree,
Are constant in your watchful care, Lord
Are daily fed by thee.

And we who are your children
Now raise our voice in praise
For food, for clothes, for shelter
All through our life-long days.

—Marie Harder Epp
September 3, 1975

22

Mother Is Dying

THE TELEPHONE RANG YET again and the hysterical voice of a sister on the other end of the line cried, "Mother is dying, Mother is dying."

"Yeah, yeah, yeah," I said to myself. This was not the first time a call like this had come; my mother was a tough lady and had not died yet. But at ninety-four, life is less certain and nothing can be taken for granted. I rushed out of the house, jumped into my pickup, and drove the three miles to the nursing home to check on my mother.

It was serious this time. Mother had suddenly sat up in her bed, became stiff, and then had fallen back on her pillow. By the time I saw her, she lay peacefully, pale, and unconscious. She looked as white and ashen as the Caucasians sitting on benches along Fifth Avenue in New York City on an early warm, summer afternoon. Four of my sisters maintained a vigil at her bedside, and I brought bouquets of flowers from the farmstead kitchen garden.

Mother had moved to the nursing home with my father, her husband of sixty-six years, when he conceded that life in the old farmhouse was too cumbersome and burdensome for my sister Martha who had ended a thirty-year career of missionary nursing in Africa to provide care. The bathroom was tiny and not wheelchair accessible, and if either Mother or Father had fallen, the door could have been blocked requiring major wall or door dismantling to provide help.

Mother was the ideal helpmate. Her life was dedicated to her husband and his needs and interests. Father seldom spoke and usually there was no discussion. In his Germanic way, he just gave orders, for he was the biblical head of the household, and that was serious business. But Mother found love and, later in life, companionship after all the children left home. In the evenings of summer, whenever we children were busy playing outside and the games were at their height of excitement, Father would once again authoritatively shout out of the kitchen door, "*Wollen lesen*! Let's read!" referring to evening devotions. Father would read aloud nightly from the Bible and then we would all kneel at our dining room chairs while he prayed. These devotions were conducted in German until the early 1950s, when Father decided to become more proficient in English so that he could become more effective in church planting in Wichita. Father and Mother would sit together and when they knelt to pray, they held hands. On occasions, after a day when Father did not speak at all and tension seemed palpable, I would peek to see if they were holding hands. They always did. Their marriage also gave Mother eight children. She loved them all dearly and I was the last. From birth, I was bonded with my mother in a special way.

In 1950, when I was eight years old, my father was elected to the board of deacons of the Emmaus Mennonite Church. Shortly after the election, my mother stopped me at the north garden gate and explained the importance and honor of that position. She emphasized that from now on we as a family needed to be examples of good behavior for the community. She told me that I could no longer be naughty. Right then and there I promised my mother that I would never be naughty again.

Toward the end of their lives, Mother accompanied Father to a lawyer to write their wills. Father dictated his and then told the lawyer to write Mother's will identical to his. Years of subservient behavior would not allow her to protest in front of the lawyer, but she had her own views about inheritance. Father had little concern about the well-being of his children, having entrusted them to God, and wanted to give his estate to mission outreach. Mother, on the other hand, was deeply committed to the welfare of her children and preferred to share the estate with them. She came home fuming, expressing her sentiment to those few of her children who were home at the time. I urged some of my sisters to take Mother back to the lawyer, which they did, and she wrote a will that emphasized her children as well as charity. When she came home she said, "And now I will pray that I will outlive John." She was granted her wish and did survive him by three years.

At Father's insistence, Mother never cut her hair after she married because there is that Bible verse that was interpreted to indicate this activity as ungodly. After Father aged sufficiently that he would not notice, Mother wheeled herself into the beauty shop of the nursing home and asked for a haircut and a permanent to make her gray hair curly and easier to manage. When asked if she wanted to save her braid, she simply said that it was too thin by now and she had spent enough years grooming it that she no longer had any interest in it.

Mother was known for her boundless level of energy, as well as self-reliance and self-sufficiency, two mantras learned early in childhood. She raised chickens, milked cows, helped with the butchering of hogs and calves, and chopped wood for the wood-burning cook stove. Water was pumped by hand and carried on washdays; the house had a cold water tap drawn from a raised storage tank filled by a windmill pump. Vegetables and fruits were raised in a garden that had been in continuous use since 1893 when Grandmother Harder initiated the gardening activity on the site. What was not consumed during the summer season was preserved in glass canning jars for use during the winter months. Before the tornado of 1941, canning was done outside the house in a small building referred to as the *Sommer Küche* or summer kitchen, which was equipped with a wood stove and a firewood-heated cauldron. It was quite logical to say the Lord's Prayer in earnest, particularly the phrase, "give us this day our daily bread." Living in Kansas on the farm during the twentieth century, Mother needed all the divine help and strength she could possibly muster. Providing daily sustenance was labor intensive. The washing facilities were in this summer kitchen as well, so that the water could be heated in the cauldron.

Mother was also the household seamstress, sewing most of the clothing for the family. I always felt that the clothes Mother sewed were power-packed, because she had to pedal with her feet to get the sewing machine to work, and she could get the sewing machine to hum. Only overalls and long johns were purchased at the general store in town. I can still remember the look of joy on her face when, after rural electrification reached our farm in 1950, she was able to purchase an electric sewing machine. She no longer had to pedal and could give her varicosed veins in her legs and ulcerated ankles a much deserved rest.

Even into the early 1940s, chicken feed was sacked in one hundred pound quantities in decoratively printed cotton cloth bags. This cloth was called "poultry linen," and the colors were wash-fast. These bags were recycled into clothing for her family or used as kitchen tea towels. Fabric was also bought by the yard in town, and sometimes Mother would allow us to select the fabric before she began sewing.

Both my mother and I loved vivid colors. One summer when I was a young adolescent, I asked mother to sew for me a summer dress shirt out of a purple, non-absorbent, synthetic-crepe material, which I proudly wore until I outgrew it. Years later I found it in my mother's rag bag. It was not sufficiently absorbent to be used even as a rag. None of my contemporaries had a shirt like that—they probably would have rather died than be seen in that color. The memory of that shirt demonstrates to me anew the creative mindset of my mother.

On Thursday afternoons once a month, Mother would go to the local church basement and join other women in a charity work group known as a sewing circle or "*Nähverein*," in the local dialect. Typical projects included tearing old bed sheets into three to four-inch wide strips and rolling them up for bandages to be sent to a medical missionary. Blankets and quilts were created and sewn out of remnants of leftover fabric from home sewing projects and recycled parts of worn-out clothing. During World War II, sewing circles in Mennonite churches throughout the United States shipped hundreds of quilts and blankets to Europe for distribution to refugees and displaced persons through the Mennonite Central Committee (MCC), the humanitarian charitable organization of the American Mennonites. Many of these needy survivors of the war were distant cousins. Mother especially loved to quilt and I am sure that along with every stitch, there was a prayer.

The people of Germany recognized with appreciation the contribution of the MCC and the many, many quilts and blankets and other charitable acts contributed to their country during and after World War II by the American Mennonites. They reciprocated in 1951 with a symbolic gift of Germany's art—*Dankspende*. The art was collected into an exhibit at Kauffman Museum, North Newton, Kansas by Reinhild Kauenhoven Janzen during 1984 and was also pictured in an accompanying exhibit catalogue.

I do not remember Mother quilting at home during my childhood. However, from my earliest days, I remember her vocalizing the desire to make a pansy quilt. Pansies were her favorite flowers. Pansies were also the class flower with class colors purple and orange chosen by the 1919–1920 freshman class at Bethel Academy; I have often wondered if Mother suggested the class flower or if her experiences at Bethel Academy encompassed her. The class motto was "Not for school, but for life we learn." Mother was indeed a lifelong student.

Mother Is Dying

When I went away to college she was still visualizing her pansy quilt. In the 1920s, Mother began to cut quilting patterns out of the *Kansas City Star*, but it was only during the 1970s and 1980s that she finally found the time to design eighteen quilt blocks with appliquéd pansies, which she embroidered herself. I remember the day she began going to fabric stores to search for the right color and texture for the backing of the quilt. After sewing all the embroidered and contrasting blocks together and fastening the whole quilt onto a quilting frame, she finally used a pattern saved from the 1920s on the solid blocks. The quilting was completed in the mid-1980s, and she was exhausted, but seemed to be spiritually fulfilled and content after she completed this work of her lifelong fascination.

Figure 40
Marie's pansy quilt with eighteen blocks of appliquéd pansies that she uniquely designed. Private collection. Source: Author's file.

There were many other ways for Mother to utilize her creative energy. When a niece needed a wedding cake, mother baked and decorated one. This garnered requests from other couples in the community who were getting married. During the 1930s and 1940s, these wedding cakes were decorated angel food cakes, so young couples would bring a basket of fifty, seventy-five, or even more eggs together with their request. Details of size and color themes were discussed and carefully followed. Mother perfected her skills by reading a lot and attending cake decorating classes sponsored by the County Extension Service, so by the time she baked and decorated her final cakes in the late 1950s or 1960s, they were classic wedding cakes with elaborate designs. For a nephew's wedding, she created a four-tiered cake with extensive free-standing frosting latticework encasing the decorated cake highlighted with white frosting roses.

Figure 41
Wedding cake for Alice and Herald Thiessen married July 14, 1957, decorated by Marie. Source: Doug Thiessen's file.

For a niece, whose chosen colors were purple and white, Mother decorated a white, tiered cake with purple cattleya orchids made of frosting. These cakes were not a business activity; they were just another avenue for Mother to share her talents with the community and celebrate the excitement of life.

When I was in elementary school, Mother and some of the neighboring farm wives began a Wednesday afternoon Bible study and prayer time, referred to as Prayer Band. Initially, the Band included six or seven women, but after ten years or so, the number decreased to two, Mother and a neighbor. These two continued to meet weekly for many years until mother felt that she no longer cared to drive a car. Sewing circle and Prayer Band were opportunities for Mother to spend time with other farm women and discuss issues pertinent to their lives as wives and mothers.

When Mother was thirteen, my grandmother bought their first car. Grandmother never learned to drive the Overland, but left that task to Mother and her sisters. This surely beat driving with horse and buggy; nothing could spook the Overland (see chapter 3). Flat tires were fixed on the spot, with the inner tube being patched and the tire reassembled and inflated with a hand air pump. When passing a specific farmhouse about five miles away, mother would occasionally comment, "We had a flat in front of that house once, and since I didn't have a pair of scissors to cut the patch, I went to the house and asked to borrow scissors. We patched the tire right there and then were on our way again."

Figure 42
The Overland with Marie's niece Lydia and nephew Bernard helping to take flowers to an event. Photo by Marie. Source: Phebe Ann Cressman's file.

One day when I was in elementary school, Mother was driving our new 1947 Chevy and I noticed she was constantly moving the steering wheel back and forth about six to twelve inches. When I asked why she didn't hold the steering wheel steady, she looked at me and smiled—as I think of the conversation now, her smile admired the innocence of a lad with so few of her life's experiences—and explained, "When I learned to drive in 1916, cars had so much play in the steering mechanism that I had to keep moving the steering wheel just to keep the car on the road even while going only fifteen miles an hour."

Mother was a good student and an avid reader. For many years my Christmas gift to her was a subscription to the *National Geographic* magazine, which she read from cover to cover. She once mused that she felt she had traveled the world by reading those magazines. The formal educational opportunities for Mother included elementary school through the eighth grade at Brainerd Elementary, which was two miles east of the farm. This was augmented with total immersion German Bible school, usually held for a month or two after the completion of the public school term. For a short period, there was also a German parochial elementary school taught by the elder of the local church, B. W. Harder, and others.

Walking or taking a buggy were the modes of transportation. While Mother and her sisters attended Brainerd they would take a buggy and leave the horse at a livery operated by Mr. Brucks. After school they would go to the livery located two or three blocks from the school where Mr. Brucks would have the horse hitched up to the buggy, and they were on their way home. Mother would read her assignments while either walking or riding in the buggy, utilizing that time to memorize classical poems like "Paul Revere's Ride" by Henry Wadsworth Longfellow. Occasionally, she would quote these poems to us and continued to recite them to the end of her life.

Mother completed the ninth grade at Bethel Academy in North Newton in 1919–20. For that year, Grandmother Harder moved to North Newton, renting a house near Bethel College so that she could care for Mother and her sister Minna while they attended school. Because Mother's interest patterns and behavior seemed so academic to me, I once asked her why she had not pursued more education particularly since, as a girl, the farm work did not depend on her. She replied simply that she knew that some day she would marry a farmer and she had all the education she needed.

Mother did indeed marry a farmer. At the age of ten, at the wedding festivities of her oldest sister Justine, Mother shared a piece of cake with a thirteen-year-old neighbor boy from across the section to the east. From that moment onwards, mother knew this boy would become her husband, claiming it was the Lord's guidance. She did marry him thirteen years later.

The intriguing events of living in a small community came to light when mother shared, while in her nineties, that Father, following the customs of the community, had asked his father to go to the parents of a young woman and ask for her hand in marriage for his son. However, this first request was for the hand of another young woman from the church community. Mother's explanation was that this other young woman always acted coquettishly whenever she became aware of romance in the community. Other young bachelors had also succumbed to her charms, but she declined all requests for her hand in marriage. After an interlude of one year, Grandfather Epp came by buggy to Grandmother Harder and requested the hand of her daughter Marie for his son John. The harshest thing my mother could say was that the other woman had died without getting married and without having any children of her own.

Is it any wonder that my mother did not encourage her children to date in high school? In fact, she discouraged it. Mother truly felt that "first loves" were the best and she wished that all her children would experience, as she had, the joy of marriage to that one special person in the whole world that had been ordained by God to be one's spouse.

Generally, Mother enjoyed good health. However, in midlife, she developed varicose veins in her legs and wore support hose daily for the rest of her life. This was not surprising when you consider all the hard work and heavy lifting of farm life, as well as bearing and raising eight children. This problem was sufficiently severe that in most years when she worked in the garden and walked in the soft soil, she would also develop an ulcer at the ankle of her right leg. With care and tending, the ulcer would normally disappear by the next spring, but when she was in her seventies, it no longer healed and eventually progressed to involve the bone. Her foot was finally amputated about three years before she died. I thought that we had lost her after surgery, because she became comatose with a high fever, but the attending physicians changed her antibiotics and she made a remarkable recovery. Her cheeks became rosy again and she was happy, spending the final years of her life without the constant pain of a sore leg.

In 1944, two years after my birth, mother had surgery to remove fibroid growths from her uterus. The doctor powdered the incision with pure sulfur to ward off infection. Unfortunately, mother was sensitive to sulfur and went into severe allergic reaction, spending twenty-one days in the hospital. But she clung to life and during that time asked Father to bring me to her. This required special dispensation because children under fourteen were not allowed as visitors in the hospital. It probably was mother's strong maternal instincts that pulled her through and enabled her to return to her children.

When mother was in her late seventies, she had her gall bladder removed. Fortunately, mother recovered well again. She continually refused all offers of pain medication and one day the doctor said to her in jest, "Do you think you are a tough old woman who will live forever?" Mother is reported to have replied that she thought she would have to live forever to get all the projects done that she had planned for herself.

Figure 43
Marie, 84, on her sixty-first wedding anniversary, April 21, 1988. Photo by Phebe Ann Cressman. Source: Author's file.

By the time she moved into a nursing home, mother had completed her project list and she had enjoyed a full life. About this time the fingers of her hands became stiffened and gnarled from age and use, and she could no longer hold a needle or crocheting hook to do hand or needlework. To try to curtail boredom, she once asked Martha for some chewing gum, commenting that she wanted to feel as though she was doing something.

In 1946, as a four-year-old, I remember mother racing around the house commenting to no one specifically, and yet to each of us within the sound of her voice, that she had now lived longer than any of her sisters. Her sister Justine died of influenza in 1919 at the age of twenty-four after giving birth to her third child. Baby Helen stayed in the hospital for eighteen days and then came to live with Mother and Grandmother for three months. Her sister Minna died of typhus at the age of twenty-seven; Mother and Grandmother took care of Aunt Minna's two sons until Mother got married and Aunt Minna's husband remarried. Her sister Helene died of cancer when she was forty-three. Mother was particularly fond of her sister Helene and when she passed away, Mother felt so alone. By that time her mother, Grandmother Harder, had also passed away, and she felt that all the people were gone in whom she could confide. Mother treated Aunt Helene's six children as if they were her own and over the years kept in close touch with them. One of her nieces, Lydia, remained in the community and she and Mother talked on the telephone nearly every day until her final years.

Several months before the final urgent call from the nursing home, I went to visit Mother at eight o'clock one evening. She was already in bed without her glasses. I walked into her dimly lit room and greeted her; I took her hand, and told her who I was. She immediately asked about my family, the farm, and about the ostrich I was raising. Then she asked if I remembered that old suitcase her father had carried to America from West Prussia as an eleven-year-old boy (see figure 9). She related that Grandfather had packed in that suitcase and carried to America a children's book of stories and riddles. As a child she had read that book on Sunday afternoons sitting on the south screened porch. One of the ditties in the book was "*Straussen Eier hart gesotten, liebt jawohl der Hutten Tutten!* Hard boiled ostrich eggs are a delicacy of the Hotten Tots!" We both had a good laugh.

Mother did not give up life easily; it took ten long days. After the episode that precipitated my sister's call, she never again opened her eyes, nor did she say another word. After ten days of anxiety, the time

The Petals of a Kansas Sunflower

came to say our goodbyes. I have always thought that the best way to say something is to use a common shared language. Mother understood and appreciated poetic verse, so I wrote a simple tribute and began the church memorial service by reading it.

Tribute to Marie Harder Epp
(1903–1998)

Born to a time that we call simpler
And four months prior to Kitty Hawk,
Was a woman I called mother.
She lived the twentieth century.
You may have also called her mother,
Or grandmother, *Tante Mimi*, Aunt Marie,
Marie or Mrs. Epp.

Thank you for joining my family in a tribute
To the very last member
Of the first generation of Harders
Born in America.

From her chair at the old pedal sewing machine,
She watched time and clothed her family.
As she pedaled through the seasons,
The sun shone on her Stonehenge.
The elevator marked the winter solstice
And the cattle barn the summer solstice.
And when her foot got too painful to pedal,
I would sit and pedal for her.
That was before rural electrification.

On that one occasion
When mother initiated work on a Sunday,
The lugs of overripe cherries arrived from Colorado
Just in time for Sunday School.
That night, she was convinced
That even the man in the full moon
Was pitting cherries.

Mother was learned.
Not by intense formal instruction,
But by a lifetime of learning.

Mother Is Dying

She was an educated woman.
She was published.
Her poem, "In Butler County on the Farm"
Appeared in the *Daily Drovers Telegram*.
She wrote a book.
She provided us a written legacy.

The Ides of March marked the beginning
Of the gardening season,
The perennial kite,
The Silver Maple whistles
Carved in the pulp after slipping the bark,
Balls of yarn and baby chicks.

It was Mother
who loved the children.
It was Mother
who nursed the children.
It was Mother
who focused her children.
It was Mother
who protected her children.

Before the word "pedophile"
Was in our vocabulary,
Mother roared her car within range
To read the license plate
Of the car stalking her children
Coming home from school.

At 13, she was chauffeuring her mother
In the newly acquired Overland,
Learned to patch tires at the roadside
And never let us forget
That at the corner of Butler and 130th
(Eric Penner's south corner)
The first local car accident occurred,
Which took human life.

Mother asked baffling questions:
How much space is required
To house the souls of all Christians
Since the beginning of time?
Will my father recognize me;

The Petals of a Kansas Sunflower

He saw me last when I was nine months old?
When I pass on,
Will my mother be the first to greet me?
Will I be able to sing in heaven?

At the age of forty-three,
She said, "I have lived longer
Than any of my sisters."
Her long arms of love
Embraced her children
And the children of her sisters.
She hugged each one,
And then she hugged them all again.

Using the technology developed in her century,
She circumnavigated the globe while in the air.
She visited Martha in Africa,
John Edwin in Hong Kong,
Bernard & Ruby in Japan,
Dorothy & John in Hawaii.
She went by bus
To Raymond's wedding in Mountain Lake.
She took the train to Chicago
To watch me graduate from Wheaton.
She drove us all to church by car.

It was the land
That gave my mother continuity.
Section 17 was her Tara.
When she asked, "What right
Do you have to the land?"
I replied, "We are all
Stewards for a time."

I am the youngest
Of the second generation
Of Harders born in America,
I am now the keeper of the gate.

—Melvin D. Epp, 07/10/1998

My sister Phebe, to whom mother gave her pansy quilt, also gave a tribute:

Tribute to Mother

While I was visiting with my mother when she was in her 80s, she asked reflectively, "What legacy am I leaving my children?" I can think of many and would like to share a few.

Mother was the family historian and taught us to appreciate our heritage.

I learned about my heritage from historical anniversaries and celebrations. I also learned about my heritage by accompanying Mother to the Harder Cemetery where she hoed the grave sites. My inquiring mind asked questions generated by the tombstones and I heard stories of persons interred there. Years ago, Mother demonstrated the importance of memories by making cedar wreaths with pink crepe paper roses and placing them on these gravesites for special events.

We learned from her photo album of the beautiful yards and gardens once gracing the farm.

Our farm had a granary shed with many fascinations. Instead of climbing a ladder, we stepped up on a broad stairway leading to the second floor. The second floor also had an antique room. Through inquiry, I learned that this was the original gathering place for the Harder family (and their neighbors) on Sundays. This worship group became the Emmaus Mennonite Church as the church organized.

As our forefathers settled in this country, the outstanding privilege they experienced was political and religious freedom. This mother repeated many times and in one of her poems entitled, "In Butler County on the Farm," the last line describes the farmer's thankfulness for freedom—still his right.

As a family we benefited from mother's love for literature and her rich repertoire of memorized poetry.

Christmas gifts brought children's classics into the home, e.g., *Little Men, Little Women, Uncle Tom's Cabin* and many more.

She seemed to have a line of poetry or a proverb for every event. When I had eleven windows to polish and I sighed after the first one, she enthusiastically instructed, "Work well begun is half-done," a concept hard for a child to understand as there were still ten windows to clean.

On another occasion, we were discussing an unkind opinion someone had made about us and she commented, "*Auch*, the empty wagon rattles the loudest." I do not remember the unkind words, but I remember the lesson she taught, which I also passed on to my family. One of my sons reminded me recently, "Didn't you say the empty wagon rattles the loudest?"

She quoted the works of poets such as Edgar Allen Poe and Henry Wadsworth Longfellow. One of her favorite Longfellow works was "Paul Revere's Ride." This poem became so familiar to me that when I visited our son in Boston and followed the historical tourist trail, which ended at the North Church, I responded with excitement, "This is where Paul Revere hung two lanterns in the belfry." I entered the church and stood in silence in honor of my mother who taught me about this historical site.

Not only did Mother know poetry, she also wrote poetry, which we as children quoted at many of your weddings, your anniversaries, and at major church events.

Mother demonstrated how to enjoy the opportunities of life.

From her photo album we learned that she once, with her brother-in-law John Thiessen, walked down from Pike's Peak. She on another occasion thrilled us children by firing a firecracker on the fourth of July. She taught us to enjoy the splendor of a sunset, the shooting stars in August, the intricacies of a blooming flower, a beautifully created and decorated wedding cake, the literary flow of a poetic line, the song of a bird, and a carefully stitched quilt block.

She was a tireless person. When there were eight children underfoot, she waited until we were all in bed and scrubbed the kitchen floor on a Saturday night at midnight. The poetry she was asked to write for celebrations was often written between eleven and one o'clock at night.

Mother enjoyed people. Living across the road from our farm when we were children were Uncle B. P. Harder and Alvin Regier. Uncle B. P., due to complications during a childhood communicable disease, was deaf and speech impaired. Alvin had a severe infant illness, which affected his gait and speech. Mother taught us how to communicate with them and consequently, how not to be afraid when these two challenged men walked onto our yard.

She enriched herself by entertaining and always gaining friends in activities in which she participated such as church planting, relief service abroad and teaching Sunday school. During World War II, when the German prisoners were in our field, the guidelines were to feed them only one meal per day. "No one can work on an empty stomach," she'd say and sent us to the fields with a pot of steaming coffee and egg sandwiches and called it "coffee break."

She demonstrated strength in crisis. It was difficult for her to lose her three sisters. Her sisters died much too young and with their passing, she became the family matriarch for eleven additional children, who, to this day, are an extended part of our family.

She and father weathered the '41 tornado with such inner resources and strength, that as an adult, I use them as an example for myself when faced with a crisis. How they responded also influenced how we as children responded at that time to the situation. My brothers, with scrap wood graded roads in our backyard. We made ramps over the sidewalks. With a wicker wheel chair and a wicker baby carriage, which were both blown out of the granary, together with a wheelbarrow, a wagon and tricycle, we raced around the graded roads. Mother, against this backdrop of tornadic destruction, stood in the kitchen door laughing at the gaiety in the back yard.

In a telephone conversation on her ninetieth birthday, I commended her continued sharp and alert mind. Her response was "The Bible says 'Delight yourself in the Lord and he will give you the desires of your heart.' My wish has always been to have an alert mind even as I age." God granted her wish.

And so today, we say, "goodbye," to Mother and the family matriarch.

—Phebe Ann Epp Cressman, 07/10/1998

One of my mother's favorite hymns was "My God and I." She had arranged for this song to be sung at their twenty-fifth wedding anniversary and again at their fiftieth wedding anniversary. In the final years of her life she wrote poems that for her would serve as the second and third stanzas of this hymn. A ladies duet sang Mother's poem during the memorial service on July 10, 1998. These words testify to her lifelong personal commitment to the Anabaptist principles to follow after Jesus and apply his teachings to her daily life.

> My God and I are keeping sweet communion,
> We walk and talk as friends along the way;
> I trust completely in his perfect guidance—
> His holy presence hallows night and day;
> I trust completely in his perfect guidance—
> His holy presence hallows night and day.
>
> My God and I will walk for aye together,
> Neither life nor death can separate us two;
> My hand in his, till I have passed the shadows—
> And reached the land of sun-kissed golden hue;
> My hand in his, till I have passed the shadows—
> And reached the land of sun-kissed golden hue.

The Harder cemetery where we laid Mother to rest on July 10, 1998, is at the end of the driveway to the farm where Mother lived during the twentieth century. The cemetery was established to reassure my great-great grandmother, Justine Claassen Bergmann Penner, who at seventy-nine immigrated with the family to America in 1876, that when she died she would have a *proper* burial. She had left two husbands buried in West Prussia in the Heubuden Church cemetery and came to American with her only son, Jacob Bergmann and family, and her only daughter, my great-grandmother Justine Bergmann Harder. Great-great grandmother lived for another eight years in America and was the first interment in the Harder cemetery in 1884.

The cemetery was originally planted with Osage orange trees around the periphery and four red cedar trees on either side of the central path. The hedge trees on the periphery were trimmed yearly to a height of about ten feet. During the early 1940s the hedge trees were pulled out one rainy day using horses and replaced with a wire fence, a gift from Marie Bergmann who was later interred in 1949. By 1998, there were only four cedar trees left. Several times during each summer Mother would take us children to the cemetery to hoe the weeds on the graves. For Memorial Day she would bring peonies from the kitchen garden and place them on the graves. If the peonies bloomed too early, she would cut the buds and take them to the cool farmhouse basement so the flowers would hold until Memorial Day.

After the funeral I asked the funeral director to drive the hearse to the middle of the farmyard. I led the procession along the driveway under the cedar trees that Mother's grandfather planted shortly after they established the farm in the 1870s, scattering flower petals on the driveway with the help of Mother's great-grandchildren. Grandsons carried the coffin, followed by my brothers and sisters and their families. When we got to the cemetery, I opened the gate on which I had hung traditional cedar wreaths with black bows—the gatekeeper function having been passed to the next generation. Through the open gate, the family took Mother to her final place of rest between her most influential mentors, her mother and her husband of sixty-seven years.

Figure 44
The Harder cemetery gates with traditional cedar wreaths and black bows on July 10, 1998. Source: Author's file.

The church community usually has a luncheon in the church basement for the family and those attending the funeral, and this time was no different. A copy of one of Mother's table graces was at each place. Since our family is large and scatted across the United States, we reserved the church basement for a social time after the luncheon to visit with family members and share memories. Phebe had Mother's pansy quilt for us to admire anew. A reading of Mother's poems was impossible since they were still scattered on miscellaneous scraps of paper and not translated into English. At five that afternoon, a severe thunderstorm moved over the church from the southwest. Although there were many bright flashes of lightning and very loud claps of thunder, it was assumed that this was just a typical midsummer storm and no one, especially those from Kansas, gave it a second thought. After the storm passed, I drove to the farm, stopping by the cemetery gate. Lightning had struck the century-old cedar tree at the foot of Mother's grave, splitting it in half. It had fallen perpendicular to the direction of the wind. One part of the tree fell north and missed all the old fragile headstones, so no damage was done. The larger part of the tree fell directly on the foot of Mother's newly filled grave, covering more than half of it.

Figure 45
Marie's newly filled grave covered with boughs from a lightning-struck century old cedar tree. Source: Author's file.

The scene was surreal. I stood for a long time in utter silence. It seemed as if nature was responding to the lessons that Mother had taught us all . . . respect for our heritage and respect for those interred that had created this heritage for us.

Appendix 1

History of My Mennonite Family

THE PROTESTANT REFORMATION BEGAN in October 1517 as Martin Luther nailed a handwritten document, *The Ninety-Five Theses*, on the Wittenberg church door. Within a few weeks, *The Ninety-Five Theses* was read throughout Germany and across Europe, thanks to the newly developed technology of the printing press. The doctrines of justification through faith, forgiveness without penance, and no indulgences were some of the concepts included in Luther's theses.

There were other religious activists who believed that Luther was too conservative and restrained. He had not included the symbolic representation of Christ in the communion bread and wine rather than a corporeal presence, the separation of church and state, and believer's baptism to replace infant baptism. By 1525, groups who supported only the baptism of adults upon their confession of personal faith were organizing across Europe. On January 21, 1525, the first such adult baptism took place in Switzerland when Conrad Grebel and Felix Mantz baptized each other. The centers of this activity were in Zurich, Switzerland, South Germany, Austria, Moravia, and Holland. Many who were baptized as adults to signify their chosen faith had already been baptized as children, so these nonconformists were called with derision "*ein Wiedertaüfer*," "rebaptizers," or "Anabaptists."

Nowhere else in Europe did as many people join the Anabaptist movement as in Holland; among them were some of my Epp ancestors. The surname "Epp" is of Friesland Dutch origin, having come from Switzerland to the Friesland area between Harlingen and Emden during the Middle Ages.

In 1536, a Dutch priest-turned-Anabaptist named Menno Simons became influential in leadership and coalesced the Anabaptist

Appendix 1

movement in Holland. Menno Simons was a scholar and a prodigious writer. The participants of this Anabaptist movement eventually took on his name as followers: Mennonites.

The common thread of theology held by all groups of Anabaptists was composed of elements of discipleship, nonresistance, and community. The starting point was discipleship, "to follow after Christ." That portion of the New Testament that reveals Christ's commands was the most important part of the Bible. When the teachings of Jesus were applied to everyday life, his concepts of love and personal respect for others, together with the separation of church from the state led to the practice of nonresistance, i.e., the absolute refusal to bear arms, to hold political office, to swear an oath of loyalty to the state, or to sue in courts of law. The third key element was the necessity of community. The Anabaptists saw themselves as a people set apart from the world. Only adults could freely join this community after they consciously chose to be baptized. Mutual aid was an integral feature of group practice.

These concepts and attitudes continued to be exemplified within the immigrant community established in Butler County, Kansas in 1876. I was very aware during my childhood in the 1940s of the continued desire to follow after Christ, the separation of church and state, nonresistance, and mutual aid to help less fortunate people.

In 1920 the Mennonite Central Committee (MCC) was organized to focus on humanitarian outreach. My grandfather, John Epp Sr., contributed the initial five hundred dollars through the local Kansas church to finance a tractor-plow unit to assist relatives suffering through a devastating drought in southern Russia (present day Ukraine) where my grandfather spent his adolescence. Most of the horses had been confiscated by the military or slaughtered for human consumption to sustain human life during this disruption of food production. His donation stimulated the first MCC development project to assist in times of need, and he shortly saw his contribution escalated into a shipment of fifty Fordson tractors and Oliver plows to southern Russia in 1922. Additional shipments followed later.

In December 1945, following World War II, my father invited other farmers to our farm for the first MCC meat canning in our community for charity/relief projects. During December 1945 and the following two months in 1946, five other farmers also held canning days on their farms, so collectively fifty-four hogs, eleven cattle, and four

Appendix 1

lambs were processed in sealed tin cans and canning jars using small stovetop pressure cookers. It took several days at each location to get all the meat processed, but the collective effort produced 4,050 pounds of cured meat, 4,900 cans of meat, 3,400 pounds of lard, 725 pounds of tallow, and 1,050 pounds of cracklings. This meat was distributed by MCC in Europe and in civil service camps here in the U.S. where young men met their commitments to the national government in alternative military service.

My parents purchased a hand-operated tin can sealer and would freely seal lids on cans of food for people in the community as they were creating charity packages to be sent to Europe. Even *Pfeffernüsse* (peppernuts), were sealed in cans to keep them fresh during the three months in shipment. After World War II, the Elbing, Kansas post office had its rank elevated, reflecting the volume of charity packages of food and supplies that were shipped to Europe from our community.

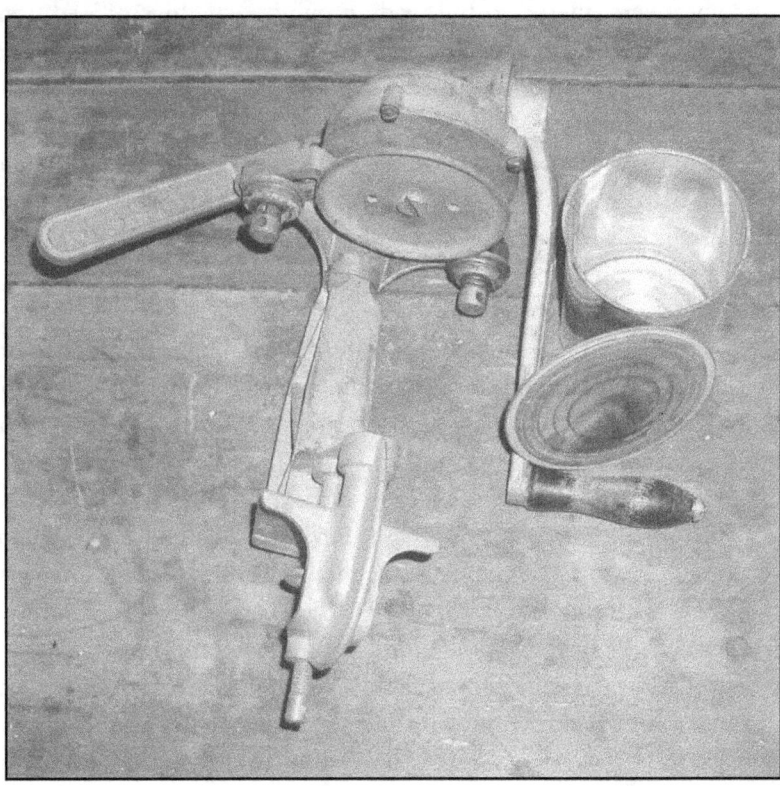

Figure 46
My parents' hand-operated can sealer. Source: Author's file.

Appendix 1

But in 1520, the Anabaptist concepts were not popular; in fact, their religious concepts were considered heresy, i.e., a cult, by the established state church and even by other new Protestants. Opposition to the movement was intense and immediate. When imprisonment and banishment did not halt the vigorous preaching of the Anabaptists, death sentences followed. In 1529, a death decree was issued against the Anabaptists by the Second Diet of Speyer. This greatly accelerated the program of persecution already in progress. An estimated four thousand Anabaptists were put to death for their faith by drowning, burning at the stake, or by torture and dismemberment. Their farms and property were also confiscated by the church/state. Thieleman van Braght as a young editor compiled the stories of nearly a thousand martyrs in 1660. In 1685 van Braght published these stories in a 1290 page, two-volume, folio-sized book. This edition of *Martyrs Mirror* was a state-of-the-art printing phenomenon at the time. One thousand identical copies were offered to the reading public. For this 1685 edition, the poet-artist Jan Luyken contributed 104 copper plate etchings to this book. With pictures and words, the meaning of living or dying for one's faith was immortalized. Thirty of these copper plate etchings are still known to exist and several can be viewed locally in the permanent exhibit "Mirror of the Martyrs" at Kauffman Museum, North Newton, Kansas. As I walked through this exhibit in silence, the truth of historical reality enveloped me like a sodden dark cloud.

When the Canadian writer Rudy Wiebe penned the novel, *Sweeter than All the World*, he included scenes of a fictional or spiritual ancestral grandmother and several other women being prepared for burning at the stake. Hot iron screws were clamped to the tongues of these condemned women while they were still in jail to prevent them from expressing their faith or singing as they were taken by ox cart to the stakes in the town square where they were chained and burned. Executions like these were theater for the local residents, and martyrs' hymns and testimonies were upsetting to the spectators. These Dutch Wiebes may well have been neighbors of my ancestral Epp grandparents; surely they shared a similar faith and worship experience. Also in this community were people with the surnames of Bergmann, Claassen, Driedger, Fast, Klassen, Regehr, Reimer, Schroeder, Toews, Van Bergen, and Warkentin.

Appendix 1

The Dutch Mennonites sought a promise of political and religious freedoms from the King of Poland and the nobility, who for a time had a minority that were Reformed. The northern cities of Danzig and Elbing were noted for relative religious tolerance. Poland was outside the Holy Roman Empire, so the ban on Anabaptists of 1529 also did not apply there. Polish noblemen who owned large tracts of swampy land needed experts to drain and make arable these unproductive acreages of sedge and willow thickets. The Polish-Prussian War (1519–1521) had completely devastated agricultural activity in the area and they needed workers. The industrious Mennonite agriculturists were suited for this reclamation. An invitation was issued from the king with tacit promises for freedom, and large groups of Mennonites anxiously left their Dutch homeland, clinging to the promises of no persecution. Concessions of religious freedom were granted to attract these expert farmers, and only after they began to prosper were efforts made to restrict their growth since their pacifism did not contribute to the growing military presence. From 1530 onward, many came to the Vistula Delta and the Vistula Lowlands. The personal cost to the first generation was high and many died of swamp fever (malaria). Since no Mennonites were ever put to death for their religious convictions in the Vistula Delta, there was continued, heartfelt thankfulness for security and religious freedoms. However, the continuation of their privileges came with the assessment of heavy taxes and legal harassment that was oppressive in many ways. A review of the ever-evolving governmental regulations and the impact of these regulations on the lives of Mennonites in the Vistula Delta is discussed in Mark Jantzen's book, *Mennonite German Soldiers: Nation, Religion, and Family in the Prussian East, 1772–1880*.

Draining swampy land was normal activity for the Dutch Mennonites since much of the land in Holland had also been reclaimed. Many settled in the vicinity of Danzig and Elbing, near or between the Vistula and Nogat Rivers, which was located within Poland in 1530, then Prussia after the First Partition of Poland in 1772, and finally, West Prussia following the Third Partition in 1795. Some estates were leased to the Mennonites by successive owners for thirty to forty-year periods until finally the Mennonites came into complete ownership of the land. In other villages, the Mennonites were able to procure their land immediately.

Appendix 1

My Epp ancestors were among those who moved from Holland to West Prussia in the 1500s and early 1600s to get away from the religious persecution and death squads. These new Dutch immigrants in Poland were subjects of the king in a foreign country. They were thankful for peace and grateful for freedom from physical persecution and death threats, worshiping as they wished in the privacy of their own homes. They were economically valuable to the state for land reclamation and so were tolerated in spite of their strange religion and Dutch language. The Netherlands was a world power when the Mennonites migrated to Poland and retaining the Dutch language was a proud identity and told the communities around them that they were different. It was well into the eighteenth century before High German replaced Dutch in the church services in the Danzig area. The unwritten dialect, *Plautdietsch* (Low German), brought from Holland, became the everyday working language of all Mennonites in Prussia; Low German is not a common vernacular of High German, but rather an amalgamation of dialects spoken by the primitive people who roamed the northern regions of Europe many centuries before Christ.

The efforts of the Dutch immigrants in land reclamation began to be noticed and over time their farms of fertile pastures and arable land reflected a strong work ethic, becoming the envy of neighbors and other governments. The Vistula lowlands developed into the bread basket of the Prussian provinces.

After Czarina Catherine the Great (1729–1796) issued a manifesto on July 22, 1763, she extended an invitation to West Prussian Mennonites and other Germans (Volga Germans) to come to the southern steppes of Imperial Russia, present day Ukraine, where there were vast areas of grassland that needed reclamation into productive agriculture. An estimated five hundred Prussian Mennonite families relocated to southern Russia between 1769 and 1804 and developed colonies (a community of villages) there, in great part because the population density of Mennonites in Prussia had exceeded the available farmland and supporting occupational opportunities. The dearth of farmland was created by Prussian law that made it almost impossible for Mennonites to buy land since they did not serve in the army. Some of my paternal ancestry followed that route in 1870 and then immigrated to the United States a short time later in 1882 and 1883. More details are included in chapter 14.

Appendix 1

Life in West Prussia was never without political tension. Early governmental directives were that Mennonites should associate only with others within their group, practice their religion quietly, and avoid any proselytizing. The Mennonites tried to conduct themselves as the "quiet people of the land" (*die Stillen im Lande*) pursuing their religious lifestyle. Intermarriage with persons of other faiths was strictly prohibited.

After Frederick William II issued his "Edict Concerning the Future of Mennonites" in 1789, Mennonites were not permitted to buy land from a Lutheran or a Catholic without special permission from the authorities to retain their pacifist status, which was seldom granted. The new owners of homes purchased from a Lutheran or a Catholic would lose the exemption from conscription. The Prussian rulers were interested in increasing state revenues and began taxing for military exemptions; they were also interested in increasing the size of their army and granting exemptions to conscription did not conform to their need for soldiers. This edict greatly stimulated the emigration of Prussian Mennonites to southern Russia.

One of the avenues available to acquire land or farms for young Mennonite men who were not in line to inherit a farm was to marry an older Mennonite widow, where, upon her death, one-half of the farmland would become the property of the young surviving husband and the other half would be the shared equally by the deceased widow's children, regardless of gender, per the Mennonite community inheritance guidelines of that time. Two of my ancestral grandfathers followed this custom for land acquisition between 1800 and 1825.

Bernhard Regier (1781–1830) married an aged widow Christine Harder (1749–1806) allegedly to acquire her farm. Folklore says that she went into this marriage already on a walking cane (Germanic idiom equivalent to "one foot in the grave") and died about one year later. Bernhard Regier subsequently married Anna Peters and they had four children. He died of tuberculosis in 1830 at the age of forty. In chapter 16, on the day of his one hundredth birthdate, my paternal great-grandfather Cornelius H. Regier was eulogized. Bernhard Regier was Cornelius's grandfather.

The widow Anna (Peters) Regier subsequently married my great-grandfather Bernhard Harder (1811–1900) who was born to Hans Harder (1764–1815) and Helene (Reimer) Harder (1790–1812). Hans and Helene had two children, Bernhard, born in 1811 and Marie, born

Appendix 1

in 1812. Helene passed away later in 1812, so these orphaned children were raised by their grandmother. Hans passed away three years later. At the age of seventeen, Bernhard went to stay with his Uncle Abraham Harder in Heubuden and lived with them until he married. He employed himself on the farm of the widow Anna (Peters) Regier, whose four children were partially grown. Bernhard endeared himself to her children and with time her grandchildren, and many years later, some of the grandchildren attended Bernhard's funeral on the farm in Kansas in 1900.

Oral history suggests that Anna Regier was impressed with Bernhard and she suggested that they get married since he was managing her farms anyway. On October 9, 1832, at the age of twenty-one, he married Anna (Peters) Regier who was twenty-eight years older than he, presumably thinking this marriage would last for only a short time, about two years. Local humor suggests that the devil had his hand on the zero, obscuring it from view. A neighboring farmer at the time reports that my great-grandfather once lamented with humor, "*Deine Frauen starben immer, und meine wird night mal krank.* Your wives always die and mine does not even get sick." They were compatibly married for twenty years and upon her death her children inherited one farm and Bernhard the other. This was the farm that Great-grandfather Harder nurtured for forty-four years before he immigrated to America with his three sons of subsequent marriages.

After Anna Regier Harder passed away on August 17, 1852, Bernhard married Agathe Regier (1830–1867) on March 8, 1853 and together had six children of which Johannes (1854–1946) and Gustav (1856–1923) survived. On November 4, 1861, Agathe passed away. "In this time when our beloved father experienced for the second time the loneliness of widowhood, he took us [Johannes, age 7 and Gustav, age 5] often with him into the prayer room [a room planned into the architecture of the homes at that time for the express purpose of prayer] and taught us in this way to take our burdens to the Lord." On July 16, 1863, my great-grandfather married Justine Bergmann (1834–1916). My grandfather Bernhard Jr. (1864–1904) was their only surviving child.

For over one hundred fifty years the Mennonites were forced to pay heavy taxes to support the Catholic and Lutheran parishes in their vicinity. They were not allowed to build a church so they gathered in homes. It is known that several congregations existed in West Prussia as

Appendix 1

early as 1549, because Menno Simons wrote a letter in that year under the byline of "The children of God in Prussia." Old Polish government documents indicate that in 1550 an invitation was issued to Mennonite farmers and laborers from Groningen to relocate to Kulm and the Schwetz-Neuenburg Niedernung, where additional congregations were initiated. These groups were initially frequently visited and served by Menno Simons himself until his natural death in 1561. By 1562 the lowland areas surrounding Tiegenhof were settled by Mennonites.

Without churches, the Mennonites were also not allowed to have their own cemeteries. Instead, they were required to pay a high fee to be interred in a special area of Catholic cemeteries. Since the state church kept records of infant baptisms, thereby creating birth and family/population records, the Mennonites were not only deprived of cemeteries, but no formal records were kept of births, baptisms, and deaths until 1668. Polish law did not require records and preferred not to have them. This lack of records kept secret the number of Mennonites that lived in Poland and who they were. Church records of adult baptisms, usually sixteen to seventeen-year-old teenagers, did not include the many infants who perished with childhood maladies; only family records included these.

Until 1700 the church services were conducted in homes entirely without music. Occasionally, itinerant preachers held services in large rooms or, in summertime, made use of machine sheds and cow barns, which were thoroughly cleaned and decorated with green foliage for these meetings. Finally, in 1744, two hundred years after establishing residency, the Mennonites were granted full rights of citizenship with reassurances that their convictions, including pacifism, would be respected. Two years later, an army general, General Gessler, tried to induct Mennonites into the army, and when the church protested to the Polish king, he reaffirmed the original privileges granted to the Mennonites.

After the first partition of Poland in 1772, much of the area where the Mennonites lived was transferred to the sovereignty of Prussia under King Frederick the Great. Exemption from military service was again guaranteed on the condition that 5,000 *Reichsthaler* was paid annually for the upkeep of the cadet school at Kulm. This order was accepted by the Heubuden church and paid annually for over one hundred years.

Appendix 1

The Dutch Mennonite immigrants had continued to use the Dutch language to express their community-set-apart philosophy until the mid-1770s. By 1780, however, the Heubuden Church services were in German and a German songbook was also introduced. Some congregations had switched to the German language a bit earlier. It had taken over two hundred years for the Dutch Mennonites in Prussia to assimilate the local language.

When the Heubuden (where my Kansas ancestors worshiped), Ladekopp, and Tiegenhagen groups got their permits to build churches in 1768, they were also required to build and maintain one for the Catholic Church. They were able to establish their own cemeteries in 1775.

The permit to build the Heubuden Church came with the stipulation, that all construction be completed within one week. The governmental regulators thought this was impossible, but underestimated the thriftiness of the Mennonites for this monumental task. The Mennonites crafted and assembled all the components of the large building on an adjacent farm and then used less than a week to assemble the prefabricated elements on the actual church site.

Yet to express gratitude for security and military exemptions, during one period of war the Mennonites contributed over 6,000 *Reichsthaler* and 6,000 yards of linen, and sent food into the hospitals for the wounded, exemplifying with actions that they wanted to heal wounds rather than inflict them.

In 1780 the "Gnaden Privilegium" was granted, in which the king guaranteed for himself and his successors that there would be everlasting freedom from conscription and military service, undisturbed freedom of religion, and protection in practicing customary trades and professions within the limits of the law and regulations of Prussia. In 1806, the Mennonites of West Prussia collected 30,000 *Reichsthaler* as a gift for war widows and orphans, which they personally presented to the West Prussian king and queen as the royal entourage was traveling through the country. When the war of 1813 erupted, universal military service was inaugurated and again the church elders appealed. With time, upon paying additional taxes, they were granted military exemption.

During the 1800s the ferment for war between regional states was constant. In 1848 a Prussian constitution declared universal conscription, precipitating the migration of hundreds of additional Mennonite families to southern Russia. The final test came in 1867 when a national conscription law was passed abolishing all exemptions. A subsequent Prussian cabinet order made possible noncombatant service alternatives within the military organization, and a grace period until 1870 to emigrate. After that, every able-bodied man between the ages of twenty and forty-five years could be drafted for military service. This ended the privileges, obtained through land reclamation and special taxation, that the Mennonites had enjoyed in West Prussia for more than three hundred years.

These new political directives led to an ideological division within the Heubuden Church, the largest West Prussian Mennonite congregation. The majority of the parishioners, tiring of their struggle for military exemptions, were ready to follow the example of their brethren in Holland who had discarded the principle of nonresistance. However, a small minority of the congregation withdrew from the church and formed the *Auswanderungs Gemeinde*, an Emigrant Congregation. The elder and all ministers of the Heubuden Mennonite Church supported this breakaway group. The tensions between dissenting factions were sufficient that the church elder dispensed with the celebration of communion during the two years before he immigrated to Beatrice, Nebraska in 1877, because he felt that only those supporting pacifism, i.e., "the teachings of Jesus," were worthy of this sacrament. Even noncombatant service within the military organization was not considered an acceptable alternative. One event that contributed to the discord occurred on Sunday, June 7, 1874, when Elder Gerhard Penner denied communion to church member Bernhard Fieguth, a freshly minted Prussian Mennonite soldier who came to church in uniform. Within a week, the local prosecutor filed charges against Elder Penner for violating the May 13, 1873 law concerning the limits of church discipline. The incident was litigated in a local court and Elder Penner's action was declared illegal and he was fined 25 *Reichsthaler*. The appeals of the local litigation went all the way to Prussia's High Court in Berlin, where Penner's denial of communion for Fieguth was upheld as illegal and Elder Penner was forced to pay the substantial fine. During the appeals, Elder Penner argued that the state was legislating changes to the Mennonites' confession of faith by requiring military service. The High Court disagreed: "The state does not demand that religious communities adjust their confessions according to the law, the state demands only that all citizens regardless of confession obey the laws."

As Elder Penner left West Prussia in 1877, he took the Heubuden Church communion set of plates and chalices with him as a symbol of his authority, feeling that it was within his church authority to prevent the set from being misused. He felt that those that remained in West Prussia were not appropriately applying the teachings of Christ and consequently were unfit to celebrate this sacrament. This communion set was used by Gerhard Penner, as the first elder at the First Mennonite Church, Beatrice, Nebraska, beginning in 1877; these sacramental utensils continued to be used in that church until 1940. The communion set is now on permanent exhibit in the Kauffman Museum, North Newton, Kansas.

In 1869, Great-grandfather Harder traveled extensively in southern Russia and visited the Mennonite colonies, looking for an opportunity to relocate, since he had sons approaching draft age. The trip itself was arduous, involving five weeks to go from West Prussia to southern Russia, and another five weeks for the return trip. While there, Great-grandfather Harder must surely have learned of the impending changes likely to occur in southern Russia. Compulsory military service for all young men was introduced in southern Russia the next year in 1870, together with a program of forced incorporation of the Russian language into education and culture. The privately run schools within the Mennonite colonies were forced to convert to the Russian curriculum. There appeared to be no acceptable opportunities in southern Russia anymore.

When the appeals to government officials in both West Prussia and southern Russia did not produce desirable and acceptable results, emigration for many appeared to be the only solution. Possible locations considered were Turkestan, New Zealand, Australia, North America, and South America. With time, a deputation of twelve men was chosen to investigate the opportunities in North America. Eleven of the chosen men were from various villages in southern or western Russia and the twelfth man was elder Wilhelm Ewert from Obernessau near Thorn, West Prussia.

Included in the Russian contingency was Leonhard Sudermann, former member of the Heubuden Church in West Prussia, who had relocated in 1841 at age twenty to Berjansk, south Russia where he was chosen a lay minister in 1860. In the fall of 1876, he with his extended family immigrated to Summerfield, Illinois, before making a decision where they wanted to settle. After traveling to Nebraska and Kansas, Elder Sudermann bought the northeast quarter of Section 9, Milton Township in the center of the fragmented West Prussian community and moved his family to Butler County, Kansas in April, 1877. He took charge and helped organize the local church within the West Prussian group that initiated worship services in Great-grandfather Harder's granary. The first Emmaus Mennonite Church building and cemetery were located on the northeast corner of Elder Sudermann's property.

But prior to his scouting tour to America in 1873, the general perception garnered from the little information available was not that positive and Sudermann wrote: "America was a country interesting for the adventurer, an asylum for convicts. How could one live in peace under his vine and fig tree amidst such people, to say nothing of the native savages? This might be possible, for those who have their pockets full of revolvers; but for a non-resistant people it would be impossible to found homes amidst such surroundings." During April and May in 1873, the twelve delegates in three groups toured the provinces of Manitoba and Ontario in Canada, and the prairie states from North Dakota to Kansas and eastward to Pennsylvania. During their travels the delegates were hosted by Mennonites in Pennsylvania and Indiana who for over two hundred years had found refuge in America from severe discrimination in Germany, Switzerland, and other parts of Europe. The delegates were very favorably impressed with the religious and political freedoms in America, and returned to West Prussia and southern Russia with agreements for inexpensive land acquisition in Manitoba, Nebraska, and Kansas, agreements for assistance from railroad companies for reduced-fare transportation, and assurances from the American Mennonites who specifically organized The Mennonite Board of Guardians to help new immigrants financially and in any other way as required. However, the delegates were unable to locate large tracts of land where the Mennonites could establish self-governing communities as they had in southern Russian prior to 1870.

When the American railroad agents arrived in West Prussia, there was excitement and a viable option presented. Sections of land offered by the railroads were up for sale across the Kansas prairies, and some homesteading was also still available. On December 28, 1872,

Appendix 1

the Atchison, Topeka, and Santa Fe Railroad completed its track across Kansas and reached the Colorado border. This secured the land grant given nine years earlier to the state of Kansas by Abraham Lincoln when he signed the Land-Grant Legislation of 1863, providing eight and a half million acres along the proposed railroad routes across Kansas, on the condition that the railroad and telegraph lines reach the Colorado border by the end of 1872. Seeing that the conditions of the stipulation were met, Kansas deeded the odd-numbered, alternate sections ten miles on both sides of their right-of-way for a total of 3.2 million acres to the Atchison, Topeka, and Santa Fe Railroad; the even-numbered sections were reserved for homesteading. The railroad in turn would sell the land to create revenue to finance the cost of building and maintaining the railroad line across Kansas. In an effort to sell these parcels of recently earned land, a gigantic advertising campaign was launched. Land agents, coordinated by C. B. Schmidt of the Atchison, Topeka, and Santa Fe Railroad Company in Topeka, Kansas, were sent across the U.S. and to Europe, including West Prussia. The agents were fluent in German and had sale fliers, also called advertising posters, in German, describing the land and the opportunities. C. B. Schmidt established land sales offices in northern Europe, and published letters in the *Frankfurter Zeitung* (Frankfurt newspaper). In 1875 he traveled through West Prussia, across Europe, and to southern Russia advertising his railroad's land to Mennonites and others of German heritage. He was targeting people with a well-developed work ethic whom he thought would utilize the services of the railroad in their agricultural business development.

In an effort to boost the sale of Kansas land to the European and Russian Mennonites, the Atchison, Topeka, and Santa Fe Railroad Company lobbied the Kansas legislature to pass an act on March 9, 1874 amending the Kansas State Militia Law, granting exemptions from military service based on religious beliefs of pacifism, as well as exemptions when required to take oaths.

These agents visited West Prussia at the time my family was seriously considering their options. Relatives and friends were among the eighteen thousand Mennonites from southern Russia who had begun immigrating to North American in 1874, so the concept of emigration was part of the historical ongoing Mennonite diaspora; however,

Appendix 1

relocation was personally monumental with another promise for religious and political freedom in a new location.

Figure 47

Land Sales Flier created by the Atchison, Topeka & Santa Fe Railroad, March, 1876, advertising land in southwestern Kansas. This flier was newspaper-sized with four pages. Only the top half of the first page is shown. The top left-hand caption reads: "The last and best opportunity for land buyers! A government grant to the Atchison, Topeka and Santa Fe Railroad Company of 3,000,000 acres of land in southwestern Kansas is for purchase with 11 years credit with 7 percent interest." Source: Mennonite Library & Archives, Newton, KS.

Appendix 2

Passage to America

THE DEPARTURE DATE WAS set for Thursday, June 15, 1876. Passage to America had been contracted on the *Norddeutscher Lloyd* (North German Lloyd) *SS Rhein*. The entire second-class cabin section had been reserved as well as additional space in the third-class (steerage level). Included in this travel package was a dedicated train chartered to take the emigrants from their nearest train station at Simonsdorf, West Prussia to the seaport of Bremen, Germany. These travelers were the initial group of emigrating members from the Heubuden Church who had aligned themselves with the *Auswanderungs Gemeinde*, the Emigrant Congregation. On the train also were well-wishers who would bid their final farewells at the Bremen docks. The train with 118 people pulled out of the station at 8:15 a.m.

The emigrants must have literally collapsed into their train seats on that soggy, rainy Thursday morning. Following years of emotional debate and evaluation, now the final months of preparation had set them on a course propelled by faith and conscience. Endless political pressure and church controversy had precipitated this exodus. In 1867 the National Conscription Law was passed, abolishing all military exemptions and ending the privileges that Mennonites had enjoyed in the Vistula Delta region for over three hundred years. The conciliatory Prussian Cabinet Order of March 3, 1868, which allowed Mennonites to serve in noncombatant roles in hospitals and quartermaster departments of the military in lieu of military service, was not an acceptable alternative for these emigrants. There was intense pressure on Mennonites to send their sons to the Prussian army and to find their primary identity in the German nation rather than the Mennonite church.

Appendix 2

What do you pack when you do not know what you will need when you get to the end of your one-way ticketed travel itinerary? So, many wooden chests and trunks were packed with items considered necessary or essential for living. My great-grandparents brought things that they perceived they would need to establish normal life in the hinterlands of America, about which they had limited information: a farm wagon with a high seat for the coachman, a Dutch ceramic house stove, a kitchen table with six chairs, a wooden clothes mangle, many featherbeds, a parlor chair for seventy-nine year old Great-great-grandmother Penner, Great-grandmother's Flow Blue china, the *Springerle* cookie rolling pin, Great-great-grandmother Penner's wine glasses, the family's communion set, wine making equipment including a grape press and bottles, many wooden chests, and vast quantities of clothing and linens because in Europe they only laundered four times a year with massive wash days.

They had trunks, chests, and boxes delivered to the train the day before their departure, a distance of about three to five miles from the farm in Gurken that Great-grandfather had just sold together with the machinery and animals. Twenty-one Heubuden families sold their properties for this June 15, 1876 departure. Mennonite-owned farms were in great demand since available land was an ongoing limiting factor and sold for a good price in 1876. Since less than 10 percent of the church membership was emigrating, those remaining could expand their holdings.

The Rev. Peter Dyck of Tiege and Abraham Claassen of Simonsdorf kept diaries during this journey. The Dyck diary is available on microfilm at the Mennonite Library and Archives, Bethel College, North Newton, Kansas, in *Mennonitische Geschichtsblätter* (1954) with translated excerpts included in *The Bernhard Regier Genealogy, 1669–1973*. The Claassen diary is available translated into English in *Abraham Claassen, Vistula to Plum Grove*.

By 8 p.m. that evening they arrived in Berlin, having endured the usual irregularities and annoyances of travel. Some scheduled stops had been omitted, other stops were announced but the lengths of stops were not communicated, and there was no light in the coaches. In Berlin the scheduled stop of twenty-five minutes never materialized. Rather, the locomotive was detached and the train was transferred to a connecting line and taken to the Lehrter station, but no one was permitted to disembark. After some passengers complained, the train personnel

Appendix 2

become more accommodating, but the train travelled on to Ratinau before a fifteen-minute stop and passengers could get out. The train arrived at Bremen shortly before 4 a.m.

Personnel of hotels near the train station greeted the travelers warmly and took charge of each family assigned to them, taking them to their rooms, and transporting the hand-carried luggage on carts. The travelers had coffee and visited a bit before they retired since they were all billeted in close proximity.

After 9 a.m. on Friday, the head of each household went to the office of the North German Lloyd. Each had to report how many were in his family, their ages, and in which coach class they had travelled to Bremen on the special train. This information was used to calculate the amount due. They were asked to return at 3 p.m. to make their payments and to receive tickets for the train trip to Bremerhaven, for the ocean steamer, and for the railroad journey in America. By 5 p.m., these transactions were completed, and upon returning to the hotel, hotel personnel took their guests on a two-and-a-half hour pleasure walk in the charming Bremen Park.

The next morning, Saturday, the travelers made a few last minute purchases, had breakfast, put their personal things back into their luggage, and went to the station to board the train bound for the harbor. They arrived at the *Norddeutscher Lloyd Wartenhalle* (North German Lloyd waiting room) at 11:30 a.m.

The group was guided to a small steamer for transport to the *SS Rhein*. Because of low tide, the ship was anchored some distance from the land. After all baggage was loaded and the 102 emigrants were on board, the *SS Rhein* departed shortly before 9 p.m. "The sixteen well-wishers waved their good wishes from the shore, while the travelers waved 'adieu' to our loved ones on shore, straining our eyes until the distance blocked our view. Our hearts were heavy, and now was the time to remind ourselves that God, our God, who never sleeps would watch over us and if it were his will would keep us safe from unforeseen danger and misfortune. With this feeling of renewed faith, we turned our eyes to new horizons." This is what the Rev. Dyck entered into his diary, realizing that most would never see each other or their fatherland again.

Appendix 2

Figure 48
The front of the *Lloyd Wartenhalle*, built in 1869 at the New Harbor in Bremerhaven. The *SS Rhein* is moored at the dock but it is difficult to identify its two masts among the many in the background. In the foreground the trains converge with baggage on the left and passengers in the middle right.
Source: www.geocities.com/mppraetorius/com-rh.htm.

More from the writings of the Rev. Peter Dyck:

> We, in the name of God, and in the hope of regaining our religious freedom had sold our earthly belongings and were now leaving the persecutor's cruel hand which had drafted so many of our youth into military service. We were given no choice: we would have to leave our fatherland and search for a country where we could retain our religious beliefs, our freedom from military service, and where we would be able to pursue our life's work as quiet citizens. In hope of all this, America was our choice and now we were departing and venturing out onto the water to a new land with the hope that God would go with us in this, our new undertaking.

The first evening was novel as the travelers watched from the deck the many ships and fishing boats passing by. Dinner was served by an attentive wait staff and the group as a whole retired late. During the night the wind began to blow and by morning many experienced their first discomforts of nausea and seasickness. None felt the distress more than Great-grandfather Harder, who lay on the deck until almost noon, covered with a fur robe and an overcoat. Shortly before noon a church service was organized in the dining salon led by the Rev. Peter Dyck, the only minister in the group. Every evening he led the group in a short period of devotions. Early Monday morning, June 19, the *SS Rhein* docked at Southampton, England.

The travelers welcomed the opportunity to tour Southampton as a reward for the successful initiation of their trip. The beauty of Southampton exceeded that of Bremen and definitely that of Danzig. Since most were farmers, some admired the many sheep and cows of fine breeding, while others were impressed with the horses, uncommonly broad and strong with sloping rumps and a long growth of hair on their legs. Other memorable impressions of this charming city were the extensive glass show windows of the elegant shops and their inability to communicate with people speaking English. By 7 p.m. the travelers were back on the ship again for dinner and then enjoyed the glorious evening on deck.

On Tuesday morning, June 20, the ship's crew was very busy loading cargo for three more hours, and then the gangway was hoisted around 10 a.m. At 11:45 the *SS Rhein* left the harbor before the ebb tide and anchored in deeper water. The water depth fluctuated by seven feet at Southampton harbor from high to low tide. At 3:30 a small steamer came from Southampton with last minute mail and some additional passengers. Shortly before 4 p.m. the ship left for New York.

The *Norddeutscher Lloyd SS Rhein* was built at the Clyde Caird shipyard by the Caird & Co., Greenock, Scotland and was launched in August 1868. She sailed her maiden voyage from Bremen to Southampton and New York on October 3, 1868. Her details were: 2,901 gross tons, length 332 feet x beam 40 feet, clipper stem, one funnel, two masts, iron construction, single screw, and a speed of thirteen knots. There was accommodation for seventy passengers in first class, one hundred in second class, and six hundred in third class, with a crew of one hundred seventeen. She was a sister ship (almost identical) to *SS Main*, *SS Donau*, and *SS Mosel*. During the 1873–74 season, her record time from New York to Southampton was nine days and ten hours. The *SS Rhein* replaced the original ship laid down with similar name, which was sold on the stocks to the Royal Mail Steamship Co. and launched in February 1868 as the *SS Neva*. The second *SS Rhein* was sold in 1891

Appendix 2

to Gray, Liverpool and in 1893 she was scrapped or broken up by Jaeger Brothers, Liverpool in Barrow-in-Furness.

In conversation with the purser, Abraham Claassen learned that the *SS Rhein* used seventy-five tons of coal daily, which would cost about $350 and for one round-trip used about four thousand pounds of oil for lubrication. There were indeed 117 crewmen; the shift in the engine room worked four hours and rested eight hours. The deck crews were on four hours and off four hours. On this particular trip there were thirty-four first cabin passengers, ninety-three second cabin passengers and three hundred eighty-seven steerage passengers.

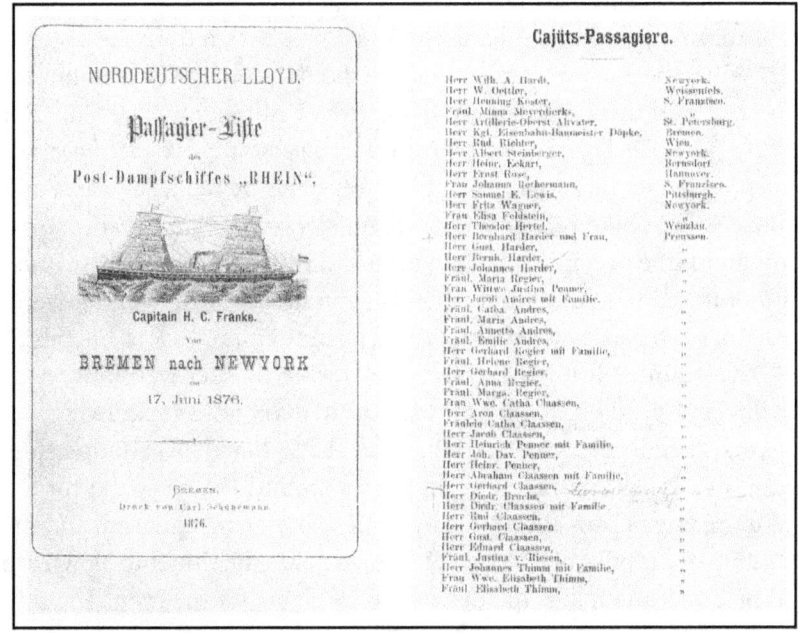

Figure 49
The passenger list of the mail steamship *Rhein* for its voyage initiated on June 17, 1876 in Bremen in route to New York. Only the cover page showing the *SS Rhein* under full sail and the page with my family listed are shown. Source: The entire passenger list is available in *The Family of Gerhard & Anna Regier, 1852–2001*. Used with Permission.

The passenger list for this voyage of the mail steamship *SS Rhein* includes a picture on its cover page of the ship under power with steam as well as fully using the wind sails, combining new and standard technologies. The captain on this crossing was H. C. Franke. Heading the

Appendix 2

list of those from *Preussen* are my mother's family, Mr. Bernhard Harder and wife, Mr. Gust. Harder, Mr. Bernh. Harder, Mr. Johannes Harder, Miss Maria Regier, and widow Justine Penner. The Harder's employee Andres Powolski traveled with the steerage passengers.

After leaving England, the sea became rough. Seasickness was almost universally experienced. Abraham Claassen records in his diary that "I went a number of times to the bow and had myself thoroughly tossed for the money I had paid. It is as if one is on a swing, when one is raised 20 to 30 feet up and then is hurled down again."

Great-grandfather Harder was so seasick during the crossing that the captain said he had never seen anyone so severely incapacitated. He spent many days at sea lying weak and helpless on the deck covered with a fur robe and an overcoat. But he did not lose his sense of humor and once said in Low German to his friend Abraham Claassen, "*Eck kun mi aever Di argere. Du steihst wie en Fuerst, un eck mot ligge wie en bettler.* I could get angry with you. You stand there like a prince and I must lie here like a beggar." Abraham Claassen's diary records that throughout the ocean trip he and others of the group from West Prussia monitored the condition of Great-grandfather with sympathy and concern, as well as assisted him to and from the ship deck to his cabin.

Entertainment for the passengers during these eleven long, endless days in transit on the Atlantic, at least items of note, included seeing flags of different colors hoisted whenever the *SS Rhein* met another ship, seeing flying fish, sharks, and porpoises around the ship, the furling and unfurling of the sails as the direction of the wind changed, and the boarding of the pilot on Friday, June 30, to guide the ship into New York harbor. The captain also handed out some cigars for the men. The ship docked at Hoboken, and at 6:00 a.m. on July 1 the harbor doctor came on board to inspect the steerage passengers. The line kept moving quite rapidly and after the passengers had breakfast, "they began unloading our things." During the afternoon the customs officials came and the travelers did not have to open anything. C. B. Schmidt and a Mr. Andres of the Santa Fe Railroad Land Sales Office in Topeka, Kansas and "two brethren (relatives) from Nebraska" also arrived.

The unloading of "our things" from the ship into the tugboat was done very recklessly. The dockhands had iron hooks with wooden handles and the chests were thrown end-over-end. They even hooked into bedding and the feathers began to fly. When Abraham Claassen

Appendix 2

complained, one dockhand who spoke German simply said, "Laß die Federn fliegen. Let the feathers fly!" Abraham then went to the tugboat captain and "remonstrated that we had not acquired the bedding to have it torn up so sinfully." This did help a bit, but the dockhands continued working with utmost speed.

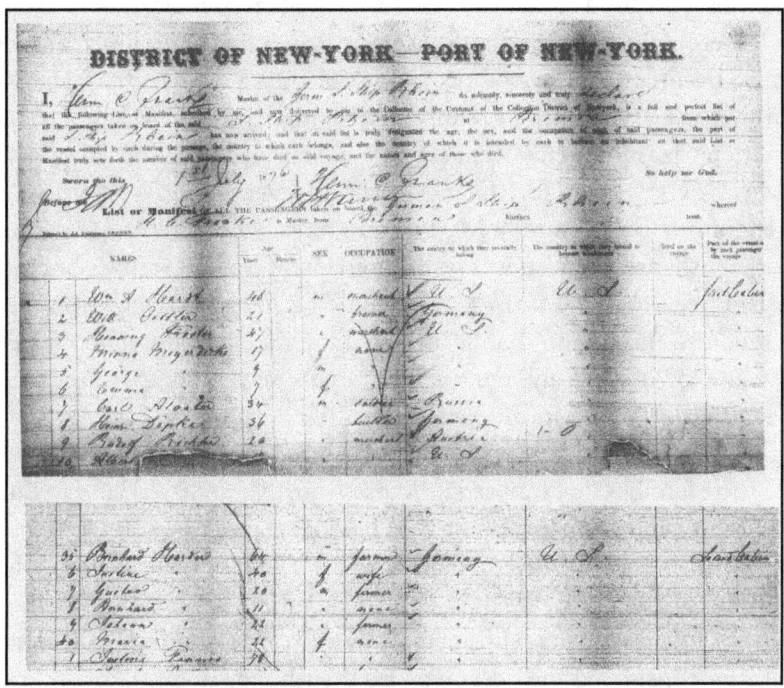

Figure 50
The manifest of passengers disembarking from the *SS Rhein* in New York on July 1, 1876. Every individual, including children and infants is recorded by a line of description. Of the 514 passengers, the Bernhard Harder family members are passengers #35–41. Their employee Andres Powolsky is #199 (not shown). National Archives Microfilm Publications, Passenger Lists of Vessels Arriving at New York 1830–1897, Roll 404. Source: Mennonite Library & Archives, Bethel College, North Newton.

When Aaron Claassen, a fellow passenger who had worked in America for several years and had returned to West Prussia to bring his mother and siblings to America, had completed his help with the officials and railroad agents using English, everyone had received their rail tickets. He and C. B. Schmidt then took many of the passengers into New York to exchange their *Reichsthaler* for American dollars and where they

399

Appendix 2

admired eight-story buildings. At 3 p.m. the group returned from the city to learn that they had to board the train immediately. Not everything had been unloaded from the ship, but things were moving rapidly and they could not remain to watch while everything was loaded into the baggage cars. Somehow, in the end, people and luggage all got on the right trains and mostly in good condition, thanks to excellent packing.

Here at the New York port the group split into two parties, traveling to two destinations. Thirty-one people, including the Bernhard Harder family, the Gerhard Regier family, the Heinrich Penner family, and the Dietrich Claassen family went directly to Halstead, Kansas, where they had relatives waiting for them. The other seventy-one West Prussian Mennonites took a train to Mt. Pleasant, Iowa where they were met by Cornelius Jansen. Jansen was well-known in Mennonite circles because he had been expelled from Russia where he so aggressively promoted Mennonite emigration that he attracted the ire of the Russian officials; he came to America and continued to focus on immigration, assisting many newly arrived immigrants in finding locations to establish new settlements.

The families that traveled to Kansas shortly purchased land in Butler County, Kansas. Most of the Mt. Pleasant travelers would with time buy farmland near Beatrice, Nebraska. A few who initially went to Iowa and later joined the group in Kansas included the Rev. Peter Dyck family with two daughters who married just prior to coming to America but who considered the ocean voyage their honeymoon, Jacob W. and Agathe (Dyck) Regier, and Bernhard and Marie (Entz) Regier. They came to Kansas in August/September, 1876. The Abraham Claassen family located permanently to Kansas in January, 1877. Johann Dyck, a fellow immigrant who was courting Helene Regier, the third child of the Gerhard Regier family and married her in 1877, also established a farm in the Kansas community.

This was July 1, 1876 and the centennial celebrations of the United States were in full evidence. The new immigrants were exhilarated as they traveled westward to their new life on the plains with locomotives decked out with flags and flowers.

Appendix 3

Tornado of June 8, 1941

SOME OF THESE STORIES and experiences were retold so often that it seemed I too had lived through this event, but I was born a year after a devastating tornado tore through the community from corner to corner. The tornado was the largest catastrophe in the local area since the grasses gave way to farming in 1876. Mother's photo album contains images of this tragedy.

Every winter during my elementary school years, I was sent to the big woodpile to break old lumber gathered from the tornado to stoke the iron potbelly stove in the kitchen. The wood was collected from the fields and the farmyard in the aftermath during cleanup prior to rebuilding the farm. Waste wood from the reconstruction of the farm was also on this pile. On other occasions, I went to the woodpile to look for scraps of wood that could be recycled into woodworking projects.

At a Farm Bureau meeting in El Dorado in the 1950s, beautifying farmyards was discussed with the suggestion that if you cannot clean it up, hide it. Mother came home and ordered spirea bushes from a mail order nursery catalog and planted a row in front of the woodpile. By 1990 when I returned to the farm, all the wood was gone and only miscellaneous metal debris remained hidden by volunteer trees growing among the spirea bushes. With time the scars on the landscape from June 8, 1941 have disappeared, but the psychological and physical scars on the people that lived through this tornado remain.

Tornadoes occur in all states east of the Rockies, but are more frequent in Midwestern states. The states of Kansas, Texas, Oklahoma, Nebraska, and Missouri are within "Tornado Alley"; more tornadoes are spawned in these states than anywhere else. Tornadoes are the most violent, least extensive, and most sharply defined of all storms. Because

Appendix 3

Kansas is rather sparsely populated and farms are large, tornadoes often occur with little or no damage to human life or habitation. More densely populated states repeatedly report more fatalities and property damage per year than Kansas.

In 1955, the city of Udall, Kansas was demolished with the loss of eighty-two lives. Since then, other cities of Kansas, including El Dorado, Topeka, Emporia, Hesston, Andover, Haysville, South Wichita, and Greensburg have been hit. The storms of 1990 and 1991 were particularly destructive. The good news remains that survival is normally possible if timely precautions are taken. Based on data from 1950 to 1995, compared to other states, Kansas ranks third for the frequency of tornadoes, eighth for the number of deaths, fourteenth for injuries, and third for cost of damages. When the data are compared based per square mile of area within states, Kansas ranks fourth in frequency of tornadoes, thirteenth for fatalities, twenty-second for injuries per area, and eighth for costs per area.

Between 1914 and 1945, five hundred tornadoes were sighted in Kansas, with the month of June registering 30 percent of the total. During this period, tornadoes occurred at all hours of the day except from 4 a.m. to 5 a.m., and were most frequent from 5 p.m. to 7 p.m., with about 16 percent occurring between 5 p.m. and 6 p.m. The characteristic vortex cloud is usually a funnel-shaped mass of air revolving at a terrific speed. The centrifugal force of this whirl, rotating counterclockwise in the northern hemisphere, creates a partial vacuum at its center. This accounts for the explosive effect as it passes over buildings. The force of the storm accounts for the many freak occurrences that result, such as wheat straw penetrating hardwood hedge fence posts, a lit lamp flying out of a window, or boards penetrating the exterior walls of a house.

In 1941, there were eighteen tornadoes recorded in Kansas with eight lives lost and an estimated property loss of $612,050. These eight lives were lost along the path of the June 8, 1941 tornado; the physical damage of this storm was estimated at $228,000 with $150,000 damage to crops and $78,000 damage to buildings.

The total path of the F4 tornado of June 8, 1941 was forty-two miles, initially touching the ground seven miles southwest of Maize, which is about eight miles northwest of Wichita. It moved northeastward with a swath of one half-mile, running about three miles southeast of Valley Center. Newspaper accounts relate and show that damage was done on many farms along its path, beginning at the Williams' property. The George Thompson farm had all the farm buildings destroyed. The C. L. Groves farm had considerable damage and Frank Jump had a barn destroyed. The large barns on the J. W. Harrison farm were completely destroyed and their house was twisted on its foundation; the Harrison family found shelter in their storm cave.

At the Charles Frazee Sr. farm, the roof was blown off the house and other buildings were demolished. One-half mile east, the Charles Frazee Jr. home, completed just six months earlier, was blown away. They were entertaining guests in their home that evening and just minutes before the tornado hit, as they were bidding the guests farewell, they sensed that a tornado was coming. Charles and his wife attempted to drive out of the path of the storm, but the wind blew their car off the road. They were forced to sit and watch their house being destroyed. However, through their efforts to drive to safety, they escaped uninjured.

The home of John Schaefer Jr. located east of Valley Center on Meridian was said to have collapsed and a friend, Haskell H. Keyes (age fifty), who had just arrived that afternoon from Oklahoma City to assist with the wheat harvest, was killed. Keyes had been in the basement, but came up to help the others. The storm hit before he got back to the basement and he was found twenty feet from the house with a broken back and leg, and a badly smashed face, dying before a doctor could get there. Those in the basement all escaped injuries except for cuts, bruises, and shock.

The Lester Smith home nearby was also destroyed. The Smiths were sleeping on the ground floor with a twenty-month-old grandson and their grown children, the Basils, were sleeping upstairs with two additional children. When Mrs. Basil heard the roar of the approaching tornado, she grabbed her seven-month-old child and yelled to her husband to get their other son. This awakened the grandparents and Mrs. Smith caught up the twenty-month-old child. They all met at the backdoor ready to run to the storm cave when the storm demolished the house. Glen, the oldest son was sucked up through the stairwell and landed west of the house with only scratches. Mrs. Smith and Mrs. Basil each held a child through the ordeal and although they felt an awful pressure pushing them down, miraculously, the whole family survived with only bad bruises. The house and its furnishings were a mass of splintered boards; not even the floor of the house was left and only three small pieces of furniture remained intact. This, together with other shattered personal items and broken machinery, was mute evidence that a tornado can wipe away the work of a lifetime in a few minutes.

At the H. H. Phillips home the barn was blown away and several horses killed. When the family tried to open the door to get to the cave, boards were hurled into the house every time they opened the door, so they stayed in the house and were safe, although the house was badly damaged. Across the road at the Roy Paff home, a large barn and several smaller buildings were destroyed and the windmill was torn down. At the J. F. Metcalf home, the garage was slightly twisted and a chicken house destroyed.

The tornado crossed the Butler county line road west of the Metcalfs and roared through a wheat field mowing the wheat, tearing up hedges and other shrubs by the roots and leveling telephone poles, stringing the wire in every direction. One mile from the county line it struck the H. E. Eshelman farm. Mrs. Eshelman took a child and ran to the basement when she heard the roar. Mr. Eschelman grabbed the other child but could not open the basement door because of the air pressure caused by the tornado, so he and the child remained upstairs. Shortly, all the windows broke and the doors were blown open, the house was wrenched and the front porch and part of the roof were torn off. A huge cedar tree west of the front porch was twisted off, and the Eshelmans felt that this tree protected the house enough to keep it from being torn down. All eleven outbuildings were destroyed and several animals were killed. A practically new combine was destroyed and a new tractor was picked up and set down with one wheel on the family car.

The funnel cloud apparently then retracted for a time of twelve to fifteen minutes and a distance of about eight to ten miles. The second time it touched down, it inundated a swath one-half mile wide and twenty miles long. It took sixteen minutes to travel the last ten miles and then dissipate near the Butler-Marion County line, five miles west of Burns. Shortly after the storm moved on, the rain clouds followed and a bright moon shone on the trail of destruction. Heavy torrential rains had fallen in the morning and again all evening and the streams were in flood stage. Highway 196 west of Whitewater was covered with two feet of water for a quarter mile.

Appendix 3

Initiating the second touch down in rolling wheat and pasture country, which offered little natural resistance to the wind's sweep, several miles of telephone and electric lines were torn down sometime after 11:00 p.m. southeast of Furley and the Whitewater community was without power.

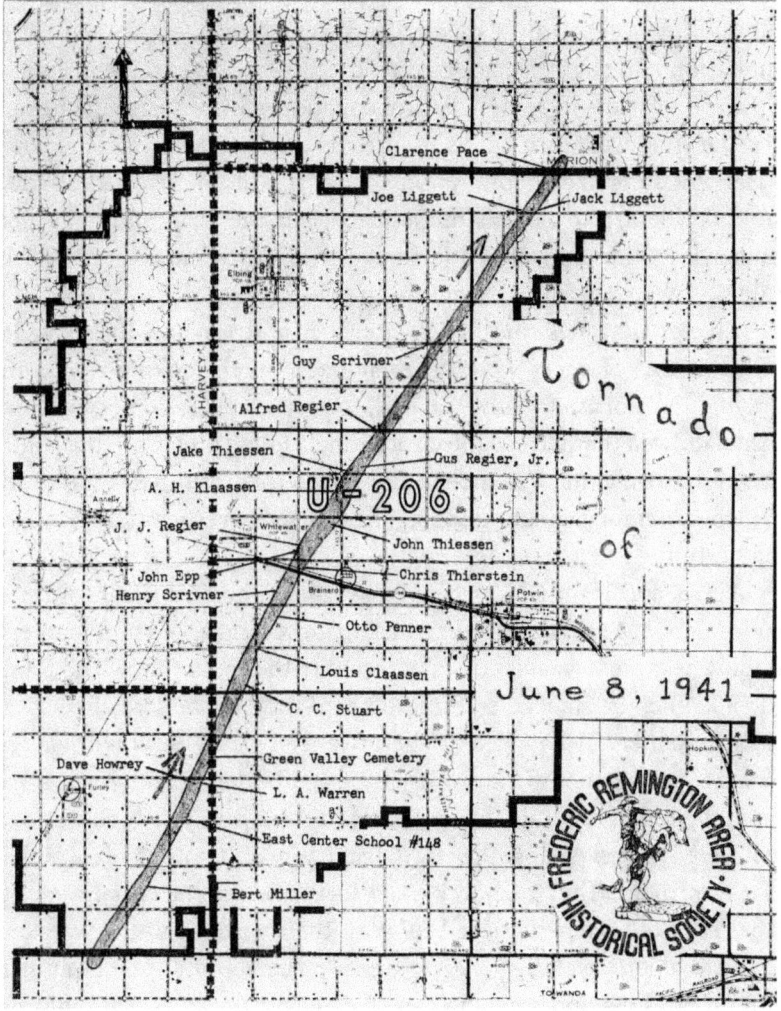

Figure 51
Path of tornado during the second touchdown on June 8, 1941. Source: The Frederic Remington Area Historical Society Library.

On the Bert Miller's farm on Section 34, a barn, a chicken house, and a windmill were destroyed, but the house remained. Also on that

Appendix 3

section, the henhouse of Harold Greese was demolished. The tornado then completely destroyed the District No. 148 East Center School House and coal house, which were located a few miles south and west of Whitewater. As the storm moved on in its northeasterly trajectory, the farm home of Dave Howrey was damaged and a barn and windmill were wrecked. One-half mile farther at the L. A. Warren farm the outbuildings were badly damaged and their house was shifted off its foundation and slightly damaged. At the Green Valley cemetery many of the monuments were tipped, broken, and destroyed, and the beautiful cedar trees were torn out by their roots and splintered. On the farms of Harry Patterson and John Hiser the farm buildings were destroyed. The C. C. Stuart house was undamaged, but the farm buildings were damaged. At the unoccupied farm of the C. A. Neiman estate, all the buildings were destroyed except for the house.

Five or six miles south of Whitewater and south of the tornado's path, the Gus Harders were on their back porch looking north and studying the storm. As they watched, the rapid succession of lightning flashes allowed them to see the dark funnel cloud come from the southwest and move along its northeasterly trajectory. But it was the sound that left a memory; it sounded like the roaring reverberation of a large freight train.

Lewis and Ruth Claassen were living on the Gus Claassen estate farm. At about 11:20 p.m., Ruth woke up Lewis and asked him to open a window because it was so hot. Lewis went to the east window and found it open. When he smelled sulfur and heard the roar, he screamed, "Run for the basement." He picked up their twenty-month-old son Elwin and started for the stairway. Ruth was at the bottom and Lewis with Elwin was at the top of the stairs when the lights went out. When all was over they were lying close together in the stairway and an outside wall was on top of them. They had all landed in the basement unharmed, but rather shocked. They managed to work their way out of the wreckage and were able to walk to Lewis' parents place about a mile away with nothing but cuts and scratches on their backs and feet. All buildings were demolished and never rebuilt.

Living on the Arnold Zuercher farm were brother and sister Otto and Marie Penner. Marie had been spending the weekend in El Dorado with her sister Martha (Mrs. Carl Steiner) and initially planned to return to the farm on Monday, but since her peas were ready for picking and canning, she returned on Sunday afternoon to give herself an early start on Monday. She was blown nearly two hundred feet by the tornado and her battered body was tossed into a hedgerow. Otto, bruised with small splinters of wood lodged in his scalp and in shock, walked to their neighbors, the Henry Scrivners, and knocked on the door where he stood without shoes and in his rain-soaked nightclothes. After giving him some clothes and shoes, the Scrivners with Otto drove to the Penner farm and picked up Marie. The Scrivners took both to the hospital in El Dorado, but Marie passed away en route. She was thirty-six years old. Her funeral was at Emmaus Mennonite Church on the afternoon of June 11, 1941. Officiating was her pastor the Rev. J. C. Kaufman with the assistance of the Rev. B. W. Harder and the Rev. Ted Roth. Her obituary in *The Independent* and rerun in the *Potwin Ledger* ended with this poem:

> I have prayed for courage,
> Longed for stability;
> I have sought for patience
> Knelt in humility
> Scourged I have been and weakened
> Weary but not for long
> Then new strength came to me
> Brought to my lips a song
> Grateful for my burdens
> Thankful for each task;
> Give me strength to bear them.
> This is all I ask.

Otto Penner died not long after from injuries received during the storm. Mrs. Mary Scrivner, and her son Henry and his new bride who had just returned from their honeymoon, lived just north of the Penners but were far enough west of the storm that they only lost a barn.

The storm continued across that section crossing the Missouri Pacific Railroad, and passed directly over the farm of C. B. Thierstein Jr. The family had just moved their household into a newly constructed garage and was sleeping there, because they were going to tear down the old 1870s house in preparation for the construction of a new house. The Thiersteins had been visiting neighbors Sunday evening and returned home after 10 p.m. The storm struck without warning about an hour later. C. B. tried to gather Pauline (age twelve), Gerald (age ten), and Eldrid (age six) around him and Mrs. Thierstein (Ella) took Myron

Appendix 3

Keith (age five months) in her arms. The eye of the storm transformed their farm into splinters and spread it though a half a mile of wheat. Ella was knocked unconscious for a short time and Myron was blown from his mother's arms by the force of the wind and flying debris as she tried to shield him from harm; he was found under debris in the yard. The storm tossed C. B. around through the trees north of the house and then laid him down on the muddy ground. He began calling each family member by name and locating them under the debris. They all stumbled towards a part of the chicken house that remained intact. It seemed to Ella that they had all been let out of a dungeon, hair twisted, barefooted with only wet nightclothes on. They tried to nestle close together as C. B. went to get help. He saw lights of an approaching car coming slowly along the old route of Highway 196.

Mr. and Mrs. Bill Joseph were slowly driving to Potwin through heavy rain along Highway 196, passing just north of the Thierstein farm. They saw the heavy black cloud ahead of them and thought they were running into another rainstorm. As they approached the path of the tornado, they were slowed down by the telephone poles and fences littering the highway, arriving at the Thierstein farm just minutes after the storm had passed. They heard C. B.'s cries for help and immediately gathered the family from the chicken house, stumbled down the debris-strewn driveway, and loaded them into the car bleeding with injuries, and with the limp baby in their arms. They drove to Whitewater, where the Josephs roused residents and search parties went out to help other victims. The darkness, the heavy rain, and the debris on the roads made rescue efforts difficult.

C. B. and Ella had severe skin bruises from the wind and flying debris, and straw had penetrated their skin. Both were hospitalized for a time. Myron died at 2:48 in the morning, about an hour after being admitted to the hospital. Pauline, Gerald, and Eldrid escaped with minor injuries. The next day *The Wichita Eagle*, evening edition, included pictures of both C. B. and Ella in hospital beds. Ella was shown with bandages on her injured hand. A picture of C. B. in his hospital bed courtesy of the *Wichita Eagle* also appeared in the *Potwin Ledger* on June 19, 1941 with the caption "C. B. Thierstein, 35, in a Newton hospital recovering from cuts and bruises after he was blown 100 yards with the rest of his family in Sunday night's tornado."

Fifty years later Ella recounted the night of the tornado:

Appendix 3

One of the hardest hit families was the C. B. Thierstein family who lost their youngest child of five months, losing their whole farm with the exception of a small piece of the chicken house.

It took C. B. up and down through trees before landing on the ground. The rest of our family was under the debris. It took our baby Myron, whom I was holding in my arms, later finding him by our daughter, Pauline, in the middle of our yard.

Where could C. B. find the rest of our family? So C. B. walked around calling each of us, calling us by our names. We then walked into the little part of the chicken house. C. B. then went to the road calling for help. It so happened a car was coming from the east [west]. Luckily, it stopped to see if we needed help.

Together they came back to pick the rest of us up to take us to Whitewater where my sister and husband (the Herman Klaassens) lived. My husband C. B. had a chest wound with a nail sticking in and I had the thumb on my right hand almost off.

There was an osteopath doctor living in Whitewater who later passed away with a fractured skull. The rest of our children stayed in Whitewater at my sister's and husband.

Even though it was a terrible experience to live through we were thankful that the rest of the family had been saved.

The funeral for Myron Keith Thierstein was held at the Emmaus Mennonite Church on Thursday, June 12 at 9:30 a.m. The Rev. J. C. Kaufman and the Rev. B. W. Harder officiated. Concluding the short obituary in *The Independent* and also in the *Potwin Ledger* was a poem:

Mine

I closely held within my arm a jewel rare
Never had one so rich and pure engaged my care.
T'was my own, my precious jewel God gave it me.
T'was mine, who else would care for it so tenderly?
But the Master came one day my gem to take
"I cannot let it go," I cried, "my heart will break."
"Nay, but I came for it, to bear above, to deck my royal diadem."
Yes, Master. Thou mayest keep my own for it is thine.
Safe in the house not made with hands
T'is thine and mine.

The Independent of July 24, 1941, mentions that the Thierstein family moved into one of the small houses south of the Brainerd store until their home, which was destroyed by the recent tornado, was rebuilt.

Appendix 3

However, with time they moved to a farm two miles east of the original farm and never rebuilt the original farm.

As the storm moved a quarter mile northeast, it destroyed the farm of John Epp Jr., my parents' farm. All the buildings erected sixty years earlier by Great-grandfather Harder were destroyed, including the initial granary that was used as their temporary home and the first worship center until the local church was built. This also was the preferred roosting site for the pair of Great Horned owls mentioned in chapter 4. Some of the 8" x 8" timbers put together with wooden pegs from this granary were found a mile farther along the path of the storm. The area where the granary had been looked as though it had been swept with a broom. All the outbuildings and the silo were leveled. Less than one-third of the horse barn remained intact. Most of the house, built by my grandfather in 1887, in which my parents and siblings were sleeping remained standing; however, the house was heavily damaged. My parents' farm must have been on the western edge of the tornado with the center of the vortex going directly over the farm across the road.

Figure 52a
The south side of the house with the dented car where a crib of corn landed. Albert is seated on the running board. Photo by Marie. Source: Author's file.

Appendix 3

Figure 52b
The north side of the house where the roof was off the lean-to kitchen. To the left was Marie's garden covered with debris. Photo by Marie. Source: Author's file.

Figure 52c
The horse barn was the only other structure surviving after the tornado with about a third of structure remaining. Photo by Marie. Source: Author's file.

The house my great-grandfather initially built on the farm had been disassembled in 1927 and reassembled on the John Thiessen farm. This house was totally demolished at that location and was discussed in chapter 5.

The first week in June, 1941, had been very stormy and rainy, with about five inches of rain already recorded since June 1. Total rainfall for the year was 14.15 inches, two inches above normal. My parents and siblings went to bed as usual on that Sunday evening, except Hildegard and Phebe who were sleeping on the floor in the south room on the main floor adjacent to my parents' bedroom because they had just come home from the hospital the day before recovering from a severe flu. Albert, John Edwin, and Martha were sleeping upstairs. Sometime after eleven o'clock, my mother recalls, the roar of the tornado awakened them and they jumped out of bed. She held on to Father as they stood there. She could feel a pull on the house floor and then it relaxed and all the window panes on the south and west side of the house flew inwards, breaking into one to two-inch shards. There was glass all over the floor where Hildegard and Phebe were sleeping. The door to Albert and John Edwin's bedroom must have slammed shut with great force since half of the door was in the stairwell. A wooden board (2 x 4) was sticking through the wall above the boys' bed, and red boards from the cowshed were under their bed. Martha remembers covering her head with her pillow because pictures hanging on the wall fell onto her bed. My brother John Edwin slept through the whole event. As my mother opened the door leading upstairs, she screamed the phrase that tornado victims seem to utter in unison, "*Kinder, sind Sie da?* Children, are you there?" Fortunately, none of the family was injured. Justina and Frieda were staying for the weekend with Aunt Helen Ruth at Grandfather Epp's house two miles away.

At the end of the Epp farm driveway is the small, private Harder cemetery. The cemetery was between the Epp and Regier homes. Nearly all of the tombstones had been toppled flat. The air pressure variations of the passing tornado funnel also caused many of the graves to cave in. Interments at the time did not involve cement vaults but rather wooden boxes and with time gravesites needed to have additional soil put on top to keep the gravesite level with the surrounding earth as the boxes decayed. The vacuum of the vortex must have drawn air out of the gravesites causing unusual settling of the earth.

Mother thought she heard voices and opened the east door of their first-floor bedroom. She gasped as she saw only empty space across the road where the house of the Jake Regier family had stood. Father took a lantern and went down the driveway where he met the seven members of the Regier family. Taking the offered lantern, the Regiers stumbled among the scattered boards and debris and came to the house where

Mother handed out dry clothes and comfort, since they were in their nightclothes, soaked with rain, and barefoot. Mother gave her bathrobe to Betty, Jakie's wife, because she was very pregnant. A healthy Ronald Roger Regier was born eleven days later as reported in the *Brainerd News*.

Jake Regier Sr. had long had a storm protection plan that he taught his family. At a previous residence there had been a storm cave one-hundred feet from the house and whenever there was an impending storm, the whole family had a routine drill with assignments for everyone to create a picnic in the storm cave. This included open-faced cheese sandwiches, dill pickles, and homemade ice cream. Part of the storm routine was to take ice and the manually operated ice cream freezer into the cave and make ice cream to occupy their time as the storm passed. But on June 8, on their present farm, Jake Sr. was awakened by something that sounded like a freight train on the Missouri Pacific Railroad track one-half mile south of the farm. Instinctively, he shouted, "Everyone to the basement!" His frightened shrill voice awakened anyone who had already fallen asleep. All seven adults in the house made a mad dash down the stairs. The last ones, Mrs. Regier and a son, Alvin, were still on the basement steps when the house was lifted off its foundation, clearing the cellar with its occupants and exploding in the vegetable garden about one hundred feet northeast of the site where the house had stood since 1880. The steps, with Mrs. Regier and Alvin, fell to the basement floor. Mrs. Regier's hip was severely bruised but not broken and she subsequently spent some time in the hospital recuperating. Everyone says, "Of course, Mrs. Regier (Justine) would have been the last one down. She was such a loving, concerned person that she would have made sure everyone was safe before she thought of herself." Having observed the destroyed Regier farm, a newspaper reporter wrote, "How any of them could have escaped death is a miracle."

With the house gone, the winds swirled sand, dirt, gravel, glass, and debris round in the basement. Much of it clung to their hair, except for an uncle who wore a toupee, which the wind sucked off and up and which was never found. The Regier family could look up out of their open basement and see the storm clouds overhead, hear the memorable roar, observe the continual lightning, and feel the hot rain coming down on them in torrents. The wind was fierce enough to roll around three or four ten-gallon food storage crocks, spilling their contents as they rolled into family members. When the debris stopped falling, Mrs. Regier was heard faintly asking, "*Lebt ihr alle noch?* Are you all still alive?" In that moment, Jake Sr. asked Jakie to return thanks to God for sparing their lives. Jakie attempted with, "Our precious Heavenly Father . . . " but could not continue; he and Betty were crouched low in the southwest corner of the cellar where Jakie had bent over Betty to protect their unborn baby as best he could.

Their immediate problem was to get out of the basement. As they collected their thoughts, they noticed that the steps that had fallen into the basement were quite sturdy. They set these against the north wall and one by one, while two people held the steps, they all got to ground level. With the light of the receding flashes of lightning they saw destruction, rubble, and heartache. Cleanup started the next day, but looters were there almost immediately during the first night. Some of their silver was later retrieved from a pawn shop in Wichita. The antique clanging kitchen clock was found nearby, stopped at 11:15. However, the Regiers were able to retrieve eighty quarts of preserved fruit and fifty-two quarts of canned meat from the open cellar the next day. A relative found Mrs. Regier's diary in a pasture, and when he returned it, the smirk on his face was really embarrassing to her.

Father walked on to the Thierstein farm a quarter-mile south; it had been Mr. Thierstein's cry for help that Mother heard. By that time they were gone, picked up by the Josephs, and on their way to the doctor and hospital. Father then walked three-quarters of a mile east to the Gus Reimer residence outside the path of the storm, and told them of the damage and the Regiers' need for help. He then walked another mile to his father's farm from where he and his brother Cornie drove a car to the John Thiessen farm. Gilbert Thiessen had already been there to ask for help.

A short time later, Gus Reimer appeared at the house to take the Regiers to the hospital for medical assistance. The Regiers were required to again walk the debris-strewn driveway to the car on the road because the debris prevented the car from passing. My father's employee spent the next whole day removing the debris from the driveway and boards from the cedars that lined it. Gus took the Regier family to the hospital in Newton in his chugging Model T Ford where Betty and Mrs. Regier were admitted.

By then the rain had stopped and the moon was shining brightly. Mother ventured out alone to survey the damage. Only the house remained with the tin roof torn off the kitchen and the roof was off the barn. She noticed that the cistern pump was gone, together with the platform, and so she covered the cistern with boards from the debris. The car was crushed on one side where the bin of corn stored above it was dumped on it. The implement shed, the chicken house, and, as already mentioned, the granary, were all gone. In the chicken house, Mother was raising next year's flock. They were just eight weeks old and were later found strewn along the driveway together with pigeons.

Some people from the community were coming home very late that Sunday night and saw the black storm clouds ahead of them. Passing through Brainerd they found a herd of cattle on the road. The men rounded up the cattle and managed to get them into the stock pens at the train siding. This would hold them until the next day when the owner could retrieve them. With the fences destroyed by the tornado, these were my father's fattened cattle, which had wandered two miles eastward. They had been contracted for purchase, but Father wanted to fatten them a bit more. Now that they were in Brainerd where they could be loaded into train stockcars and sent to Wichita, Father sent word to the buyer, "The steers are coming." These cattle escaped injury, but a considerable number of animals including horses, cows, and hogs were killed outright or had to be destroyed due to injury.

Father returned home early the next morning bringing the sad news of Susan Thiessen's injuries. He and mother tried to relax and get some sleep; mother had a mild form of the flu and was running a fever, but with the crises around her, she never checked her temperature again. As dawn broke, relatives and neighbors were there to help. An uncle went out to milk a cow and came back with a bucket of pink liquid; there was blood in the milk. It was not an internal injury as first suspected, but rather a cut on the udder and if bandaged during milking, there was no blood in the milk. Another neighbor brought a hog shed, knowing Father raised pigs and needed items like shelter and fences. A youngster, Bernie Regier, who came with his father to help, remembers seeing neighbors loading my father's fat hogs onto farm wagons drawn by horses and presumably driving them to the Brainerd railhead for shipment to market in Wichita. Some pigs had boards in their sides. These were sent to the desiccating company. Friends walked the fields to pick up boards and debris. Nails on the ground were a real hazard for the horses that got lame and tractor tires that were punctured, and even five years later, my father was still rewarding us children with candy when we had picked up one hundred nails in the farmyard.

Among Mother's papers was a poem written in 1947 that describes the impact of the tornado on my parents' farm. The authorship is undetermined, presumably a sibling, but it does describe our place. A cat did jump into the kitchen through a window with broken panes during the night after the tornado and had a litter of kittens on a stack of gloves in a corner of the coat closet.

A Cyclone

Six years ago on the eighth of June
A large dark cloud hid away the moon.
As we did sleep
The winds did leap
Into a cyclone of destruction and ruin.

The evening air seemed so hot and still.
Suddenly a breeze came o'er the hill.
The cyclone was coming
Through the treetops running
Destroying everything just at will.

No heed or warning, no signal of alarm
Yet it rapidly approached our farm.
Buildings were ripped
The house was stripped
And it blew the lid right off the barn.

The cyclone sped on; it did not detain.
Leaving a pussy cat out in the rain.
As quiet as a mouse
She jumped into the house
Through a hole in the broken window pane.

—Author Unknown

During the summer that followed, women from the church community canned vegetables for my mother since her garden was covered with debris. Others brought fresh produce in season. Some brought

Appendix 3

baked goods. Several took the family laundry and washed it for Mother. My parents wanted to say "thank you" to these kind people who so selflessly helped with the recovery, and ten years later invited them with lasting appreciation to their silver wedding anniversary celebration.

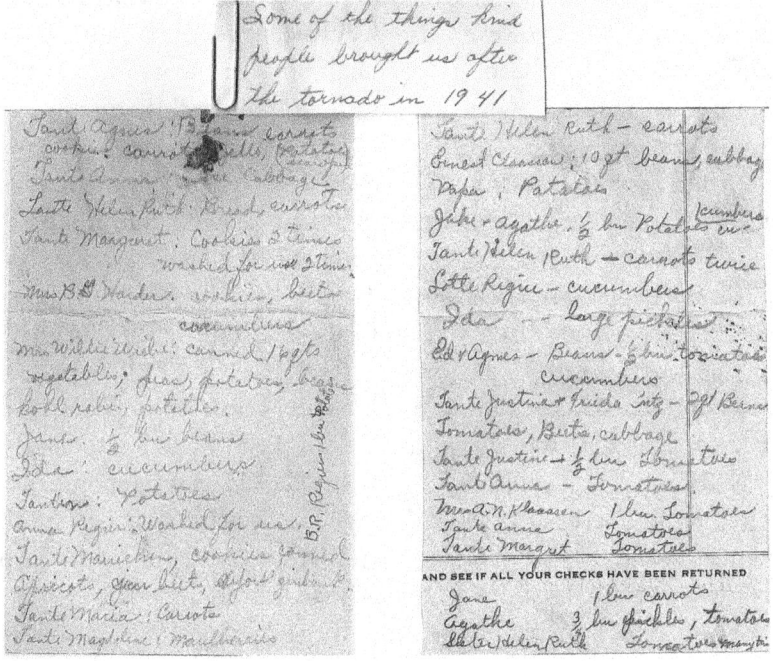

Figure 53
The community sharing with Mennonite compassion.
"Some of the things kind people brought us after the tornado in 1941"
and the list that Marie kept on front and back of a piece of paper
cut from the bottom of a bank statement. Source: Author's file.

The winter wheat and barley were nearly ready to harvest in early June. Within the half-mile swath of the tornado, if the crops had been cut, bundled, and stooked, the shocks were all tangled up with telephone and fence wire, and wooden debris and not salvageable. If the nearly ripe wheat was still standing in the field, the wind simply flattened it into the mud and it too was unsalvageable. Fields of green alfalfa were also flattened, but these plants could erect themselves and regrow.

The rampaging tornado continued to the John Thiessen farm and completely leveled it. Several family members were injured and one daughter, Susan, sustained severe injuries. As *The Independent*

Appendix 3

reported, "their loss was total, all buildings being swept away." Many details are included in chapter 5. Looting was a major problem. There had been hams hanging in the attic curing; a spectator was observed carrying away two hams from the debris in the field. The local sheriff provided some order on Sundays, when the number of spectators was at its peak. There were, however, also benevolent spectators in neighbors and friends who helped locate personal items in the debris and took them home to clean, as well as to wash clothing and then return the items to the family.

After their release from the hospital, Thiessen family members stayed with different relatives. In the *Brainerd News* on June 26, 1941, is an entry that John Thiessen's sister and family, the Ed Claassens whom we met in chapter 14, had a shower for the Thiessen family on Friday, June 20. Many people responded and they received many useful gifts to help them start over.

John Thiessen's mother lived in a small house on the Jake Thiessen farm. That farm was also in the path of the tornado but the houses received only minor damage. Grandma Thiessen was temporarily relocated to the Bethel Home of the Aged in Newton and Uncle John and his children moved to her house until they could build a garage on their own farm. By July 24, they relocated to that garage while their new house was rebuilt on the foundation of the previous house using the same floor plan. The house was completed by the end of 1941. During the months that the family lived in the garage, there were additional thunderstorms. Obviously the family was very sensitized to stormy weather and very apprehensive and frightened. One evening when Uncle John was reading aloud from the Bible to his children, a storm passed over their farm. To create a calming influence, Uncle John just kept reading and reading and reading aloud until the storm had passed.

In the summer of 1972, while moving things out of this 1941 Thiessen house, a notebook used by Gilbert was found by his siblings. Gilbert had passed away in Spokane, Washington on October 7, 1962. In the notebook was a poem "Tornado," which he identified as "A review as I recall the tornado of June 8, 1941." The notebook entry was dated April 25, 1946. None of his siblings knew that he had written it.

Appendix 3

Tornado

The day was Sunday, the eighth of June
It had been raining ever since noon;
But then at night the sun broke through
Made the grass and flowers look like new.
So we all thought that the time was here
The rain was gone and the skies would clear.

Then after the chores our supper we ate
And since at that time it was not late
They gathered about in the dining room neat
While Herald and I were fixing a treat
As in the kitchen the popcorn we popped
Which really tasted what I called top.

And when at ten, it was bedtime you see
We noticed that it was lightning as hard as could be
But we were not troubled for we did not think
That within that night we were asked to drink
Of the cup of disaster, which made us sink
Because our chain of plans was broken in its strongest link.

And as we were sleeping on that fateful night
We were all awakened with sudden fright,
A queer sound of thunder so loud and strong
We were afraid there was something wrong.
And as our custom has always been
The folks called us down in storm and rain.

So we settle down on the floor to sleep,
Until the storm would pass on to the deep;
We were not there but just for a jerk
When everything began to perk—
When by the window we could see
Boards and rubbish fly, including a tree.

And oh! The wailful cry of Daddy that night
As he cried, "*a tornado*," and then what a fright,
Then the house began to raise and we did fly
We would grab for this board and brick as they flew by
But to no avail, nothing could help we knew
And we thought of a lot as they always do.

Appendix 3

> We thought of this and we thought of that
> And finally we were lying flat,
> On a pile of wreckage which used to be
> The home of Daddy, sisters, brothers and me,
> When during one minute the change had been made
> And I wondered where the others of the family lay.
>
> One by one we found our way
> To the ones who were hurt, and the place they lay.
> Bernard had a gash on his head we could see
> All seemed to be hurt but Lydia and me.
> Susan the worst, was in awful pain
> And our efforts to help were all in vain.
>
> After the ambulance finally came
> The doctor, too, Stalman by name,
> We finally got started on to Newton we did go
> The whole hospital force was on their toe.
> There the wounds were fixed with needle and thread
> And some of the others were put into bed.
>
> That is the way it all happened you see
> It still is fresh in my mind for me
> The lesson I learned was a very large dose
> Because the end of my life seemed very close.
> But now we see it was a God-sent disaster
> To draw us closer to our Savior and Master.
>
> —Gilbert Thiessen

On the next farm, belonging to the Abe Klaassens, some buildings were completely wrecked and others badly damaged. The Klaassens were visiting in Iowa, but two sons were at home and asleep upstairs. The house was moved off the foundation and sitting at a thirty to forty degree angle leaning against a large locust tree. Since the stairs were pushed to a crazy angle, the two boys, who were unharmed, were afraid to descend the steps fearing they would fall to the basement, so they escaped out the window on the side of the house with a rope made of knotted bed sheets. They then stumbled a half mile south through the muddy debris-strewn field to the John Thiessen farm and received help.

Continuing on its course, the tornado hit the Jake Thiessen farm next. An old tile silo remained standing while a new one and a large barn were demolished. Other buildings, including their house and the house of Grandma Thiessen, were somewhat damaged, but no one was injured. Across the road to the north at the "almost model farm home of Gus H. Regier," three walls of the house were left standing but the roof was blown off and most of the other buildings were destroyed. A newspaper reporter described the house as "a tangled mess of wreckage. How an individual or other animal life could have escaped death is either a freak of the storm or the hand of God." Further to the northeast, the Alfred Regier farm was badly damaged with a barn destroyed and other buildings leveled.

There were no farms in the path of the storm for the next two miles, only a few hedgerows, which were uprooted, until the tornado reached the Guy Scrivner farm. All Scrivner buildings were torn to pieces except one chicken house and one barn to the north. The windmill was twisted into a tangle. During the afternoon, the Guy Scrivners had celebrated their twenty-third wedding anniversary and Mrs. Scrivner's forty-first birthday. They had married on her birthday in 1918. Everyone was asleep in the one-story frame construction house when the tornado struck.

A neighbor, Charles W. Barker, stood in the door of his storm cave and watched from three-quarters of a mile north. The lightning in the clouds sporadically lit the area. He observed that the house "went to pieces like it had exploded when the wind hit it. It seemed to fly in every direction." He clearly recalled the sounds of the storm, the roar. Because the telephone lines were down, he could not contact his neighbors, so Charles walked to the Scrivner farm with a flashlight and lantern. Searching alone he located the victims. Mr. Scrivner was blown two hundred yards and was badly injured with a suspected broken leg. He was lying unconscious under a tractor for a time, and Charles pulled him by his legs out from under the debris. The falling rain revived him. He was taken to the Axtell Christian Hospital in Newton where x-rays indicated his leg was not fractured.

Charles continued his search for the others. Their bodies were scattered four hundred yards in the field north and east of the house. Killed were Edna Marie Krueger-Scrivner (Mrs. Guy Scrivner, age forty-one); Margarite Marie Jessen-Krueger (age sixty-four), Mrs. Scrivner's mother; Margaret Mary Scrivner (age twenty) and Betty Jean Scrivner (age sixteen), daughters; and Janet Lee Paulson (age three) daughter of neighbors Virgil and Marjorie Paulson, who was an overnight guest at the Scrivner home. The bodies were put on a pickup truck and driven to the mortuary in Whitewater with much difficulty due to debris and power lines on the road. Two other Scrivner children escaped injury because they were not home that night. Billy was visiting in Wichita and Hazel was in the Halstead Hospital for treatment.

The funeral for Mrs. Krueger was on June 11 at 10 a.m. in the St. Mary's Catholic Church in Newton with burial in St. Mary's Cemetery. Mrs. Scrivner, her two daughters, and Janet Paulson were eulogized on June 12 at 2 p.m. at the Federated Church in Whitewater with the Rev. Myron Settle officiating with the assistance of the Rev. J. A. Hartman. This mass funeral, as the tabloids called it, drew one thousand mourners. The church is small, but is reported to have accommodated four hundred in the sanctuary and Sunday school rooms. Another three hundred were seated in the basement and another three hundred stood on the lawn. Loudspeakers were used. As the two-hour service ended, a light rain continued for half an hour. During this time, those who stood on the lawn remained with bowed heads waiting their turn to join the viewing procession that marched for a full forty-five minutes beside the four flower-banked caskets. Janet Paulson was interred in the Newton Greenwood cemetery. Mrs. Scrivner and her daughters were interred in the Pleasant View Cemetery east of Elbing. The funeral procession to Elbing stretched for two miles. Rain continued and the friends of this family stood with bared heads while the rain fell quietly as the Rev. Settle officiated at the graveside services.

The tornado traveled further to the northeast passing between the two Leggett farms. Some of the buildings were damaged, but until the funnel dissipated near the Marion County line about five miles west of Burns, no other farms were struck nor was anyone else injured.

After its final touchdown, the tornado dissipated after sixteen minutes on the ground causing a quarter to a half mile swath of damage. S. E. Anderson, the Potwin Kansas Gas and Electric technician, was awakened by a bell ringing in his house indicating that there was a power outage. At the substation, an electric clock attached to the power line had stopped at 11:24 p.m. caused by the power line being blown down south of Whitewater in the Furley area. In the Peabody substation, the electric clock stopped at 11:40 p.m. when the power lines at the extreme north end of the tornado's path were blown down.

The residents of Whitewater and the farmers living adjacent to the path of the tornado heard the terrific roar of the funnel cloud and knew that a tragedy was occurring. The torrential rains made quagmires of roads, rescue crews walked in six inches of mud, and it was not until dawn that the full extent of the horror was realized.

The community rallied with assistance. Since most of the damaged farms in the last half of the storm were within the Mennonite church community, this whole community provided assistance. Relatives and friends opened their homes, providing lodging and food. Assistance was provided for rebuilding or repairing houses and farm buildings, as well as with farmwork to speed the return to agricultural productivity of those that experienced devastation. Most farms were covered with some insurance, with the largest carriers being Mennonite Aid Plan, Midland Mutual, and Farmers Alliance.

The Independent on June 12, 1941, ran a call for volunteers for cleanup at the Henry Scrivner, Arnold Zuercher, and Louis Claassen farms. This was organized by a relief committee of the Whitewater Chamber of Commerce. Also, an invitation was printed inviting the community to an aid shower for Guy Scrivner in Elbing. The Red Cross organization of Butler County conferred with their representatives in Whitewater, advertising that the Red Cross stood ready to be of service to those in need. After the local committee "made an intensive survey of the disaster," the American Red Cross provided $250.00 "in the rehabitation work."

The bereaved families expressed their appreciation to the community for sympathy, kindness, floral tokens, and cards with individual notes collected into one column in the July 19 issue of *The Independent*. In that same newspaper there was a heartfelt expression of appreciation for help from Chris Thierstein, the father of C. B. Thierstein Jr. He also apologized to the community volunteers because on the Tuesday morning after the tornado, Chris Thierstein had asked the men who were voluntarily beginning to clean up the fields around the Thierstein farm to stop their benevolent activity. C. B. Thierstein Jr. who had been hospitalized with injuries after he had stumbled in the darkness to the road to get help for his family, had not seen his destroyed farm in daylight and wanted to view it before cleanup began. C. B. and his family were finally able to view their farm on Thursday after the memorial service for Myron Keith. Chris Thierstein concluded his expression of thanks

Appendix 3

with "Then on Friday when a great crowd of sympathizing men again came to clean up after the family had seen all the disaster, I could hardly do anything, only to see the eager men working and several times could hardly withhold tears caused by the love of the community and so once more I want to thank the whole community and especially those that have taken active part in the aid, for their dear Lord [will] richly reward everyone."

The following week in the June 26, 1941 *The Independent*, all families touched by the tornado collectively thanked the community. "We hereby express our sincere and heartfelt thanks and appreciation to our many neighbors, friends, and relatives, far and near, for their sympathy, encouragement and help in taking care of the wounded and cleaning up the chaos caused by the tornado."

On June 15, 1941, the Sunday afternoon following the tornado, several thousand people from across Kansas wanted to see the aftermath of the storm. It was reported that twelve to twenty cars were parked near each of the destroyed farms and one hundred fifty to two hundred cars parked at the Guy Scrivner home. At all farms, volunteer cleanup work was evident with huge piles of wrecked lumber being visible in the fields. Repairs to buildings also were evident. At my parents' farm, Mother had a notebook and siblings asked each spectator who walked past the house to sign their name; nearly one thousand names were entered and only three people refused to sign.

After tornados there always are observations that seem inexplicable. Lewis and Ruth Claassen found a set of glass mixing bowls all nested together at least seventy yards from the house without a chip or a crack. A bedroom slipper of theirs was found three miles northeast of their place. The high school graduation certificate of Marie Penner was found near Cedar Point, Kansas about forty miles northeast of Whitewater. At the Thierstein farm, a barrel used as a hog waterer, situated on a cement slab between the barn and the silo, was left standing while the barn and the silo were destroyed. The poultry house on the Guy Scrivner farm, which was located a short distance north of the house, was not disturbed; there were four hundred fifty young chickens in it. The house and other buildings beyond the chicken house were totally destroyed.

Some time later, the Bank of Whitewater received a card from a H. J. Hooper stating that eight miles southeast of Alta Vista his son had picked up a canceled Whitewater Bank check written by Gus. H. Regier Jr. Alta Vista, Kansas is located northeast of Harrington. The wind had carried the canceled check for nearly one hundred miles. Also, Charley W. Schoof who lived ten miles southwest of Council Grove in Morris County sent a letter to Gus H. Regier Jr. stating that while plowing, "Today, I found two old checks dated July 1934 and December 1935, one $17 and one $5.00 drawn on the Whitewater bank with your signature. Also, I found a Kodak picture of a bride & groom. A neighbor found a group picture. I thought you and your neighbors would be interested in knowing how far these articles were carried." He offered to return these items.

There also was a letter from L. A. Hanna addressed to Mrs. Claassen:

> On the 10th of this month, I was out in my pasture fixing fence and I found a paper on which was printed a program of the Emmaus Young People's Society of Christian Endeavor for April 3, 1938, Whitewater, Kansas.
>
> This program had not been folded so I came to the conclusion that the tornado of last Sunday night had carried the paper to this location. Then too our neighbor found a piece of white painted siding and some shingles on his farm.
>
> The reason I am writing this to you is that your name appears as pianist on the program.

Lydia Thiessen, an officer of the group, had on file a notebook of these programs but her pages were punched for a ring binder. The paper that was found apparently was not punched, so from which house it originated is not clear.

A cattle broker of the Kansas City firm of Maxwell-Furnish Commission was traveling in the Topeka area where a client said that he had found a picture lying in their pasture and asked if the broker recognized the people in the photo. The broker who did business in our area and was familiar with the families involved in the tornado, recognized it as a photograph of the John Thiessen family and returned it to them.

This tornado was imbedded in the poetry that Mother wrote. "In Kansas on the Farm" in chapter 2, she wrote "When the thunder clouds are rolling and the twisters have their way." In "The Pair of Owls" in chapter 4, the granary blew away where these two owls preferred to roost at night. In chapter 5, the twenty-fifth anniversary of Susan's employment with permanent disabilities that were incurred during the

Appendix 3

tornado is celebrated. The twenty-fifth wedding anniversary poems of the Alfred Regiers and Gus Regiers in chapter 13 mention the destruction of their farms. This is also true for the fiftieth wedding anniversary poem for the Jake Thiessens in chapter 14. Additionally, Mother wrote poems for persons years before they experienced the tornado like the Jacob Regiers in chapter 13 and John Thiessen in chapter 6. She also wrote poems for people who had experienced the tornado but did not mention it, as in the wedding poems for Lydia Thiessen and Bernard Thiessen in chapter 12.

In addition to the physical damage, the tornado truly tore a swath through the heart of the community my mother called her own, including the farm that was a part of her cherished heritage.

Appendix 4

Eye on the World

THERE ARE MANY GOOD reasons why Mother had incredible recall of historical facts, family events, and dates. She was a very talented woman; however, she also used information techniques that embellished her memory. She actively wrote down observations that she wanted to reference later. In her world without a computer and limited paper, she would use scraps of paper or the backs of business letters for a writing medium. These were then stored in a drawer in the farmhouse or a bedroom dresser drawer.

A special tool that augmented record keeping for Mother was the gift of a box camera from her brother-in-law John Thiessen. John married Mother's sister Helene in 1917 and lived in Great-grandfather's original house on the Harder farm until 1926. (See figure 7.) Great-grandmother had passed away in 1916, vacating that house. No doubt, John considered this camera a gift to keep his energetic younger sister-in-law creatively challenged as she grew to maturity in rural Kansas.

Looking at the pictures, the earliest photos date from the early 1920s. Mother's niece and nephew, Lydia and Bernard as toddlers, born in 1918 and 1920 respectively, were some of Mother's first photographic subjects. Mother had the camera in 1923 when Mother accompanied the John Thiessens on a trip to Colorado Springs, Colorado.

The most ingenious use of the camera was for a self-portrait of Mother and her new family taken in September 1928. By tying the camera to the picket fence and attaching a string to the shutter trip lever, Father could operate the camera with his left hand.

This was the only camera that Mother every used. The rolls of Kodak film allowed for eight exposures. Exposed rolls were taken to

Appendix 4

Newton for shipment to be developed and returned in two to four weeks. It was with this camera that Mother created a photographic history of her family and the world around her.

Figure 54
Marie's No. 2A Brownie Camera. The shutter was controlled with the lever on the right and the manual film advance was achieved by turning the knob at the lower middle of the camera. To maintain the integrity of the original box for the camera, Marie sewed the corners with thread and then glued strips of cloth over. Private collection. Source: Author's file.

Appendix 4

Figure 55
Marie taking a picture of her family in September 1928 when Hildegard was six months old. Source: Author's file.

Chronological List of Poems

by Marie Harder Epp

1929—*Für Carl J. Claassen zum Wassertopf*

1929—*Für Paul U. Claassen zum Buttertermameter*

1930—*Für John & Elsies Fruit Shower, 17 Januar 1930*

1930—*Zu John T. Reimers Fruit Shower, 17 Januar 1930*

1930—*Zu Geburtstag von Onkel Christ Thierstein, 17 Dezember 1930*

1930—*Rückerinnerungen*

1932—*Für Ernest Wiebe zu Deckel, April 1932*

1932—*Für Schwager Hans Thiessen, 15 Mai 1932*

1932—*Für Edna zum Handtuch, 26 Mai 1932*

1932—*Zu Jacob J. Regiers Silberhochzeit, 24 Oktober 1932*

1932—*Für Herman A. Wiebes, 12 November 1932*

1932—*Für John Thiessen zur Kammbox, 24 Dezember 1932*

1933—*Für Marilyn Wiebe, 13 Januar 1933*

1933—*Für Jake Wiebes, 17 Juni 1933*

1933—*Zu Onkel Gerhard Regiers Goldenehochzeit, 25 Oktober 1933*

1934—*Zu Großmutters Erinnerungs 100ste Geburtstag, 6 Juli 1934*

1935—*Für Edward Regiers Hochzeit, 12 Dezember 1935*

1937—*Jake Regiers zum 30ten Hochzeitstag, 24 Oktober 1937*

1937—*Zu Weihnacten*

1938—*Albert & Bertha zu Hochzeit, Erste Gedicht, 16 März 1938*

by Marie Harder Epp

1938—*Albert & Bertha zu Hochzeit, Zweite Gedicht, 16 März 1938*

1938—*Für Onkel Bernhard & Tante Justine, 27 Juli 1938*

1938—Bilingual Poem

1939—*Zu Albert Entz & Frieda Busenitz Hochzeit, 12 Januar 1939*

1940—*Für Papa's Goldenerhochzeitstag, 6 März 1940*

1940—Farewell to Uncle Lester and Aunt Agnes, August 1940

1941—*Die Beiden Eulen*

1942—*Zu Großpapas 100sten Geburtstag, 16 Oktober 1942*

1943—*Goldenehochzeit von Onkel Johannes & Tante Emilie, 26 Oktober 1943*

1944—*Zu Onkel John Harders 90sten Geburtstag, 11 Januar 1944*

1944—*Für Waldo & Lydia, 31 Augu'st 1944*

1944—*Für Onkel Abraham Entz 100sten Geburtstag, 27 November 1944*

1944—Emil Wiebes' Silver Wedding, October 30 1944

1945—*Gedichte Aufgesagt für Anna Regier am 29 Juli 1945*

1946—*Für Waldimar & Ester Wiebe, 25 Juli 1946*

1947—*Für Geburtstag von Tante Herman Dyck, 25 April 1947*

1947—Our Feathered Friends, May 7, 1947

1947—For the Wedding of Gerhard & Olga Busenitz, May 31, 1947

1947—Welcome, December 25, 1947

1948—For Sister Helen Ruth's Fiftieth Birthday, April 20, 1948

1948—Prayer for Berean Academy, May 28, 1948

1949—For the Wedding of Bernard & Ruby, June 16, 1949

1950—Golden Years, June 7, 1950

1950—Twenty-fifth Wedding Anniversary of Henry & Maria Wiebe, November 6, 1950

1951—These Seventy-five Years, July 8, 1951

1951—Twenty-fifth Anniversary of Nursing for Aunt Helen Ruth, September 28, 1951

by Marie Harder Epp

1951—Wedding of Aunt Louise Entz & Uncle Howard Wedel, October 10, 1951

1952—*Silberhochzeitsgedicht, 8 April 1952*

1952—*Der Vierzigster, 12 November 1952*

1952—For Ed Claassens' Golden Wedding Anniversary, December 18, 1952

1953—The Wedding Poem, July 31, 1953

1954—Hitherto the Lord Has Helped Us, October 3, 1954

1954—Wedding Reception of Elvin and Ann Wiebe

1955—Anniversary of the Berean Bible Church, June 5, 1955

1956—Margaret Ann Tannahill's Wedding Invitation, March 16, 1956

1956—Dr. & Mrs. Mann's Farewell, August 30, 1956

1957—For Lois Roth's Farewell, September 1, 1957

1957—Alfred Regiers' Silver Wedding, November 24, 1957

1958—For Eldon Wohlgemuths' Wedding Reception, September 7, 1958

1959—Willie Busenitz Silver Wedding Anniversary, May, 1959

1959—For Marline Dyck and Larry Lutz, May 2, 1959

1959—In Memory of my Father, May 21, 1959

1959—Edna Regier and Martin Graber Wedding, August 4, 1959

1959—Delora Busenitz for her Grandmother's Birthday, November 1959

1959—For J. E. Thiessens' Golden Anniversary, November 23, 1959

1960—Gus & Edna Regier's Silver Wedding Anniversary, September 12, 1960

1960—*Die Kuh ist Frisch*

1962—Herman A. Wiebes' Golden Wedding, (Poems I, II, and III), November 27, 1962

1963—Edgar Busenitzs' Silver Wedding Anniversary, March 1, 1963

1963—For Albert Busenitzs' Twenty-fifth Wedding Anniversary, March 16, 1963

by Marie Harder Epp

1963—Herman and Elvira Klaassen's Twenty-fifth Wedding Anniversary, November 19, 1963

1965—Waldo Harders' Twenty-fifth Wedding Anniversary, August 28, 1965

1965—Henry Wiebes' Fortieth Wedding Anniversary, October 29, 1965

1965—B. E. Busenitz Silver Wedding Anniversary, December 30, 1965

1967—For Willie Harders' Golden Wedding Anniversary, May 11, 1967

1967—Welcome Poem, December 1967

1968—Mrs. Ed Harder's Eightieth Birthday, February 6, 1968

1969—Berean Academy School Song, April 1969

1970—Oct 21, '70

1971—Fifty-fourth Birthday of Rev. Amstutz, February 17, 1971

1971—Berean Academy, 1946–1971

1972—The Home, Willard Thiessen Silver Wedding Anniversary, March 12, 1972

1972—*Polterabend* (Nuptial Eve) For Sharon Graber and Brad Graber, July 1972

1973—Della Busenitz and Brian Loewen Wedding

1975—Table Grace I, II, and III, September 3, 1975

1977—J. S. Harders' Golden Wedding Anniversary, June 28, 1977

1977—*Polterabend* (Nuptial Eve) For Clarence and Twila Busenitz, August 4, 1977

1977—Melvin Claassens' Silver Wedding, August 14, 1977

1978—Susan's Twenty-fifth Anniversary with the "Go Ye" Mission, January 8, 1978

1978—Pattern for Living

1981—Father and Son Banquet, Berean Academy, February 21, 1981

1981—For Walter Harder's Birthday, October 4, 1981

by Marie Harder Epp

    1984—Gregory and Caroline Epp Wedding, April 21, 1984

    1985—Steven and Kimberly Epp Wedding, December 28, 1985

    1987—For Lisa Harder, June 27, 1987

    1987—Michael and Corinne Cressman Wedding, June 27, 1987

    1991—James and Lisa Epp Wedding, August 24, 1991

    Undated Doughnuts

    Undated Golden Wedding Anniversary of Ted Nickel's Parents

    Undated Happy Birthday Song

    Undated In Butler County on the Farm

    Undated Just a Little Wish

    Undated Kansas

    Undated Kansas Certified Seed

    Undated Verses two and three for *My God and I*

Bibliography

Chapter 1

Claassen, Ernest, et al., eds. "90th Anniversary." In *History of the Emmaus Mennonite Church: Whitewater, Kansas, 1876–1976*. Hillsboro, KS: M. B. Publishing House, 1978.

Epp, Marie Harder. *Lest We Forget*. Whitewater, KS: n.p., 1992.

———. "Reasons for Immigration (The Decision)." Unpublished document in author's collection, 1951.

Hartzler, Arlene, and John Gaeddert. *The Children's Hymnary*. Newton, KS: Faith and Life Press, 1967.

Wobus, Reverend R. *Lesebuch für Evangelische Schulen, Unterstufe*. Chicago: Eden, 1885.

———. *Schreib=Lese=Fibel mit besonderer Berüchtigung der Lautiermethode*. Chicago: Eden, 1885.

Chapter 2

Dick, Gary. (Butler Rural Electric Cooperative.) In discussion with the author, October 21, 2006.

Emmaus Mennonite Church. *In Commemoration of Seventy-Five Years in America, 1876–1951*. Whitewater, KS: n.p., 1951.

Epp, John, Jr., Mrs. "Golden Years." *The Independent* (Whitewater, KS), June 15, 1950.

———. "In Butler County on the Farm." *The Kansas City Daily Drovers Telegram*, September 12, 1961.

Epp, Marie Harder. *Lest We Forget*. Whitewater, KS: n.p., 1992.

Everhart, Mike. "Oceans of Kansas Paleontology." December 1996. Online: http://www.oceansofkansas.com.

Harder, Agnes Wiebe. *The History of Brainerd*. Whitewater, KS: n.p., 1985.

Kansas Geological Survey. "Kansas Geologic Timetable." Online: http://www.kgs.ku.edu/Extension/geotopics/timeChart.html.

K-State Research and Extension. "Climatic Maps of Kansas." Online: http://www.oznet.k-state.edu/wdl/climate/climate2.asp.

Miner, Craig. *Kansas: The History of the Sunflower State, 1854–2000*. Lawrence: University Press of Kansas, 2002.

Wohlgemuth, Marge, ed. *Whitewater, Kansas: 1890-1990*. Shawnee Mission, KS: Kes-Print, 1990.

Bibliography

Chapter 3

Arndt, Karl J. R., and May E. Olson. *The German Language Press of the Americas, 1732-1968: History and Bibliography*. Vol 1. Munich: Verlag Dokumentation, 1976.
Blakeslee, Donald. In discussion with the author, August 13, 2008.
Claassen, Ernest. *Abraham Claassen: Vistula to Plum Grove*. Whitewater, KS: n.p., 1975.
Claassen, Ernest, et al., eds. *History of the Emmaus Mennonite Church: Whitewater, Kansas, 1876-1976*. Hillsboro, KS: M. B. Publishing House, 1978.
Department of Anthropology, Wichita State University. "Artifacts of Kansas." Online: http://www.ksartifacts.info.
Doerkson, Darrel. In discussion with the author, February 18, 2007.
Driedger, Abraham. *Heubuden Church Records*. Unpublished document. 2003.
Dyck, D. Frederick. *Jacob J. Dyck: Am Trakt to America*. Washington, KS: n.p., 2000.
Dyck, Peter. "Unsere dritte Reise nach Kansas am 10 Oktober, 1876." *Mennonitsche Geschichtsblätter* 11 (1954): 43-47.
Emmaus Mennonite Church. *In Commemoration of Seventy-Five Years in America, 1876-1951*. Whitewater, KS: n.p., 1951.
Entz, Selma Thiessen. In discussion with the author, April 10, 2007.
Entz, Wynona Claassen. In discussion with the author, March 15, 2007.
Epp, John, Jr., Mrs. "These Seventy-Five Years." *In Commemoration of Seventy-Five Years in America, 1876-1951*. Whitewater, KS: Emmaus Mennonite Church, 1951.
Epp, Marie Harder. *Lest We Forget*. Whitewater, KS: n.p., 1992.
Esau, Elbert. In discussion with the author, July 12, 2007.
Harder, Agnes Wiebe. *The History of Brainerd*. Whitewater, KS: n.p., 1985.
Harder, Gustav. "Obituary of Bernhard Harder, 1811-1900." *Christlicher Bundesbote* (Newton, KS). September 20, 1900.
Hunsicker, Henry A. "Among the Kansas Mennonites." Letter in *Der Vulksfreunden Beubachter* (Lancaster, PA) August 5, 1877. Translated by John F. Schmidt in *Mennonite Life* 40/1 (March 1985): 9-11.
Jantzen, Mark. "'Whoever Will Not Defend His Homeland Should Leave It!' German Conscription and Prussian Mennonite Emigration to the Great Plains, 1860-1890." *Mennonite Life* 58/3 (September 2003): n.p. Online: http://www.bethelks.edu/mennonitelife/2003Sept/jantzen.php.
Janzen, Reinhild Kauenhoven, and John Janzen. *Mennonite Furniture: A Migrant Tradition (1766-1910)*. Intercourse, PA: Good Books, 1991.
Jennings, Bob. "The Last Indian Raid on Kansas Soil." *Kansas Country Living* 58/9 (September 2008): 8, 30-33.
Kaufman, Edmund G., ed. *General Conference Mennonite Pioneers*. North Newton, KS: Bethel College, 1973.
———. "Harder, Gustav (1856-1923)." In *The Mennonite Encyclopedia*, edited by Cornelius Krahn, 2:660. Scottdale, PA: The Mennonite Publishing House, 1956.
Kaufman, Edna [Ramseyer]. *Melting Pot of Mennonite Cookery, 1874-1974*. North Newton, KS: Bethel College Women's Association, 1974.
Loewen, Royden. *Hidden Worlds: Revisiting the Mennonite Migrants of the 1870s*. North Newton, KS: Bethel College, 2001.
Miner, Craig. *Kansas: The History of the Sunflower State, 1854-2000*. Lawrence: University Press of Kansas, 2002.
Murray, Elmo. *Welcome to Elbing*. Elbing, KS: n.p., 2007.

Bibliography

Neufeldt, V., and D. B. Guralnik. *Webster's New World Dictionary of American English, Third College Edition.* Cleveland: New World, 1988.
O'Brien, Patricia J. *Archeology in Kansas.* Lawrence, KS: University of Kansas, 1984.
Penner, Horst. *Die ost-und-westpreussischen Mennoniten.* Vol 1. Berkely, CA: Mennonitischer Geschichtsverein, 1978.
Penner, Mil. *Section 27: A Century on a Family Farm.* Lawrence, KS: University Press of Kansas, 2002.
Potts, George, and Bob Gress. "American Bison." n.p. Online: http//www.gpnc.org/ambison.htm.
Regier, Arnold, and Helen Regier. *Elbing—Next Stop.* Elbing, KS: n.p., 1994.
Schmidt, C. B. "Kansas Mennonite Settlements, 1877." *Mennonite Life* 25/2 (June 1970): 51-58.
Thiesen, John D. *Prussian Roots/Kansas Branches: A History of First Mennonite Church of Newton.* Newton, KS: Historical Committee of First Mennonite Church, 1986.
Thiessen, Susan. *Our Roots: "A Goodly Heritage".* Tahlequah, OK: The "Go Ye" Mission Print Shop, 1986.
Torline, John. In discussion with the author, December 13, 2007.
U.S. Census Bureau. "1880 United States Census Household Record." Online: www.familysearch.org/Eng/Search/census/household_record.asp?.
Walters, George J. *Wir Wollen Deutsche Bleiben.* Kansas City, MO: Halcyon, 1982.
Waltner, John D. "The Process of Civilization on the Kansas Frontier: Newton, KS. 1871-1873." Master's thesis, University of Kansas, 1971.
Wohlgemuth, Marge, ed. *Whitewater, Kansas: 1890-1990.* Shawnee Mission, KS: Kes-Print, 1990.
Zornow, Frank. *Kansas: A History of the Jayhawk State.* Norman: University of Oklahoma Press, 1957.

Chapter 4

Hunsicker, Henry A. "Among the Kansas Mennonites." Letter in *Der Vulksfreunden Beubachter* (Lancaster, PA) August 5, 1877. Translated by John F. Schmidt in *Mennonite Life* 40/1 (March 1985): 9-11.
Pearson, T. Gilbert. *Birds of America.* Garden City, NY: Garden City Publishing Company, 1936.
Peterson, Roger Tory, and Virginia Marie Peterson. *A Field Guide to the Birds of Eastern and Central North America.* 5th ed. New York: Houghton Mifflin, 2002.
Voth, Nada. In discussion with the author, April 15, 2006.

Chapter 5

"Are Injured in Tornado." *Wichita Eagle,* June 9, 1941.
"Attends Easter Service at Emmaus Church." *The Independent* (Whitewater, KS), April 5, 1942.
Entz, Walter. In discussion with the author, August 30, 2007.
Epp, Marie Harder. *Lest We Forget.* Whitewater, KS: n.p., 1992.
Klaassen, Lydia Thiessen. In discussion with the author, December 6, 2006.

Bibliography

"Miss Susie Thiessen Slowly Regaining Strength." *The Independent* (Whitewater, KS), July 24, 1941.
Thiessen, Susan. In discussion with the author, December 4, 2006.
Thiessen, Susan. *Our Roots: "A Goodly Heritage"*. Tahlequah, OK: The "Go Ye" Mission Print Shop, 1986.
"Tornado Sweeping Through Nearby Community Leaves Only Death and Destruction in its Wake, Cutting Path One-fourth Mile Wide and Ten Miles Long; Killing Seven; Injuring Eight; Rising Near Butler-Marian Line, Takes Sixteen Minutes to Travel Ten Miles." *Potwin Ledger*, June 12, 1941.
"Tornado Sweeps Through Kansas, Eagle Cameras Cover Deadly Tornado." *Wichita Eagle*, June 9, 1941.
"Tornado Takes Eight Lives Sunday Night—Injures Many Others." *The Independent* (Whitewater, KS), June 12, 1941.

Chapter 6

Epp, Marie Harder. *Lest We Forget*. Whitewater, KS: n.p., 1992.

Chapter 7

Epp, Marie Harder. *Lest We Forget*. Whitewater, KS: n.p., 1992.
Rogers, Maureen. *Herbalpedia 2004*. CD-ROM. Silver Springs, PA: The Herb Growing and Marketing Network, 2004.

Chapter 8

Loewen, Royden. *Hidden Worlds: Revisiting the Mennonite Migrants of the 1870s*. North Newton, KS: Bethel College, 2001.
Peterson, E. H. *The Message: The Bible in Contemporary Language*. Colorado Springs: NavPress, 2002.

Chapter 10

German Wedding Traditions: Poltrabend. Online: http://www.wedding-ideas.org/?p=3.
Voth, N. J. *Mennonite Foods and Folkways from South Russia*. Vol 2. Intercourse, PA: Good Books, 1991.

Chapter 11

"Advertisement for Midwest Deutsche Oktoberfest." *Kansas Traveler*, (Summer 2007): 4.
Barkman, Sue. "Mennonites, Food, and Hospitality." *Mennonite Heritage Village: Preserving Our Heritage* 11/1 (July 2003).

Epp, Marie Harder. *Lest We Forget*. Whitewater, KS: n.p., 1992.
Gaeddert, Joyce Regier. *The Bernhard Regier Genealogy, 1669-1973*. Topeka, KS: n,p., 1973.
Keys, Linda. J. *The Family of Gerhard and Anna Regier, 1852-2001*. Topeka, KS: n.p., 2001.
Miner, Craig. *Kansas: The History of the Sunflower State, 1854-2000*. Lawrence: University Press of Kansas, 2002.

Chapter 12

Emmaus Mennonite Church. "Wedding Dress Display Guide." For the 125th Anniversary of the Emmaus Mennonite Church, Whitewater, KS. 2001.
Epp, Marie Harder. *Lest We Forget*. Whitewater, KS: n.p., 1992.
Graber, Edith Claassen. "Gustav Harder." *Mennonite Life* 7/4, (December 1952): 176-79.
Harder, Gus. In discussion with the author, March 6, 2007.
Kaufman, Ed G. *General Conference Mennonite Pioneers*. North Newton, KS: Bethel College, 1973.
———. "Harder, Gustav (1856-1923)." In *The Mennonite Encyclopedia*, edited by Cornelius Krahn, 2:660. Scottdale, PA: The Mennonite Publishing House, 1956.
Regier, Elfriede. "When the Sky Fell: Recollections of June 8, 1941." In Frederic Remington Area Historical Society Library, Whitewater, KS. January 1982.
Riley, Glenda. *The Female Frontier*. Lawrence: University Press of Kansas, 1988.
Spahn, Martin. "The Thirty Years War," *Catholic Encyclopedia* 14 (1912): n.p. Online: http://www.newadvent.org/cathen/14648b.htm.
Wiebe, Wilbert. In discussion with the author, April 7, 2008.

Chapter 13

"Buying Liberty Bonds is not an Act of Charity." *The Independent* (Whitewater, KS), June 17, 1917.
Claassen, Ernest, et al., eds. *History of the Emmaus Mennonite Church: Whitewater, Kansas, 1876-1976*. Hillsboro, KS: M. B. Publishing House, 1978.
Emmaus Mennonite Church. *In Commemoration of Seventy-Five Years in America, 1876-1951*. Whitewater, KS: n.p., 1951.
Emmaus Mennonite Church. "Wedding Dress Display Guide." For the 125th Anniversary of the Emmaus Mennonite Church, Whitewater, KS. 2001.
Entz, Margaret. "War Bond Drives and the Kansas Mennonite Response." *Mennonite Life* 30/3 (September 1975): 4-9.
Epp, Albert H. "Letter to the Editor." In *Mennonite Weekly Review* (Newton, KS). October 5, 1995.
Epp, Helen Ruth. *My Mother—1971*. Unpublished document.
Epp, Johann. *Brief Sketches of my Life*. Unpublished document. February 1923.
Epp, Johann. *Communion Sunday*. Unpublished document. May 29, 1921.
Epp, John, Jr., Mrs. "Golden Years." *The Independent* (Whitewater, KS), June 15, 1950.
Epp, Marie Harder. *Lest We Forget*. Whitewater, KS: n.p., 1992.
Foerster, Norman, ed. *American Poetry and Prose*. Boston: Houghton Mifflin, 1957.

Bibliography

Friesen, Wilma Harder. In discussion with the author, January 3, 2008.

Gaeddert, Joyce Regier. *The Bernhard Regier Genealogy, 1669–1973*. Topeka, KS: n.p., 1973.

Harder, Agnes Wiebe. *The History of Brainerd*. Whitewater, KS: n.p., 1985.

Harder, Bernhard. "Oral Interview on the American Flag Incident at the Harder Homestead, 1918," *Mennonite Life* 57/3 (September 2002). Online: http://www.bethelks.edu/mennonitelife/2002sept/harder-interview.php.

Harder, Gustav. "Obituary of Bernhard Harder 1864–1904." *Christlicher Bundesbote* (Newton, KS), May 19, 1904.

Homan, Gerlof, D. *American Mennonites and the Great War 1914–1918*. Scottdale, PA: Herald, 1994.

Hostetler, John A. *Hutterite Society*. Baltimore: The Johns Hopkins University Press, 1974.

Jantzen, Johann. *Diary of Johann Jantzen*. Beatrice, NE: n.p., 1887.

Juhnke, James C. "Mob Violence and Kansas Mennonites in 1918." *Kansas Historical Quarterly* 43/3 (Autumn 1997): 334–50. Online: http://www.kshs.org/p/kansas-historical-quarterly-mob-violence-and-kansas-mennonites-in-1918/13278.

———. *A People of Two Kingdoms: The Political Acculturation of the Kansas Mennonites*. Newton, KS: Faith and Life, 1975.

Keys, Linda. J. *The Family of Gerhard and Anna Regier, 1852–2001*. Topeka, KS: n.p., 2001.

———. "Johann P. Epp, 1862–1943." n.p., 1995.

Mennonite Central Committee. "Mennonite Relief Sale, April 7 & 8, 1995." Flier. Newton, KS: Mennonite Central Committee, 1995.

Miner, Craig. *Kansas: The History of the Sunflower State, 1854–2000*. Lawrence: University Press of Kansas, 2002.

Peachey, Titus, and Linda Gehman Peachey. *Seeking Peace*. Intercourse, PA: Good Books, 1991.

Peters, A. B. "A Tribute to Johannes P. Epp." *Christlicher Bundesbote* (Newton, KS), September 1943.

Prieb, Wesley J. "The Man behind the Tractors." *Mennonite Weekly Review* (Newton, KS), August 24, 1995.

Schrag, Paul. "Who's Fundamental?" Editorial. *Mennonite Weekly Review* (Newton, KS), June 18, 2007.

Stucky, Harley J., ed. *The Centennial Treasury of Recipes, Swiss (Volhynian) Mennonites*. North Newton, KS: Mennonite Press, 1973.

"That the People May Know." *The Independent* (Whitewater, KS), May 2, 1918.

Thiesen, John D. *Prussian Roots, Kansas Branches: A History of First Mennonite Church of Newton*. Newton, KS: First Mennonite Church, 1986.

"U.S. Liberty Bond Button is Your Badge of Honor." *The Independent* (Whitewater, KS), June 17, 1917.

VanDyke, Jim. *More Than a Pile of Stones: 50 Years of Berean Academy in Elbing, Kansas 1946–1996*. Elbing, KS: n.p. 1995.

Zion Mennonite Church. *Centennial Reflections: Zion 100*. Elbing, KS: n.p., 1983.

Chapter 14

Ensz, Roland H. "Whitewater, Kansas: Past and Present." Unpublished manuscript. North Newton, KS: Mennonite Library and Archives, Bethel College, 1954.
Epp, Helen Ruth. "My Mother—1971." n.p.
Epp, Marie Harder. *Lest We Forget*. Whitewater, KS: n.p., 1992.
Epp, Melvin D. "The Heritage of a Garden: Replicating a West Prussian Garden among the Tall Grasses of Kansas." *Mennonite Life* 63/2 (Fall 2008). Online: http://www.bethelks.edu/mennonitelife/2008fall/epp.garden.phg.
Gaeddert, Joyce Regier. *The Bernhard Regier Genealogy, 1669-1973*. Topeka, KS: n.p., 1973.
Harder, Agnes Wiebe. *The History of Brainerd*. Whitewater, KS: n.p., 1985.
"Obituary of Justine Bergmann Harder 1834-1916." *Christlicher Bundesbote* (Newton, KS). April 13, 1916.
Thiesen, John D. *Prussian Roots, Kansas Branches: A History of First Mennonite Church of Newton*. Newton, KS: Historical Committee of First Mennonite Church, 1986.
Thiessen, Susan. *Our Roots, "A Goodly Heritage"*. Tahlequah, OK: The "Go Ye" Mission Print Shop, 1986.
Wohlgemuth, Marge, ed. *Whitewater, Kansas: 1890-1990*. Shawnee Mission, KS: Kes-Print, 1990.
Zion Mennonite Church. *Centennial Reflections: Zion 100*. Elbing, KS: Zion Mennonite Church, 1983.

Chapter 16

Dyck, A. J. "Hoffnungsau in Kansas." *Mennonite Life* 4/4 (October 1949): 18-19, 46.
Gaeddert, Dale A. "Biography of Abraham J. Dyck." Unpublished manuscript. North Newton, KS: Mennonite Library and Archives, Bethel College, 1959.
"Rev A. J. Dyck: In Memorium." *Mennonite Weekly Review*. Mar 21, 1959: 8.
Toevs, Bertha. In discussion with the author, September 12, 2006.

Chapter 17

Ensz, Roland H. "Whitewater, Kansas: Past and Present." Unpublished manuscript. North Newton, KS: Mennonite Library and Archives, Bethel College, 1954.
Epp, John, Jr., Mrs. "Prayer for Berean Academy." *The Berean*, 1/2 (1948): 5.
Epp, Marie Harder. *Lest We Forget*. Whitewater, KS: n.p., 1992.
Harder, Agnes Wiebe. *The History of Brainerd*. Whitewater, KS: n.p., 1985.
Peterson, E. H. *The Message: The Bible in Contemporary Language*. Colorado Springs: NavPress, 2002.
Rempel, Herman. *Kjenn jie noch Plautdietsch? A Mennonite Low German Dictionary*. Winnipeg, MB: Mennonite Literary Society, 1984. Online: http://www.mennolink.org/doc/lg/.
Rice, John R. *Bobbed Hair, Bossy Wives, and Women Preachers*. Murfreeboro, TN: Sword of the Lord, 1941.
Sharp, John. (Historian, Hesston College). In discussion with the author, September 27, 2006.

Bibliography

Thiessen, Jack. *Mennonite Low German Dictionary*. Madison: University of Wisconsin Press, 2003.
VanDyke, Jim. *More Than a Pile of Stones: 50 Years of Berean Academy in Elbing, Kansas 1946-1996*. Elbing, KS: n.p., 1995.
Wedel, Peter J. *The Story of Bethel College*. North Newton, KS: Mennonite Press, 1954.
Wohlgemuth, Marge, ed. *Whitewater, Kansas: 1890-1990*. Shawnee Mission, KS: Kes-Print, 1990.

Chapter 18

Claassen, Ernest, et al., eds. *History of the Emmaus Mennonite Church: Whitewater, Kansas, 1876-1976*. Hillsboro, KS: M.B. Publishing House, 1978.
Clinesmith, Lois. In discussion with the author, September 26, 2006.
Harder, Gerhard. In discussion with the author, September 26, 2006.
The Holy Bible. New International Version. Grand Rapids: Zondervan, 1984.
Mennonite Central Committee. "Mennonite Relief Sale, April 7 & 8, 1995." Flier. Newton, KS: Mennonite Central Committee, 1995.

Chapter 19

Claassen, Milton. In discussion with the author, October 5, 2006.
Claassen, Ralph. In discussion with the author, September 20, 2007.
Schuler, Steve F. "Producing Kansas Certified Seed." Online: http://www.kscrop.org/resources/How%20to%20Produce%20Certified%20Seed.pdf.

Chapter 20

Claiborne, Craig, ed. *The New York Times Cook Book*. New York: Harper & Row, 1961.
Epp, Frieda. *Mother's Favorite Recipes*. Leavenworth, KS: n.p., 1993.
Kaufman, Edna (Ramseyer), comp. *Melting Pot of Mennonite Cookery 1874-1974*. North Newton, KS: Bethel College Women's Association, 1975.
Showalter, Mary Emma. *Mennonite Community Cookbook*. Scottdale, PA: Mennonite Community Association, 1957.
Voth, Norma Jost. *Mennonite Foods and Folkways from South Russia*. Vol 1. Intercourse, PA: Good Books, 1994.
Voth, Norma Jost. *Peppernuts Plain and Fancy: A Christmas Tradition From Grandmother's Oven*. Scottdale, PA: Herald, 1978.

Chapter 21

Calovich, Annie. "Giving Thanks by Saying Grace: Prayers of Gratitude." *Wichita Eagle*. November 27, 2003.
Converse, Charles C. "What a Friend We Have in Jesus." In *Worship and Service Hymnal*. Chicago: Hope, 1960.

Kaufman, Edna (Ramseyer), comp. *Melting Pot of Mennonite Cookery 1874–1974*. North Newton, KS: Bethel College Women's Association, 1975.
Peterson, E. H. *The Message: The Bible in Contemporary Language*. Colorado Springs: NavPress, 2002.
Stucky, Harley J., ed. *The Centennial Treasury of Recipes, Swiss (Volhynian) Mennonites*. North Newton, KS: Mennonite Press, 1973.

Chapter 22

Bethel College. *The Graymaroon 1920*. Newton, KS: Bethel College, 1920.
Janzen, Reinhild Kauenhoven. *The Art of Sharing, the Sharing of Art: Responses to Mennonite Relief in Postwar Germany*. North Newton, KS: Kauffman Museum, 1984.
Sergei, I. B. "My God and I." In *A Collection of Gospel Songs for Solo, Duet, Trio, Quartet and Group Singing*. Compiled by John W. Peterson. Grand Rapids: Zondervan, 1971.

Appendix 1

Alexander, Edwin, ed. "Atchison, Topeka and Santa Fe, the Early Years 1860–1899." Online: http://edwin.theeds.net/Trains/ATSF/early.htm.
Claassen, Ernest. *Abraham Claassen: Vistula to Plum Grove*. Whitewater, KS: n.p., 1975.
Claassen, Ernest, et al., eds. *History of the Emmaus Mennonite Church: Whitewater, Kansas, 1876–1976*. Hillsboro, KS: M.B. Publishing House, 1978.
Driedger, Abraham. *Heubuden Church Records*. n.p., 2003.
Dyck, D. Frederick. *Jacob J. Dyck: Am Trakt to America*. Washington, KS: n.p., 2000.
Emmaus Mennonite Church. *In Commemoration of Seventy-Five Years in America, 1876–1951*. Whitewater, KS: n.p., 1951.
Epp, Marie Harder. *Lest We Forget*. Whitewater, KS: n.p., 1992.
Estep, William R. *The Anabaptist Story*. Grand Rapids: Eerdmans, 1975. Online: http://www.reformedreader.org/history/anabaptiststory.htm.
Ewert, Bruno. "Four Centuries of Prussian Mennonites." *Mennonite Life* 3/2 (April 1948): 10-18.
Gaeddert, Joyce Regier. *The Bernhard Regier Genealogy, 1669–1973*. Topeka: n.p., 1973.
Harder, Agnes Wiebe. *The History of Brainerd*. Whitewater, KS: n.p., 1985.
Harder, Gustav. "Obituary of Bernhard Harder 1811–1900." *Christlicher Bundesbote* September 20, 1900.
Harder, Gustav. Speech given at the anniversary of Bernhard Harder's One Hundredth Birthday, March 17, 1911. n.p.
Jantzen, Mark. *Mennonite German Soldiers: Nation, Religion, and Family in the Prussian East, 1772–1880*. South Bend, IN: University of Notre Dame Press, 2010.
Jantzen, Mark. "'Whoever Will Not Defend His Homeland Should Leave It!' German Conscription and Prussian Mennonite Emigration to the Great Plains, 1860–1890." *Mennonite Life* 58/3 (September 2003): n.p. Online: http://www.bethelks.edu/mennonitelife/2003Sept/jantzen.php.

Bibliography

Jantzen, Mark, and William Eash. "Reviving Songs of Peace from the Vistula Delta." *Mennonite Life* 62/2 (Fall 2007): n.p. Online: http://www.bethelks.edu/mennonitelife/2007fall/jantzen%20eash.php.

Kaufman, Edmund G., ed. *General Conference Mennonite Pioneers*. North Newton, KS: Mennonite Press, 1973.

Loewen, Royden. *Hidden Worlds: Revisiting the Mennonite Migrants of the 1870s*. North Newton, KS: Bethel College, 2001.

Mennonite Central Committee. "Mennonite Relief Sale, April 7 & 8, 1995." Flier. Hutchinson, KS: Mennonite Central Committee, 1995.

Oyer, J. E., and R. S. Kreider. *Mirror of the Martyrs*. Intercourse, PA: Good Books, 2003.

Prieb, W. J. "The Man Behind the Tractors." *Mennonite Weekly Review*. August 24, 1995: 8.

Regier, James Peter. "Mennonitische Vergangenheitsbewätigung: Prussian Mennonites, the Third Reich, and Coming to Terms with a Difficult Past." *Mennonite Life* 59/1 (March 2004): n.p. Online: http://www.bethelks.edu/mennonitelife/2004Mar/regier.php.

Ruth, John L. "America's Anabaptists: Who They Are." *Christianity Today* 34/15 (October 22, 1990): 25–29.

Ruth, John L. *Forgiveness*. Scottdale, PA: Herald, 2007.

Saul, N. E. "The Migration of the Russian-Germans to Kansas." *Kansas Historical Quarterlies* 40/1 (Spring 1974): 38–62. Online: http://kancoll.org/khq/1974/74_1_saul.htm.

Schmidt, C. B. "Kansas Mennonite Settlements, 1877." *Mennonite Life* 25/2 (April 1970): 51–58.

Schrag, D. R., J. D. Thiesen, and D. A. Haury. "The Mennonites: A Brief Guide to Information." North Newton, KS: Bethel College, 1994.

Schroeder, William, and Helmut T. Huebert. *Mennonite Historical Atlas*. 2nd ed. Winnipeg, MB: Springfield, 1996.

Sudermann, Leonhard. *From Russia to America: In Search of Freedom*. Translated by Elmer F. Suderman. Steinbach, MB: Derksen, 1974.

Sudermann, Leonhard. "Introduction to Emmaus Record Book No. 1." Translation, manuscript 49, 1888. North Newton, KS: Mennonite Library and Archives.

Tanner, Beccy. "A Legacy of Faith and Hard Work." *Wichita Eagle*. July 9, 1999.

Thiessen, Jack. *Mennonite Low German Dictionary*. Madison: University of Wisconsin Press, 2003.

Unruh, Mark. "A Story of Faith and the Flag: A study of Mennonite Fantasy Rhetoric." *Mennonite Life* 57/3 (September 2002): n.p. Online: http://www.bethelks.edu/mennonitelife/2002sept/unruh.php.

Walters, George J. *Wir Wollen Deutsche Bleiben*. Kansas City, MO: Halcyon House, 1982.

Wiebe, Rudy. *Sweeter Than All the World*. Toronto: Knopf, 2001.

Appendix 2

Claassen, Ernest. *Abraham Claassen: Vistula to Plum Grove*. Whitewater, KS: n.p., 1975.

Dyck, Peter. "Beschreibung meine Auswanderung nach Amerika, 1876." *Mennonitische Geschichtsblätter* 11 (1954): 43–44.

Emmaus Mennonite Church. *In Commemoration of Seventy-Five Years in America, 1876-1951*. Whitewater, KS: n.p., 1951.
Gaeddert, Joyce Regier. *The Bernhard Regier Genealogy, 1669-1973*. Topeka, KS: n.p., 1973.
Heibert, Clarence, ed. *Brothers in Deed to Brothers in Need: A Scrapbook about Mennonite Immigrants from Russia, 1870-1885*. Newton, KS: Faith and Life, 1974.
Jantzen, Mark, and William Eash. "Reviving Songs of Peace from the Vistula Delta." *Mennonite Life* 62/2, (Fall 2007): n.p. Online: http://www.bethelks.edu/mennonitelife/2007fall/jantzen%20eash.php.
Keys, Linda. J. *The Family of Gerhard and Anna Regier, 1852-2001*. Topeka, KS: n.p., 2001.
"Notes on *SS Rhein*." Online: http://www.aquila.net/rayhent/HENThtml/notes.html.
Palmer List of Merchant Vessels. "*Rhein* (1868)." September 16, 1999. Online: http://www.geocities.com/mppraetorius/com-rh.htm.
U.S. National Archives and Records Service, General Service Administration. *Passenger Lists of Vessels Arriving at New York 1820-1897*. Microfilm No. 237, Reel 404, no. 597. North Newton, KS: Mennonite Library and Archives, Bethel College, n.d.

Appendix 3

"Aid Shower for Scrivners Monday Night at Elbing." *The Independent* (Whitewater, KS), June 12, 1941.
"Appreciation of Sympathy." *The Independent* (Whitewater, KS), June 19, 1941.
"Are Injured in Tornado." *Wichita Eagle*, evening edition, June 9, 1941.
"Brainerd News." *The Independent* (Whitewater, KS), June 26, 1941 and July 24, 1941.
"Calling for Volunteers." *The Independent* (Whitewater, KS), June 12, 1941.
"Cards of Thanks." *The Independent* (Whitewater, KS), June 19, 1941.
Claassen, Lewis, and Ruth Claassen. "Letter to William J. Regier." n.p.: Frederic Remington Area Historical Society, March 1, 1978.
Cressman, Phebe Ann. In discussion with the author, April 24, 2008.
Ensz, Roland H. "Whitewater, Kansas: Past and Present." Unpublished manuscript. North Newton, KS: Mennonite Library and Archives, Bethel College, 1954.
Epp, Marie Harder. *Lest We Forget*. Whitewater, KS: n.p., 1992.
"Families in Sedgwick Vicinity Left Homeless When Roaring Tornado Strikes." *Sedgwick Pantagraph*, June 12, 1941.
Flora, S. D. "Climate of Kansas." *Report of Kansas State Board of Agriculture* 67/285 (1948).
"Freak Incidents of the Storm." *Sedgwick Pantagraph*, June 12, 1941.
"Funeral Service for Storm Victims." *The Independent* (Whitewater, KS), June 12, 1941.
Hanna, L. A. "Letter to Mrs. Claassen." In Frederic Remington Area Historical Society Library, Whitewater, KS. June 12, 1941.
Harder, Gus. In discussion with the author, March 6, 2007.
"In Appreciation." *The Independent* (Whitewater, KS), June 26, 1941.
Inglish, Howard, ed. *Year of the Storms: The Destructive Kansas Weather of 1990*. Hillsboro, KS: Hearth, 1990.
"Injured Persons Are Improving, Survivors of Storm in Newton Hospitals; Announce Funerals." *Evening Kansan-Republican* (Newton, KS), June 10, 1941.

Bibliography

"Josephs First to Storm Victims Aid." *Potwin Ledger*, June 12, 1941.
"Kansas Tornadoes: 1950-1995." Online: http://www.disastercenter.com/kansas/tornado.html.
"Kansas Tornado Kills Eight; Five of Victims Struck Asleep in Farm House North of Wichita." *New York Times*, June 10, 1941.
"Kansas Tornado Kills Eight." *Wichita Eagle*, evening edition, June 9, 1941.
Klaassen, Lydia Thiessen. In discussion with the author, December 6, 2006.
"Loving Hands Laid Storm Victims to Rest." *Potwin Ledger*, June 19, 1941.
"Many Visitors at Storm Scene Sunday." *The Independent* (Whitewater, KS), June 19, 1941.
"Mass Funeral Rites for Four Storm Victims." *The Independent* (Whitewater, KS), June 19, 1941.
Miner, Craig. *Kansas: The History of the Sunflower State, 1854-2000*. Lawrence: University Press of Kansas, 2002.
"Mrs. Margarite Krueger—Obituary." *Evening Kansan-Republican* (Newton, KS), June 14, 1941.
"No Stick Left Standing After Twister Strikes." *Wichita Eagle*, sunrise edition, June 9, 1941.
"Notes and Freaks of Sunday Tornado." *The Independent* (Whitewater, KS), June 19, 1941.
"Red Cross Renders Assistance." *The Independent* (Whitewater, KS), June 26, 1941.
"Red Cross Workers are Busy." *The Independent* (Whitewater, KS), June 12, 1941.
Regier, Elfriede. "When the Sky Fell: Recollections of June 8, 1941." In Frederic Remington Area Historical Society Library, Whitewater, KS, January 1982.
Regier, William J. "Tornado of '41." In Frederic Remington Area Historical Society Library, Whitewater, KS, March 6, 1978.
Schoof, Charley W. "Letter to Mr. Gus H. Regier, Jr." In Frederic Remington Area Historical Society Library, Whitewater, KS, June 20, 1941.
"Seven Die in Series of Tornadoes." *Wichita Eagle*, sunrise edition, June 9, 1941.
"Seven Lives Lost in Storm." *Evening Kansan-Republican* (Newton, KS), June 9, 1941.
"Severe Local Storms, June 1941." *Monthly Weather Review*. Online: http://docs.lib.noaa.gov/rescue/mwr/069/mwr-069-06-0197.pdf.
Silver, Diane, ed. *Kansas Storms: Destruction, Tragedy and Recovery, 1991*. Hillsboro, KS: Hearth, 1991.
"Storm Damage Estimate at $228,000." *The Independent* (Whitewater, KS), June 12, 1941.
"Storm Toll." *Wichita Eagle*, June 9, 1941.
"Tells of Babe's Death." *Wichita Eagle*, evening edition, June 9, 1941.
Thiessen, Susan. In discussion with the author, December 4, 2006.
Thiessen, Susan. *Our Roots, "A Goodly Heritage"*. Tahlequah, OK: The "Go Ye" Mission Print Shop, 1986.
Toews, Nick N. "Butler County—The Tornado of 1941." *El Dorado Times*, millennium edition, December 14, 1999.
"Tornado Leaves Trail of Death at Whitewater." *Wichita Eagle*, evening edition, June 9, 1941.
"Tornado Sweeping Through Nearby Community Leaves Only Death and Destruction in its Wake, Cutting Path One-fourth Mile Wide and Ten Miles Long; Killing Seven; Injuring Eight; Rising Near Butler-Marian Line, Takes Sixteen Minutes to Travel Ten-Miles." *Potwin Ledger*, June 12, 1941.

Bibliography

"Tornado Sweeps Through Kansas, Eagle Cameras Cover Deadly Tornado." *Wichita Eagle*, evening edition, June 9, 1941.
"Tornado Takes Eight Lives Sunday Night—Injures Many Others." *The Independent* (Whitewater, KS), June 12, 1941.
"Wichita Area Counts Toll of 8 Dead, Heavy Property Damage in Path of Tornado." *Wichita Eagle*, morning edition, June 10, 1941.
"Wichita Area is Soaked Again as Wheat Hard Hit." *Wichita Eagle*, morning edition, June 9, 1941.
Wohlgemuth, Marge, ed. *Whitewater, Kansas: 1890-1990*. Whitewater, KS: Kes-Print, 1990.

Subject/Name Index

Note: Whenever possible, women are entered under their married name. Unless otherwise stated, all relationships given are from the author, Melvin Epp. Poems written in German are entered under both the German title and the English translation of the title.

A

absolute refusal, to bear arms, hold political office, swear an oath of loyalty to the state, or to sue in courts of law, 378
accomplishment, struggled for a feeling of, 1
adjustments, in setting up a new household, 126
adult baptism, in Switzerland in 1525, 377
advertising song, on subject of certified seeds, 340
affection, within the Germanic Mennonite community, 168
agoraphobia, 75
agrarian lifestyle, idealized, 30
agricultural advances, increased production of food, 353
"Agriculture During Pioneer Days," 211–213
agronomists, 30
Albert & Bertha zu Hochzeit, Erste Gedicht (poem), 126
Albert & Bertha zu Hochzeit, Zweite Gedicht (poem), 127
Alexanderwohl Mennonite Church, 188
Alfred Regiers' Silver Wedding (poem), 192–195

allspice, popular in European cooking, 105
alternative service, in Russia, 257
America
    known as an asylum for convicts, 389
    passage to, 392–400
American Legion, honored Emil Wiebe, 178
American Mennonites and the Great War 1914-1918, 234
Americanization, of our local church community, 316–317
Amstutz, Rev. L. R., 282–284
Anabaptist concepts, 380
Anabaptist principles, Mother's personal commitment to, 374
Anabaptists, 31, 377
ancestral grandfathers, land acquisition between 1800 and 1825, 383
Anderson, S. E., 422
Andres, Mr., 24, 398
anise cookies, 348
Annelly, Kansas, 47
anniversaries
    time for reflection, 239
    of weddings, 157–208
Anniversary of the Berean Bible Church (poem), 332–333
apple and peach trees, in the garden, 297
arbor, first choice by parents of courting children, 296
Atchison, Topeka, and Santa Fe Railroad, 24, 33, 390, 391
attached pairs, of peppernuts, 347
Auswanderungs Gemeinde (Emigrant Congregation), 387, 392

Subject/Name Index

B

B. E. Busenitz Silver Wedding Anniversary (poem), 205
baby screech owls, 79
baking soda, leaving out of cookies, 105
Baldwin, Nereus, photographer, 21
baptisms
    of adults upon confession of personal faith, 377
    no formal records kept until 1668 in Prussia, 385
Barker, Charles W., 421
bashfulness, of Melvin Epp as a child, 342
Basil family, during tornado, 403
Berean Academy, 321, 326, 327
Berean Academy (poem), 327-330
Berean Academy School Song, 326-327
Berean Bible Church, in Wichita, 332-333
Bergmann, Dietrich, great-great grandfather, 36, 291
Bergmann, Jacob, 35, 222, 299, 374
Bergmann, Margarethe, 263
Bernhard Harder house and floor plans, 291-294
The Bernhard Regier Genealogy, 1669-1973, 393
Bethel Academy
    B. W. attended for high school, 227
    converted into Bethel College in the spring of 1946, 321
    Mother completed the ninth grade, 364
    North Newton, Kansas, 4, 5
Bethel College, 167, 233, 317
Bethel Deaconess Hospital (Newton), 83, 275, 317
"Bethel Old Folks Home," 72
Bethesda Hospital (Goessel), 317
Bible Institute of Los Angeles, 227
Bible study and prayer time, 362
Bilingual Poem (1958), 6-8
birds, poem about, 76
birth dates, remembering special people on, 291-315

birthday poems, posthumous, 123
birthdays, celebration of, 263-290
births, records kept in Prussia, 385
bison, in Kansas, 27
"Black Hawk Waltz," 10
Bontrager, Manassas E., 233
boundary, around homesteads from prairie fires, 47
box camera, Mother's, 427
Brainerd, Kansas, 16, 47
Brainerd elementary school, 6, 319, 320
bridal shower gift, poem used for in 1987, 98-99
brothers, marrying sisters, 222
Brownie Camera, Mother's, 428
Brucks, Mr., 364
Brucks, Mrs., 121
Brudertal congregation, founding of, 34
bud vase souvenir, photo of, 62
Buffalo alfalfa, 340
Busenitz, Albert, 125, 128
Busenitz, Albert and Bertha, poems for, 202-203
Busenitz, Albert and Justine, 130
Busenitz, Ben E., 204-205
Busenitz, Bertha Regier, 125, 309
Busenitz, Carolyn, 166
Busenitz, Clarence, 116
Busenitz, Delora, 279
Busenitz, Elma Regier, 201, 343
Busenitz, Emilie Ruth, Father's niece, 204-205
Busenitz, Emma Wiebe (Mrs. Willie), Mother's cousin, 195
Busenitz, Franz, 229
Busenitz, Gerhard, 138, 279-280
Busenitz, Judy, 205
Busenitz, Justine, 128
Busenitz, Leroy, 166
Busenitz, Marie Sudermann, 279, 280
Busenitz, Olga Wiebe, 138, 279-280
Busenitz, Phyllis, 205
Busenitz, Sammy, 116
Busenitz, Twila, 116
Busenitz, Velma, 183, 186
Busenitz, Verna Marie, poem recited by, 148

Subject/Name Index

"But God!" Mother said upon Susan's prognosis, 84
Butler County, Kansas, physiographic map of, 15
Butler Rural Electric Cooperative (REC), 16
butter thermometer, poem on the gift of, 3

C

C. A. Neiman estate, tornado destruction, 406
cake decorating by Mother, 148, 362
camera, Mother's, 427, 428
car. *See also* Overland; Pontiac
    crushed on one side by tornado, 415
    Father driving, 139
    Mother driving, 363
Cassoday, Kansas, "The Prairie Chicken Capital of the World" sign, 79
Catherine the Great, Czarina, 23, 257, 382
cedar tree at the foot of Mother's grave, struck by lightning, 375
celestial changes, observation of, 75
cemeteries, in Prussia, 385, 386
cemetery. *See also* Harder cemetery
    built by Great-grandfather Harder, 35
    Green Valley, 406
    Zion Mennonite Church, 214
Certified Class seeds, 339
cherry trees, in the garden, 298
Cheyenne raid, through Kansas (1878), 27
Chicago, Kansas & Nebraska Railroad Company, 47
Child Evangelism Fellowship, Inc, 335–336
children, effects of knowledge and a global outlook on, 320
children's chair, from Aunt Helen Ruth, 274

children's classic books, in the home, 371
children's program, at church, 342
Chisholm Trail, 28
chorister (*Vorsänger*), 34, 167
Christlicher Bundesbote (German language newspaper), 25, 260
Christmas cactus, in full bloom, 240
Christmas card, Melvin's special, 343
Christmas carols, singing of, 1, 9
Christmas celebration
    on Christmas Eve for the Thiessens, 86–87
    family, 349
    at home on the evening of December 24, 344
    two church services, 342
Christmas gifts, from Susan Thiessen to her family, 82
chronological list of poems, by Marie Harder Epp, 430–434
church attendance, as priority number one, 117
church membership, guidelines for former combatants, 234
church services, conducted in homes entirely without music until 1700, 385
church weddings, held in the evenings, 157
cicadas, sound of, 17
cistern pump, gone after tornado, 415
civilization, absence of the sounds of, 16
Claassen, Aaron, 399
Claassen, Abraham, 393, 397, 398–399, 400
Claassen, Arnold, 340
Claassen, Carl, 340
Claassen, Dietrich, 25, 26, 37, 400
Claassen, Edward Sr., 25, 26
Claassen, Elwin, 406
Claassen, Herbert, 340
Claassen, James, 208
Claassen, Kurt, 240
Claassen, Lewis and Ruth, 406, 424
Claassen, Louis, 423

Subject/Name Index

Claassen, Melvin, 206–208
Claassen, Mrs., 425
Claassen, Mrs. Ed, father's cousin, 240
Claassen, Paul, 340
Claassen, Ruthie, 208
Claassen, Steve, 207
Claassen, Vangie, 207
Claassen, Walter, 340
Claassen, Wynona, 240
Claassen brothers, certified seed on their Golden Rule Farms, 340
Claassen diary, available in *Abraham Claassen, Vistula to Plum Grove*, 393
Claassens, Ed, shower for the Thiessen family, 418
Clinesmith, Lois (Roth), 337
coal-powered steam locomotives, perpetual fire hazard, 47
communion set, of a pewter chalice and plate (photo), 36
community, 25, 31, 378
community bonds, poems reaffirming the strengths of, 106–107
community village, recreating, 27
compulsory military service. *See also* universal conscription, introduced to Russia, 23, 257, 388
Congo, Africa, 280
construction, often timed with wedding festivities, 113
continental climate, 14
cookies
  anise, 348
  baking soda, leaving out of, 105
  Springerle (Anise) recipe, 348
  Springerle cookie rolling pin, photo of, 347
cooking, for one's husband, 98–99
corn, roasting ears of, 30
County Extension Service, cake decorating classes, 362
courtship, as a big event, 199
cow, responsibility for milking, 102–105
The Cow is Fresh (poem), 104
coyotes, sounds of, 17
creative process, 4
Cressman, Corinne, 154–155
Cressman, Michael, 149, 154–155
Cressman, Phebe Ann Epp, 366, 370–373
criminal element, in the American heartland, 28
A Cyclone (poem), authorship unknown, 416

D

daily sustenance, labor intensive on the farm, 359
deaconess, described, 275
deaths, records kept in Prussia, 385
"The Decision" (historical skit), 11
deed, for sale of Section 17, Milton Township, 32–33
deep wells, as a new concept for immigrants, 31
Della Busenitz and Brian Loewen Wedding (poem), 149
Delora Busenitz for her Grandmother's Birthday (poem), 280
Der Fibel, reading a set number of pages from, 6
Der Herold (German language newspaper), 25
Der Vierzigster, 12 November 1952, 165–166
devotional, on birthdays given by Mother, 288–290
devotional poem, commemorating twenty-fifth anniversary of Heinrich Wiebes, 180
Die Beiden Eulen (poem), 80
Die Kuh ist Frisch (poem), 104
discipleship, to follow after Christ, 378
divine directive, to write poetry, 1–2
divorce, 157–158
Domestic Laundry, on East Douglas in Wichita, 233
donuts, joy of eating, 100–101
double wedding ceremony, 221

Subject/Name Index

Doughnuts (poem), 101
Dr. and Mrs. Mann's Farewell (poem), 336–337
Dull Knife, Cheyenne Chief, 27
Dutch ceramic tile stove, 292–293
Dutch Mennonites, 381
Dyck, Alma Regier, 145–146
Dyck, Herman, 270–271
Dyck, Johann, courting Helene Regier, third child of the Gerhard Regier family, 400
Dyck, John, son of Rev. Peter, 213–214
Dyck, Margaret Schmidt, wife of Abraham J. Dyck, 316
Dyck, Marie Wiebe, 270
Dyck, Peter, son of Rev. Peter, 213–214
Dyck, Rev. Abraham J., 316, 317
Dyck, Rev. Peter, 26, 31, 47, 400
    America was our choice, 395
    helping with early Sunday worship services, 35
    kept diaries during this journey, 393
    organized a church service in the dining salon, 396
    thoughts on immigration, 394
    two sons of, fatal accident, 213–214, 313
Dyck, Rev. Peter and Mrs., 313
Dyck, Rev. Walter H., 282
Dyck diary, available on microfilm, 393

E

eating on the sly, 101–102
Eaton, Mrs. E. T., 32
Edgar Busenitzs' Silver Wedding Anniversary (poem), 201–202
Edna Regier and Martin Graber Wedding (poem), 148
educational opportunities, for Mother, 364
efficiency, in creative crafting of verses, 137
ein Wiedertaüffer, 377
eine Laube (arbor or bower), 296

Elbing, Kansas, 47
elders, Mennonite, 38, 227
electric sewing machine, purchased in 1950, 359
elementary school
    Brainerd, 6, 319, 320
    Christmas program, 344
    on section adjacent to land purchased by great-grandfather Harder, 32
Ellis county, Kansas, "German Capital of Kansas," 135
Ellsworth, McPherson, Newton, and Southeastern Railroad Company, 45–46
Emigrant Congregation, breakaway group in Prussia, 387
emigrating members, initial group from the Heubuden Church, 392
Emil Wiebes' Silver Wedding (poem), 179–180
Emmaus Mennonite Church, xiii, 10
    first building in 1878, 38
    first interment by 1880, 35
    photo of second building erected in 1908, 39
    photo of third building in 1929, 39
employees, on farms, 30
Emporia State College, 227
engagement dinner, 119
English
    after changing to, Mother's reuse of lines, 137
    increased, 135
    learned at school, 6
Entz, Abraham, 313–315
Entz, Marie Busenitz, 313
Entz, Walter, 81
environment, awareness of, 75
Epp, name of Friesland Dutch origin, 377
"Epp," Dutch origins of, 30
Epp, Agnes, Father's youngest sister, 124
Epp, Agnethe Andres, passed away on January 12, 1875, 257

453

Subject/Name Index

Epp, Albert, 108
    marriage in South Dakota, 140–142
    photo of, 109, 184
    photo seated on the running board, 410
    poem recited by, 131–132
    sleeping upstairs night of tornado, 412
Epp, Anna
    assumed role of the mother-in-law to Mother, 163
    birthday on January 1, 164
    took over household at the death of grandmother Epp in 1907, 163
Epp, Anna Regier (1869-1907)
    Father's mother, 9, 129, 254, 257, 259
    grandmother Epp, 304
    passed away giving birth to the youngest daughter, 256
    photo prior to her marriage on March 6, 1890, 255
    walked barefoot while plowing, 256
Epp, Caroline, 149
Epp, Cornie, Father's brother, 275, 414
Epp, David, July 4th 1976, in St. Louis, 43–44
Epp, Frieda, 108, 137
    with Aunt Helen Ruth night of tornado, 412
    photo of, 109, 184
    poems recited by, 135, 138–139
Epp, Gregory, 149
Epp, Helen Ruth
    negotiated with Grandfather Epp on education, 274–275
    ordained as a deaconess, ordination photo, 276
    role model for all her nieces, 279
    surrogate grandmother in Father's family, 274–279
    twenty-fifth anniversary in nursing, 279
Epp, Hildegard, 91, 108, 146
    photo of, 109, 184, 429
    poems recited by, 124, 129, 188, 260

    recovering from severe flu night of tornado, 412
Epp, James, 149, 150, 155–156
Epp, James and Lisa, wedding of, 19
Epp, Joann, wife of brother Albert, 140
Epp, Johannes (John) Sr. (grandfather), 9, 199, 254, 255, 275, 378
    charitable contributions, 259–260
    "Egyptian eye disease" childhood bouts of, 274
    enforced rigidity of the discipline excessive for Mother's spirit, 163
    life experiences of, 257–262
    married Margarethe Toews, 259
    photo of, 256
    portable set of steps for reception, 161
    remembered for his regal deportment, 163
    seven daughters, 159
Epp, John and Marie Harder
    golden wedding celebration invitation, photo of, 209
    twentieth wedding anniversary, 183
    twenty-fifth wedding anniversary portrait, 184
Epp, John Edwin, 108, 370
    photo of, 109, 184
    slept through tornado, 412
    poems recited by,132–134
Epp, John (Father), 119, 122, 199–200
    attended Hesston Academy, 320
    Berean Academy supported by, 322
    birth date shared with niece Marilyn Wiebe, 98
    on board of deacons of the Emmaus Mennonite Church, 358
    driving fifty-five miles per hour, 139
    elementary education, 319
    farm buildings destroyed by tornado, 410
    fattened cattle, 415
    first marriage proposal, 364–365
    first meeting with Mother, 364

Subject/Name Index

gasoline a precious, costly commodity, 344
gift of milking stool to Mother, 103
giving up German difficult, 6
growing up with seven sisters, 163
lost three fingers in a farm accident, 104–105
maternal grandparents, 304
MCC meat canning, 378
not liking unstructured, non goal-oriented activity, 100
oldest sister, twentieth wedding anniversary, 162
photo of, 184, 428, 429
praying with Mother, 358
purpose on earth, 100
role of, 330
weekday evenings away from home, 10
will of, 358

Epp, Justina, 108
with Aunt Helen Ruth night of tornado, 412
photo of, 109, 184
poem for English class written with Mother's help, 323–324
poem for her thirtieth birthday, 105
poems recited by, 139, 181

Epp, Kimberly, 152–154

Epp, Lisa, 150, 155–156

Epp, Margarethe Toews, 259

Epp, Marie Harder (Mother), 119, 122
baking frenzy of Christmas goodies, 344
continuing to quote "Paul Revere's Ride," 235
courtship and wedding of, 199–200
discouraged from openly expressing joys, 100
driving, 363
elementary education, 319
encouraged Father and helped in other ways, 322
energy and self-reliance, 359
family self-portrait taken in September 1928, 427, 429
"first loves" were the best, 365
first meeting with Father, 364
flu and temperature night of tornado, 415
garden covered with debris after tornado, 411
going by train from Whitewater to Elbing, 95
good student and an avid reader, 363–364
growing up without brothers or the presence of a father in the household, 163
hair, cutting, 358–359
health of, 365–366
life dedicated to her husband, 357
life summary of, 4
list of things people brought to them to help after tornado, 417
love of vivid colors, 360
not giving up life easily, 367–368
outliving her sisters, 367
photo of, 184, 366, 429
photo of her children, 109
recall of historical facts, family events, and dates, 427
relationship to recipients included with poems, 107
reuse of lines, 137
school picture of, 5
self-confidence of, 163
shopped in El Dorado, Newton, and Wichita for Christmas gifts, 344
stiff knees, 102
taking a picture of her family in September 1928, 428
treating Aunt Helene's six children as her own, 367
white wedding dresses, 159
will of, 358

Epp, Martha, , xi, 91, 108, 357, 367, 412
in first graduating class of Berean Academy, 322
photo of, 109, 184
poems recited by, 261, 322
valedictory speech, 322

Subject/Name Index

Epp, Melvin, 108, 320, 342, 354, 370
   born a year after tornado of June 8, 1941, 401
   first spanking, 163–164
   July 4th 1976, in St. Louis, 43–44
   love of vivid colors, 360
   photo of, 109, 184
   poems recited by, 141, 181
   poem written with assistance from Mother, 324–325
Epp, Peter, 257
Epp, Peter and Agnethe, photograph, 258
Epp, Phebe Ann, ix, 108, 370, 375
   photo of, 109, 184
   poems recited by, 40, 126, 223, 267, 271, 311
   recovering from severe flu night of tornado, 412
Epp, Steven, 149, 152–154
Epp, Sylvia, July 4th 1976, in St. Louis, 43–44
Epp, Terry, July 4th 1976, in St. Louis, 43–44
Epp ancestors, 382
Eshelman, H. E., farm, 404
espionage law, during World War I, 232
ethnicities, viewed with fear early in the twentieth century, 233
Europe, devastated in post-World War I period, 334
evening services, complementing work schedules, 157
evil spirits, driving away with loud noise, 112
Ewert, Rev. Wilhelm, 34, 388
exodus, from Europe, 392

F

familial relatedness, extensive among Mennonites, 107
families
   Christmas celebration, 349
   division of labor, 330
   eating meals together as, 120
   first going to Kansas, 25
   marriage and, 205–206
family historian, Mother as, 371
The Family of Gerhard & Anna Regier, 1852-2001, 397
Farewell to Uncle Lester and Aunt Agnes (poem), 335
farm animals, moving to market, 47
farm buildings, building material to construct, 213
farm wagons, taking place of modern automobiles, 212
Farmers Alliance, 423
farmhouse, move out of, 4
farming, 30, 31
farms
   ebb and flow of life on, 197
   eldest son inherited the whole in Prussia, 304
   insurance for, 423
farmyard, photo of, 295
Fast, Heinrich, initials of on chalice, 36
Father and Son Banquet (poem), Berean Academy, 330–331
fellowship hall, completed in 1929, 157
female participation, allowing in church, 40
Fido, Justine's dog, 295
Fieguth, Bernhard, Prussian Mennonite soldier, 387
Fifty-fourth Birthday of Rev. Amstutz (poem), 283–284
firecracker, firing on fourth of July, 372
first cousins, marriage of, 222
first loves, as best, 365
First Mennonite Church, in Newton, 304
flat tires, repairing, 363
floods, in West Prussia, 20
Fluegel grand piano, 167
For Albert Busenitzs' Twenty-fifth Wedding Anniversary (poem), 202–203
For Brother-in-law John Thiessen (poem), 94–95
For Carl J. Claassen for the Water Pitcher (poem), 2–3

Subject/Name Index

For Christmas (poem), 351–352
For Ed Claassens' Golden Wedding Anniversary (poem), 240–242
For Edna about the Towel (poem), 96
For Edward Regiers' Wedding (poem), 125
For Eldon Wohlgemuths' Wedding Reception (poem), 144–145
For Ernest Wiebe to the Lid (poem), 96–97
For Grandpapa's One-hundredth Birthday (poem), 309–311
For Herman A. Wiebes (poem), 165
For J. E. Thiessens' Golden Anniversary (poem), 243–247
For Jacob J. Regiers' Silver Wedding Anniversary (poem), 174–176
For Jake Regiers' Thirtieth Wedding Day (poem), 177–178
For Jake Wiebes (poem), 161
For John & Elsie's Fruit Shower (poem), 93
For John T. Reimers' Fruit Shower (poem), 92–93
For John Thiessen about the Comb Box (poem), 97
For Lisa Harder (poem), 99
For Lois Roth's Farewell (poem), 337–338
For Marilyn Wiebe (poem), 98
For Marline Dyck and Larry Lutz (poem), 146–147
For Papa's Golden Wedding Anniversary Day (poem), 261–262
For Paul U. Claassen for the Butter Thermometer (poem), 3
For Sister Helen Ruth's Fiftieth Birthday (poem), 277–278
For the Albert Entz & Frieda Busenitz Wedding (poem), 131–132
For the Birthday of Mrs. Herman Dyck (poem), 272–274
For the Birthday of Uncle Christ Thierstein (poem), 264–265
For the Wedding of Albert & Bertha, (poem), 140
For the Wedding of Albert & Bertha, Poem 2, 128
For the Wedding of Bernard & Ruby (poem), 140
For the Wedding of Gerhard & Olga Busenitz (poem), 138–139
For Uncle Abraham Entz's One-hundredth Birth Date (poem), 315
For Uncle Bernhard & Aunt Justine (poem), 130
For Uncle Gerhard Regier's Golden Wedding (poem), 210, 218–221
For Uncle John Harder's Nineteenth Birthday (poem), 269–270
For Waldimar & Ester Wiebe (poem), 137
For Waldo & Lydia (poem), 134
For Walter Harder's Birthday (poem), 285–286
For Willie Harders' Golden Wedding Anniversary (poem), 251–252
The Fortieth (poem), 166
Foundation Class seeds, 339
fragrant flowers, in orderly beds, 298
Franke, H. C., 397
Frankfurter Zeitung (Frankfurt newspaper), 24, 390
Frazee, Charles Jr., home blown away, 403
Frazee, Charles, Sr. and wife, 403
Frederick the Great, 385
Frederick William II, "Edict Concerning the Future of Mennonites" in 1789, 383
freedom to worship, 15–16
Friesen, Kaete (Katie), 65, 227
fruit shower, 91–92
funerals, comforting the bereaved as another core activity, 123
funnel cloud, 16–17, 81
Für Carl J. Claassen zum Wassertopf (poem), 2–3
Für Edna zum Hantuch (poem), 95
Für Edward Regiers Hochzeit (poem), 124
Für Ernest Wiebe zu Deckel (poem), 96

Subject/Name Index

Für Geburtstag von Tante Herman Dyck (poem), 271–272
Für Herman A. Wiebes (poem), 164
Für Jake Wiebes (poem), 161
Für John & Elsies Fruit Shower (poem), 93
Für John Thiessen sur Kammbox (poem), 97
Für Marilyn Wiebe (poem), 98
Für Onkel Abraham Entz 100sten Geburtstag (poem), 314
Für Onkel Bernhard & Tante Justine (poem), 129–130
Für Papa's Goldenerhochzeitstag (poem), 260–261
Für Paul U. Claassen zum Buttertermameter (poem), 3
Für Schwager Hans Thiessen (poem), 94
Für Waldimar & Ester Wiebe (poem), 136
Für Waldo & Lydia (poem), 133
Furley, Kansas, 47

G

garden, 296, 297, 299
garden house, 298
Gateway to the West, arch symbolizing, 44
Gedichte Aufgesagt für Anna Regier am 29 Juli 1945 (poem), 311–312
gemütlichkeit (inner comfort and peace), in perpetuating pleasant memories, 291
General Conference (Mennonite), 167, 317
geological impact, Kansas expressing variation in, 14
German
  language used until 1940, 5
  reading, as prerequisite for driving a car, 6
German Bible school, total immersion, 364
German Christmas carols, singing of, 1, 9
German hymn, 282
German prisoners, Mother's treatment of, 373
German school, 225, 227
German tradition, of Christmas cookies, 347
Germantown near Philadelphia, xiv
Germany's art - *Dankspende*, symbolic gift of, 360
Gesangbuch mit Noten (songbook with notes), 267
Gesangbuch ohne Noten (songbook without notes), 167
Gessler, General, 385
gifts, short poems complementing, 91
"Giving Thanks by Saying Grace: Prayers of Gratitude" (newspaper article) *The Wichita Eagle*, 354
"Gnaden Privilegium," granted in 1780, 386
"Go Ye" Mission, Susan Thiessen working as secretary, 87, 88, 89–90
God
  all good things a gift from, 353
  bringing people together, 150
  controlling all aspects of the physical world, 150
Goertz, David, 275
golden wedding anniversaries, celebration of, 209–262
Golden Wedding Anniversary of Ted Nickel's Parents (poem), 254
Golden Wedding Anniversary of Uncle Johannes and Aunt Emilie (poem), 224
Golden Years (poem), 236–239
Goldenhochzeit voin Onkel Johannes und Tante Emilie (poem), 223
Goldschaar (Golden Plowshare), 79
Goossen, Alvin, 187–191
Goossen, Elsie, 190
Goossen, Hildegard Epp, 188
Goossen, Paul, 190
Goossen, Susie, 190
Gospel Missionary Union, 337

Subject/Name Index

Graber, Brad, 114–115
Graber, Edna Regier, 147–148
Graber, Martin, 147–148
Graber, Sharon Busenitz, 114–115
grace (prayer), 354, 355. *See also* table graces
Grace Bible Institute (Grace University), 202
granary (*Speicher*), 34
granary shed, antique room on the second floor, 371
"Grandma Epp," as Mother's signature on one poem, 150
Grandmother Harder's Peppernuts (recipe), 346
grandparents, lauded by grandchildren, 247
grand-sons, wedding poems requested by Mother's, 149
grape vines, two rows of, 297
gratitude, for agriculture, 14–15
Great Blue Herons, 79–80
Great Depression, time of, 191
Great Horned Owls, 80
Grebel, Conrad, baptism of, 377
Green Valley cemetery, tornado damage, 406
Greese, Harold, tornado damage, 406
Gregory and Caroline Epp Wedding (poem), 150–152
Groves, C. L., farm, tornado damage, 403
Gus and Edna Regier's Silver Wedding Anniversary (poem), 197–199

H

Halbstädt (Molotscha Colony), southern Russia, 257
Halstad, Kansas, newspapers, German language, 25
hand-operated can sealer, photo of, 379
Hanna, L. A., letter to Mrs. Claassen, 425
Happy Birthday Song, written by Mother, 263
"Harder," name indigenous to West Prussian Mennonites, 30
Harder, Abraham, 384
Harder, Agathe Regier (1830-1867), married great-grandfather Bernhard Harder, 384
Harder, Anna Peters Regier, married great-grandfather Bernhard Harder, 304
Harder, B. P., deaf and speech impaired, 372
Harder, B. W., 231, 235, 364, 407, 409
  dispatched his son John S. to purchase a flag, 229
  encouraged members to buy bonds, 229
  father of John Schiller Harder, 252
  heart problems, 235
  led the singing of patriotic hymn "America," 230
  Linda Marie, granddaughter of, 228
  lived by himself for a period, 235–236
  Mother's former school teacher, 45
  papers of, 44
  went out and faced the mob, 230
Harder, B. W. and Minna
  fiftieth wedding anniversary, 224–232
  photo of twenty-fifth wedding anniversary, 226
Harder, Bernhard (great-grandfather), 22, 25, 26, 33, 291, 299, 304, 383
  challenges of winds, rains and temperatures, 298
  decided to immigrate to American, 23
  falling backward off a wagon, 26
  family, passengers #35-41, 399
  family went directly to Halstead, Kansas, 400
  house, floor plans, 293–294
  Johannes oldest son of, 210
  journey to the new farm (September 1876), 34
  looking for high ground, 20
  married Anna (Peters) Regier, 384

459

Subject/Name Index

Harder, Bernhard –continued
   photograph of, 21
   seasickness, 396, 398
   stayed with his Uncle Abraham Harder in Heubuden, 384
   traveled extensively in 1869 looking for an opportunity to relocate, 388
Harder, Bernhard Jr. (grandfather), 46, 160, 299
   double wedding ceremony, 221
   elementary school, 32
   emigrated as an eleven-year-old boy, 43
   farm photo in 1915, 37
   house, 37
   house, photo, 295
   second marriage for, 222
   suitcase, photo of, 44
   surviving child, 384
Harder, Catherine Wiebe, 250
Harder, Christine (1749-1806), 383
Harder, Eduard, 280–281, 314
Harder, Elna Jane, 236
Harder, Emilie Epp, father's sister, 252
Harder, Frieda, 282, 284
Harder, Gustav, 22, 46, 231, 314, 384
   delivering a sermon, 167–168
   Helene's father, 167
   interred in the Harder cemetery, 168
   ordained as a minister in 1884, 167
   sharing devotional thoughts, 296
Harder, Gustav and Helena Kroeker
   silver wedding anniversary, 168
   silver wedding anniversary portrait, 169
Harder, Hans (1764-1815), 383
Harder, Helene Kroeker, wife of Gustav Harder, 167, 168, 169
Harder, Helene (Reimer) (1764-1815), 383
Harder, Helene Wiebe (grandmother), 100, 119, 160, 199–200, 222, 270
   black dress on her wedding day, October 26, 1893, 159

double wedding ceremony, 222
peppernut recipe, 345
rented a house near Bethel College, 364
Harder, John and Gustav, 222
Harder, John and Marie (Regier), 225
Harder, John Schiller (1901-1993), 228
   as Americans, 231
   Mother's cousin married Father's sister Emilie, 252
Harder, John Sr. (Johannes) (1854-1946), 22, 25, 26, 210, 284–285, 384
   celebration for his nineteenth birthday, 265
   doubts about necessity of education, 227
   wedding portrait of, 266
Harder, Justine Bergmann (great-grandmother), 35, 62, 222
   anniversary of her one-hundredth birthday, 291
   enjoyed entertaining, 295
   invasive surgery, 299
   married great-grandfather, 384
   photo ca. 1885, 292
   remembered for New Year celebrations, and the celebration of her birthday in July, 295
   third wife of Bernhard Harder Sr., 291
Harder, Justine Bergmann, 222
   first wife of Bernhard Harder Jr. (grandfather), 222
   marriage in Beatrice, NB, 222
   passed away March 29, 1889, 222
Harder, Katharina Regier, 265
Harder, Katherine (adopted), married Gustav Harder, 314
Harder, Kenneth and Luella, 314, 315
Harder, Kenneth Roy, 335
Harder, Linda Marie, 228, 253
Harder, Lisa, 99
Harder, Marie Regier, 210, 265, 383–384
   wedding portrait of, 266

Subject/Name Index

Harder, Marie Wilhelmine Entz, married Eduard Harder, 313–314
Harder, Marilyn, 140, 285
Harder, Minna (Mother's sister), 364
 died of typhus at the age of twenty-seven, 367
 food items prepared for her wedding, 120–122
 photo of, 295
Harder, Minna Wiebe, 225, 235
Harder, Mr. Bernhard and wife, on ship passenger list, 398
Harder, Mr. Gus, on ship passenger list, 398
Harder, Mr. Johannes, on ship passenger list, 398
Harder, Mrs. Eduard (Marie Wilhelmine Entz Harder), 280
Harder, Priscilla, 280
Harder, Stanley, 253
Harder, Waldo, 202–4, 280
Harder, Walter, 284–86
Harder, Wesley, 285
Harder, Willie, 250
Harder, Wilma, 250
Harder cemetery, 35, 168, 299, 374–376. *See also* cemetery
 origins of, 35
 photo in 1998, 375
 tornado damage, 412
Harders, joined Mennonite community in Prussia, 31
Harms, Mr., well digger, 31
Harrison, J. W., tornado damage, 403
Hartman, Rev. J. A., 422
Hawes, Mary, 225
Hector, Justine's dog, 295
Heimat (homeland), idea of leaving, 23
Helene's daughters (Mother's sister's daughters), inherited gift of storytelling and laughter, 100
Henry Wiebe's Fortieth Wedding Anniversary (poem), 181–183
herd of cattle, on the road after tornado, 415
heritage, we are product of our, 43

Herman A. Wiebes' Golden Wedding (poem), 247–250
Herman and Elvira Klaassen's Twenty-fifth Wedding Anniversary (poem), 200–201
Hesston Academy, 320, 321
Hesston College, flag display altercation, 233
Heubuden Church in West Prussia, 34, 38, 386, 387
Hillsboro Old People's Home, 67
Hiser, John, farm buildings damaged, 406
historian, Mother as, 371
historical poem, for fortieth wedding anniversary of Henry Wiebes, 180
Hitherto to Lord Has Helped Us (poem), For Alvin Goossens' Silver wedding Anniversary, 188–191
hoarfrost, as devotional subject, 283
hogs, hauling in a farm wagon, 47
Holden post office, in Milton Township, 32
Holden School (1871), 32
Holland. *See also* Netherlands, Anabaptist movement, 377
Holstein Friesian cattle, 214
Homan, Gerlof D., 234
The Home (poem), 206
Homestead Act of 1862, 27
Hooper, H. J., 424
horse barn, surviving after tornado, 411
horses, Molly, Lady, Prince, Saul, Nellie, Tom, 69
hot oil, making of doughnuts in, 101–102
houses
 built by my grandfather in 1887, 295, 410
 north side photo after tornado, 411
 shipped to Idaho, 250
 West Prussia residential features, 291–292
Howrey, Dave, tornado damage, 406

461

Subject/Name Index

humanitarian outreach, Mennonite focus on, 378
Hunsicker, Henry, 79

I

ice cream, homemade, 295–296
"In Butler County on the Farm" (poem), 12–14
    changed to "In Kansas on the Farm," 19
    printed in the column: "Kernels and Cobs" of the Kansas City *Daily Drover Telegram*, 19
In Memory of my Father (poem), 317–318
Independence Day, July 4th 1976, in St. Louis, 43
The Independent (Whitewater, Kansas), 19, 224, 228
Indians. *See also* Native Americans
    encounters with, 212
    not roaming freely in Kansas, 27
information outside of a biblical context, considered dangerous, 319
information techniques, used by Mother, 427
Inman Home for the Aged, 317
interest, high rate of, 212
Interstate 70, 14

J

J. S. Harder's Golden Wedding Anniversary (poem), 253–254
Jake Regiers zum 30ten Hochzeitstag (poem), 177
James and Lisa Epp Wedding (poem), 155–156
Jansen, Cornelius, 400
Jansen, Marie J. (Regier, Frantz), 334
Janzen, Reinhild Kauenhoven, 360
Japanese descent, internment of persons of, 233
Jefferson, Thomas, surveying system originated by, 26
Jessen-Krueger, Margarite Marie, killed by tornado, 421
Jesus, teachings on complying with governmental obligations, 229
Joseph, Mr. and Mrs. Bill, 408
Jost, Ann (Mrs. Arlo Voth), 283
journal, with a chronological sequence of poems, 2
joy of cooking, for one's husband, 98–99
Jump, Frank, barn destroyed by tornado, 403
Just a Little Wish (poem), 123
Justine Harder Reimer's Peppernuts (recipe), 346

K

Kansas
    arrival of families in July 1876, 22
    divinely blessed, 15
    first families going to, 25
    frequency of tornadoes, 402
    Mother's enjoyment of, 12
    open spaces of south central, 13
    opened for agricultural settlement in 1854, 29
    poem reflecting the pastoral aspects of living on the prairies, 17–19
    statehood on January 29, 1861, 29
Kansas (poem), 18
Kansas Anabaptists, 233
Kansas Certified Seed, 339
Kansas Certified Seed (song), 340–341
Kansas communities, "patriotic activists" alienating resident Mennonites, 232
Kansas Crop Improvement Association (KCIA), 339
Kansas Gas & Electric Company (KGE), 16
Kansas State University, plant breeding to improve crops, 339
Kansas Wreford chert (flint), 29

Subject/Name Index

Kauffman Museum, North Newton, Kansas, 360, 380, 388
Kaufman, Marilyn Harder, 285
Kaufman, Marvin, husband of Marilyn Harder, 285
Kaufman, Rev. and Mrs. J. C., Susan's Christmas gift for, 85
Kaufman, Rev. J. C., 85, 132, 282, 407, 409
Keyes, Haskell H., killed by tornado, 403
Klaassen, Abe, tornado damage, 420
Klaassen, Elvira (Regier), 199, 200–201
Klaassen, Herman, 200–201, 409
Klaassen, Kathy, 87
Klaassen, Lydia Thiessen, 113, 132
Klaassen, Waldo, 113, 132
Kliewer, Katharina ("Tien"), 47, 48
    photo of, 64
Klingenburg, Viola, 201
Kodak film, allowed for eight exposures, 427
Kopper, Helen, poet from the Plum Grove area, 107
Krueger, Mrs., funeral for, 422
Krueger-Scrivner, Edna Marie (Mrs. Guy Scrivner), killed by tornado, 421

L

Ladekopp, got permits to build churches in 1786, 386
land
    sections available for purchase or homesteading, 27
    viewed as a divine instrument, 30
Land Grant Legislation of 1863, 24, 390
Land Ordinance of 1785, 26
land sales flier, created by the Atchison, Topeka & Santa Fe Railroad, March, 1876, 391
Landis, Melvin, 320–321
lawlessness, in Russia between 1875 and 1882, 257
legal harassment, oppressive in Prussia, 381

Lest We Forget (book), 11
Lester Smith home, destroyed by tornado, 403–404
Liberty bonds, dilemma among the Mennonites, 229
life, enjoying the opportunities of, 372
life and longevity, envisioned as divinely granted gifts or privileges, 263
life expectancies, late 1800s and early 1900s, 209–210
lightning, causing prairie grass fires, 47
Lincoln, Abraham, 27, 354, 390
lines, reuse of, 138
literature, Mother's love for, 371
Litsewitz homestead, 313
Little Bighorn battle (1876), 27
Little Wolf, Cheyenne Chief, 27
Lloyd Wartenhalle, built at the New Harbor in Bremerhaven, 395
Loewen, Brian, 149
Loewen, Della Busenitz, 149
Loggerhead Shrikes, 79
Longfellow, Henry Wadsworth, 235, 364, 372
looting, after the tornado, 414, 418
Low German, 382
Luther, Martin, 377
Lutz, Larry, 146–147
Lutz, Marline Dyck, 146–147
Luyken, Jan, copper plate etchings of, 380

M

Madrid yellow sweet clover, 340
males, early church leadership and organization restricted to, 40
manifest of passengers disembarking, from the *SS Rhein* in New York on July 1, 1876, 399
Manifesto of 1793, 23
Mann, Dr. and Mrs., 335–336
Mantz, Felix, baptism of, 377
Margaret Ann Tannahill's Wedding Invitation (poem), 111

Subject/Name Index

marriage
    celebration of, 117–156
    and the family, 205–206
    Mother's views of, 129
    requirements for, 110
    of strangers as noteworthy, 109
Martens, Gustav, 66–67
Martyrs Mirror, 380
marzipan, Mother's handmade, 349
Matthew 6:11, 353
Matthew 20:1, 335
MCC (Mennonite Central Committee), 334, 360, 378
McLains. Kansas, 47
meals, eating together as a family, 120
Melvin Claassens' Silver Wedding (poem), 207–208
Memorial Day, Mother placing peonies on graves, 374
Mennonite agriculturists, suited for reclamation, 381
Mennonite Aid Plan, 423
Mennonite Board of Guardians, 389
Mennonite Central Committee (MCC), 334, 360, 378
Mennonite family, history of Melvin Epp's, 377–391
Mennonite farmers, becoming laborers themselves in America, 40–41
Mennonite German Soldiers: Nation, Religion, and Family in the Prussian East, 1772-1880 (Jantzen), 381
Mennonite immigrants, prevailing attitudes, 234
Mennonite institutions of higher education, suffering at the hands of patriotic activists, 233
Mennonite men, marrying an older Mennonite widow, 383
"Mennonite name game," 107
Mennonite schools, Russians converting into governmental institutions, 23
Mennonite-owned farms, in great demand in Prussia, 393

Mennonites
    followers of Menno Simons, 378
    found refuge in America, 389
    lost privilege of exemption from military service in 1867, 257
    not known for tactile interactions, 164
    in some communities realigning economical associations, 232
    from southern Russia had begun immigrating to North America in 1874, 390
Mennonitische Geschichtsblätter (1954), 393
Metcalf, J. F., tornado damage, 404
Meyer, Mrs., 45, 47, 61, 62
Michael and Corinne Cressman Wedding (poem), 154–155
Midland Mutual, 423
military service, compulsory for all young men in Russia, 23, 257, 388
milking stool, photo of Marie's (Mother's), 103
milking the cow, responsibility for, 102–105
Milky Way, viewed from Kansas, 16
Miller, Bert, tornado damage, 405
Miller, Herman, 193
Miller, Samuel H., 233
Milton Township, Section 17, Butler County, Kansas, 12, 17, 29, 32
mind, Mother's continued sharp and alert, 273
"Mine" (poem), 409
ministerial organization in the local church, 282
"Mirror of the Martyrs," exhibit at Kauffman Museum, 380
mission Sunday school, establishing in the Wichita area, 332
missionaries
    to China, 335
    first from the local church, 334
    to India, 240
    to Morocco, 250, 337
missions, increased interest during 1850 to 1875, 286

Subject/Name Index

modernism, one sign of, 319
Moody Bible Institute in Chicago, 227
Morocco, missionary in, 250, 337
Mother. *See* Epp, Marie Harder (Mother)
Mrs. Ed Harder's Eightieth Birthday (poem), 281–282
music
    Mother not singing but surrounding with, 10
    words vocalized with expressive varieties, 106
mutual aid, integral feature of group practice, 378
"My God and I" (hymn), 183, 273

N

N. Baldwin & Son studio, 21
Nachrichten aus der Heidenwelt (German language newspaper), newspaper, German language, 25
nails on the ground, after the tornado, 416
Nancy Lee, Alfred Regiers' granddaughter, 195
"*naschen*" (eating on the sly), 101–102
national conscription law (1868), in Prussia, 23, 313, 387, 392
National Geographic, Mother reading from cover to cover, 363–364
Native American artifacts, from section 17, Milton Township, 29
Native Americans. *See also* Indians
    hungry, fed by Mennonite pioneers, 28
    working among in Montana, 334
nausea and seasickness, discomforts of, 395–396
neighborliness, jeopardizing bond issue, 229
neighbors, being good, 229
neighbors and relatives, eating together with, 120
Neiman, I. H. (postmaster), 32
Netherlands, 382. *See also* Holland

New Year's festivities, Justine giving each grandchild a *Reichsthaler* (silver coin), 296
New York Times, 25
newspapers, German language, 25
Newton, Kansas
    Bethel Academy, 4, 5
    Bethel Deaconess Hospital, 83, 275, 317
    cowboys turning into a cowtown of incredible violence, 28
    First Mennonite Church in, 304
    German language newspapers, 25
    Kauffman Museum, 360
    model prairie town by 1876, 28
Newton Anzeiger (German language newspaper), 25
Nichel, Rose Ann, asked Mother for poem, 254
Nichel, Theodore "Ted" D., 254
nighthawks, observing, 76
The Ninety-Five Theses (Luther), 377
noncombatant service, not considered an acceptable alternative, 387
noncombatants, severely harangued by other combatant draftees, 234
nonresistance, practice of, 378
Norddeutscher Lloyd (North German Lloyd) SS Rhein, 392, 396
Norddeutscher Lloyd Wartenhalle (North German Lloyd waiting room), 394
notebook, used by Gilbert Thiessen, found by his siblings, 418–420

O

Oct 21, '70 (poem), 105
oleanders, 48, 63
Omaha, wedding in, 139
one flesh, concept of, 109–110
one paid minister system, adopted in 1939, 282
one-room advanced parochial school, B. W. conducted, 227
oral delivery, 108, 109

Subject/Name Index

Osage orange trees, cemetery planted with, 374
ostrich, ditty about, 367
Our Feathered Friends (poem), 76–78
Overland. *See also* car, Grandmother's first car, 363, 369
owls, 79, 80

P

pacifists, programs in the event of another war, 234
Paff, Roy, tornado destruction, 404
The Pair of Owls (poem), 80
pansies, 360–361
pansy quilt, 360–361, 375
  photo of, 361
paper, scarcity of, 2
parents' wedding, photo of invitation, 119
parochial education, mission of, 319–333
passenger list, of the mail steamship *Rhein* for its voyage on June 17, 1876, 397
patriarch, honoring, 316–318
patriarchal tradition, inculcated in Germanic Europe, 40
patriotic acts, 230
patriotic fervor (1917-18), not exclusively anti-(German) Mennonite, 233
Pattern for Living (poem), 286–288
Patterson, Harry, tornado damage, 406
"Paul Revere's Ride" (Longfellow), 235, 364, 372
Paulson, Janet Lee, 422
  killed by tornado, 421
Peach, Guernsey cow named, 102
pecking patterns, of woodpeckers, 76
Penner, Elder Gerhard, 222, 387, 388
Penner, Heinrich, 25, 26, 259, 400
Penner, Justine, on ship passenger list, 398

Penner, Justine Claassen Bergmann (great-great grandmother), 35, 36, 299, 374
Penner, Marie
  high school graduation certificate found forty miles northeast of Whitewater, 424
  obituary poem, 407
Penner, Otto, died from injuries received during the tornado, 407
Penner, Otto and Marie, 406
people from the community, requesting poems, 106–110
peppernut cutter, 344–345
peppernuts (*Pfeffernüsse*)
  attached pairs of, 347
  baking, 344
  at Christmas, 342
  cutter for, 344–345
  sealed in cans to keep fresh during shipment, 379
perpetual immigrants, Mennonites viewed as, 118
persons, older addressed as "uncle" or "aunt," 263
Peters, A. B., 257, 260
phenology, 17
Phillips, H. H., tornado damage, 404
photographic history, of Mother's family and world, 428
piano, Mother playing, 9–10
picket fence, house surrounded with, 294
Pike's Peak, Mother walked down, 372
Plautdietsch (Low German), 382
Poe, Edgar Allen, 372
A Poem recited for Anna Regier (poem), 312–313
poems. *See also* titles of individual
  chronological list of, 430–434
  final, 150
  first to brothers Carl and Paul, 2
  first two, dated October 1929, 9
  focus on writing, 2
  intended for communication of ideas, 4

Subject/Name Index

memorizing classical, 364
paid for writing, 108
putting words into new sequences, 106
requests for, 106–110
second and third stanzas of "My God and I," 373–374
for seventy-fifth anniversary of the local church (1951), 40
written in German, best read in German, 8
Poland, 381, 385
Polish-Prussian War (1519-1521), 381
political and religious freedom, experienced in America, 371
Polterabend (Nuptial Eve), 112
Polterabend (Nuptial Eve) For Clarence & Twila Busenitz (poem), 115–116
Polterabend (Nuptial Eve) For Sharon Busenitz and Brad Graber (poem), 114–115
Pontiac, keys to, 83
porcelain and ceramics, breaking to make as much noise as possible, 112
postal service, pioneers having access to, 32
post-tornado baby, Melvin Epp as, 17
Potwin. Kansas, 47
"poultry linen," 359
Powolski, Andres, 48–49, 67–74, 399
  photo of, reading a German newspaper, 71
  on ship passenger list, 398
prairie chickens, flocks of, 79
prairie grass, 26, 213
prairie wind, in poetic sails, 44
Prayer Band, 362
Prayer for Berean Academy (poem), 322–323
presents, for children at Christmas, 349
printing press, as newly developed technology, 377
productivity, struggled for a feeling of, 1

program welcome, for the Christmas children's program, 343
project list, Mother's completion of, 366–367
prose, gift of writing, 10
Protestant Reformation, 377
Proverbs 22:6, 319
Prussia. *See* West Prussia
Prussian Cabinet Order of March 3, 1868, 392
Prussian constitution, declared universal conscription in 1848, 386
Prussian Mennonite immigrants, leaving for America, 23
Prussian rulers, interested in increasing state revenues, 383
public high school, established in Whitewater in 1900, 319

Q

quiet people of the land (*die Stillen im Lande*), 383

R

railroad companies, agreements for assistance from, 389
rain, timeliness of, 14
"Reasons for Immigration" (skit, 1951), 10
rebaptizers, 377
reception, tape recorded in 1953, 141
recitation, of poems, 108, 109
red cedar, only native Kansas evergreen, 242
Reformed Seminary, 227
Regier, Alfred, 191, 192, 222, 421
Regier, Alma, 210, 218
Regier, Alma Claassen, 283
Regier, Alvin, severe infant illness, 372
Regier, Anna Ensz, 210
Regier, Anna Peters, 383, 384
Regier, Anna (Regier) (1845–1920), 304, 305, 311

467

Subject/Name Index

Regier, Bernhard, married Justine Busenitz, 128–129
Regier, Bernhard (1781-1830). 283
    married an aged widow Christine Harder (1749–1806), 383
    married Anna Peters subsequently, 383
Regier, Bernhard and Marie Entz, 400
Regier, Bernhard R. Jr., 304, 306
Regier, Bernie, 415
Regier, Bertha, sister to Edna, 147
Regier, Bertha (daughter of Justine), 95
Regier, Betty, Jake's wife, very pregnant, 413
Regier, Catharine Wiebe, grandmother Harder's oldest sister, 210–211
Regier, Cornelius H. and Anna (Regier), 256
    fiftieth wedding anniversary photo, 305
    firstborn son, grave in West Prussia, 306
    immigration undertaken to achieve a better life for their children, 306
    parents of Anna, 255
Regier, Cornelius H. paternal great-grandfather, 20–21, 304, 305
    Bernhard Regier, his grandfather, 383
    Bernhard Regier, older brother of Cornelius died at age 16, 304
    elected as a lay minister, 306
    ordained by Bernhard R. Regier Jr., father, 306
Regier, Delbert, 166
Regier, Donice, 194
Regier, Dr., 83
Regier, Edna, 95, 197–199
Regier, Edward, 125
Regier, Elfried, 178
Regier, Emilie Wiebe, 221
Regier, Fremont, 193–194
Regier, Gerhard, 25
    family went directly to Halstead, Kansas, 400
    father of Gerhard, 210
    seeing two Indians on horses, 28
Regier, Gerhard and Anna (Ensz), 270
Regier, Gerhard (Jr.)
    asked in 1926 to reminisce about "Agriculture During Pioneer Days," 211–213
    married childhood friend and cousin, Catharine Wiebe, 210
    my mother's uncle by marriage to Catharine, 210
Regier, Gladys Penner Awy, 11
Regier, Gus, 197–199
Regier, Gus H. Jr., 421, 425
Regier, Helen, 95, 125, 128
Regier, Helene Harder, 167, 168
Regier, Ione, 191
Regier, J. G., organist, 167
Regier, Jacob J., 168, 231
Regier, Jacob W., 26
Regier, Jacob W. and Agathe (Dyck), 400
Regier, Jake Sr., 81, 413, 414
Regier, John and Gustav, 211
Regier, John H., 95, 291, 304
Regier, John (Johannes), lifelong interest in education, 222
Regier, John (Johannes) and Emilie, 191, 222–224
    double wedding ceremony with Bernhard Harders, 160, 221
Regier, Justine Harder (Mother's sister)
    death of, 95, 367
    married John H. Regier, 304
    visiting between 1914 and 1919, 95
Regier, Louise, John H. Regier's sister, 95
Regier, Louvina, 193, 195
Regier, Marie Harder, 304
Regier, Marie J., 222
Regier, Miss Maria, on ship passenger list, 398
Regier, Mr. Jacob, 167
Regier, Mrs. G. H. (as a child), 38
Regier, Nancy, 343
Regier, Rev. Cornelius H. and Anna, 129

Subject/Name Index

Regier, Ronald Roger, born eleven days after tornado, 413
Regier, Sara Mae, 193–194
Regier, Wilbert, 178
Registered Class of seeds, 339
Reichstaler notes, exchanging for American dollars, 24
Reimer, Elsie, 91, 92–93
Reimer, Gus, 414
Reimer, John, son of John T., 91, 121
Reimer, John T., 91, 92–93
Reimer, Justine Harder, peppernut recipe, 345
Reimer, Mina, , 91
Reimer, Raymond, , 91
relatedness, issues of, 107
relatives, interconnectedness or bonding of, 291
religious activists, believing Luther to be too conservative and restrained, 377
religious community, core activities, 117
relocation, monumental choice, 391
Remembering Grandmother on her One-hundredth Birth Date (poem), 302–304
Reminiscences on the Past (poem), 44, 60–74
review of history, giving a reference point in time, 45
rhythms of nature, sounds playing out, 17
Rice, John R., 320
rolling pin, brought along from West Prussia in 1876, 347
Roth, Rev. Ted, 407
Rückerinnerungen (poem), 49–60
"Rumbling Evening," 112
rural electrification (1950), 16
Russia
  compulsory military service, 23, 257, 388
  devastating drought, 334
Russian Mennonites, origins in West Prussia, xiii

S

salt-and-pepper sets, Susan's collection of, 85
Santa Fe Railroad, 3,200,000 acres to sell, 24
Schaefer, John Jr., home collapsed, 403
Schmidt, Agnes, 225
Schmidt, Arthur, wife and twins died, 66
Schmidt, Carl Bernhard (C. B.), 398
  coordinated land agents, 390
  established land sales offices in Europe, 390
  general agent of the German Department of the Land Office in Topeka, 24
  getting travelers onto trains, 25
  showing land, 25–26
  taking passengers into New York to exchange *Reichsthaler* for American dollars, 399
  targeting people with a well-developed work ethic, 390
  toured German Mennonite settlements, 37
Schmidt, Cornelius, 65–66
Schoof, Charley W., 425
school songs, composed for Berean Academy, 326
schools. *See also* elementary school; specific
  consolidation of local, 19
  early, 227
  German, 225, 227
  Mennonite in Russia, 23
  public high, 319
screech owls, antics and sounds of baby, 79
Scripture Memory Mountain Mission, 335
Scrivner, Billy, 422
Scrivner, Guy
  farm, damage to, 421
  shower for, 423
Scrivner, Hazel, 422
Scrivner, Henry, 407, 423

Subject/Name Index

Scrivner, Margaret Mary, killed by tornado, 421
Scrivner, Mary and son Henry, 407
seamstress, Mother as household, 359
seasickness, 395–396, 398
Second Diet of Speyer, 380
"the secret room," on second floor of the Bernhard Harder house, 293, 294
sections, odd and even numbered, 27
seed certification service, 339
self reference, in bilingual poem, 8
self-reliance, 353
sense of humor, poems reflecting Mother's, 100
separation of church, from the state, 378
sermonette, in German, 282
Settle, Rev. Myron, 422
sewing circle *(Nähverein")*, 286, 360
shivaree, organized by Mother, 113–114
shrikes, 79
siblings, names of Melvin Epp's, 108
Silberhochzeitsgedicht (poem), 185–186
Silent Night, singing of, 1
silver wedding anniversary celebration, Mother invited those who helped with tornado recovery, 417
Silver Wedding Anniversary Poem, 186–187
Simons, Menno, 377–378, 385
singing
    B. W. Harder led for patriotic hymn "America," 230
    of Christmas carols, 1, 9
    Mother's perception of being vocally challenged, 9
Sister Kati, deaconess, 84
slavery, 29–30
social activity, Mennonites cherished, 118
social aspect, to attending church, 117–118
socks and tires, gift for use in patching both, 135
Sommer Küche (summer kitchen), 359

South Dakota, marriage in, 140
Southampton, beauty of, 396
Spanish American War, member who volunteered and served, excommunicated, 234
sparks, igniting dry grasses along the tracks, 47
sparrows, mating, 110
speaking cues, in a poem, 146–147
speeches, composing difficult for Martha, 322
Speicher, granary
    photo of, 37
    Sunday worship in, 34
spouses, chosen from the community, 118
spring thaws, in Europe, 20
Springerle (Anise) Cookies (recipe), 348
Springerle cookie rolling pin, photo of, 347
Springerle rolling pin, brought along from West Prussia, 348
SS *Donau* (ship), 313, 396
SS *Main* (ship), 304, 396
SS *Mosel* (ship), 396
SS *Rhein* (ship), 24
    departure of, 394
    moored at the dock, 395
    under power with steam as well as wind sails, 397
    transport to, 394
Stalman, Dr, 83
"Star of the East," 10
Steiner, Martha (Mrs. Carl), 406
Steven and Kimberley Epp Wedding (poem), 152–154
streams, crossing flooded, 213
strength in crisis, demonstrated by Mother, 273
Stuart, C. C., tornado damage, 406
Suderman, Elder and Mrs. Leonard, 38
Sudermann, Leonhard, 37–38, 388–389
Sudermann, Margaretha, 63
    photo of, 64
sulphur, Mother's allergic reaction to, 365
Sunday school, Mother's teaching of, 10

Subject/Name Index

surrogate grandmother, in father's family, 274
surroundings, poems recording interaction with, 12–14
Susan's Twenty-fifth Anniversary with the "Go Ye' Mission (poem), 89–90
sustained bonding, celebration of, 157–208
Sütterlin script, laborious to read, 5
swampy land, draining, 381
Sweeter than All the World (novel), 380
Swiss Mennonite Church, 335
Swiss Mennonite Church community, 337

T

Table Grace I (poem and song), 355
Table Grace II (poem), 356
Table Grace III (poem), 356
table graces, at each place for Mother's funeral luncheon, 375
Tabor College, main building burned, 233
talk with God, Mother's, 9, 10
Tannahill, Margaret Ann, 111
    husband, Dean Rensberger, 111
taxes, in Prussia, 381
temperatures, fluctuating widely within a day, 14
Teutonic Knights, Harders invited to colonize the Vistula Delta by, 30
Thanksgiving, traditions followed, 354
thanksgiving grace, 355
"That the People May Know," newspaper apology to Mennonite community in April 1918, 231–232
theology, common to all groups of Anabaptists, 378
These Seventy-five Years (poem), 41–43
"they are one flesh," Mother's comment about marriage details, 109
Thierstein, C. B. Jr., 423
    cry for help that Mother heard, 414

family of, 409
farm of, 407–408
organist, 167
tornado injuries, 408
Thierstein, Chris, father of C. B. Thierstein Jr., 423–424
    sixtieth birthday of, 263–265
Thierstein, Eldrid, 407, 408
Thierstein, Ella, 407, 408–409
Thierstein, Gerald, 407, 408
Thierstein, Myron Keith, 407–409
    died from injuries received during the tornado, 408
    funeral for, 409
    obituary poem, 409
Thierstein, Pauline, 407, 408, 409
Thierstein family, never rebuilt original farm, 409–410
Thiessen, Agnethe, *Tante Thiessen*, 259
Thiessen, Alice and Herald, 362
Thiessen, Bernard, 82, 83, 139, 427
Thiessen, Dorothy
    Susan's Christmas gift for, 85
    visiting a cousin night of tornado, 82
Thiessen, Gilbert, 82, 83, 414
    Susan's Christmas gift for, 85
Thiessen, Grandma, temporarily relocated to the Bethel Home for the Aged, 418
Thiessen, Heinrich, 259
Thiessen, Helene and John, 299
Thiessen, Helene Harder
    Bernard, son of, 139
    died of cancer at forty-three, 367
    known for contagious laughter, 100
    Mother's sister, 81, 427
    photo of, 295
Thiessen, Henry, 227
Thiessen, Herald, 82, 83
    Susan's Christmas gift for, 85
Thiessen, Jacob, wedding, 159
Thiessen, Jacob E., brother to Mrs. Ed Claassen, 242
Thiessen, Jake, tornado damage, 420–421

471

Subject/Name Index

Thiessen, John, 83, 94
    comb box, gift for Christmas, 97
    family of, 81–82
    family photograph found in the Topeka area, 425
    farm completely leveled, 417–418
    farm of, 81–82
    house totally demolished, 411
    Lydia's dad, 132
    mother lived in a small house on the Jake Thiessen farm, 418
    Mother's brother-in-law, 372, 427
    Susan's Christmas gift for, 85
Thiessen, Lillian, 243
Thiessen, Lydia, 83, 84, 183, 302, 367, 425
    Bernard's sister, 139
    one of Mother's first photographic subjects, 427
    Susan's Christmas gift for, 85
Thiessen, Marie Renatha Wiebe, 242
Thiessen, Martha, 201, 343
Thiessen, Mrs. Jake, black dress in 1909, 159
Thiessen, Peter, 167, 259
Thiessen, Ruby and Bernard, 139–140
Thiessen, Susan (Susie), 82–88
    Bernard's sister, 139
    graduation picture from Grace University in 1949, 88
    injuries from tornado, 415, 417
    and other siblings, 81
    photo in the "Go Ye" Mission office, 88
    photo with salt-and-pepper collection, 86
    poem about, 89–90
    working as secretary, 87, 88, 89–90
Thiessen, Tante, father's aunt, 242
Thiessen, Willard, 206
Thiessen family members, after tornado, 418
thirtieth wedding anniversary, poem for Jacob Regiers,' 170
Thirty Years War (1618-1648), 170, 177
Thompson, George, all farm buildings destroyed, 403
Tide, box of, as a wedding present, 148–149
Tiegenhagen, got permits to build churches in 1786, 386
Tiegenhof, surrounding lowland areas settled by Mennonites, 385
Tien. *See* Kliewer, Katharina ("Tien")
tin can sealer, hand-operated, 379
tireless person, Mother as, 372
Toevs, Bertha Dyck, married Herman Toevs, 317
Toevs, Herman, 317
Toevs, Kenneth, 317
Toevs, Rosella Dyck, 317
Tornado (poem), by Gilbert Thiessen, 419–420
Tornado Alley, 401
tornado of June 8, 1941, 16–17, 401–426
    after its final touchdown, 422
    damage to farms from the tornado, 402–423
    damage to Regier farm, 191
    demolished the Jacob Regier's home, 168
    demolished Thiessen farm, 242
    destructive, 197
    effect on the Thiessen home, 82
    embedded in the poetry that Mother wrote, 425–426
    looting after, 414, 418
    Mother and Father weather with inner resources and strength, 273
    night of June 8, 1941, 81
    path during the second touchdown, 405
    total path of, 402
tornado of June 8, 1941 deaths
    Jessen-Krueger, Margarite Marie, 421
    Keyes, Haskell H., 403
    Krueger-Scrivner, Edna Marie (Mrs. Guy Scrivner), 421
    Paulson, Janet Lee, 421
    Penner, Marie, 407
    Scrivner, Betty Jean, 421
    Scrivner, Margaret Mary, 421

Subject/Name Index

Thierstein, Myron Keith, 408
tornadoes, described, 401–402
Towanda, Kansas, 32
towns, established along railroad, 47
tractors and plows, shipped to southern Russia in 1922, 378
train transportation, from Brainerd to Wichita by 1885, 21
transgression, public confession of, 158
transportation, to school for Mother and her sisters, 364
travels, of mother and father, 17
Tribute to Marie Harder Epp (1903-1998), written by Melvin Epp, 368–370
"Tütchen," given to each child, 343–344
Twenty-fifth Anniversary of Nursing for Aunt Helen Ruth (poem), 279
twenty-fifth wedding anniversary celebration invitation, of John and Marie Harder Epp (photo), 184
Twenty-fifth Wedding Anniversary of Henry and Maria Wiebe (poem), 181

U

Udall, Kansas, demolished in 1955 by a tornado, 402
Ukraine, grassland needing reclamation, 382
ulcer, at the ankle of Mother's right leg, 365
unique event, every poem a, 109
United States Postal Service, establishing mail delivery in 1854, 32
universal conscription. *See also* compulsory military service, in Prussia, 386
unloading from the ship, done very recklessly, 398–399
Unruh, Reverend P. H., 188
U.S. Geological Survey, bench mark post, 14

V

van Braght, Thieleman, stories of martyrs in 1660, 380
varicose veins, Mother's requiring support hose, 365
vegetable patch, 296
village poet, Mother as, 107
"vineyard," conceptualizing mission work, 334–335
Vistula Delta, 22, 381
Vistula lowlands, 381, 382
visualized pathway, to a successful marriage, 130
vocally-challenged, Mother's perception of being, 9
volunteer cleanup work, evident at all farms, 424
volunteer work, writing poems for other, 107
Vorsänger (chorister), 34, 167

W

Waldo Harders' Twenty-fifth Wedding Anniversary (poem), 203–204
war bonds, presented as a volitional act, 229
war effort, collection of interest from, 229
Warren, L. A., out-buildings badly damaged and house shifted off its foundation, 406
water pitcher, poem on the gift of, 2–3
wedding
    festivities as another core activity, 118
    of Mother's oldest niece Bertha Regier to Albert Busenitz, 125–128
wedding anniversaries
    celebrating, 157–208
    poems for, 19
wedding cakes, decorated by Mother, 148, 361–362

473

Subject/Name Index

"Wedding Dress Display Guide," 132, 250, 252–253
wedding dresses, dark prior to 1920, 159
wedding invitation, for a neighbor in 1956, 111
Wedding of Aunt Louise Entz & Uncle Howard Wedel (poem), 140
wedding picture, of John Epp and Marie Harder Epp (Mother and Father), 122
The Wedding Poem, recited by Melvin Epp, 141–142
wedding poem, request for, 107–108
wedding poems
    last written and recited in German, 135
    presented in chronological sequence, 123
wedding portrait, of grandparents Bernhard Jr. and Helene Wiebe, 160
Wedding reception of Elvin and Ann Wiebe (poem), 143–144
wedding receptions
    in a cleaned up machine shed or barn, 113
    poems recited or read at, 123
wedding wish, short poem summarizing, 123
Wedel, Howard, 140
Wedel, Louise Entz, 140
The Weekly Budget, 233
Welcome (poem), 343
welcome sign, 294
wells, construction of, 31
West Prussia
    life never without political tension, 383
    not easy leaving, 23
West Prussian Mennonites, from the Heubuden Church, xiii
West Prussian settlement, in Butler County, 37
Western District Conference of the General Conference Mennonites, xiii, 275
Western Interior Sea, sea bottom of the ancient, 14
"What a Friend We Have in Jesus"
    grace sung to, 354–355
    tune for Happy Birthday Song, 263
white wedding dresses, appearing after 1900, 159
Whitewater, Kansas, 16, 47
Whitewater business leaders, apology to the Mennonite community, 230–232
Whitewater Chamber of Commerce, relief committee, 423
Whitewater patriotic rally, highlighting issues triggering mob action, 229
Whitewater patriots, embarrassed to be "out-Americanized," 230
Whitewater River, crossing the swollen, 213
Wiebe, Agathe Epp, 159
Wiebe, Alfred and Agnes, 334
Wiebe, Ann, from Holland, 142
Wiebe, Catharine, 250
Wiebe, Elvin Roy, 142, 178–180
Wiebe, Emil, military service, 178
Wiebe, Emilie, 234
Wiebe, Ernest, 96
Wiebe, Ester, 137
Wiebe, Francis, 181–183
Wiebe, Frieda and Paula, sisters of Emma, 195
Wiebe, Heinrich, 180, 222
Wiebe, Henry, wedding ceremony of, 159
Wiebe, Herman A., 247–250
Wiebe, Jacob
    family, 270
    father of Minna Wiebe Harder, 225
Wiebe, Jake, 159
Wiebe, Margarete Regier, sister of Gerhard and John Regier, 222
Wiebe, Margarethe and Emil, home of, 275
Wiebe, Margarethe Epp, twenty-fifth anniversary celebration, 178
Wiebe, Maria Epp, 180

Subject/Name Index

Wiebe, Marilyn, 98, 181
Wiebe, Mrs. Henry, brown silk dress, 159
Wiebe, Peter, 25
Wiebe, Renathe Ensz, 270
Wiebe, Rudy, 380
wife, role of, 96
Willard Thiessen Silver Wedding Anniversary (poem), 206
Willie Busenitz Silver Wedding Anniversary (poem), 196–197
wind, sound of, 16
Wohlgemuth, Eldon, 144
Wohlgemuth, Jan Diller, 144
women from the church community, canned vegetables for Mother after tornado, 416–417
work, demarcation lines between male and female, 135–136
World War I
    anti-German sentiment, 135
    patriotism, 228
    young men served as noncombatants, 234
World War II
    anti-German sentiment encouraged integration of English language, 135
    local young men enrolled in alternative service programs or military service, 235
    quilts and blankets to Europe, 360
writing
    legacy of, 11
    while working, 10
Wüst, Rev. Edward, 286
Wuthrich, Lester and Agnes (Harder), 335

Y

Yotter, 66

Z

Zaccheus (poem), 325
Zaire, Melvin Claassens in, 207–208
Zion Mennonite Church, 214, 306
Zu Albert Entz & Frieda Busenitz Hochzeit (poem), 131
Zu Geburtstag von Onkel Christ Thierstein (poem), 264
Zu Grossmutters Erinnerungs 100ste Geburtstag (poem), 299–301
Zu Grosspapas 100sten Geburtstag (poem), 306–308
Zu Jacob J. Regiers Silberhochzeit (poem), 171–173
Zu John T. Reimers Fruit Shower (poem), 92
Zu Onkel Gerhard Regiers Goldernhochzeit (poem), 215–218
Zu Onkel John Harders 90sten Geburtstag (poem), 267–268
Zu Weihnachten (poem), 350–351
Zuercher, Arnold, 406–407, 423
Zur Heimat (German language newspaper), 25

www.ingramcontent.com/pod-product-compliance
Lightning Source LLC
Chambersburg PA
CBHW052111010526
44111CB00036B/1650